A Thousand Miles on an Elephant in the Shan States

A Thousand Miles on an Elephant in the Shan States

by

Holt S. Hallett

With a Preface

by Virginia M. Di Crocco

White Lotus Press

White Lotus Co. Ltd.
G.P.O. Box 1141
Bangkok 10501
Thailand

Telephone: (662) 332-4915 and (662) 741-6288-9
Fax: (662) 741 6607 and (662) 741-6287
E-mail: ande@lox2.loxinfo.co.th
Webpage: http://thailine.com/lotus

Printed in Thailand

ISBN 974-8495-27-2 pbk White Lotus Co. Ltd., Bangkok

Front cover: On the way to the high plateaus
Back cover: At school

Pages i - iii include an enlarged portion of the original folded map.
The original frontispiece map has been reproduced on a smaller scale.

Preface

A Thousand Miles on an Elephant in the Shan States by Holt S. Hallett presents an excellent overview of the topography, economy, peoples and customs, legends and local histories of Northern Thailand in the latter part of the nineteenth century. Consequently it is immensely valuable to anyone interested in the area, and has long been recognized for its merit by scholars. Indeed, in the Nineteen Twenties the great French art historian and epigraphist George Coedès wrote that Hallett's account was one of the two significant works in English on Northern Thailand.[1]

The book, first published in 1890, resulted from Hallett's thorough fact-finding trip through the region in 1876 when he was in search of the best route for a railway by which British goods would be transported from Burma to Thailand, and more especially to China, where a great and lucrative market was anticipated. The route he finally selected would go from Moulmein in Southern Burma to Tak and then across to Payao and Chiang Saen, terminating at Ssumao on the China frontier. This line, however, would constitute but one section of a great railroad system which would begin at the Persian Gulf and cross India and Burma. Ssumao in turn would be the starting point for a railway network which would spread through the western central and southern provinces of China. Not only would the establishment of the railroads assist the

---

1. Coedès, George, "Documents sur l'histoire politique et réligeuse du Laos occidental," **B.E.F.E.O.,** Tome XXV, 1925, Nos. 1-2. The other writer mentioned was the British colonial officer and explorer, Dr. D. Richardson, whose route to Mae Sarieng Hallett followed.

economy at home in England, but it would help the British industries in India and thwart French designs on Northern Thailand.

Hallett was qualified for his undertaking. A trained civil engineer, precise in his habits and work, he had retired from a career as a British colonial officer whose posting for a long period as head of the Tenasserim Division of Burma had given him intimate knowledge of the political and economic issues at stake. He was joined in his campaign to support British industries by Mr. Archibald R. Colquhoun. The latter undertook two research trips himself, one from Canton to Ssumao and ultimately Mandalay, and another from Moulmein via the Salween River and its tributaries to the Karen town of Paphun and thence eastward to Mae Sarieng, crossing the Salween by the Dagwin Ferry. From there he had gone to Chiang Mai, Payao, Nan, Chiang Saen and Chiang Rung. His trips resulted in two books, **Across Chryse, Being the Narrative of a Journey of Exploration Through South China Border Lands from Canton to Mandalay,** and **Amongst the Shans,** published in 1883 and 1885 respectively. The latter book included supplementary chapters by Hallett on the history of the "Upper Shan."

A Thousand Miles on an Elephant in the Shan States both reinforces the material on Northern Thailand presented to the British public in **Amongst the Shans** and gives much new information about places visited by Colquhoun, plus details on sections in Northern Thailand to which he did not go. In his journey Hallett took a different route from his colleague. He went from Moulmein up the Salween and then turned toward Hlaingbwe, where he picked up his elephants, and proceeded overland from Mae Sarieng. This was only the first leg of his journey, which would take him over much of the territory of present-day Northern Thailand, from Mae Sarieng north to Fang, east to the Mekhong River, and south to Tak and thence to Bangkok. By the "Shan States" he refers to the political entities, many still ruled by local princes, which existed in the region. Both he and Colquhoun were of the impression that the Shans were the major ethnic group in the area. Thus both authors emphasized the word "Shan" and inferred that since the people for the most part were linguistically the same as those in the British Shan States in Burma, a British presence was more correct than a French one with their ideas of "Western Laos." The misconception about the Shans as being the dominant people, rather than the Tai-Yuan, stems from that of the prominent linguistic authorities of the time, such as the Rev. J.N. Cushing, D.D., an eminent Shan scholar, who acted as Hallett's interpreter for much of the trip. He wrote in the introduction to his **Elementary Handbook of the Shan Language,** published in 1888, that the language of the "British Shan Branch of the Tai family" was spoken from the Salween to the Mekhong.[2] Probably this idea was fostered by the fact that the Khün script of the then British Shan State of Kengtung is identical to that used by the Tai-Yuan of Chiang Mai and the Tai-Lü of Sipsongbannā.[3] Furthermore, Burmese naturally transliterate "Siam" as "Shan."

The author has included eight maps, the first of which gives the proposed French and English railways in Southern China and Indochina. The others show the routes Hallett followed in Thailand. On each he has recorded the altitudes of the mountains and the significant economic aspects noted in each area through which he passed. Moreover, the book abounds in carefully and well drawn sketches depicting the landscapes and the peoples. Especially fine are his detailed drawings of fishing equipment and other types of basketry. The reader will note the differences in the rendering of place names in the area from what is customary now; for example,

---

2. Cushing, the Rev. J.N., D.D., **Elementary Handbook of the Shan Language,** Rangoon: American Baptist Mission Press, 1888, p.1.

3. Mangrāi, Sāimöng, **The Pādeng Chronicle and The Jengtung State Chronicle Translated,** Ann Arbor: The U. of Michigan Center for South and Southeast Asian Studies, 1981, pp.3-4.

the Burmese Zimme for Chiang Mai, Penyow for Payao, Lakon for Lampang, Kiang Hai for Chiang Rai, Haut for Hot, etc.

At the time when Holt Hallett was writing, the British shipbuilding demand for teak was spurring a marked increase in the teak industry and had sparked the movement of many Karens to the area east of the Salween. Hallett notes that most of the elephants used in the logging were owned and handled by Karens and that the latter had set up numerous villages in what had been Lawa land. The center of much of the teak forestry business was Mae Sarieng, known then as Maing Loongyee,[4] and the main port of export Moulmein. Logs from as far away as the great forests in Chiang Saen were being sent out through that port.

Throughout his writing the author attempts to inform the reader about the age of the cities visited and their development; for example, he points out that the Mae Sarieng he visited was a relatively new stockaded town with suburbs to the north. South of it were two ancient cities which had once formed part of a Peguan kingdom. He says that according to the Lamphun Chronicle one of the old cities together with 400 Peguans was handed over to the Shan Chief of Lamphun as a dowry when he married a daughter of the King of Pegu in 1289. This reader has found no such reference in the Lamphun Chronicle as translated by Camille Notton.[5] Colquhoun, on the other hand, says that the city, Yunsaleen,[6] which was formerly part of the old Kingdom of Pegu, was given at a remote period as a dowry of the Mon princess to a chief of Chiang Mai. The Chiang Mai Chronicle seems to corroborate this. It says that King Mangrai was given in marriage a princess of Pegu and a

---

4. A Karen term (U Bokay, Consultant, Pagan) still used by many Burmese.

5. Notton, Camille, **Annales du Siam, Vol.II: Chronique de Lam:p'un. Histoire de la dynastie Chamt'evi,** Paris: Charles-Lavauzelle & Cie, 1930.

6. Hallett, p. 35, gives the name Yain Sa Lin.

large dowry; however, no mention is made of a city being part of it.[7]

From Hallett comes much data about the Lawa, who at that time were much less integrated into Thai Society than presently is the case. Especially significant are the facts about Lawa mining and metal production. The production of iron by the Lawa in the Bô Luang area has often been cited, as it is by Hallett, but this reader has not seen any other reference to mining iron by the Lawa in the Vieng Papao area and the subsequent manufacture of metallic goods. The author also includes observations about Lawa religious and burial customs. Important in the wake of the many wooden coffins found in Northern Thailand is his statement that at that time the Lawa hollowed out a log in which to bury the dead and that they buried all the dead person's personal effects of importance with the corpse. He repeats the well-known Lawa legends about Queen Chamadevi and the Lawa Chief Khun Luang Viranga, sometimes known as Milunga, and yakshas Pu Saeh and Ya Saeh.

One aspect of Hallett's writing that may well annoy readers is his propensity to prudishness, perhaps but a reflection of 19th-century English morality. He does not to say why the garment which Chamadevi sent to her Lawa suitor should weaken him, and he looks upon local maidens as being unchaste and even flagrantly bold when they swim undressed or playfully flirt. He tends also to be very supercilious about local beliefs, not really understanding Buddhism, and often is condescending about the manners and intellect of the princely rulers.

His description of the walled city of Chiang Mai gives both pleasure and regret. One comes to realize what a beautiful city it was at the time and is filled with sadness that one has missed the

---

7. Colquhoun, Archibald R., **Amongst the Shans,** London: Field & Tuer, 1885, p. 35.

opportunity to see it as it once was. Hallett characteristically notices and describes correctly that Chiang Mai houses have the peculiar feature of inclining the walls slightly outwards from the floor to the roof. He points out that the city had been deserted for several years in the latter part of the 18th century. In fact, the desertion of Northern Thailand's cities and the general depopulation of the area is one of his frequent themes.[8]

Particularly interesting are the trade statistics given: Annually 700 - 1,000 laden mules and ponies came to Chiang Mai from Yunnan and 7,000 to 8,000 from Kengtung, Chiang Rung and other places in the then British Shan States; 1,000 elephants were employed in carrying goods to and from Chiang Saen, chiefly for transhipment to Luang Prabang and elsewhere; 5,000 porters and 500 - 6,000 laden oxen went to Lower Burma, etc. There were fully 8,000 elephants in Chiang Mai and also in Lampang, and even more in Nan, with about half that amount in Phrae. A thousand boats plied between Chiang Mai and Tak, many of them proceeding to Bangkok. Salt was an important item of trade and currency. Indeed, Hallett says that up to 1874 salt from Nan was used as currency for purchases in the Chiang Mai market and was bought by the Yunnanese.

One hundred years ago travel from Bangkok was amazingly time-consuming. In the rainy season one could expect to spend 45 days proceeding from Bangkok to Hot, south of Chiang Mai, and two months in the dry season. From Hot to Chiang Mai took six days in the dry season. In the rains one always went by elephant.

Immediately north of Chiang Mai Hallett found two ancient cities, and still others in the Fang area. There he noted seeing over 320 ruined temples and thousands of images. Fang itself had been destroyed by the Burmese in 1717 and lay deserted for over a

---

8. Notton, Camille, **Annales du Siam, Vol.III, Chronique de Xieng Mai,** Paris: Paul Geuthner, 1932, part 2, p. 52.

century only to be resettled in 1880. Chiang Dao, a palisaded city at the time of his visit, had also been resettled.

The once populous area around Chiang Saen and Chiang Rai had been left virtually destitute of inhabitants by the wars at the end of the 18th century. At the time he visited the walled city of Chiang Rai, Hallett found that it had only 300 houses and was just beginning to regain a semblance of prosperity. Evidence of devastation was everywhere in Chiang Saen, which had been reoccupied in 1881. The author writes of the splendid bronzes scattered about in every direction, the massive ruined walls and the excellence of the stucco work. At Payao, which had been resettled from Lampang, he found ancient cities and evidence of ceramic production.

One of the more exciting passages is that describing travel on the River Ping. In the days prior to its emasculation by the Bhumibol Dam, the Ping was a formidable river whose rapids were full of terrifying potentialities and whose defiles commanded respect. The majesty of the river is in part captured by Hallett's drawings.

The author did not choose to travel from Tak to Moulmein although he decided that the railway that he espoused should come from Burma to Tak via Moulmein; rather he relied on the information readily available to him. We learn from his accounts that the journey from Moulmein to Tak took about six days over an area whose mountains were easy to cross and through which there were not less than eleven distinct caravan routes, information which might interest those puzzling about the recent ceramic finds in the region.

Hallett's description of the life of most of the population in Bangkok is an extremely negative one. It reflects partially what he saw himself and partially the accounts of the British officials in the city. He was much impressed, however,with the King and Prince Devawongse, and foresaw that they would carry out many reforms.

Over the century since Hallett wrote, much information has been gathered from which new views have come to replace many theories set forth as background material in his introduction. Yet certain of the ideas once held prick interest. One of these is his statement that Ayutthaya was built on the site of a deserted Cambodian city called Vieng Lek. These days most historians discount this idea. However, it is interesting to note that in both great Burmese chronicles, U Kala's **Mahayazawingyi** and the **Hmannan Mahayazawindawgyi (The Glass Palace Chronicle of the Kings of Burma),** reference is made during the reign of the 11th-century Pagan king, Kyanzittha, to the country of the Gywans (the Khmer) to the southwest called **Ayawsa.** In their translation of the latter chronicle Pe Maung Tin and Gordon H. Luce transliterate the name of the country as **Ayoja.** Could **Ayoja (Ayawsa)** be an early rendering of Ayodhya?[9]

At the end of the book Hallett presents the many accolades given him by various vested interests for his work of promotion. Ironically, **A Thousand Miles on an Elephant in the Shan States** did not bring about the desired railway to Ssumao. Instead it achieved for the author an esteem as an astute observer and capable writer. His testimony is a work of great historical value. It is indeed a pleasure to see it become available after having been out of print for many years.

Virginia M. Di Crocco

---

9. Kala, U, **Mahayazawingyi,** Rangoon: Burma Research Society, 1960, Vol.I, p. 212, and **Hmannan Mahayazawindawgyi,** Rangoon: Pyigyi Mandaing Pitaka, 5th ed., Vol.I, p. 204, and Pe Maung Tin and Gordon H. Luce, **The Glass Palace Chronicle of the Kings of Burma,** Rangoon: Burma Research Society, 1960, p. 106.

Map of
SOUTHERN CHINA
and
INDO CHINA.
Showing Proposed
FRENCH & ENGLISH RAILWAYS.
Finished Railways.
Projected do.
English Miles.
NOTE. The census figures do not include the hill tribes which are numerous in Kwangtung, Kwangsi, Kweichau, Yunnan and Szechuen.
Longitude East 100 of Greenwich
T I B E T
Lhassa
Himalaya Mountains
I N D I A
CALCUTTA
Mouths of the Ganges
BAY OF BENGAL
UPPER BURMA
Mandalay
Bhamo
LOWER BURMA
Rangoon
Gulf of Martaban
MAULMAIN
SHAN STATES
SIAM
Pop. 7.000.000
Bankok
Gulf of Siam
Isthmus of Kraw
CAMBODIA
Pop. 2.000.000
Saigon
FRENCH COCHIN CHINA
COCHIN CHINA
Hue
TONG KING
Hanoi
GULF OF TONG KING
HAINAN
Paracel Islands
C H I N A
SZE CHUEN
Pop. Cen. 1885: 71,073,730
CHUNG KING
HUPEH
KWEICHAU
YUNNAN
Yunnan Fu.
KWANG SI
KWANG TUNG
HONAN
KIANG SI
Hong Kong
CANTON
INDIAN OCEAN
Andaman Islands
Nicobar Islands
Mergui Archipelago
MALACCA STRAIT
MALAY PENINSULA
SUMATRA
Malacca
Singapore & Strait
Anamba Islands
Nantuna Islands
BORNEO
Sarawak
CHINA SEA
Maulmain to London 25 days
Singapore to London 28 days
Hong Kong to London 35 days
Shanghai to London 39 days

F. S. Weller.

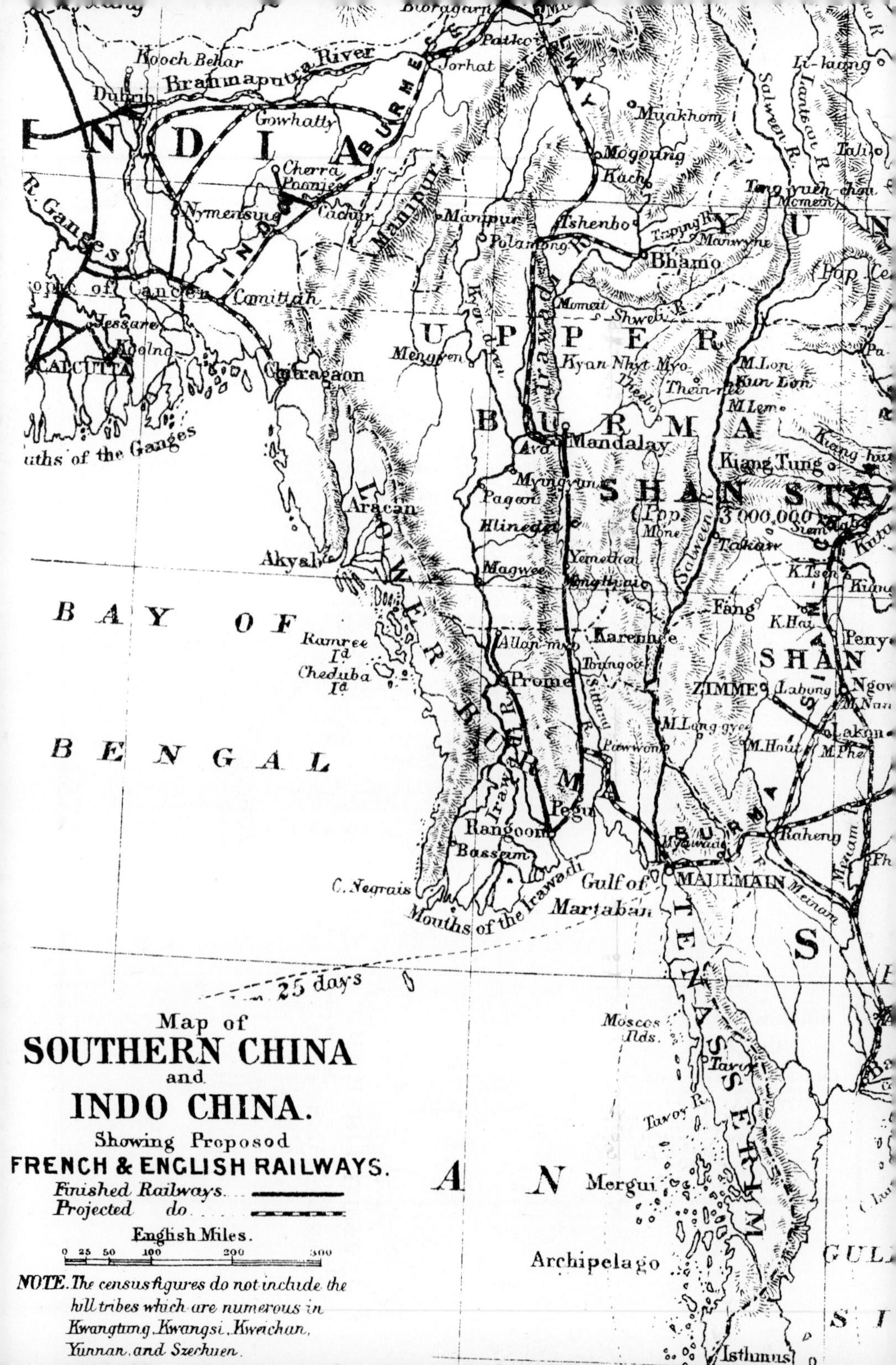

Map of
SOUTHERN CHINA
and
INDO CHINA.
Showing Proposed
FRENCH & ENGLISH RAILWAYS.
Finished Railways
Projected do
English Miles.
0 25 50 100 200 300
NOTE. The census figures do not include the hill tribes which are numerous in Kwangtung, Kwangsi, Kweichau, Yunnan, and Szechuen.
INDIA
BURMESE
UPPER BURMA
LOWER BURMA
SHAN STATES
BAY OF BENGAL
Brahmaputra River
Kooch Behar
Dubrib
Gowhatty
Jorhat
Patkoi
Cherra Poonjee
Nymensing
Cachar
Manipur
Camillah
Jessare
Koolna
CALCUTTA
Chittagong
Mouths of the Ganges
R. Ganges
Tropic of Cancer
Muakhom
Mogoung
Kach
Tshenbo
Polamong
Bhamo
Tapping R.
Manwyne
Momein
Momeit
Shweli R.
Salween R.
Li-kiang
Lantsan R.
Tali
Kyan Nhyt Myo
Theebo
Mengyen
Mandalay
Ava
Myingyan
Pagan
Hlinedet
Magwee
Yemethen
Aracan
Akyab
Ramree Id.
Cheduba Id.
M. Lon
Kun Lon
M. Lem
Kiang Tung
Mone
3,000,000
Takaw
K. Tsen
Fang
K. Hai
Karennee
Allan-myo
Toungoo
Prome
Sittang R.
ZIMME
Labong
Lakon
M. Long-gyee
Pawwon
M. Hout
Pegu
Rangoon
Bassein
Irawadi R.
Raheng
Myawadi
MAULMAIN
Menam
C. Negrais
Mouths of the Irawadi
Gulf of Martaban
25 days
Moscos Ids.
Tavoy R.
Mergui
Archipelago
TENASSERIM
Isthmus

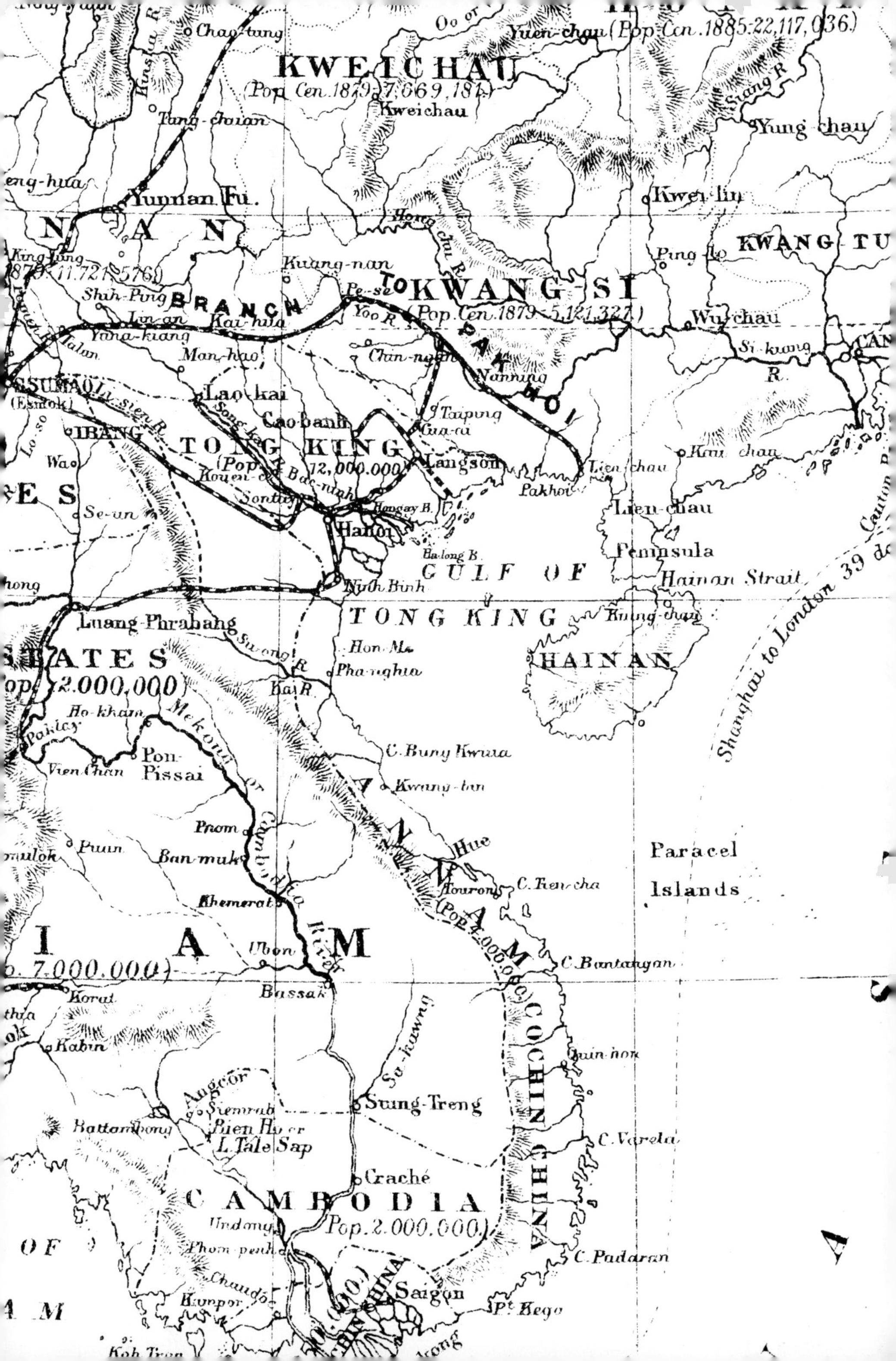

Chao-tung
Oo or
Yuen-chau (Pop. Cen. 1885: 22,117,036.)
KWEICHAU
(Pop. Cen. 1879: 7,669,181.)
Kinsha R.
Kweichau
Siang R.
Tung-chuan
Yung-chau
eng-hua
Yunnan Fu.
Kwei-lin
N A N
Hong-chui R.
King-tung
1879: 11,721,576)
Kuang-nan
Ping-lo
KWANG-TU
TO KWANG-SI
Shih-Ping
BRANCH
Pe-se
Lin-an
Kai-hua
Yoo R.
(Pop. Cen. 1879: 5,121,327)
Wu-chau
Yuna-kiang
PAKHOI
Talan
Man-hao
Chin-ngan
Si-kiang R.
CAN
SSUMAO
(Esmok)
Lao-kai
Nanning
Lo-so
Li-sien R.
Taiping
IBANG
Cao-banh
Cua-ai
TONG KING
Song-koi R.
Langson
Wao
(Pop. 12,000,000)
Kouen-ce
Bac-ninh
Lien-chau
Kau-chau
Pakhoi
ES
Sontay
Hongay B.
Lien-chau
Se-un
Hanoi
Peninsula
Balong B.
GULF OF
hong
Ninh Binh
Hainan Strait
Luang-Phrabang
TONG KING
Kiung-chau
Shanghai to London 39 d
Su-ong R.
Hon Me
STATES
Phanghia
HAINAN
(Pop. 2,000,000)
Kai R.
Ho-khan
Mekong
Pakley
C. Bung Kwua
Pon-
Vien Chan
Pissai
ANNAM
Kwang-bin
Prom
Hue
Paracel
Islands
mulok
Puun
Ban-muk
Cambodia River
C. Tien-cha
Tourons
Khemerat
(Pop. 2,000,000)
I A M
Ubon
(Pop. 7,000,000)
C. Bantangan
Bassak
Korat
thia
Se-kawng
ok
Kabin
COCHIN CHINA
Quin-hon
Angcor
Stung-Treng
Siemrab
Battambong
Bien Hoer
L. Tale Sap
C. Varela
Craché
CAMBODIA
(Pop. 2,000,000)
Udong
OF
Phom-penh
C. Padaran
Chaudó
Saigon
Kampor
FR. CHINA
Pt. Kego
A M
Koh Tron

TO

THE AMERICAN MISSIONARIES IN BURMAH,
SIAM, AND THE SHAN STATES,

I DEDICATE THIS BOOK,

AS A MARK OF THE

HIGH ESTEEM IN WHICH I HOLD THE NOBLE WORK

THE AMERICAN BAPTIST MISSION AND

THE AMERICAN PRESBYTERIAN MISSION

ARE ACCOMPLISHING

IN CIVILISING AND CHRISTIANISING

THE PEOPLE OF INDO-CHINA.

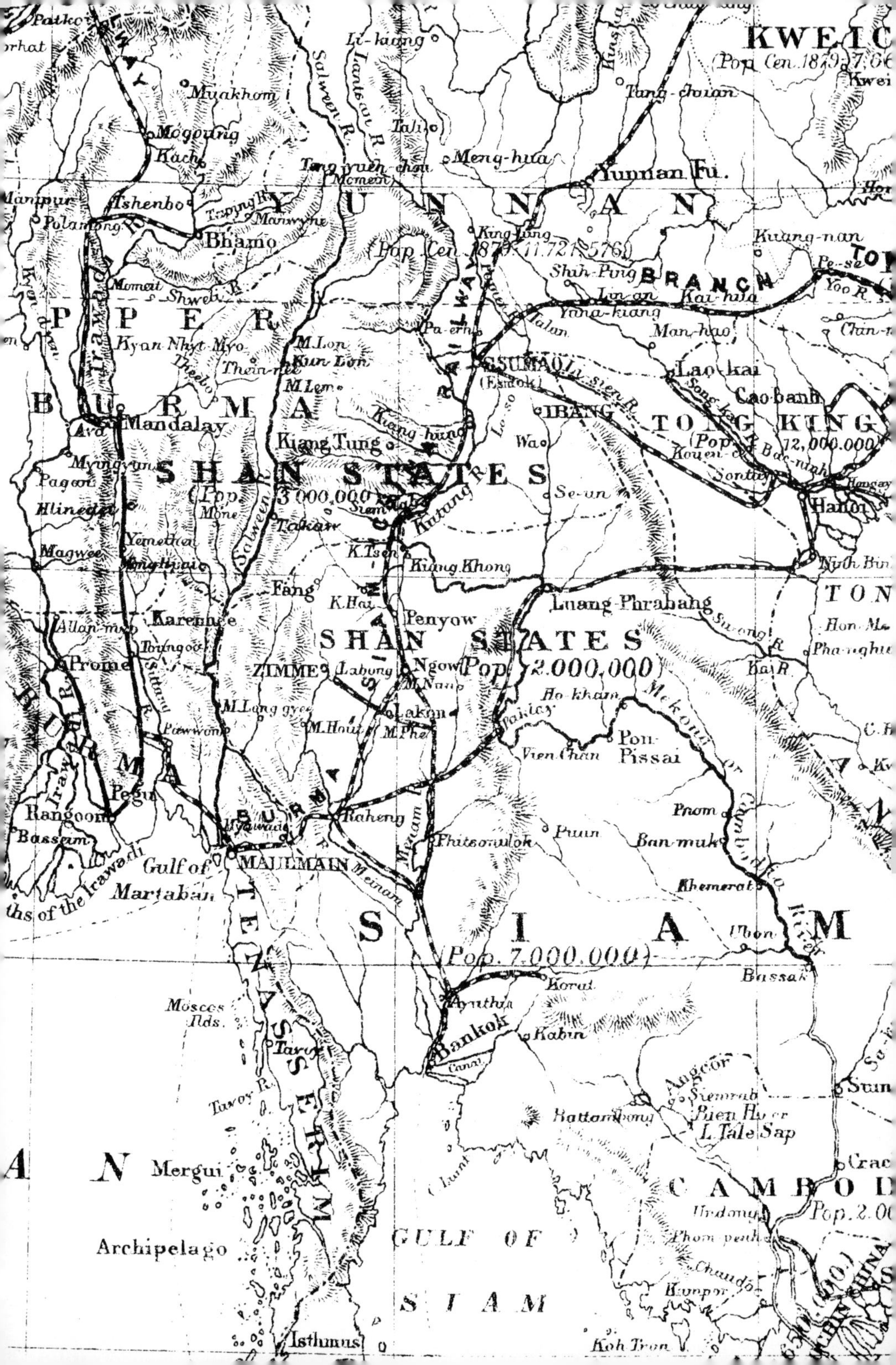

KWEIC
(Pop. Cen. 1879. 7,66
Patkoi
Li-kiang
Muakhom
Mogoung
Kach
Tali
Tang-choian
Meng-hua
Yunnan Fu.
Tang-yueh-chau
(Momein)
Salween R.
Lantsan R.
Manipur
Ashenbo
Polamong
Bhamo
Manwyne
YUNNAN
(Pop. Cen. 1879 11,721,576)
King-tung
Kuang-nan
Shih-Ping
BRANCH
Lin-an
Kai-hua
Yoo R.
Momeit
Shweli R.
UPPER
Yuna-kiang
Man-hao
Talan
Kyan Nhyt Myo
Theebo
Thein-nee
M. Lon
Kun Lon
M. Lem
Pa-erh
SSUMAO
(Esmok)
Lao-kai
Cao-banh
Song-ka
BURMA
Ava
Mandalay
Kieng-hung
Kiang Tung
IBANG
Wa
TONG KING
(Pop. 12,000,000)
Myingyan
Pagan
SHAN STATES
(Pop. 3,000,000)
Se-un
Sontay
Hanoi
Hlinedet
Mone
Takaw
Kutang
Yemethen
Magwee
Ninghyan
Salween
K. Tsen
Kiang Khong
Ninh Bin
Fang
K. Hai
Luang-Phrabang
TON
Allan-myo
Karennee
Penyow
Toungoo
SHAN STATES
Prome
ZIMME
Labong
Ngow
(Pop. 2,000,000)
Sittang
Su-ong R.
Kai R.
M. Nang
Ho-kham
M. Lang gyee
Lakon
Pawwon
M. Hout
M. Phe
Vien-Chan
Pon-Pissai
Mekong or Cambodia River
Irawadi
Pegu
BURMA
Rangoon
Raheng
Prom
Bassein
Myawadi
Menam
Phitsanulok
Puun
Ban-muk
Gulf of Martaban
MAULMAIN
Meinam
Khemerat
Mouths of the Irawadi
SIAM
Ubon
(Pop. 7,000,000)
Bassak
Korat
Moscos Ids.
Ayuthia
TENASSERIM
Tavoy
Bankok
Kabin
Canal
Angcor
Siemrab
Tavoy R.
Battambong
L. Tale Sap
AN
Mergui
CAMBOD
Pop. 2,00
Udong
Archipelago
GULF OF SIAM
Phom-penh
Chaudo
Kampot
Isthmus
Koh Tron

PREFACE.

THE importance of the Eastern markets to European commerce has long been recognised, and since the famous Portuguese navigator Vasco da Gama rounded the Cape of Good Hope at the close of the fifteenth century, and the Portuguese occupied Malacca and established factories or trade depots in Burmah at Martaban and Syriam, the trade of Western China and Indo-China has been a prize which has attracted the commercial aspirations of every maritime mercantile community in Europe.

In 1613, the Portuguese were ousted from Burmah, and six years later, the English and Dutch established factories in that country. Some years afterwards the Dutch were expelled, and in the middle of the next century the French became our rivals for a short time. In 1756 the chief of their factory was executed, and their factory was destroyed, never to be resuscitated.

The first Englishman whose name is recorded in history as travelling in Siam and the Shan States is Thomas Samuel, who happened to be at Zimmé when that place was recaptured by the Burmese in 1615. In Purchas's 'Pilgrims' it is related that he had proceeded from Siam to Zimmé "to discover the trade of that country." From that time to 1687, when the English were turned out of Siam for killing some of the natives in a scuffle, many English merchants resided there.

Whilst the coast of Burmah was under native dominion, our traders had to content themselves with travelling along the great rivers; and it was not until 1829, three years after we had annexed the Burmese provinces of Tenasserim and Arakan, that steps were taken by us to establish overland trade with Northern Siam, the Shan States, and China. In that year Lord William Bentinck, the Governor-General of India, ordered a mission to proceed, under Dr Richardson, from Maulmain to the Siamese Shan States, to ensure friendly relations and trade in that direction; and in 1837, Lord Auckland, then Governor-General, despatched Captain (late General) MacLeod, *viâ* Zimmé and Kiang Hung to China, with the view of opening up trade with that country. Notwithstanding the favourable reports of these and subsequent missions, and the frequent petitions of our mercantile community asking for the connection of Burmah with China by railway, no action has been taken by the Indian Government in the sixty years that have elapsed since Dr Richardson's mission, for improving the overland routes leading from Burmah to the great undeveloped markets which immediately border our possessions on the east. Burmah might as well have remained for these sixty years in native hands, for all the good that its acquisition has been to the furtherance of our trade with the neighbouring regions.

When I retired from Government service at the end of 1879, the French were again in the field. They had annexed the south-eastern corner of Indo-China, had seized Cambodia from the Siamese, were determined to wrest Tonquin from China, which they have since succeeded in doing, and had openly avowed their intention to eject British trade from Eastern Indo-China, and to do all they possibly could to attract the trade of South-western, Southern, and Central China to French ports in Tonquin, where prohibitive duties could be, and have since been, placed upon British goods. It was under these circumstances that Mr Colquhoun and I took up the question, placed the necessity of connecting India with Burmah, Siam, and China before the public, and with the aid of the mercantile community determined to carry out a series of exploration-surveys to prove whether or not Burmah could be connected with these countries by railway at a reasonable expense, and to select the best route, financially and commercially, for the undertaking. The present volume deals with my exploration-surveys in Siam and the Shan States.

The country through which I passed, besides being of interest from a commercial point of view, was at the time of my visit shrouded with that glamour which invests all little-known regions; and an accurate knowledge of its physical features and political relations promised to be of great importance in view of the action of France in Tonquin, and our threatened embroilment with that nation in Upper Burmah.

Before commencing the narrative of my journey, in which the manners, customs, and habits of the people will be portrayed, I will, from information recently acquired by myself and other travellers, and from other sources, give a slight sketch of the ethnology and history of the interesting races met with by me on my journey.

The first mention in history of Lower Indo-China is in the 'Annamese Chronicles,' where it is stated that Founan —the early Chinese name for Cambodia—in B.C. 1109 was under the rule of a native queen. The next we hear of it is in A.D. 69, at the time when a Brahman from India, named Prea Thong, who is said to have been the fugitive son of the sovereign of Delhi, married the then ruling queen. This Brahman is believed to have introduced Brahmanism, architecture, sculpture, and astronomy into Cambodia. At that time Cambodia consisted of an agglomeration of seven States, which were constantly at war with each other. On the death of the Brahman's son, the commander-in-chief of the army made an end of the principalities, and was elected to the joint throne.

From B.C. 125 there are many accounts of embassies passing between China and Cambodia, and the country seems rapidly to have reached a height of prosperity and Eastern splendour. In the third century Chinese ambassadors mention palaces, towers, and theatres having been erected for the reception and amusement of the guests, and meeting merchants in the ports from countries as far west as the Roman Empire. The people were described by the Chinese as an active and robust small black race, with long hair knotted on the top of the head; the rich wearing only a silk loin-cloth, and the poor one of cotton. The women had head-coverings, and decked themselves with beautifully wrought silver jewellery set with precious stones. The men excelled in making jewellery, gold and silver vases, furniture, and domestic utensils—and were honest, and hated theft above all things. They worshipped Hindoo gods, and offered up human sacrifices.

This small black race, the Cham or Siam, was of the Malay stock, doubtless darkened by interbreeding with the Negrito aborigines, and perhaps with Dravidian colonists from the Madras coast. Remnants of the Negrito aborigines, evidently akin to the Australioids, are still found in the hilly districts of the Malay Peninsula, as well as in some of the adjacent islands: and the Kha, or Ka, in the neighbourhood of Luang Prabang; the Trao, to the east of Bienhoa in Cochin China; the Hotha Shans, in the Chinese Shan States; and one of the native races in Formosa,—are, according to Professor Terrien de Lacouperie, representatives of the same stock, and akin to the Tiao, a race of pigmies, with whom the Chinese (Peh Sing tribes) became acquainted when they entered North-eastern China more than 4000 years ago.

To the north of the Chams, the country from an early period was occupied by the Lawa, a race with Mon affinities and probably of the Mon stock, who, according to their own traditions, and the beliefs and traditions of their neighbours, are the aborigines of the region stretching southwards from Yunnan, and eastwards from the Salween to the Meh Kong, and perhaps even to the China Sea. Many of the names of principalities and deserted cities are said to have been derived from the Lawa; and fierce battles were fought between them and the Shans before the former were conquered or driven into the hills. In a few years the language of this interesting race will be extinct, as the race have gradually been absorbed into the Shan and Peguan population, and Shan as well as Lawa is now being spoken in their few remaining distinct villages.

To the west of the Lawa were the Mon or Mun, a Mongoloid race of Malaysian affinities, whose scattered tribes spread from Indo-China into Western Bengal and Central India, where they are now known as Kolarian. Their first kingdom in Lower Burmah was founded at Thatone, an ancient seaport on the east of the Gulf of Martaban, by an Indian dynasty from the Madras coast, in the sixth century B.C. About the end of the first century of our era, Mon tribes drove the Burmese from Prome, which had been their capital from B.C. 483. These tribes were probably descendants of the Ngu race, including the Pang, Kuei, and Miao tribes, who, with the Shan, Yang or Karen, and King or Chin tribes, formed the chief part of the population of Central and Southern China during the struggle for empire —604-220 B.C.—between the Dukes of Tsi, Dsin, Ts'in, and Tsoo, which ended in the ruler of Ts'in becoming the first Supreme Emperor of China. Some of the wars waged by Ts'in during this period seem to have been wars of extermination; and many tribes must have sought safety by moving southward and south-westward out of the area of turbulence. In one campaign 240,000 heads are said to have been cut off; in another, 140,000; and in others, 60,000, 80,000, and 82,000 heads.

In A.D. 573, the Mon founded a separate kingdom at Pegu, which, with the Thatone kingdom, was destroyed by the Burmese King of Pugan in the middle of the eleventh century; from that time to 1287, when Pegu was conquered by the Shan King of Martaban, Lower Burmah remained under the Burmese. In 1540 it was reconquered by the latter, and formed part of their empire for 200 years. In 1740 the Mon, aided by the Karen and Gwe Shan, rebelled against Burmah, and, electing a Gwe Shan as their king, commenced the great fight for supremacy, which lasted till 1757, and left the Burmese supreme in the country until we annexed it.

The language of the Mon is now nearly extinct in Lower Burmah. The Mon or Peguans, who sided with us during the first Burmese war, were mercilessly ill-treated by the Burmese when we evacuated Martaban and Pegu: those who did not escape into Tenasserim, Zimmé, and Siam, were either murdered or forced to learn and speak the language of their oppressors.

To the north of the Mon race, in the district of the Middle Irawadi, the country was occupied from an early date by Burmese tribes of Tibetan origin, who were gradually welded together by warlike Kshatriya princes, who invaded the country from Northern India. According to the Tagaung Raza Weng, their first capital in Burmah was founded at Tagaung by Abhi Raja, one of the Sakya Rajas. This prince came from Kapilavastu with an army, and, B.C. 923, built the city. One of his sons founded a dynasty in Arakan, and a grandson established another at Kalê in the Kubo valley. The destruction of the first monarchy at Tagaung was due to the irruption of tribes, probably Shans, from the East. This is said to have happened in the sixth century B.C.

About this time a second band of Kshatriyas arrived from Gangetic India, whose chief, Daza Raja, married the widow of the queen of the last dynasty, and some years later, B.C. 523, built old Pugan, near the site of the ancient capital. His successor was expelled and driven south by the Shans, and founded a new capital, B.C. 483, at Prome, in the north of Lower Burmah. Upper Burmah was thus left in the possession of the Shans, many of whose cities in the Shan States lying to the west of the Salween were founded about this time. Moné is said to have been built as early as B.C. 519.

Thirteen years after the Burmese were turned out of Prome by the Mon, they created a new capital, A.D. 108, at Pugan, where the Burmese monarchy continued until 1291, when it was expelled by the Shans, who governed Burmah from that time until 1554. From thence until we annexed the country, Upper Burmah was under Burmese rulers.

The Karen tribes who are found scattered amongst the hills in Burmah and Siam from the latitude of Mandalay southwards, are called by the Burmese Karen or Kayen; by their other neighbours they are known as Yang, pronounced sometimes nasally as Nyang. These people are believed to have been a branch of the Chau or Djow, which entered the north-west of China about B.C. 1276. The Djow displaced the Shang dynasty in China B.C. 1122, and remained supreme over the agglomeration of principalities forming the Chinese Empire until B.C. 336, when some of the States acknowledged Ts'in as their lord. Djow was ultimately overthrown, in B.C. 255, by the Prince of Ts'in, who took possession of Djow's sacrificial vessels and the nine tripods, the symbols of empire. During their rule the Djow preserved their ancient faith in divination, and the augurs in the courts of the principalities occupied a distinguished position. No expedition or any business of importance was entered into without first consulting the fates.

The Yang or Karen—who gave their name to the Yang-tsze Kiang, and settled on its banks—at the time of the destruction of Tsoo, the great principality which covered Southern China, by the Shensi State of Ts'in, B.C. 221, occupied the country to the south of the river in the provinces of Kiangsu, Anhwei, and Kiangsi. They were driven away by the Shan and Mon population of the eastern provinces, 210-206 B.C., and were finally expelled from China by the Shan King of Nanchao, *viâ* Yungchang, a city on the Bhamo route, A.D. 778. They have since spread southwards into Lower Burmah and Siam. At the time they left China, they are said to have numbered 200,000 families.

The traditions which are repeated from father to son in metrical verse by the Yang, have evoked great interest among the American missionaries, who have done such good work in converting them to Christianity. From the creation until after the flood these traditions are intrinsically the same as the Mosaic accounts. Some people firmly believe the Karen to be the ten lost tribes of Israel; but as their ancestors are known to have been in China some 550 years before the ten tribes were lost, it is much more reasonable to believe that they received their traditions from the Mohammedans of Yunnan, or that before their entrance into China they followed the tracks of the Peh Sing tribes, and had their earlier home in the neighbourhood of the Semite tribes, and there acquired their knowledge. The two other races which have extended southwards from China into Indo-China are the Jung and the Shan. The former was already on the borders of China, and some of its tribes had settled about the southern bend of the Hoang Ho at the time when the Peh Sing Chinese tribes arrived from their long journey from the neighbourhood of Chaldea. The Jung, according to Professor Terrien de Lacouperie, were originally of the same white stock as ourselves, and have become hybrid by intermixture with the neighbouring races. They were so warlike in their disposition that their name became amongst the Chinese equivalent to that of warriors. In the seventh century B.C. they were spread across the north of China from the extreme west of Kansu to the neighbourhood of Pekin. Many of their tribes were absorbed by the Ts'in—the Seres of the Greeks and Romans—of the province of Shensi, whose State name Ts'in has been by Europeans corrupted into China.

The people of Ts'in claimed kinship with the Niao-suk (Nila-Cakas or black Sakœ), and with the Fei or Bod, the people of Tibet. About B.C. 770, Ts'in was incorporated in the agglomeration of dukedoms or States forming the Djow dominion, and rapidly increased in strength by conquest, and partly by the absorption of the neighbouring Jung tribes. It then grew in power at the expense of the eastern States, and brought them into subjection. It further carried its sway across the Yangtsze B.C. 279, and conquered Tsoo. Its duke became Supreme Emperor of Ts'in B.C. 220.

The Jung tribes which were not absorbed by Ts'in, gradually pressed southwards amongst the Shan tribes in Szechuen, and are now found, under the tribal names of Mo-so, Lissu, Lolo, La-hu, La-wa (Lahs and Wahs to the north of Kiang Tung), &c., in the west of that province, and in Yunnan, Kweichau, and the Shan States as far south as the latitude of Zimmé, and as far west as the Salween river. These tribes speak a Tibeto-Burmese language.

The Shan race, known by the self-names of Tai, Pai, Lao, &c., occupies an area of country six times as large as the United Kingdom; yet, owing to the trading propensities of the race, the dialects spoken by the Shans differ so slightly that travellers from the Tonquin hills, Kwangsi, Yunnan, and Bhamo can converse with people at Zimmé and at Bangkok.

In the earliest times we hear of the Shans under their tribal names stretching across China from east to west, and occupying the country between the Yangtsze and the Hoang Ho. From 1766 to 1122 B.C. they are supposed to have been the dominant power in China, since the Shang, or traders, the ruling dynasty during that period, were presumably of their race. Later on they spread over Southern China, forming a large ingredient in the kingdoms of Tsoo, Tsen or Tien, and Nan-Yueh, and extended into the valleys of the Irawadi, Salween, Meh Nam, and Meh Kong.

The last of their tribes to leave Central China for Indo-China appear to have been the Chau Tai or Siamese, who were expelled from their seat in Kiangsi and Anhwei in the tenth century of our era. They were driven to the south-west into Kwangsi and Kweichau, where some of their tribes are still found, and a large body ultimately migrated into the Shan States to the south of Kiang Hsen.

In the latter half of the thirteenth century the country occupied by the Shans was in a state of turmoil and unrest. The ancient principalities in Yunnan had been conquered by Kublai Khan 1253-54; the Shan States to the south and west of Yunnan had been attacked, and a consequent great displacement of the population occurred. At that time the agglomeration of States formed by the Ngai Lao or Lao Shans stretched southwards from the latitude of Kiang Hsen to the northern confines of Cambodia or La-Wek, which then included a number of principalities in the valley of the Meh Nam, as well as in that of the Meh Kong. About 1281, according to the Shan records at Zimmé, the Prince of Kiang Hsen advanced southwards and conquered Lapoon, and in 1294 founded the present city of Zimmé. The Lapoon Shans fled into Martaban, and, headed by one of themselves, attacked the Burmese governor, slew him, and made their leader Wa-re-ru King of Martaban, A.D. 1281. Six years later, this Shan king conquered Pegu, and Shan kings reigned over the joint kingdom from that time until they were conquered by the Burmese in 1540. Upper Burmah was likewise under Shan kings from A.D. 1290 to 1554.

It was about the time of the conquest of Lapoon, according to Siamese history, that the Siamese were expelled from Kiang Hai by the Prince of Sittang. The Siamese fled southwards, and founded a new capital at Muang Pehp or Pet, opposite the present city of Kamphang Pet on the Meh Ping. In 1320 they deserted that city and founded another in the neighbourhood, and thirty-one years later migrated to the south, built their new capital at Ayuthia, on the site of a deserted Cambodian city called Viang Lek, founded dukedoms or *Muangs* at Soo-pan-Boo-ree and Lop-Boo-ree, and joined the confederation formed by the Ngai Lao States, over which the King of Sukkhothai was then suzerain. This king had attacked Cambodia in 1296, pillaged its cities in the valley of the Meh Nam, driven the Cambodians to the eastward, and thus rendered the country available for the Siamese settlements.

As time went on the Siamese became the predominant State in the kingdom, and entered on frequent wars of aggression with Cambodia, Annam, Vieng Chang, and Zimmé. In 1546, six years after the Burmese King of Toungoo had conquered Pegu, the Siamese commenced the series of wars with Burmah which ended in nearly exterminating the population of both countries.

Every able-bodied man who did not take refuge in flight was forced into the ranks, either to defend his country, or to attack that of his neighbours, or the neighbours of the power to which his own State was tributary. Armies, from forty thousand to two hundred thousand men strong, ravaged the land, and swept away, as in a great net, those of the inhabitants who were not killed in battle. In vast tracts not a man, woman, or child remained; and elephants, rhinoceroses, tigers, deer, wild cattle, and other wild animals took possession of the devastated country. At length the Mon armies of Burmah, who hated forced service, mutinied, and, taking their wives and children with them, fled into Siam; and Zimmé, which had been under Burmah, except in times of rebellion, from 1558 to 1774, threw off the yoke and asked for the protection of Siam. To such an extent was the population thinned out by the incessant warfare, that when we annexed the Burmese province of Tenasserim, which borders Siam and Zimmé, we found in it barely seventy thousand souls.

Burmah is blessed with a fruitful soil and a bounteous rainfall. It only requires increased population to make it the garden of the East; and every chief commissioner, from Sir Arthur Phayre downwards, has advocated its connection with China by railway, as the means for supplying that want from the most industrious and enterprising people in Asia, the Chinese.

I take this opportunity to record my deep sense of gratitude to the Rev. J. N. Cushing, D.D., and the Rev. D. M'Gilvary, D.D., who accompanied me as comrades and interpreters during part of my explorations, for their friendly endeavour to secure the success of my undertaking; and I have much pleasure in expressing my heartfelt appreciation of the frank cordiality and unwearying kindness accorded me by all the American Missionaries and Missionary Ladies during my stay in the country.

CONTENTS.

CHAPTER I.

CHAPTER II.

CHAPTER III.

CHAPTER IV.

CHAPTER V.

CHAPTER VI.

CHAPTER VII.

CHAPTER VIII.

CHAPTER XIII.

CHAPTER XIV.

CHAPTER XV.

CHAPTER XVI.

CHAPTER XVII.

CHAPTER XVIII.

CHAPTER XIX.

CHAPTER XX.

CHAPTER XXI.

CHAPTER XXII.

CHAPTER XXIII.

CHAPTER XXIV.

CHAPTER XXV.

CHAPTER XXVI.

CHAPTER XXVII.

CHAPTER XXVIII.

CHAPTER XXIX.

CHAPTER XXXII.

CHAPTER XXXIII.

CHAPTER XXXIV.

ILLUSTRATIONS.

LIST OF MAPS.

A THOUSAND MILES ON AN ELEPHANT IN THE SHAN STATES.

CHAPTER I.

DR CUSHING'S ARRIVAL—A-HENG—LEAVE SHOAYGOON—GOLD AND SILVER CARRIED—FLOOD OF 1877—A BAD DRIVER—DOG OFFERED TO DEMONS—SOUSED IN THE HLINEBOAY—HLINEBOAY—TRADERS—MR BRYCE'S PARTY—ASKED TO JOIN PARTIES—DR CUSHING IN CHARGE OF COMMISSARIAT—LABELLING AND SORTING BASKETS—THE LUGGAGE—MEDICINES—KAREN INTERPRETER—LOADING THE ELEPHANTS—PORTOW AND LOOGALAY—MADRAS BOYS GOOD FIGHTERS.

"Dr Cushing here, sahib! boat coming:" so gasped Veyloo and Jewan, my Madras servants, as they came racing up the staircase of the teak-built court-house at Shoaygoon, where I was enjoying a smoke whilst reclining in my table-armed folding-chair. This chair, which was a miracle of comfort and convenience, together with my camp-bedstead, had been designed and constructed for me by A-heng, a very clever and honest Chinese contractor, who for many years had been employed by me in constructing bridges, court-houses, jails, bazaars, and various other public buildings whilst I was in charge of the Tenasserim division of Burmah. This division, measuring 630 miles in a north and south direction, forms the eastern portion of Lower Burmah, and is bordered on the east by Siam and the Siamese Shan States, through which I was about to journey in search of the best route for a railway to connect Burmah with South-western China.

Following the boys, who had rushed off as soon as they had given me the news, I scrambled down the steep bank of the Salween river, which forms the western boundary of the garden of the court-house, and reached the water's edge some minutes before the boat stranded at my feet.

"Here we are, together at last!" I exclaimed, as I helped my future companion from the boat; "I do hope you are better. I was so glad you succeeded in persuading the doctor to allow you to come,—I should have been helpless without you."

"Thanks; I feel better already, and hope to be all right in a day or two," said Dr Cushing. "Jungle-life was what I wanted: my illness, although partly the after-effects of fever, was mainly due to being cooped up for months at indoor work. Have you got the elephants?"

"Yes," I replied, "they are at Hlineboay, and I have arranged for seven carts to take our things there to-morrow. We can have them packed after lunch, and see if we shall require more. Come along; the boys have lunch ready."

Meanwhile the boys had been welcoming Ramasawmy, Dr Cushing's Madras servant; and Shoay Wai and Portow, the Shan interpreters, who had been hired for the expedition, were aiding the boatmen to unload the boat and carry the things to the court-house.

The next morning, the 21st of January, we were away early, Dr Cushing and I leading the way in the cart which carried our bedding and the treasure; the latter consisting of fifteen bags, each containing a hundred rupees, packed away in the tin boxes and waterproof bags amongst my clothing, and a heavy burden of gold-leaf, which for safety I carried on my person. How glad I was to place the gold in the custody of the missionaries at Zimmé when I arrived there! Very few men would care to be rich if they had to carry their wealth in bullion about them.

After continuing northwards along the river-bank for two miles we turned eastward, crossing the low land that lies between the Salween and the high laterite ground which separates it from the basin of the Hlineboay river. The highest point passed by the cart-road between Shoaygoon and Hlineboay is less than a hundred feet above the former place. The great flood of 1877 rose two feet six inches above the bank of the Salween at Shoaygoon, or to a level twenty feet above the ground in the interior; but owing to the breadth of the valley and the slope of the country, the flood-water passed off in a stream a mile in breadth and about ten feet deep.

Leaving the valley, we proceeded over laterite ground, amongst small trees and scrub-jungle. Before reaching the Hlineboay river we had been pretty nearly jolted to death by our abominable driver, the worst and most apathetic of his kind I have ever suffered from. The carts, as is usual in Burmah, were springless, and ordinary jolts might be expected; but this creature drove us against trees and over tree-roots a tyro might have avoided. I was particularly annoyed, as Dr Cushing was only just recovering from an attack of liver complaint. It was no use expostulating (though expostulate we did), for there only came bang, bang, bang over another tree-root. We had to laugh, the man seemed so utterly irreclaimable. Loogalay, my half-breed Burmese Mohammedan, who was walking by the cart, assured us that it was no use talking to the man,—"He was *yainday* (a country lout); born a bullock, and would die a buffalo"—that is, he was born a bumpkin and would die a blockhead.

On passing near the village of Quanta, which is situated about eleven miles from Shoaygoon, Dr Cushing called to me to hold my nose,—the Karens, to propitiate the *nats* (demons, gnomes, and fairies) of the vicinity, had sacrificed a dog to them, and the air for a hundred yards was reeking with the stench from the crucified remains.

A mile and a half farther on we entered the low ground bordering the Hlineboay river, and shortly afterwards came to the stream. The banks, even where cut away for the cart-road, were steep, and the ford was narrow. Here was a chance for our Jehu. When racing down the bank, instead of attending to the oxen he gazed back at the other carts. The cattle, turning sharply at the ford, dragged the cart into the deep water up-stream. We were soused up to our waists, our bedding was drenched, and I incurred three hours' unexpected labour in cleaning and readjusting my surveying instruments, which would otherwise have been ruined by their bath. Our Handy Andy was not in the least discomposed by his achievement; it was an everyday feat to him: his countenance was a picture of impassive stolidity; he showed no signs of being horrified or even delighted at the effects of his carelessness. What could we do but laugh? He was indeed born a bullock, and fast merging into the buffalo. A mile and a half down-stream from the ford, skirting the river, brought us to Hlineboay, where we put up in the court-house, which the *myook*, or native judge and magistrate, had courteously placed at our disposal.

Hlineboay, a village of seven or eight hundred inhabitants, chiefly Karens, being the headquarters of a township, contains a court-house and police station. It lies at the junction of the thoroughfares from Thatone and Maulmain to the Shan States and China, and is at the navigation head of the Hlineboay river, and 111 miles distant by water from Maulmain. In the dry season, which lasts for half the year, it has a large local market and carries on a considerable trade. People congregate there from all directions. Scattered before the court-house you may see natives of India from Maulmain with cotton goods and twist; Burmans and Talaigus from the same place, with oil, salt, dried and salt fish, tinned provisions, and other commodities; Karen villagers with fowls, ducks, and pigs from the neighbouring districts; Shan and Toungthoo cattle-dealers from Thatone on their way to the Shan States; Chinese with mule-caravans from Yunnan; parties of Shans from Zimmé, with packs of beautifully worked silk garments, and others returning with woollen and cotton piece-goods and sundry articles of peddlery: the whole scene teeming with life and colour. In the rains trade becomes slack, and the Myook moves his quarters to Shoaygoon, opposite which the great teak-rafts drift down the Salween from Siam, the Shan States, and Karenni to the timber-yards at Maulmain.

Moung Tsan Yan, the Myook, an old acquaintance of mine, came to see us on our arrival, and told me that he had secured fourteen elephants, six for our party and eight for that of Mr Bryce, the head manager of the Bombay Trading Company, who had asked me to join parties with him, so that we might travel together as far as Zimmé. Dacoits might be lurking on the frontier: the more Europeans there were together, the less liable should we be to attack. I accordingly halted until the 23d, when, hearing that he was delayed, I determined to start, making short journeys in order to enable his party to overtake us.

Dr Cushing kindly took over the commissariat from me, and we set to work to sort and rearrange the baggage. Previous to leaving Maulmain I had purchased forty *pahs*, or baskets made of pliable wicker-work, each being about twenty inches long, fifteen inches broad, and ten inches deep, which would fit easily into the howdah of an elephant. These, after sorting, we labelled and numbered, entering the contents of each in my note-book.

Method in packing saves a great deal of trouble and time when on a journey. I never met a more methodical man than Dr Cushing. His arrangements were admirable. Everything was kept in its place. Each elephant-load was stacked separately throughout the journey. Each driver had charge of his own load, and was held responsible for it.

Stores for several weeks' supply were packed separately, two *pahs* together containing what was likely to be required each separate week; and no other *pahs*, except those in charge of the cook, were allowed to be opened without our consent. The cooking utensils, crockery, a dozen of brandy for medicinal purposes, two dozen of whisky, and some of the medicines, were packed in straw in small wooden cases. These, together with the *pahs*, two waterproof bags, and a tin box for clothes and money, my office-box, rugs, bedding, chairs, and camp-bedstead, and our two selves, formed the load of the six elephants which were to convey us and our belongings to Maing Loongyee, where fresh steeds had to be procured.

The medicines, purchased by me chiefly in England, were the usual ones carried in Indo-China. They consisted of quinine, Warburg's tincture and arsenic for fever, ipecacuanha, Dover's powder and laudanum for dysentery, Eno's fruit-salt, Cockle's pills and chlorodyne for lesser ailments; pain-killer for dispelling the agony of bites from noxious insects such as the huge dairy-keeping red ants that milk syrup from plant-lice, centipedes and scorpions; Goa powder for ringworm, the most general and contagious plague in the far East; and vaseline and Holloway's ointment for abrasions of the skin and ordinary casualties so frequent on a journey. Dr Cushing was a doctor of souls: he knew, and would know, nothing of physic; he abhorred it. His wife had been the general practitioner on his former journeys. There was no help for it; I must be the physician as well as the leader of the party.

At daybreak on the 23d of January, having finished our packing and procured a Karen guide who could speak Burmese and Talaing to serve as my interpreter as far as Maing Loongyee, we had the elephants brought in and loaded. Here Dr Cushing's power as an organiser became apparent. The baggage had been stacked into six loads, two smaller than the others for the elephants which were to be ridden by us. The howdahs, however, proved of unequal size, and some of them would not hold the tin boxes and cases which were intended for them. The air was filled with complaints and remonstrances. Each of the Karen mahouts, naturally, wished his beast to carry less than its portion. Each objected to have another burden foisted on him. Loogalay and Portow were worse than useless: both made confusion worse by fussing about, tugging at the Madras

Portow.

boys, and putting them out of temper by imperious commands mixed with abuse. Ignorance, according to the copy-books, is boastful, conceited, and sure. I never saw the proverb better exemplified than by these two men throughout the journey. It was impossible, in Portow's opinion, that Portow could be mistaken; he knew everything; he was always ready and eager to advise, and equally ready to jeer at and snub any one else who ventured to do so: but although he had been the head-man of his village, and was an egregious blockhead and an egotistical bumpkin, he was eminently good-natured, and bore no malice when plagued, as he frequently was, by our Madras boys.

Loogalay, or Moung Loogalay, as he liked to be called, was a hectoring, swaggering blade, as gaily dressed as a game-cock, and as vain as an actor. A well-built lad of about two-and-twenty, who had been brought up in an English school, tall and good-looking, thoughtless, gay, and careless, in his gaily coloured Burmese costume he looked the beau-ideal of a dashing youth. His hair tied in a chignon on the top of his head, and festooned with a loosely arranged silk kerchief; his *putso,* or plaid, serving as a petticoat, with the end jauntily thrown over his shoulder; his clean white cotton jacket with gold buttons, and the flower stuck in his ear,—how could one help enjoying the sight of him, however much one might be put out by his indolence!

Madras boys, particularly those who have been attached to the officers of a native regiment, and have seen more or less of the world, generally have a pretty good opinion of themselves. Some are good wrestlers, and most of them can use their fists. Loogalay was employed as my henchman, or *peon*—not to do domestic service, but to attend to my wants on the journey; to pick up geological and botanical specimens, measure the depth and breadth of streams, help me when photographing, and carry instructions to the rest of the party. His salary was greater than that of the boys, and he looked upon himself as head boss over them. Anyhow, to him they were *kulahs,* his natural inferiors, mere savages or outer barbarians; he was a *loo*—a man and a Burman. Instead of giving orders as emanating from me, he constantly put their backs up by assuming mastery over them, and issuing orders as from himself.

"Heh! Kulah! put those here, not there. What are you about?—*yainday!*" he vociferated, as the boys were handing up the things to the elephant-drivers. The boys treated his orders with sullen disdain, and went on quietly attending to their business. Loogalay was stamping about and slapping his thighs, becoming more flushed every minute, and looking more and more like an enraged turkey-cock. I was enjoying the fun, sitting quietly smoking in my chair up in the court-house, and would have liked to have watched its further development. There is nothing like a thunderstorm to clear the air, or a good determined school-fight to put the young folk at their ease and knock sense into them. Dr Cushing, however, being in charge of the marching arrangements, put an end to the cabal by appearing on the scene and bundling Loogalay and Portow off to attend on the other elephants.

With his presence order came out of chaos, and by half-past seven we were ready to start. A quarter of an hour later Dr Cushing stepped off the verandah of the court-house on to the head of his elephant, sprawled over the greasy Karen mahout to the seat that had been prepared for him, said good-bye to the Myook, and headed the train of elephants as they commenced their journey.

CHAPTER II.

SURVEYING — THANKFUL FOR A HALT — LEAVE HLINEBOAY — KAREN HOUSES INFESTED WITH BUGS—HALT NEAR WELL—RIGGING UP SHELTER FOR THE NIGHT—TENT LEFT BEHIND—TEAK-FOREST—YUNNANESE—A SCARE—EXPLODING BAMBOOS—TREES 130 FEET HIGH—A MID-DAY HALT—THE BRITISH GUARD-HOUSE—A NIGHT CAMP—GLUTINOUS RICE, MODE OF COOKING AND CARRIAGE—ELEPHANTS FEEDING—HEAVY DEW—JOURNEY DOWN THE YEMBINE VALLEY—MOTION OF ELEPHANTS—DIFFICULT SURVEYING—A PRACTICAL JOKE—RAILWAY TO RANGOON AND MANDALAY—HEATHEN KARENS—NO LONGER A MISSIONARY—DIFFICULTY IN CONVERTING BUDDHISTS—VENISON FOR DINNER—STUNG BY BEES—PASS BETWEEN THE THOUNGYEEN AND THE SALWEEN—TREES 25 FEET IN CIRCUMFERENCE—LIMESTONE CLIFFS—OFFERING TO THE DEAD—DESCENT TO THE THOUNGYEEN—THE FORD.

SURVEYING by time-distances and a prismatic compass, when on the march, requires a steady hand, a quick judgment for selecting an object for your angle, and a good memory. If the hand is unsteady, the ring of the compass, which is balanced on a needle, will not come to rest. In a jungle-clad country you must watch the foremost elephant as it winds through the trees, and rapidly select the point for your next angle as the animal is just passing from view. A good memory is required, otherwise in noticing the trees, rocks, by-paths, width and depth of streams, breadth of fields, size of villages, and taking sketches of, and angles to, neighbouring hills, you will forget the object, twig, branch or trunk of tree, that you have aimed at.

Having taken your angle, you must catch up the last elephant—for you are taking your distances by the time it takes in passing over the ground—and observe the time and your next angle on arriving at the object you had formerly chosen. This constant observation, continuing from dawn to dark with one interval for refreshment, is a great strain upon one's attention, and when joined with the necessity of taking heights from the aneroid barometer, and temperatures from the thermometer at every change of level, makes one thankful for a halt at the foot or summit of a mountain pass, where one has to check the height by the boiling-point thermometer.

For the first hour after leaving Hlineboay we passed over slightly undulating ground, covered with stunted trees and scrub-jungle, and then entered paddy-fields through which we proceeded to Quambee, a Talaing, or Pwo, Karen village in a rice-plain over half a mile in breadth. To the east of the plain amongst the forest appeared many isolated hills and knolls, backed up by a boldly defined peaked range of hills, the Dana Toung, distant about fifteen miles, which forms the water-parting between the Thoungyeen and Salween rivers.

There being no *zayat*, or rest-house, in the village, and Karen houses being generally infested with bugs, we decided to camp in a grove of large trees in the vicinity of a well, from which we could draw water for bathing and cooking. After the elephants were unloaded and we had finished our supper, a shelter for the night was quickly formed with a few bamboos, roofed with two large waterproof sheets which I luckily had with me. My tent had been left behind in Maulmain through an oversight of the boys; and although the Bombay-Burmah party kindly brought it with them to Hlineboay, it may be still at the latter place, as they had not carriage sufficient to bring it farther. A tent is a cumbersome and costly thing to carry about, and we managed very well for several months without one.

The next day we resumed our short stages, hoping that Mr Bryce's party would catch us up. The country continued of much the same character as between Hlineboay and Quambee—only, cultivated fields became rarer, isolated hills more numerous, and teak-trees were frequently interspersed in the forest. The first night from

Quambee we spent in a *zayat* on the bank of the Hline river.

Towards dark a party of Chinese from Yunnan, who had sold their goods at Zimmé, came scampering by, armed with Shan *dahs* or swords, spears, and very antiquated horse-pistols. They were conducting a caravan of between forty and fifty mules and ponies to Maulmain, intending to bring them back laden with piece-goods and general articles of merchandise. They ultimately camped about half a mile from us, as several times in the evening we heard from that direction what we considered to be the discharge of fire-arms. Chinamen were not likely to waste powder in frightening off dacoits or wild beasts when they had any simpler, equally efficient, and cheaper means at command; and next morning we learnt our mistake in a very unexpected and alarming manner. We were suddenly awakened by a fusilade of reports around our camp. I jumped up, seized my Winchester, and rushed out, thinking that our party was being attacked. I found the boys squatting quietly round the fire, grinning like monkeys, and heaping on joints of green bamboos. The liquid in the cavities turning to steam under the influence of heat, caused them to explode, thus giving rise to the reports which had startled us. The rascals had learnt the trick from Portow, and were amusing themselves at our expense, being evidently bent on giving us a good fright.

Leaving the *zayat* a little before seven, we crossed the river and clambered over a low hillock, and continued through the forest, with teak-trees still appearing at intervals. Small hills and spurs from the Kyouk Toung range were occasionally seen to the east, backed up by the Yare-they-mare hill, a great spur of the Dana range, some four miles distant. About half-past eight we crossed the Hlineboay river for the last time, and shortly afterwards ascended 80 feet to the crest of the high ground, 300 feet above sea-level, and seventeen miles from Hlineboay, which forms the water-parting between the Hlineboay and Yambine rivers.

Thence we passed through the forest, still occasionally interspersed with teak-trees, following the course of the

Yingan stream, with hills at times bordering on either side, and halted at half-past eleven for breakfast by the side of the stream, under a magnificent clump of *thyt-si* trees, which produce the celebrated black varnish. These monarchs of the forest, 130 feet in height, owing to great buttresses springing from the stem some feet from the ground, were of enormous girth, and looked truly magnificent. Here was a perfect place for a mid-day halt: hill, forest, and water scenery all combined; a cool stream as a bath for the elephants and ourselves; shelter from the heat of the sun; a pleasant glade for a ramble whilst breakfast was being prepared. Nothing was wanting but the songs of birds and the rippling chatter and laughter of girls to make our picnic all that could possibly be desired. Day after day, month after month, we enjoyed such picnics on our travels.

We struck camp at a quarter past two, and after a little more than an hour's journey, still following the stream, reached Teh-dau-Sakan, the halting-place close to the Lan-ma-Gyee Garté, the last British police post on our road to the Shan States—having thoroughly enjoyed our day.

The police station, which is situated twenty-four miles from Hlineboay, consists of two thatched buildings built of bamboo, and surrounded with a dilapidated stockade, which would have been useless as a defence against dacoits. It was occupied by ten or twelve Madras constables, who complained much of the feverishness of the locality, and begged for quinine, saying they were out of it. I never met less intelligent men in my life; they seemed to know nothing of the locality, and the idea of a map was utterly incomprehensible to them—they had not been educated up to it. There was no getting any information from them; the whole current of their thoughts ran towards *carna* and *pice* (food and money), and their bodily ailments.

We erected our shelter for the night about a hundred yards from the station, in a grove of *thyt-si* trees, each measuring from 30 to 40 feet in circumference five feet from the ground. A large party of Shans from Lapoon encamped near us, and came over in the evening for a chat with our men. Camp-fires were dotted around us in all directions.

Each elephant had, besides the mahout, an attendant to look after its wants, lop branches off banian and other trees for its food, shackle its fore-feet when we halted, and aid in its morning, noonday, and evening bath.

Each couple of men built a fire for themselves, and kept it alight during the night, partly for warmth and partly to scare wild beasts that might be wandering around. *Kouknyin*, the glutinous rice eaten by the Karens, is steamed, and not boiled. An earthen pot, or *chatty*, is placed upon three stones or clods of earth, which serve as a tripod; on the top of the pot is placed the basket containing the rice, and the junction is made air-tight with a wet cotton rag. A fire is then lighted under the pot, and the steam from the water in the pot rises into the rice and cooks it. Whilst hot the rice is stuffed into joints of green bamboos about a foot in length, and eaten when required. Joints of green bamboos likewise serve them for kettles: placed slanting over a fire, the water soon boils. The elephants feeding in the neighbourhood could be heard crashing through the bushes, rending off branches that suited their fancy. These animals were our sentinels, and would trumpet if a tiger came roving in their neighbourhood.

It would have been pleasant to sit in the open air and watch the stars as they twinkled through the trees, if it had not been for the heavy dew which commenced to fall soon after sundown. Loogalay's mosquito-curtains, made of stout cotton cloth, were dripping wet the next morning, and he came with a long face and wrung them out before us. Portow merely jeered at him, and asked why he had not erected a leaf-shelter, as the other men had done. It is worse than useless complaining of the effects of one's folly in a company of wits.

Next morning, the 26th of January, we ordered two of the elephants to be got ready to take us on an excursion down the Yembine valley, the farther end of which I had visited on a tour up the Salween. This would give me a chance of learning to survey from the top of an elephant. At first thoughts one would deem such a feat to be impossible; the pitching and rolling of the huge beast, which goes along like a Dutch lugger in a chopping sea, would prevent the compass being brought to rest, and most likely jam it into one's eye. Yet, by giving way to the swaying movements of the brute, I managed to get as perfect results as when surveying on foot. From thenceforth, during my land journeys, I surveyed from the back of an elephant.

The boys, in packing our breakfast for us, perhaps out of fun, omitted not only to put in my cigars, but also our knives, forks, and spoons, forcing us to improvise some out of slips of bamboo to avoid having to feed native-fashion, with our fingers.

Following the stream of the Yingan till it joined the Yembine, we continued down the valley of the latter, accompanied by the mournful wailing of the gibbons in the forest, the plain gradually opening out to more than a mile in width, but contracting at times to a quarter of a mile, as spurs jutted in from either side. After travelling for three hours and a half, we halted for breakfast at the Karen village of Nga-peur-dau, which is beautifully situated on the hillside to the south of the valley.

The hills opposite the village were bold, and in some places precipitous, appearing as though they had been punched up from below, and were most likely mural limestone. Clay-slate, limestone, and sandstone are the chief rocks in this part of the country. Silver, copper, lead, and iron pyrites are found in Bo Toung, a hill some miles to the north of Nga-peur-dau, and felspar and porphyry are met with along the Salween some distance above Yembine.

We were now within eight miles of the village of Yembine, which is situated at the junction of the Yembine with the Salween. After walking about a mile and a half farther along the hillside, it became evident that a railway could be carried from Yembine to Teh-dau-Sakan with the greatest ease, meeting no difficulties in its path. I had previously ascertained, by visiting Yembine, that the Salween could be crossed in the defile to the south of it by a bridge of four or five hundred feet span; and, from my former experience in the country, I was aware that a line could be carried from the Rangoon and Mandalay Railway to this crossing through one continuous plain. It remained to be seen whether such a line could be continued along the course we were taking to South-western China, or whether the better course lay eastwards from Maulmain to Raheng, and thence northwards to the same goal.

We learnt from the Karen villagers that the Karens in the hamlets scattered through this region, and those to the north and the east, are still heathens, and I was glad to find that the missionaries are now on their scent. Most of the Karens elsewhere in Lower Burmah have become Christians, and the American Presbyterian and Baptist missionaries, who have so well worked the field, are turning their attention to Upper Burmah, Karenni, the Shan States, and Siam. I was amused by reading in a missionary report some months ago the complaint of a missionary that all the Karens in his district had embraced Christianity, and he had not another one to convert. He was a pastor, but no longer a missionary.

The Karens, Shans, Kakhyens, and other hill tribes, who are spirit-worshippers and not Buddhists, are the stocks from which converts are produced in Burmah and Siam. If you wish to have Burmese Christians, it is necessary to train them in mission schools from childhood. A Burmese adult behaves like a goat in the sheep-fold. He skips in and out as it suits him. Too often he merely enters to see what he can get from the shepherd. It is said to cost more to convert a Burman than it does to convert a Jew. A Roman Catholic missionary told me some years ago that he very much doubted whether his mission had ever made a real convert out of an adult Burman. As the sapling is bent, so the tree grows.

Having finished the inspection, we returned to camp, where I regaled myself with my long-wished-for smoke. The boys, when scolded for their delinquencies, pretended to look chapfallen; but I am afraid I had a twinkle in my eyes when rebuking them, as I saw the three convulsed with laughter before they were many paces away. During our absence the other elephant-drivers had shot a deer, and on our return presented us with a leg. This was a delightful surprise, as we had been subsisting on fowls and tinned provisions for several days.

The next day was Sunday, so we had a delightful day's halt. I sent some of the Karens off to the neighbouring villages to obtain sufficient fowls and rice for our journey to Maing Loongyee, where we could obtain a fresh supply. Veyloo and Jewan went off on a lark, but soon returned in a dismal plight to seek my aid. In attempting to get honey, one had been stung on the eyelid, the other on the neck. An application of Perry Davis's pain-killer acted like magic, taking away the pain; and a little ointment sent them off again light-hearted—putting down their punishment, I hope, to their yesterday's conduct.

On Monday we started a little before seven, and followed the Yembine and its branches to the crest of the pass over the range which divides the drainage of the Salween from that of the Thoungyeen. The pass—32 miles from Hline-boay—has its crest 612 feet above sea-level, or 446 feet above our camp at Teh-dau-Sakan. On our way we met a party of Shans proceeding to Maulmain. A descent of about 50 feet from the crest brought us to the plateau, interspersed with detached hills, which is separated from the narrow plain through which the Thoungyeen runs, by a row of cliff-faced masses of limestone 1000 and 2000 feet in height, between which the drainage of the country flows to the river.

Close to the northern foot of the pass we came to the Tee-tee-ko stream, flowing through a pretty and pleasantly wooded valley, along which we proceeded. Turning up a northern affluent, when the Tee-tee-ko turned to the east on its way to the river, we halted for the night under some noble Kanyin trees. These trees, from which a brown resin and superior wood-oil is procured, have stems, often 25 feet in circumference, rising straight as a dart 120 feet from the ground to the first branch. The dense foliage completely shuts out the rays of the sun, thus affording a splendid shade for a mid-day halt. You do not realise their enormous size until from a distance you notice how dwarfed people camping under them appear. An elephant by their side looks like a pig under an ordinary tree.

The next morning, at a distance of two miles from the pass, we crossed the Meh Pau, a stream 60 feet wide and 7 feet deep, which, flowing from our right, enters the Thoungyeen some distance below the Siamese guard-house and below our point of crossing. We then clambered up a circular knoll rising 700 feet above the plateau, and had a fine view of the Pau-kee-lay Toung—one of the precipitous limestone masses lying three-quarters of a mile to the east. Descending from the knoll, which is ascended by the track to save half a mile of extra distance, we breakfasted on the bank of the Koo Saik Choung, just above its rapid descent between two great limestone precipices to the river.

At the junction of one of the many roads which diverged to Karen villages and the Thoungyeen from our track after leaving the pass, we noticed the death-offering of some Sgau Karens belonging to a neighbouring village. The offering was a propitiatory one to the spirit of the deceased, and proffered in order to induce it not to return and haunt the village. A silver coin had been placed in the ground beneath a rudely carved figure, on the top of which narrow strips of red and white cloth were hung; around the figure was a tiny fence, roofed in with a small bamboo platform. Miniature jackets and trousers were suspended from small poles at the sides of the fence. Food, which had been placed on the platform, was no longer there—the thieving birds having most likely deprived the poor ghost of it.

After breakfast we entered the defile, and descended from the plateau in the bed of the Koo Saik Choung, which falls 135 feet in the distance of a mile in a series of gentle cascades, separated by ice-cold running pools as clear as crystal; the towering precipices on either side looming through the trees, with their crests hidden by the dense foliage, and the natural colonnade formed by the evergreen forest through which we were passing rendering the air delightfully cool. How charming it would have been to have breakfasted in this pleasant retreat among the lichen-covered limestone boulders, mosses, and ferns! Leaving the defile, we followed the Thoungyeen down-stream past the Siamese guard-station, which lies on the other bank—the river forming the frontier—to the ford.

The river at the ford is 250 feet wide from bank to bank, with the channel reduced to 70 feet by a great shoal of boulders, now uncovered, stretching from the western bank. The current being swift and the water chest-deep, some of the men were nearly swept away whilst crossing. The boys went in up to their hips, and stood trembling, afraid to proceed farther. I therefore told them to return to the strand, and I would send elephants from the camp to bring them across.

The bank of the river is about 206 feet above mean sea-level at Maulmain. After passing the ford, we crossed the Meh Tha Wah, passed the guard-house, and camped about half a mile off, near the stream and some rice-fields. As soon as the elephants were unloaded, I sent two back for the boys; but meanwhile they had found their way to the ferry, and crossed the river in a boat. The guard-house is 38 miles from Hlineboay.

CHAPTER III.

REV. D. WEBSTER'S PARTY DETAINED — SIAMESE OFFICIALS EXPECT BRIBES—PHOTOGRAPHIC PLATES ALL SPOILT—VISIT FROM KARENS—JOINED BY THE B.B. PARTY—SIAMESE POLICE POST—GORGES IN THE THOUNGYEEN AND MEH NĬUM—RAPIDS STOP NAVIGATION—FORESTS AND ELEPHANTS — DWARF RACES — KAMOOK AND KAMAIT SLAVES HIRED BY OUR FORESTERS—MIGRATION OF LAOS FROM TONQUIN—THE KHAS OF LUANG PRABANG—SACRIFICES TO DEMONS—DRINKING THE HEALTH OF STRANGERS—KING OF SIAM ALLOWS SLAVE-HUNTING—MISSIONARIES REQUIRED IN THE MEH KONG VALLEY—LEAVE THE GUARD-HOUSE—CROSSING THE WATER-PARTING—WILD TEA—KAREN VILLAGES BUILT DISTANT FROM ROAD—COUNTRY FORMERLY LACUSTRINE—SHELTER FOR THE NIGHT—HEAVY RAIN—A SHOWER-BATH IN BED—ELEPHANTS CROSSING STEEP HILLS—WILD ANIMALS—REACH THE MEH NIUM—KAREN PIGS—REMAINS OF A LAKE-BOTTOM—THE MAING LOONGYEE PLAIN — EPIDEMIC OF SMALLPOX — VILLAGES TABOOED — ARRIVE AT MAING LOONGYEE — MOUNG HMOON TAW'S HOUSE—A TIMBER PRINCE AND THE MONEY-LENDERS.

THE *sala*, or traveller's rest-house, we found occupied by the Rev. David Webster, who with his wife and pretty little golden-haired daughter was on his way to Zimmé by a route to the south of that we intended taking. Mr Webster is a missionary of the American Baptist Mission, which together with the American Presbyterian Mission has been highly successful in civilising and converting the Karens in Burmah. He was now on his way to the Siamese Shan States, as he had heard from some of his converts that there were many Karens in Central Indo-China.

In Burmah he had only been able to hire elephants to carry them as far as the frontier, and was therefore at the mercy of the Siamese official in charge of the guard. He had omitted on principle to grease this petty potentate's palms, with the result that he had been detained waiting for thirteen days. Having lost patience, he had endeavoured to hire the elephants direct from the Karens instead of waiting for the Jack-in-office to take action, but found the Karens were afraid to let them on hire to him for fear of rousing their tyrant's anger, or having to part with a portion of the hire.

I stopped over the next day to allow the Bombay Burmah party to join us, which they did in the afternoon. In the morning I unpacked my photographic apparatus, and took views of the country, guard-station, and Mr Webster's party, which included several Karen girls who were attached to their schools. When unpacking the dry plates, I was dismayed to find many adhering to the tissue-paper covers, and all of them spotted by damp. As I opened packet after packet on my journey, I found them all in the same plight, and before I reached Zimmé ceased photographing, and sent the views—some fifty in number—that I had taken, to Mr Klier, the photographer in Rangoon, who had kindly promised to develop them for me.

In the afternoon a Karen man with his little boy and girl came to visit our camp. The children were greatly pleased with the bead necklaces which I gave them. Messrs Bryce and Ross, who had with them ten elephants and eleven ponies and mules—the latter purchased from the Chinese caravan which had passed us when halting on the Hlineboay river—arrived towards dusk, and camped near us.

The Siamese frontier post consists of five buildings, enclosed by a bamboo stockade. The officer in charge of the Laos or Shan police did not inquire for our passports, and allowed Mr Bryce's large treasure-guard to march by unquestioned. He had no hope of squeezing anything out of the party, and therefore paid no attention to it.

Our intention had been to proceed from the guard-station down the Thoungyeen to its junction with the Meh Nium, and up the latter river to Maing Loongyee; but on inquiry we learnt that such a route was utterly impracticable. The numerous rapids in both rivers rendered them impassable for boats, and even for canoes. Neither elephants nor men could follow the banks, as the rivers passed through great gorges—the cliffs from both sides rising from their beds. We had therefore to turn eastwards, and following branch valleys and spurs, cross the Karroway Toung, or Parrot's Hill, into the valley of the Meh Ngor, which enters the Meh Nium above the defiles, through which it escapes from the hills.

A large amount of teak timber has for many years been taken from the forests in the Thoungyeen valley. The Siamese had lately raised the tax from five to six rupees a log: their revenue in 1884 from this source amounted to upwards of two lakhs of rupees. Two hundred and sixty elephants were at work in the forests, which, like other forests in Siam, Karenni, and the Shan States, are worked by our Maulmain Burmese foresters. There is a large sale amongst the foresters of tinned milk, salmon, sardines, butter, and biscuits—all coming from Maulmain.

The Kamooks and Kamaits, who attend to the elephants and fell the timber, belong to the dwarf races of Indo-China, and are brought by their masters from their homes in the neighbourhood of Luang Prabang, and hired to our foresters at from sixty to a hundred rupees a-year; each master keeping twenty-five rupees or more out of each year's salary, and the foresters find the men with food.

The Khas, who include the Kamooks and Kamaits, are doubtless the aborigines of the country lying between the Meh Kong or Cambodia river, and the Annam and Tonquin seaboard. They are supposed to have been ousted from the plains and driven into the hills by hordes of Laos, an eastern branch of the Shans, migrating from Tonquin when it was conquered by the Chinese about B.C. 110.

According to the American missionaries who have visited Luang Prabang, the Khas are harmless and honest but ignorant, and despised by their Laos masters. Their villages are erected within stockades, on the summits of the mountains. The majority, however, live in isolated houses, which with their clearings stand out in bold relief against the sky. They cultivate rice, cotton, tobacco, vegetables, fruit, and betel-nut trees; collect stick-lac from the *pouk* and *zi* trees, and gold from the torrent-beds; and prepare cutch for chewing with the leaf of the seri vine, betel-nut, and lime. They are likewise great cattle-breeders, and many of the fine buffaloes met with in Burmah have been brought from Luang Prabang.

The Kha villages form the wealth of the Laos, who reside in the valley of the Meh Kong, to the east of the river. The Khas are known to the Siamese as Kha Chays, or slaves, and are treated as such. According to the Laos chief of Luang Prabang, the seven tribes of Khas in his territory are four times as numerous as his Laos subjects. Dr Neis, who has traversed a great part of his State, believes this opinion to be within the mark. Each Kha has to pay a tribute to his Laos or Siamese master. Without the Khas, their lazy, pleasure-loving, opium-smoking masters would have to work, or die of hunger. The extortion practised upon these kindly-dispositioned people has frequently driven them into revolt. In 1879 they joined the Chinese marauders in their attack upon the Laos; and also in 1887, when they sacked and destroyed Luang Prabang, the chief town and capital of the Shan State of that name.

The Khas, like all the hill tribes in Indo-China, offer sacrifices to evil spirits, who, according to them, are the cause of all the ills that man is heir to. In a single case of sickness as many as ten or twelve buffaloes, or other animals, are at times offered up.

They do honour to their guests and distinguished visitors by calling together the young men of the neighbourhood to drink their health in rice-spirit. Those whom I met were happy, cheery, hard-working men with pleasant faces, which, although flat, were not Mongolian, but, I think, Dravidian in type. Their expression betokened freedom from care, frankness, and good-nature. Those measured by me averaged four feet and nine inches in height, and, like the Negritos of the Andaman Isles, few exceed five feet. Their limbs were symmetrically formed, and altogether the Khas looked vigorous, pliant, and active little men. The Kamooks whom I saw, dressed in jackets and trousers dyed blue similar to those worn by the Burmese Shans, and wore their long hair drawn back from their forehead and fastened in a knot at the back of the head.

As long as the King of Siam allows the harmless hill tribes to the east of the Meh Kong to be hunted down, and held and sold as slaves by his subjects, so long should he be abhorred and placed in the same category as the ferocious monsters who have been and are the ruling curses of Africa. The sooner missionaries, American and English, are sent to Luang Prabang, and other places in the valley of the Meh Kong, the sooner will the King of Siam be shamed into putting a stop to the proceedings of the slave-dealers, who, according to French travellers up the Meh Kong, are fast depopulating the hills. There can be little doubt that the Khas, being spirit-worshippers like the Karens, and not Buddhists, would flock into the Christian fold in the same manner that the Karens have done.

During our stay near the guard-house, the temperature in the shade varied between 46° and 81°, the extreme cold being at daybreak, and the greatest heat at two o'clock in the afternoon.

On the morning of the 31st of January we left early, and following the Meh Tha Wah, and its northern branch the Meh Plor, and crossing two spurs for the sake of shortness, reached the summit of the pass over the great spur that separates the drainage of the Meh Tha Wah from that of the Meh Too, which enters the Thoungyeen two or three miles below the guard-house—the crest of the pass being 46 miles distant from Hlineboay, and 2060 feet above sea-level. The spur can easily be avoided by following the valley of the Meh Too.

Leaving the pass, we descended along the Tsin-sway, or Elephant-tusk, stream to the Meh Too, dropping 300 feet in the mile and a half. Proceeding up the Meh Too, we camped for the night at the forty-ninth mile.

The next morning we left early. A mile on, the stream forked, and we followed the intervening spur, which gradually flattened out and spread until we reached the foot of the pass over the Karroway Toung. A short climb of 400 feet past an outcrop of limestone, led us to the crest, 2817 feet above the sea, and 52 miles from Hlineboay, from whence we had a magnificent view of the country to the west. Here Mr Bryce's party passed us, and we did not see it again until we reached Maing Loongyee.

Having taken some photographs, we followed a rivulet and descended 260 feet in a mile to the Oo-caw, a small stream which flows eastwards into the Meh Ngor, where we halted for breakfast. During the descent from the pass the Shans brought me branches of the tea-plant, which was growing wild in the hills. Its long narrow leaves reminded me of the willow. The men told me that it was likewise found on the route from Maulmain to Raheng, as well as in the ranges to the north of the pass right up to China. Some of the plants were fully 15 feet in height.

From the Oo-caw we should have descended to the Meh Ngor, and followed the stream to the Meh Nium, as Dr Richardson had done on his journey to Zimmé in 1829; but the elephant-drivers said that the route was overgrown, the Karens preferring to keep open the hill-path, along which, owing to the shallowness of the streams, they could proceed throughout the year. Since leaving the Thoungyeen we had met a few parties of Karens, but had not seen any of their villages, as they build them away from the main tracks.

From the Oo-caw the road passes over a series of great spurs, separated by narrow steep-sided valleys, often merely a dip to the stream-bed. From the crests of the main spurs, which were occasionally higher than the summit of the pass, we had magnificent views of the country, which has the appearance of the desiccated remains of a great rolling plateau, the crest of the spurs following the wave-line across the main valley of the Meh Ngor.

There can be no doubt that the hill-bounded plateaux and valleys in the Shan States were at one time lakes, which were subsequently drained—some by subterranean channels, the stream reappearing on the other side of the hills, and others by great rifts made across the hills by earthquake action. The numerous mineral and hot springs we passed, and the earthquakes which still occur at times in the country, bespeak the continuance of unrest near the surface.

After scrambling over six great spurs, we halted for the night near a small mountain-stream. The strata seen since leaving the Thoungyeen had been limestone, sandstone, and shales, each appearing at various times. Many fine tree-ferns were noticed during the day.

The next day rain commenced at half-past three in the morning, and the showers continued until noon. Our howdahs were without covers during this stage of the journey, so we could not creep into them to escape from the storms which occasionally happen in the hills. Our shelter for the night consisted of a few lopped branches of trees, stuck in the ground, serving as rafters and wall-plates for our covering of waterproof sheets, while plaids hanging from the wall-plates formed the walls. This was amply sufficient to keep off the heavy dewfall, but enough care had not been spent on it to secure us from rain. I had turned in much fatigued, having stayed up late inking over the pencil notes in my field-book and writing up my journals, and had slept through the first shower, when I was awakened at half-past five by Dr Cushing, who told me I had better turn out as it was raining in torrents. I merely replied " All right," and went to sleep again. Soon the water gathering on the waterproofs, which we had rigged up as a shelter, weighed them down and came pouring on to my mosquito-curtains, and, soaking through them, effectually brought me out of dreamland ; but I got no compassion from my companion, who absolutely roared with laughter at my being ducked. A change of clothes and a peg of whisky were at hand, and having lit a cigar, I was ready to crouch out the storm cheerfully.

Rain again commenced to pour down at seven o'clock, but we could not afford to delay, so struck our camp and departed. After crossing four spurs, we halted for breakfast at eleven near two deserted houses. The path, owing to the rain, was rendered so slippery, and was so steep, that the elephants at times had to slide down on their bellies, with their legs stretching out behind and before them. To see these great clumsy-looking brutes constantly kneeling down, crouching on their haunches, and then rising again, as they ascended and descended the hillsides, in order to keep their equilibrium and reduce the leverage; never making a false step; putting one foot surely and firmly down before lifting another, and moving them in no fixed rotation, but as if their hind and fore quarters belonged to two independent bipeds; every movement calculated with the greatest nicety and judgment,—forced one to admire the sagacity and strength of the animals, and the wonderful manner in which their joints are adapted to their work.

As soon as breakfast was over we resumed our march, and crossing two more spurs, descended from the last one to the Meh Ngor, a stream 100 feet broad with banks 18 feet high. After following this stream for a mile, we camped for the night. Limestone and sandstone, with occasional shales, were the only rocks previously noticed: here trap cropped up for the first time, and teak-trees again appeared in the forest. We were now 66 miles from Hlineboay, and 396 feet above the sea.

Elephants, rhinoceroses, tigers, wild cattle larger than buffaloes, elk-deer, pigs, and other wild animals, are said to abound in these hills. We had heard tigers and deer round our camp nearly every night since we left Teh-dau-Sakan. The boys were at first frightened, and used to borrow my gun to scare the tigers away, but now had become accustomed to the peril, and ceased bothering me. Pea-fowl were plentiful, as we frequently heard them screeching in the morning.

Next morning, starting a little after seven, and skirting the stream for four miles, we crossed the Meh Ngor not far from its junction with the Meh Nium, and soon after entered the teak-clad Huay Ma Kok hills, which separate the Meh Ngor from the Meh Laik. Up and down again we went over hill and valley, instead of following the level path along the Meh Nium; past the Huay Ma Kok, which is a circular subsidence or depression 150 feet wide and 20 feet deep, on the top of a spur, until we came to and crossed the Meh Laik, by which we camped near a cliff of blue slate rock. The rocks exposed in the latter part of the journey were indurated clays and sandstones, both veined with quartz and shales and conglomerates.

The following morning a two miles' march over a hill in a dense mist brought us to Meh Ka Tone, a good-sized house on the banks of the Meh Nium. The river is here about 150 feet broad, with banks 12 feet high, and water 3 feet deep. Meh Ka Tone lies 76 miles from Hlineboay, and 451 feet above sea-level.

The house belonged to a forester who was absent, having left a Kamook slave in charge. Two Karen pigs, small, hairy, slate-coloured creatures, with dark bristling manes, were tied up by perpendicular strings under the house, so that they could neither lie down nor walk until the strings were slackened. As we had been feeding on tinned meat for the last two days, some of our fowls having been quietly appropriated by the Karens, we tried hard to persuade the man to sell us one of the pigs and a few of the fowls that were scuttling about, but all in vain,—they were his master's property, and he dared not part with them at any price without his consent.

Resuming the march and proceeding up the valley, now and then crossing hill-spurs and river-bends for the sake of shortness, at the eighty-third mile we again entered cultivated land, near the deserted village of Meh Kok, the site of which is now only marked by cocoa-nut and mango trees. The crests of the main spurs of the ranges of hills on either side appeared to be three miles distant; but on the west, a curious parallel range or formation, rising some 500 or 600 feet above the plain, lies between the main range and the river. On visiting these hills from Maing Loongyee we found them a perfect maze of equal elevation, looking like a gigantic Chinese puzzle, composed solely of friable earth, and rapidly frittering away,—there could be no doubt that we were looking at the remains of an old lake-bottom.

The plain, which is adorned with a great variety of flowering trees and shrubs, like the rest of the country we had passed through, containing much valuable timber besides teak, gradually increased in breadth as we proceeded, and is a mile and a half wide at Maing Loongyee. Several Karen and Lawa, and a few Shan, villages are dotted about it, but the cultivation is insufficient for the wants of the people, most of whom are engaged in forest operations. Rice has therefore to be imported from Zimmé.

Many of the villages in the plain were placed under taboo, owing to an outbreak of smallpox, a disease much dreaded by the hill tribes. The paths leading to such villages are stopped by a branch of a tree being thrown across them, and magical formulæ are stuck up in order to keep the evil spirits who propagate the disease from the village. No stranger dare enter a village so guarded. Should he do so, and death or illness subsequently happen, he would be held responsible. Life, or the price of life, for life, is exacted in such cases.

We halted for the night on the bank of the river, and starting early, reached Maing Loongyee the next morning. Finding that the *zayat*, or rest-house, was occupied by the Bombay Burmah Company, we despatched a messenger to Moung Kin, a relation of the celebrated Moulmain forester Moung Hmoon Taw, who works the Maing Loongyee teak-forests, and he at once hospitably placed the best part of his premises at our disposal. This arrangement proved very fortunate, as I was thus enabled to procure the most reliable information about the country.

The dwelling-house consisted of three separate buildings, built of teak and shingle-roofed, erected on a large square platform raised eight feet from the ground on posts. The house was situated in a compound enclosed by a stockade, separated from the river by a broad cattle-path, and surrounded on two sides by an orchard fringed with a fine hedge of roses eight feet in height. Two of the buildings on opposite sides of the platform, separated from each other by a broad passage, served as residences for the family. One of these, consisting of three rooms, was handed over for our use. The third building was situated near the north end of the platform, and served as a cook-house and servants' quarters. We felt quite in clover after our spell of camp life.

Moung Hmoon Taw, to whom the house belonged, was one of the kings of the teak trade. During the last three years, owing to scarcity of rain, he had been unable to float his timber out of the forests, and was therefore unable to repay the loans he had received from the *Chetties,* or Native of India Bankers. By no means alarmed at his position, he had lately astonished the bankers by sending them a letter through his solicitor demanding a further loan, and stating that unless he received it at once, he would be unable to pay them the sums they had advanced him. There was small doubt that the bankers would be compliant, as they could not afford to lose the 25 lakhs of rupees (£200,000) that was then due from him. The crash was, however, only put off for a time, as last year he became bankrupt. Poor Moung Hmoon Taw! poor bankers! I know who suffered most—*not* Moung Hmoon Taw. The bankruptcy proceedings were subsequently withdrawn.

CHAPTER IV.

MAING LOONGYEE TRAVERSED BY WAR-PATHS—DR RICHARDSON'S VISIT—PRICE OF SLAVES—DR CUSHING'S VISIT—RAIDED BY KARENNIS—THE CITY AND SUBURBS—VISIT THE GOVERNOR—THE SHAN STATES—GOVERNMENT — SUCCESSION TO THE THRONE — TITLES — MODES OF EXECUTION — ZIMMÉ FORMERLY EXTENDED FROM THE SALWEEN TO THE MEH KONG—THE GOVERNOR AND HIS BROTHER—THE BAZAAR—DISTRIBUTING SEEDS—INFORMATION FROM FORESTERS—COLLECTING VOCABULARIES — MOUNG LOOGALAY — PORTOW — A MAGICIAN — DR CUSHING AT WORK AND EXASPERATED—VISIT TO ANCIENT CITY AND TO THE EARTH-HILLS—CROSSING THE RIVER—A DANGEROUS WALK—PINE-TREES — NUMBER OF LAWA, KAREN, AND SHAN VILLAGES — POPULATION—A KAREN DANCE—ENTICING A LAWA—DESCRIPTION—SIMILARITY BETWEEN KAMOOK AND LAWA LANGUAGES—VISIT TO THE GOVERNOR—EFFECT OF A TELEGRAM—ELEPHANTS HIRED FOR FOREST WORK FROM KARENS — MODE OF ATTACK OF MALE AND FEMALE ELEPHANTS.

THE *muang*, or principality, called Maing Loongyee by the Burmese, and Muang Nium by the Shans, is traversed by war-paths leading from Burmah to Zimmé and Siam, along which great armies of invaders have passed; it was, moreover, subject to frequent inroads of man-stealers from Karenni, an independent State, which borders the *muang* on the north-west.

Dr Richardson, who visited Maing Loongyee in 1829, three years after we had annexed Maulmain, found it nearly deserted, containing, besides the hill denizens, only 200 houses, distributed among eight villages: the one occupying the site of the city had only ten or twelve dwellings in it.

The teak-forests were then unworked, and its principal export was black cattle—from 2000 to 8000 of these being yearly taken to Karenni and exchanged for slaves, ponies, tin, and stick-lac. Seven bullocks were bartered for a young man, and from eight to ten for a young woman; the very best bullock being valued at five shillings.

When Dr Cushing passed through the *muang* in 1870, the Burmese Shans, now British Shans, and Karennis had recommenced their raids into the country; and the Siamese Shans and our foresters had been shut up in the city for six months, not daring to venture into the district except in large bodies capable of defending themselves. These hostilities, lasting nine or ten years, had ceased four years previous to my visit, and the *muang* was recovering from their effects.

The city, which is built in the form of a parallelogram placed nearly true to the cardinal points, and stockaded on all four sides, measures 1740 feet from north to south, and 1050 feet from east to west. It lies 96 miles by road from Hlineboay, and is situated on a knoll, rising 15 feet above the plain and 635 feet above sea-level, in the northern angle formed by the junction of the Meh Sa Lin with the Meh Nium. It is occupied chiefly by Zimmé Shans, and contains 66 houses and two monasteries.

Like all Zimmé Shan towns, it has a peculiar air of regularity and neatness; the ends of the Shan houses invariably facing north and south, and the edges of the roofs, when of leaf or thatch, being accurately trimmed. The roads are well laid-out, ditched on either side, and attended to. A strict system of conservancy is in force, and no refuse is allowed to be heaped outside the houses and palisaded gardens. Aqueducts convey water from the upper course of the Meh Sa Lin, and distribute it through the town. The greater part of the cultivation in the Shan States is carried on by means of such irrigating channels, and in this way two crops of rice are raised in the vicinity of the town.

The suburbs, which are built at the north and west of the city, and outside the stockade, include 104 houses, mostly well built and of teak, chiefly occupied by our foresters and British Shan traders. Three monasteries in the Burmese style, and a pagoda, have been built by the Burmese *thitgoungs*, or head foresters, in the northern suburb, and another monastery was in course of erection. The people of Maing

Loongyee are said to feed on teak, the teak timber trade forming their chief means of support.

Having dismissed the elephants, we went into the city to call on the Siamese official, who was acting as deputy-governor during the absence of the chief at Bangkok. Chow Rat Sampan, the chief, a first cousin of the late Queen of Zimmé, is looked upon as the ablest man in the kingdom. Backed by the influence of the queen, he had gone to Bangkok to get himself appointed second King of Zimmé by the Siamese monarch.

The Shan States are small kingdoms, each containing a number of principalities or *muangs*. Each State is ruled in a patriarchal fashion by a court, comprising the first and second kings and three other princes of the blood-royal.

The succession to the throne primarily depends upon the person chosen by the court and people being of princely descent—all such are called *chow* or prince; secondly, upon his influence and wealth, the number of his serfs and slaves, business capacity, integrity, and his popularity with the serfs; lastly, and now chiefly, upon his interest at the Siamese court.

The first and second king usually select the other three chiefs, but their choice has to be confirmed by the King of Siam. The governors of Muang Nium, Muang Pai, Kiang Hai, and other principalities, are appointed by the King of Zimmé, who, like the King of Nan, has been granted the title of Chow Che Wit, or lord of life, by the King of Siam. The chiefs of Lakon, Lapoon, Peh, Tern, and Luang Prabang have only the title of Chow Hluang (Chow Luong or great prince). The title of Chow Che Wit was only allowed to the King of Zimmé in 1883. A Chow Che Wit can order a criminal to be decapitated. Chow Hluangs can only order execution by piercing the heart with a spear.

The Siamese Shan State of Zimmé at the beginning of the eighteenth century extended from the Salween to the Meh Kong. It had jurisdiction over the whole of the States lying in the basins of the upper portions of the Meh Nam, the Meh Ping, and the Meh Wung, comprising Zimmé, Nan, Peh, Lapoon, Lakon, and Tern; their governors being appointed by the King of Zimmé. The disruption of the kingdom resulted from the anarchy reigning in the middle of the eighteenth century, when Zimmé, then tributary to the Burmese, threw off its allegiance and became feudatory to Siam. Zimmé has now hardly a nominal supremacy over Lapoon, Lakon, and Tern, although the rulers are appointed from the same family; and Nan and Peh are perfectly independent of it, owing allegiance only to Siam.

We found the Siamese potentate squatting cross-legged, like a great apathetic indolent toad, upon a raised section of his covered verandah, in company with his brother, the headman of the Siamese frontier post at Daguinseik. Daguin-

An execution.

seik is the ford where the main track from Pahpoon to Zimmé crosses the Salween. No greeting was accorded us, no approach to the semblance of courtesy was shown us by these two unmannerly boors, who, like all low-minded Jacks-in-office, considered arrogance and incivility necessary in upholding their dignity.

Dr Cushing, who accompanied me as interpreter on the expedition, was naturally annoyed at the rudeness and grumpiness of our reception, and was intentionally brusque in expressing our requirements. These comprised six fresh elephants to carry us to Muang Haut, or, if possible, to Zimmé. The governor, who had been up night after night at the *poay*, or play, which was being given in honour of a youth who was about to join the priesthood, merely yawned in our faces, and left the answering to his brother.

We were assured that there would be great difficulty in getting our elephants, as Mr Bryce's party required ten, and would have to be served first as they had arrived the day before us; that the elephants were a long distance off working in the forests, and could not arrive for three days at the earliest. I replied that every day was of importance to us, that there were many elephants dawdling about the place, and that I saw no necessity for us to be kept waiting. He said that the elephants I had noticed belonged to the foresters, not to the Karens, and could not be hired to us. We then departed without either of the human toads rising from his haunches.

Meanwhile the boys had been rambling about the town making their purchases and bargaining from stall to stall; everything was double, or more than double, the Maulmain price, and hardly anything in the shape of edibles was to be got. Pork had been sold off in the early morning; no cattle had been killed, therefore beef was not to be had; fowls and ducks were not sold at the stalls, but hawked round to the different houses by the Karens who brought them in. Onions, beans, mustard-leaves, and pumpkins were all the vegetables they could procure: these, with eggs, dried fish, and wafer-bread, they had brought back with them. It would have been only tinned meat again for dinner had not Moung Kin come to the rescue and presented us with some fowls. At the same time, he told us that he would have a cow milked, and we should have fresh milk with our tea next day.

Disappointment came with the morning. The cow kicked the milk-pail over, so we got no milk. Seeing how scarce vegetables were in the bazaar, and considering it likely that we should be kept for several days waiting for the elephants, I sowed a crop of mustard and cress, which we reaped and enjoyed before we left. The curator of the Rangoon Public Gardens had kindly given me a large parcel of English vegetable seeds, and another of Liberian coffee, which I distributed at the various places we stopped at, on the promise that the villagers would plant and attend to them; and I trust that future travellers through the country will find cause to thank me. During our stay at Maing Loongyee, which lasted from the 5th to the 13th of February, I gathered information from the foresters about the country; collected vocabularies of the Kamook, Lawa, and other languages; and made a few short excursions. Loogalay thoroughly enjoyed himself, starring about amongst the Burmese in his best plumage, boasting of the great position he held in the expedition, and joining in the festivities that were going on day and night during our stay. Portow was in his element. He set up as an oracle, and was accordingly consulted. He knew, or thought he knew, what I was about, and the why and the wherefore of everything I was doing. I have no doubt that he led the people to look upon me as a powerful magician.

Dr Cushing, who is the greatest living Shan scholar, was accompanying me as interpreter in order to study the different Shan dialects, and was hard at work, when not at meals or out for a stroll, from morning to night.

Although the delay was rasping to me, as I was eager to be off, and Dr Cushing was exasperated at Mr Bryce's party getting elephants two days before us, we all enjoyed our stay at Maing Loongyee.

One day we visited the remains of the two ancient cities of Yain Sa Lin, situated about a mile to the south-east of the town, and surrounded and divided from each other by moats and ditches. Their area, which is now overgrown by a forest of great trees, is much larger than that of Maing Loongyee, but contains no visible ruins of ancient date. The small pagodas and ruined temples are modern, having been built in recent times by villagers occupying and cultivating part of the enclosure. The cities were situated on a knoll, and the western ramparts have been swept away by the encroachments of the river. The old city, together with 400 Talaings, or Peguans, according to the 'Lapoon Chronicle,' were handed over to the Shan chief of Lapoon as a dowry when he married the daughter of Thoo-tha Thoma, the King of Pegu, in A.D. 1289.

Another day we crossed the river, which lies to the west of the town, to visit the earth-hills and take photographs of the country from the platform of a pagoda, which stands out well against the sky. The water was about three feet deep, and the bottom covered with large pebbles, giving a rather insecure foothold. I was carried across perched on the shoulders of two men. Dr Cushing waded the stream, and resumed his nether garments on the other bank. I could not help glancing slily at him as he tottered along, his predicament being so ridiculous for such a grave and learned man, and his action so like that of the pilgrim who had not boiled his peas.

The path over the hills was covered with small rounded gravel washed out of the earth, which rendered it very slippery for shod feet. The hills were crested with large pine-trees, the first we had seen, and their sides were crumbling away in great landslips caused by the small streams, which carried off the rainfall, undermining the friable earth. Some of the spurs we passed along were barely two feet wide at the top, with slopes often nearly sheer descents. Walking along these, and peering at times into the abysses, I suddenly became dizzy, and had to take a man's hand to help me along until I reached a broader track. On and on we went, trying to reach the pagoda. The hills proved to be maze-like in character; so at last we gave up the attempt, and I took the photographs from another position. I was not sorry when we got back to the house without a mishap.

From the foresters, purposely summoned by Moung Kin to give me the information, I procured the names of thirty-three Lawa villages, forty-six fixed Karen villages, and eleven Shan villages, including the city, in the basin of the Meh Nium, and its branches. The Lawa villages contained on an average forty-two houses; the Karen, twenty houses; and the Shan, thirty-six houses. None of these foresters were working in the valley of the Meh Ngor, so its fixed villages are omitted.

The villages which are occupied by the Karen Yain—the wild or timid Karens—were said to contain as many people as the rest of the villages put together; but as these villages are temporary erections, only occupied for a year or two at a time, no accurate account could be given of them.

I was assured that the average number of people living in a house was seven; but even allowing only five, there would be upwards of 13,000 people in the fixed villages on my list, and as many more among the wild Karens. Taking into account the fixed villages not on my list, the gross population in the basin of the Meh Nium cannot fall far short of 30,000 souls.

The Siamese deputy, on being questioned on the subject, said that he had no list of the villages or census of the people; but there must be at least 3000 Zimmé Shans, 4000 Lawas, and 5000 fixed Karens, chiefly of the Sgau and Pwo and Sho tribes, in the *muang*. He could make no guess at the number of the Karen Yain; but they were very numerous. His estimate of the Shans and fixed Karens tallied well with the account given by the foresters; but the Lawas are twice as numerous as he thought they were.

The villages of the Sgau and Sho tribes of Karens are found scattered through the hills far down into the Malay Peninsula. One of their dances resembles the sword-dance of the Highlanders of Scotland, and is thus described by a gentleman who was present at it in a Karen village in the hills behind Petchaburee: Two smooth straight bamboo poles were placed parallel to each other on the ground, about eight feet apart. Across these, and at right angles to them, smaller bamboo sticks are laid—two in a place—so as to form spaces about ten inches wide between each pair of sticks. The musicians take their seats on the ground, by the sides of the parallel poles, and each takes an end of the short cross-sticks in each of his hands. These sticks he first taps together, then shifts them right and left so as to strike those of his neighbours on each side, to make a tapping musical noise, all keeping perfect time together.

The dancers, who are dressed in their most fantastic style, with painted faces, feathers in their turbans, &c., then take their places, and one after another dance into these spaces and along between the parallel poles. As they leap up, the sticks pass under their feet, and they must use their feet so dexterously as not to touch the cross-sticks which are constantly passing to and fro under them. As many as four or five dancers would be leaping up and down, across from end to end, at once, and all keeping perfectly together.

Day after day we tried to inveigle a Lawa into the house, but in vain. At length Moung Kin succeeded in enticing one there who had come with some friends on business to the city. We were elated; we had at last got a real live Lawa—one of the aborigines of the country: what should we get out of him?

He proved to be a tall, good-looking, well-built stripling, aged eighteen, with hair cut in the Siamese fashion and thrown back from his square perpendicular forehead, and eyes with no Mongolian incline about them, but slightly more opened at the inner corners than those of Europeans. He looked painfully shy, and very much ill at ease when he saw the trap he had got into.

I offered him a cigar, which he accepted and nervously twiddled about in his fingers, looking every now and then over his shoulder to see whether any of his companions had followed him, or to calculate the chance for escape. After striking a light for him, I said we were very interested in his people, and wished to learn what we could about their manners and customs, and a few words of their language; and that, if he gave me the information, I would pay him for his trouble, and give him some beads to take to his people.

He grew gradually more composed, but still appeared very uneasy. He said their customs were precisely similar to those of the Shans. Like them, they were now Buddhists, and had monasteries in the larger villages. They called themselves *L'wa;* water they called *ra-own;* fire, *ngau;* man, *pree-ra-mee;* woman, *pa-ra-peum;* day, *meu-sun-nyit;* and night, *thom.*

He then implored me to let him go, as his friends were waiting for him; and he promised to come again in the evening with a friend, and give us further information. A bird in the hand, particularly such a shy bird as this Lawa, is worth two in the bush; but as he was growing more restless and uneasy every moment, I gave him a rupee and a couple of bead necklaces, and promised him more if he kept his appointment. We then said good-bye, and he hurried off with his presents to join his companions. True to his word, he brought a comrade in the evening, and, being quite at his ease, gave us all the information we required. All our questions were answered in a frank, intelligent manner.

There was nothing very peculiar about their aspect. With complexions slightly darker than the natives of Burmah, their front faces were rather square, remarkable for their high and broad cheek-bones; their side faces seemed flat, owing to the prominence of their perpendicular foreheads; their noses were longer than those of the Burmese; and a line drawn from the top of their foreheads would leave the tips of nose, lips, and chin outside. The under jaws, far from being heavy, were slightly more angular than those of the neighbouring races. The bottom of the ear was about level with that of the nose; and the noses of the race vary greatly from well-formed straight ones, with the nostrils slightly expanding, to perpendicular for half the length, then ordinary pug for the remainder. I was altogether pleasantly disappointed with the race, having from previous accounts expected to see an ill-favoured, ill-shapen, cumbersome-looking people. The Lawa villages are permanent residences, having been occupied by them as far as tradition reaches. Their language has a strong affinity to that of the Kamook, many of the words, such as fish, foot, dog, cry, hand, mother, rice, pony, deer, river, names for other races, &c., being identical. They are, however, in appearance distinct races, and it is not unlikely that the Kamook acquired their present language from the Bau Lawa when the latter were the ruling race in Central and Southern Indo-China, and before the majority of the Lawas lost their own language and acquired that of the Shans.

The day Mr Bryce's party left we went to the Governor's house to have it out with him. He being absent, we went up-stairs and sat in the verandah awaiting his return, nursing our wrath to keep it warm. Presently his brother of Daguinseik came in without a jacket, wearing the dirtiest dishclout of a petticoat I have ever seen. His body was otherwise bare, and he looked a slovenly, unkempt savage.

He said they had been doing their utmost to procure elephants for us, but without success. This I knew to be false, as Mr Bryce had told me that their attention had been solely applied to the festivities that were going on, and that for three days after his arrival they had merely yawned over his requirements, and made no ghost of an attempt to aid him in procuring the animals.

Just as we were in the middle of our expostulations, a police constable arrived with letters and a telegram for me, forwarded in all haste by the Deputy-Commissioner at Pahpoon. I may here state that during the journeys letters were frequently sent after and from me by relays of special messengers, and in no case was a letter lost. The arrival of the constable worked like a charm, and had an immediate effect upon the manners of the Siamese official. Asking to be excused for a few minutes, he hurried away, and soon returned with his now not yawning brother, who came along buttoning up his blue-cloth police jacket, which he had not deigned to wear before, seemingly wide awake and anxious to help us.

He said that he had been doing his best, and hoped to get the elephants for us by the following day, or by the next morning at the latest; and when we talked of leaving our things to follow us and proceeding at once to Muang Haut on foot, begged us to wait till the next day, when he would let us know the upshot of his endeavours.

As soon as we had returned home, a messenger came to Moung Kin, asking him to proceed at once to the Governor's house. On his return, he informed me that an arrangement had been made whereby the Governor would hire to us three elephants, at thirty rupees each, to take us to Muang Haut, and he, Moung Kin, would let us have three more for forty rupees each. These would be ready at dawn the day after to-morrow. Thirty rupees is the usual hire for the journey; we were therefore fleeced out of thirty rupees in this little bargain, but as time was precious, I grinned and bore it.

Most of the elephants working in the teak-forests are

owned by Karens, who hire them out to the foresters at from fifty to seventy rupees a-month. The price includes the driver, but not the attendant, or any expenses incurred for the elephant.

In talking of the wages given in the forest, Moung Kin told me that larger wages had to be given to the drivers and attendants of vicious female elephants than even to those of rogue male elephants. It appears that male elephants close their eyes when they charge, and, lowering their heads in order to use their tusks, afford an opportunity for the driver to scramble up to his seat on the neck, and thus regain his mastery of the beast. Not so with the females. They approach open-eyed, use their trunks as weapons, and lash about with them — or with a sudden grip seize a man, crunch him *à la* boa-constrictor, and throw him lifeless, or nearly so, on the ground, to be trampled on.

CHAPTER V.

LEAVE MAING LOONGYEE—A HUNDRED-FOOT WATERFALL—A BEAUTIFUL HILL-TORRENT—A LUGUBRIOUS TALE—GIBBONS—GIGANTIC TREE-FERNS—SHANS CRUEL ELEPHANT-DRIVERS—METHOD OF DRIVING—DROVES OF PIGS AND LADEN CATTLE—LOI PWE—AN ACCIDENT—WILD RASPBERRIES — SHANS BARTERING GOODS — THE MEH LAIK VALLEY—A FALL OF 2049 FEET—PATHS FOR THE RAILWAY—LAWA VILLAGES—ABORIGINES—BURIAL CUSTOM—HUMAN SACRIFICES IN THE SHAN STATES AND CHINA—LEGEND CONCERNING THE CONQUEST OF THE LAWAS BY THE SHANS—THE VIRGIN OF THE LOTUS FLOWER—GAUDAMA SACRIFICED TO AS THE GODDESS OF MERCY—SACRIFICES TO ANCESTORS AND DEMONS—SIMILARITY OF SUPERSTITIONS IN ANCIENT CHALDEA AND THE SHAN STATES—PHOTOGRAPHING LAWAS—CLOTHING WORN FOR DECENCY'S SAKE—COSTUME OF LAWAS—COLD NIGHTS — VIEW OF THE HILLS — BAU-GYEE — IRON-MINES GUARDED BY DEMONS—A YOUNG BLACKSMITH.

On the 13th of February the elephants were brought leisurely in one by one from the forest, where they had been tethered for the night, the last arriving about ten o'clock. A few minutes later everything was packed, and, facing eastwards, we were again off over the hills and far away.

After fording the Meh Sa Lin near the town, and passing through Yain Sa Lin, we crossed the Meh Gat, and proceeded along a good road over a spur, where limestone, slate, and claystone, veined with quartz, cropped up, to the Meh Ka Ni. This stream, turning to the north at the point we first crossed it, tumbles over a couple of falls, one 70 feet, the other 100 feet high, and flows through a ravine into the Meh Sa Lin.

The valley of the Meh Ka Ni, up which we ascended, is narrow, the crests of the hills on either side being barely two miles apart. The hill-slopes are well wooded with large and valuable timber. Many of the trees give a splendid shade, and are evergreen. Down the valley, in a bed of granite 30 feet broad, strewn with great granite boulders, leaps and dashes a foaming torrent in the rainy season. At the time of our visit it was but a rivulet falling in little cascades, dancing round the rocks, sparkling in the sunlight, and flowing gently through pleasant pools, delightful to bathe in. For five miles we journeyed through the deep shade of the forest, frequently crossing the stream, and then halted for the night at Pang Hpan. On our way we passed several parties of Kamooks and Karen villagers, and met large caravans of laden oxen conveying paddy and betel-nut to Maing Loongyee.

The camping-ground, situated in an open plain near the meeting-place of several side valleys, lies 105 miles from Hlineboay, and 1753 feet above the sea. The highest shade-temperature during the day had been 73°, and our ride up the pretty glen had been extremely pleasant.

After dinner, in the course of conversation, Dr Cushing, thinking, perhaps, that I was a Mark Tapley, and that a lugubrious tale might cheer me up, told me that he was a most unlucky companion to travel with. All his former comrades had died on the journey, or soon afterwards. He then backed up his statement with three instances. Kelly, a missionary, was drowned one day's journey from Moné; Lyon, another missionary, had died of consumption at Bhamo; and Cooper had been killed by one of his guard at Bhamo. I instanced his wife, who was then in America, as an exception. It was of no use—she was his better half—I was a doomed man.

Next morning the thermometer stood at 48°, the same as it had been at Maing Loongyee. The trees, however, were shedding their leaves far less in the upper valley than in the lower country. Starting about eight o'clock, accompanied by the mournful wailing of gibbons, who were practising the trapeze from tree to tree far above our heads, and making astounding leaps, we continued up the glen, passing large droves of Karen pigs, and caravans of laden cattle, until the stream forked, and we ascended the intermediate spur to the crest of Loi Kom Ngam—the Beautiful Golden Mountain—the hill-range dividing the drainage of the Meh Sa Lin from that of the Meh Laik.

Gigantic tree-ferns, and the first chestnuts we had seen, were passed as we clambered the spur; and we noticed trees in bloom bearing a red flower, and a large periwinkle - blue creeper which, spreading over the largest trees, spangled them with blossoms. Before reaching the summit we had a magnificent view down the nine miles of valley we had been ascending, extending across the Meh Nium valley to the hills beyond the Salween river. The pass, which is 109 miles from Hlineboay, is 3609 feet above sea-level.

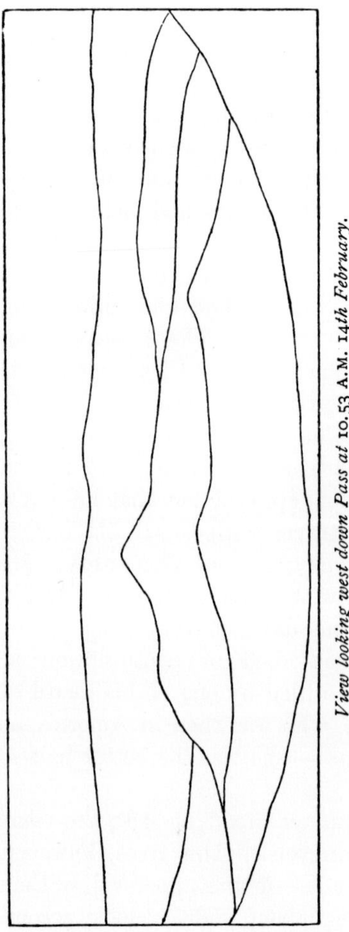

View looking west down Pass at 10.53 A.M. 14*th February.*

A short descent of 70 feet brought us to a little valley, which we crossed; then following a spur, we descended to the Meh Hau, a small stream draining into the Meh Laik here at a level of 2638 feet above the sea. We had fallen nearly 1000 feet in less than three miles. Crossing the spur which separates the Meh Hau from the Meh Lye, we halted for the night near some springs at the 115th mile.

Left the next morning at seven o'clock and descended for

a mile to the Meh Lye, passing on our way 109 laden cattle. The Meh Lai—River of Variegated Water—is 20 feet wide and five feet deep; sandstone and quartz outcrop in its bed. Looking down-stream to the south, we had a pretty view, bounded by pine-clad spurs, into the Meh Laik valley.

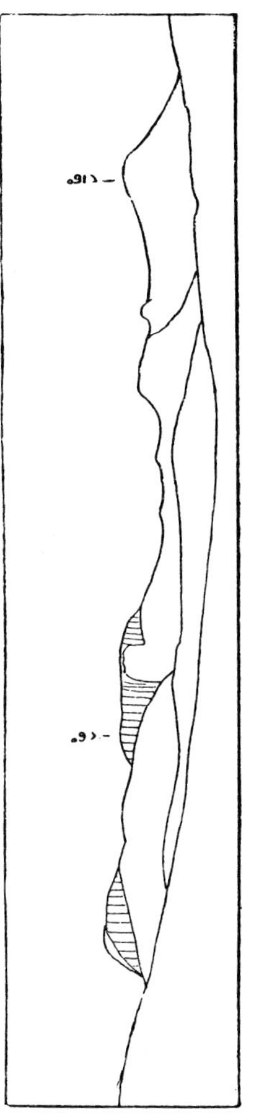

Loi Pwe seen over a spur at 9.57 A.M. 15*th February.*

Note.—< 6° and < 16° imply angles to the east of north, north being 0° and 360°—90° is east, 180° is south, and 270° west from the point whence they are taken.

Our Karen mahouts had been replaced by Shans at Maing Loongyee. The Shans proved much more cruel drivers than the Karens. The latter seldom used the cruel-looking hammer-hook, or *ankus*, they all carry, but coax and talk to the elephants; whilst the Shans correct the slightest misdemeanour by a blow that draws blood, and seek for obedience solely by bullying the beasts. The drivers, both Shan and Karen, urge their elephants on by a continuous irritation of the creature's ears with their toes, which are worked in an incessant pendulous movement at the back of them. They likewise assume all sorts of attitudes on the animal's head. Squatting on one leg with the other dangling down, lolling over the bump on its forehead, straddle-legged, and side-saddle fashion, but for ever with one set of toes or the other, or both, titillating the brute's ears.

From the Meh Lai we ascended a small glen for a little more than a mile, and shortly afterwards entered a narrow defile, where we halted for a few minutes to allow 135 laden cattle and a drove of 40 pigs to pass. Leaving the defile, a magnificent panorama spread out before us. Looking west, the eye ranged over the spurs we had crossed since leaving the pass. To the north about eight miles distant, over the hills bordering the Meh Sa Lin valley, stood out clear against the sky the bald-headed and partly precipitous summit of Loi Pwe. Here was a chance, not to be lost, for taking sketches and photographs and fixing the lie of the country.

Loi Pwe is the nucleus from which many of the spurs and minor ranges stretching into the valleys of the Meh Nium and Meh Laik have their origin. It is joined on to the Bau plateau by spurs some 15 miles in length, radiating in straight lines. Most of the hills in this region are approximately of similar elevation, their crests seeming to be the remains of a great rolling table-land eaten into valleys by centuries of erosion in the stream-beds.

On remounting the elephant, the howdah, owing to the slackness of the girth, commenced to lose its equilibrium, and I should have been precipitated to the ground, a distance of 11 feet, if I had not stepped on to the head of the beast and saved myself from falling by clinging to the greasy perspiring mahout. I had presence of mind sufficient to pocket my watch and instruments, or they would have inevitably been ruined.

Ten minutes after restarting we reached the summit of Loi Tone Wye, or Loi Tong Wai, situated 118 miles from Hlineboay and 3885 feet above the sea. Great fern-trees, 50 feet in height, the highest I have ever seen or heard of, adorned the crest of the hill. Portow brought me a handful of wild white raspberries he had just picked for me to eat. Before reaching the summit we noticed a Lawa village nestling on a hill-slope to the north of us.

On the narrow plateau forming the summit of the hill, we found a large encampment of Shans with many laden cattle. Some of the men had opened their packs and were bartering their merchandise with a number of Karens who had come from the neighbouring villages. Startled by our sudden appearance, most likely never having seen a white-face before, the latter took to their heels, fleeing as if the devil was after them, and did not venture from their hiding-places until after our breakfast, when we were preparing to resume our march. Then they came, as shy and inquisitive as cattle, and had a good look at us from a respectful distance.

From Loi Tong Wai we had a magnificent view of the hills in all directions. The great plateau of Bau, 15 miles to the east, and about the same level as the ground we were standing on, was clearly outlined against the sky; and the great trough of the wave between it and us was filled with a multitude of great spurs, crested with fine timber and divided from each other by steep-sided narrow valleys.

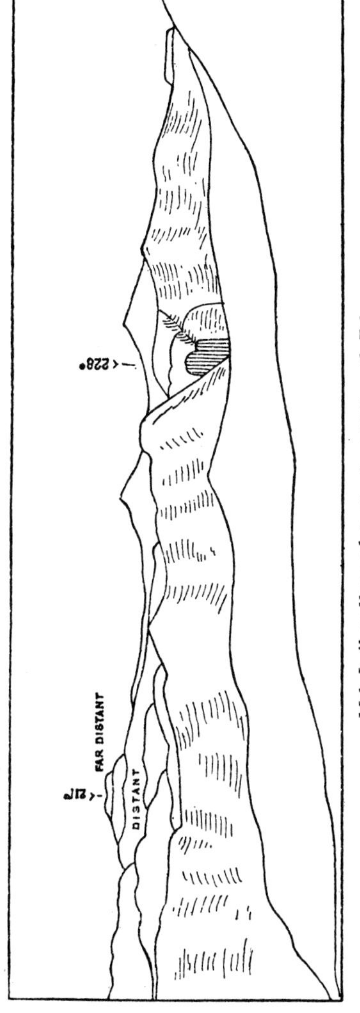

Meh Laik valley and gorge at 1.3 P.M. 15*th February.*

To the south-west, 10 miles distant, was the gorge where the Meh Laik passes through Loi Kom Ngam on its way to the Meh Nium; beyond was a sea of hills stretching as far as the eye could reach to the high peak lying to the south-east of our pass over the Karroway Toung. The cliff-faced gap through which the river rushes, tumbling hundreds of feet at a time, is impassable even to the sure-footed Karens. In the 24 miles' course of the stream between our two crossings its bed falls 2049 feet. The greater part of this drop is said to occur in this short gorge, which must be one of the wildest and grandest scenes in the world.

If the railway from Maulmain is carried up the valley of the Meh Laik, gradually rising along the hill-spurs, a gallery cut in the face of the gorge would enable the line to proceed towards Zimmé without passing, *viâ* Maing Loongyee, over the hills we have been crossing since we left the city. A better path, however, most likely exists up one of the valleys to the north of Loi Pwe, which would cross the Zimmé hills, descending by the valley of the Meh Sai, which lies between Loi Kom and the Bau plateau.

A gradual descent for four and a half miles brought us to the Meh Laik. Sandstone and quartz, and claystone veined with quartz, cropped up on the sides of the plateau and its spurs, but the bed of the river, 15 feet broad and 4 feet deep, is composed of black-speckled white granite. Our crossing lies 123 miles from Hlineboay and 2508 feet above the sea.

Leaving the stream, we ascended a few feet, and, continuing for half a mile through pine-forest, descended to a rice-plain, where the road traversed in 1879 by Colonel Street and Mr Colquhoun, when on their mission to Zimmé, joins our route. Crossing the Meh Tha Ket, a small stream which flows through the plain, and two dry streams which exposed a great depth of soil, we passed to the north of the Lawa village of Bau Sa Lee, and, fording the Meh Hto, camped for the night on its bank, 125 miles from Hlineboay. A thousand feet down-stream from our camp the Meh Hto is joined by the Meh Tyen. Both streams flow in a bed of granite boulders, and the village is situated at their junction.

In the evening I enticed two of the head-men to the camp, and gained some information about them and the features of the country. They told me the Lawas still occupied the village sites held by them before the Shans and Karens settled in the country. They had no written language, and were now Buddhists like the Shans, and had the same manners and customs. Their villages are scattered through the hills and plateaux as far south as the latitude of Bangkok, and they believed themselves to be the aborigines of the country.

The only difference between their customs and those of the Ping Shans lay in their always burying their dead, whereas the Ping Shans, except in cases of death from infectious diseases or in child-birth, burn them. Burial, however, is still observed by the British Shans. When a Lawa dies, a coffin is made by scooping out the log of a tree, and the corpse is placed in it and covered with a stout lid. After three days the priest is called and the body buried. As amongst the Karens, the personal property of the deceased is interred with the corpse.

The practice of burning their dead amongst the Shans must be of recent date, for in the middle of the sixteenth century, when they first became feudatory to Burmah, burial was the rule—elephants, ponies, and slaves being interred with the chiefs. The Burmese emperor Bureng Naung strictly prohibited the continuance of the custom. Similar observances were usual in olden times amongst the Turkish or Hiung Nu and Scythian tribes in Asia, and with the Tsin dynasty in China as well as amongst the ancient Greeks, as evidenced by Homer's 'Iliad.' The latest record of such human sacrifices in China concerns the obsequies of the Emperor Chi Hwang, B.C. 209, when all the members of the harem having no sons had to follow him in death.

The following legend concerning the conquest of the Lawas by the Shans was told me by Chow Oo Boon, the sister of the Queen of Zimmé, who was the spirit-medium and historian of the Royal Family.

LEGEND OF NAN CHAM-A-TA-WE.

Nan Cham-a-ta-we, a virgin of the lotus-flower, had two sons, who were born at Lapoon. At that time the whole of the country was occupied by the Lawas. The Lawa king met and fell desperately in love with the virgin, and for many years urged his suit. She, being unwilling to accept him as her husband, pleaded the youth of her children making it necessary for her to be constantly in attendance on them, as an excuse.

When the lads became young men, the king still tormenting her with his wooing, she promised to become his bride if he proved able to cast three spears from the top of Loi Soo Tayp, a hill to the north-west of Zimmé rising 6000 feet above the plain, into the centre of the city of Lapoon, a distance of 18 miles. His first cast being successful, she determined to foil him in his further attempts, and accordingly wove a hat out of her cast-off garments and coaxed him to wear it, saying it would greatly add to his strength. His next throw fell short of the city, and, his strength decreasing through the magical powers of the hat, his third spear fell at the foot of Loi Soo Tayp.

The king becoming weaker and weaker, the two sons of the virgin, named A-nan-ta-yote and Ma-nan-ta-yote, being enraged at the Lawa monarch for his pursuit of their mother, determined to drive him from the country. This they were enabled to do through the great merit accruing to them from their birth, which gave them magical powers.

As soon as the elder was born, a large white elephant came and voluntarily served as his domestic animal. Leaves thrown from him turned into fully equipped soldiers, and handfuls of kine-grass became armies as he breathed on them. Having created a great host, he mounted his white elephant, and forced the Lawa king to flee, and pursued him.

On reaching Kiang Hai, the elephant being heated and excited with the chase, the people of the place fled like sheep chased by a dog, shouting out "Chang Hai," wild elephant. Continuing the chase through Kiang Hsen, the elephant roared so loudly that the people scattered in all directions screaming "Chang Hsen," roaring elephant.

Having banished the Lawa king from the country, the kine-grass soldiers founded the city of Muang Poo Kah, the kine-grass city, the remains of which are still visible some distance to the north of Kiang Hsen. The virgin of the lotus-flower became ruler of Lapoon, and her eldest son went to Pegu, where he is still worshipped at festivals with dancing, mirth, and music.

Lapoon is named from La, or Lawa, and *poon*, a spear;

Kiang Hai from the elephant being vicious; and Kiang Hsen from its trumpeting.

The virgin of the lotus-flower is depicted by the Shans and Siamese as a mermaid holding a lotus-flower in her left hand, presumably in connection with the belief amongst the Chinese that Kwan-yin, the goddess of mercy, the offspring of the lotus-flower, terminates the torments of souls in purgatory by casting a lotus-flower on them.

In China, miniature offerings are laid before images of this goddess as a hint for her to convey the articles implied by

A virgin of the lotus-flower.

their likenesses to the spirits of friends or relations. The offerings, frequently accompanied by a scroll stating who the articles are for, consist of miniatures cut out of paper, of money, houses, furniture, carts, ponies, sedan-chairs, pipes, male and female slaves, and all that one on this earth might wish for in the way of comfort. In Siam and the Shan States there being no temple to this goddess, Buddha, who is generally depicted as sitting on a lotus-flower, is besought to do her work, and similar articles are heaped on his altar—but cut out of wood, or formed of rags or any kinds of rubbish, as paper is not so easily obtainable.

The same miniature images are offered by the Shans and hill tribes to the spirits of their ancestors and the ghosts and demons which haunt their neighbourhood, and food and flowers are left in the little dolls' houses which are erected for them. If neglected and uncared for, the spirits become spiteful, and bring disease, misfortune, or death to those living in or passing through their neighbourhood.

To any one travelling with his eyes open in China and Indo-China, it becomes evident that Buddhism is merely a veneer, spread over the people's belief in ancient Turanian and Dravidian superstitions. The belief in divination, charms, omens, exorcism, sorcery, mediums, witchcraft and ghosts, and in demons ever on the alert to plague and torment them individually, is universal, except perhaps amongst the highly educated classes, throughout the country. Comparing these beliefs with those appearing in the Accadian literature of Chaldea, B.C. 2230, as given by George Smith in his History of Babylonia, one is astonished at the perfect sameness of the superstitions.

The next morning, as one of the elephants had strayed away during the night and had to be tracked and brought back, I visited the village of Bau Sa Lee to take photographs of the people. The men had not the slightest objection to being taken; but the women, particularly the younger ones, skurried off as soon as they heard what I was about, and hid themselves in their houses. At length, by the gift of a necklace and a few small silver coins, I persuaded an old woman to fetch two little girls and stand for her portrait with them.

The Lawa women are the only natives in Indo-China whom I have seen wearing their hair parted in the middle, in the mode general amongst women in England a few years ago. Their hair is gathered up and tied in a knot at the back of the head, like that of the ladies amongst the Burmese and Shans. Unlike the Siamese and Zimmé Shans, the Lawa women wear upper clothing for decency's sake, and not solely for the sake of warmth. Their dress consists of a short skirt reaching to their knees, and a black tunic having a dark-red stripe on the outer edge. Some of the elder women wear a piece of cloth on their heads folded into a sort of turban.

The nights were rapidly getting colder; at five in the afternoon the thermometer showed 70°, at six in the morning it had fallen to 38°. We had to sleep dressed in our clothes under our plaids to keep warm; and the men sat huddled up, chatting and toasting themselves by the fires, for many hours towards the morning.

Leaving the Meh Hto, we ascended 1150 feet by an easy spur, through a nearly leafless forest of hill-eng and teak, to the top of Loi Kaung Hin—the Hill of the Stone-heap—so called from a cairn on its summit.

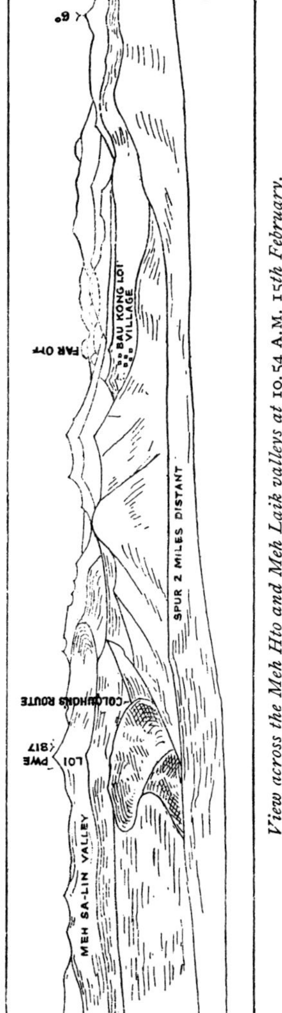

View across the Meh Hto and Meh Laik valleys at 10.54 A.M. 15*th February.*

Cresting the hill, we were again amongst the fragrant pine-forest. The air was deliciously cool, and the view was superb; I therefore decided to halt and sketch the country from an orchid-covered crag above a precipice several hundred feet in depth. Across the valleys of the Meh Hto, Meh Lyt, and Meh Sa Lin, nearly due north-east and distant 13 miles, we could see Loi Pwe, giving rise to numerous valleys. Between it and due north, on the slope of a great flat-topped spur in the valley of the Meh Tyen, lay the Lawa village of Bau Kong Loi, and beyond the Zimmé hills stretched away till lost in the haze. The whole country looked like a chopping sea of hills, in which it would be impossible, without actual survey, to settle the direction of the drainage. The main range was so cut up by cross-valleys that any one of the valleys I had not visited might drain either into the Meh Ping or the Meh Nium.

After continuing for two miles along the crest of the hill, we descended to the Meh Tyen, and halted for the night on its banks in some rice-fields near the junction of one of its branches. Our camp was situated 131 miles from Hlineboay, and 2831 feet above the sea.

The bed of the Meh Tyen is 20 feet wide and 6 feet deep, and is composed of boulders of quartz and granite.

The following morning at six o'clock the thermometer stood at 36½°. The breeze as we ascended a spur, through the hill-eng and scanty pine-forest, to Bau Koke, chilled us to the bone. Bau Koke is a small catch-pool on the crest of the Bau plateau, 3400 feet above the sea, draining into the Meh Tyen.

The air every moment became hotter as the sun rose and darted its rays through the clear sky, the soil of the plateau was of a deep red colour, and the glare where the forest had been cleared soon became distressing. Continuing along a ridge bordering the northern edge of the plateau, we reached Bau-gyee at eleven, and halted to inspect the village and for breakfast.

Bau-gyee, as the Burmese call it, or Bau Hluang as it is termed by the Shans—" Hluang " and " gyee " both meaning " great " — is situated 137½ miles from Hlineboay and 3704 feet above sea-level. It is in three divisions—two of 30 houses each, and one of 21 houses. The villagers are Lawas, and gain their livelihood as blacksmiths and miners, procuring and smelting the ore at a hill lying to the north of Loi Pwe, two days' elephant journey from the village.

The mines are said to average 50 feet in depth, and to be guarded by demons who have to be propitiated by offerings of pigs or fowls. If the ore dug up is poor, the sacrifices are repeated so as to persuade the *pee*, or demon, to allow it to yield more iron. The ore is smelted at the Lawa village of Oon Pai, situated near the mines. No stranger is allowed to watch the process lest the *pee* should be offended ; and the ingots are carried on elephants to the Lawa villages, where it is manufactured into various articles which find a sale throughout the country. The ore mined is the common red oxide of iron.

Whilst breakfast was being prepared we went into the village to have a chat with the people and watch them at their work. The houses are of the ordinary pattern occupied by the Zimmé Shans, built on posts, with the floor raised several feet from the ground, the sides of the building slightly inclining outwards as they rise towards the roof, which is steep and high. Many of the houses are small and dirty, and have pig-pens beneath them.

We found several of the men at work making chains, but they stopped as we appeared. After we had talked with them for a little while, a lad, of about twelve years of age, heated some iron, and seizing a hammer, forged several links of a chain as skilfully and quickly as any man of mature age could have done. An old man showed us several specimens of the ore, but would not allow us to take them away for fear the demons of the mine should be offended.

Their bellows and other implements are curious ; the anvil is three inches square and two inches high, formed of a large spike driven into a log of wood. Another implement shaped like a triangular hoe at the top, five inches long and one and a half inch at the base, was likewise spiked into a log of wood, exposing six inches of the spike ; this was used for forging hooks and elephant chains.

The bellows, two on each side of the charcoal fire, consisted each of a slightly sloping bamboo four inches in diameter, rising two feet from the ground, with a rag-covered piston working inside it and forcing the air out of a small hole. Each pair was placed three feet apart, and worked by a lad.

There is a dip in the plateau near the village where paddy is grown on a slip of land about two miles long and 150 feet broad. It is irrigated by small springs, the water being led to the fields through bamboo pipes.

CHAPTER VI.

PATH FOR A RAILWAY—LAWA SIVAS—LEGENDS OF POO-SA AND YA-SA, AND OF ME-LANG-TA THE LAWA KING—STORY OF A YAK—DESCENT FROM THE BAU PLATEAU—A COURAGEOUS LADY—WEIRD COUNTRY—RUBY-MINES—REACH MUANG HAUT—CABBAGES—TOBACCO-CUTTING—A BOBBERY—FABLE OF THE PEACOCK AND THE CROW—SKETCHING THE COUNTRY—CONVERSING BY SIGNS—INTERVIEWING THE HEAD-MAN—BOAT-HIRE ON THE MEH NAM—COST OF CARRIAGE—RAIN-FALL—PRODUCE OF FIELDS—A SHAN TEMPLE—METHOD OF MAKING IMAGES—BARGAIN FOR BOATS—TEMPERATURE IN SUN AND SHADE.

LEAVING Bau, we continued along the undulating plateau for two and a half miles through the pine-forests, shallow valleys at times commencing on either side. After passing some springs and large white-ant hills, and catching a glimpse of Loi Pah Khow, a great dome-shaped hill ten miles distant to the north, we came to the edge of the plateau, where a great trough or undulation separates it from Loi Kom, the Golden Mountain. Through this pass, which is about 1000 feet lower than the Bau plateau, I consider a railway might be carried from Maing Loongyee to Zimmé.

Loi Kom stands considerably higher than the Bau plateau, or appeared to do so. Looking sideways across the valley, the hill resembles a very long roof sloped at the ends as well as at the sides.

This mountain forms a link in the Zimmé chain of hills, and is the seat of the celebrated Lawa Yak or "genius" Poo-Sa, whose wife Ya-Sa inhabits Loi Soo Tayp, the great hill behind the city of Zimmé.

LEGEND OF POO-SA AND YA-SA.

These genii are said to be the spirits of an ancient Lawa king and queen, who at their deaths became the guardian spirits of the hills. Previous to the advent of Gaudama Buddha to the Lawa country, Poo-Sa and Ya-Sa were devourers of mankind, insisting upon receiving human sacrifices. On his arrival, Gaudama exhorted them to give up this evil practice; since then they are said to be content with buffaloes. The people, however, have doubts on this point, and at times fear that these powerful spirits, who can prevent the water from coursing down the hill-streams to irrigate their fields, have still a hankering after their old diet. The missionaries at Zimmé told me that the previous year the people had petitioned the King of Zimmé to hasten the execution of some malefactors in order to induce Poo-Sa to allow a larger supply of water to flow from the hills, as their fields were suffering from drought.

A Yak.

There is an annual sacrifice of animals to these genii, every house in the region being obliged to pay two annas, or twopence, towards the expenses. The money is kept in the court-house until June, when the sacrifices are made.[1]

[1] In his 'New Studies of Religious History,' Ernest Renan points out that the ruins of Ancor, in Southern Indo-China, "are now ascribed with certainty to the ninth, tenth, and eleventh centuries of our era. In them Sivaism and Buddhism are blended; and Sivaism appears here before Buddhism." There can be no doubt that Sivaism, or the worship of the hero-gods of the hills, in

LEGEND OF ME-LANG-TA.

Another legend of the local genii runs as follows: On the Shans' first entering the Zimmé country, they found the city of La-Maing, which had recently been founded by Me-lang-ta, the king of the Lawas, deserted. At that time the whole of the country to the south of the Burmese Shan States belonged to the Lawas, who resided in the hills in the dry season and cultivated the plains in the rainy season. Overrunning the plains at a time when cultivation was not going on, the Shans occupied La-Maing, the ruins of which adjoin the present city of Zimmé, as well as Lapoon and other similarly deserted Lawa towns.

The Lawa king gathered a great army in the hills to drive the Shans out of his country, but finding them strongly intrenched and in great force, he offered to form an alliance with them if they would cement it by giving him in marrage Nang Sam-ma-tay-we, the beautiful and accomplished daughter of the Shan Prince of Lapoon.

The Shan chief haughtily rejected the offer of the Lawa king, and marched with a great host into the hills, attacked Me-lang-ta, scattered his army, and slew him. The place where he was killed is known as La-wat, "the Lawa destroyed"; and the king became the Pee Hluang, or tutelary deity of the region, and resides in a cave at Loi Kat Pyee, a hill to the north-east of Zimmé. Unlike Poo-Sa and Ya-Sa, he is not a reputed cannibal, but is satisfied with sacrifices of pigs every third year and fowls in the intervening period.

The Yaks of Indo-China are close kin to the giants in our nursery tales, and the Buddhist stories relating to them and other mythical beings would compare well with our own nursery tales. To show what fearful beings they are, I take the following story from 'Nontuk Pakaranam,' the

China and Indo-China, is connected with the ancient religion of the non-Aryan Himalayan hill tribes. Siva was not incorporated by the Brahmans into their pantheon until about the commencement of our era.

translation of which appeared in the 'Siam Repository' for 1873:—

STORY OF A YAK.

"Aupata Racha Tirat, a son of royalty, went forth to conquer a kingdom. He had four servants to accompany him. A Yak, taking the form of a beautiful woman, beset his path. She enticed the servants one by one to leave their master, and ate them. She purposed to entrap the royal heir, but failed. She then went on before to the royal city, found favour in the sight of the king, and killed and ate all the people in the palace—ladies, nobility, and the king himself. The people saw the bones, and came together to see whence came all this desolation. The king's son came forward and told the story how the Yak ate his servants and wished to eat him, but was not allowed. The king had been taken with her beauty, and so lost his life and the lives of all who had died with him. They took Aupata Racha Tirat and made him king."

A Siamese king.

The ridge bordering the Bau plateau on the north-east continues at the same level for three miles, gradually turning into a great spur. The path which we descended follows a broad plateau sloping gradually down alongside the north slope of the spur, and bordered by the valley of the Huay Sai, which lies between it and Loi Kom. Descending rapidly for the first fifty feet, with granite outcropping on both sides, we crossed the Huay Pa-lat, a small stream five feet broad and one foot deep, flowing in a granite bed.

The slope then became easy, but granite masses were still exposed. Continuing through the pine-forest, we crossed two small brooks, the first flowing over a bed of white granite, and the latter dry. The pine and other trees here commenced to be moss-laden, and *zi*, cotton, and evergreen trees began to appear in the forest. Reaching Pang Ee-moon, a swampy shallow valley, we halted for the night. Our camp, 142 miles from Hlineboay, lay 2685 feet above sea-level. The temperature at 5 P.M. was 78°, and at 6 A.M. 45½°, or considerably higher than on the other side of the table-land. Near the camp are the ruins of an old pagoda, and a small stream flowing over a tough rock, which is used by the people for making hones to sharpen their knives and weapons. Still following the sloping plateau, I noticed that pine ceased to be seen in the forest at the point, a mile from the camp, where the plateau commences to throw off spurs on either side, and a steep descent amongst outcrops of granite and boulders begins. The top of the descent lies 2545 feet above the sea.

Small valleys gradually formed and deepened on either side of us as we descended slowly, halting at times for caravans of laden cattle to pass us. After crossing a torrent 40 feet broad and 3 feet deep, flowing from the great spur on the north, we camped for breakfast on the bank of the Meh Pa-pai, at the corner of the elbow-bend where it turns east. At our crossing, 145½ miles from Hlineboay and 1672 feet above the sea, this stream flows in a solid bed of granite, 82 feet broad, with banks 6 feet high.

When halting at this spot with Dr Cushing, his wife had a narrow escape. During the heat of the day she was startled from sleep by feeling something crawling over her. She at once suspected that it was a snake, and had the courage and presence of mind to remain perfectly still while it crawled up her arm, and over her face, and away from her temple. Then, unable to restrain herself longer, she jumped up and screamed as she watched the large spotted viper disappearing in the grass.

After breakfast we followed along the flat slopes on the

side of the stream—the crests of the undulations of the rolling plain we had descended to being at times 50 and 60 feet above us, and small hills occasionally jutted in from both sides. In places where, in order to cut the bends of the stream, we crossed the undulating plateau, which was evidently part of an old lake-bottom, the elephants had worn the path down as deep as themselves, exposing the earth formation, which is mixed with small rounded gravel.

The country was weird in the extreme, the grass parched up ; the trees, the bamboos, and even the great creepers strangling the trees, leafless ; and the stream looking like burnished steel in its lavender-coloured granite bed. There was a dead stillness about the scene ; the orange-red flowers of the *pouk* trees seemed to flame out of the forest.

After following the stream for five miles, we left it flowing to our right, and proceeding over the undulating ground, crossed a low hillock lying between it and the Huay Sai, a stream 30 feet broad and 5 feet deep. Crossing this stream, we entered the ruby-mine district. The ground as far as the Huay Bau Kyow is covered with sharp fragments of quartz, sandstone, and granite, which have been broken by people in search of the gems. Many of great value are said to have been found here. The workings have been merely on the surface and in the banks of the stream ; if scientifically worked, the mines might prove very valuable.

Beyond the Huay Bau Kyow—"the stream of the ruby mines"—we entered the rice-fields of Muang Haut, and crossing the Meh Haut, 60 feet wide and 5 feet deep, were cheered by the sight of trees once more in leaf. The bright red flowers of Pin-leh-Ka-thyt, the tree under which the Devas dance in Indra's heaven until intoxicated with pleasure, now flamed in rivalry of the *pouk*, and the banks of the Meh Ping were fringed with orchards and noble clumps of graceful, plume-like bamboos. Passing through the fields, which are bounded on the west by five little knolls, each crested by a pagoda, we skirted the monastery, temple, and pagoda at the entrance of the town, and passing through it, halted for the night at a fine *sala*, or rest-house, built near the bank of the river.

Muang Haut lies 154 miles from Hlineboay, and 743 feet above the sea. The river opposite the *sala* was 600 feet broad, the water 3 feet deep, and the banks 12 feet high.

After we had been thoroughly inspected by all the loafers about the place, who had luckily had the edge of their appetite taken off by the Bombay-Burmah party, which had only left on the previous day, we were able to stroll about whilst dinner was being got ready. Seeing some fine cabbages in a Chinaman's garden near our *sala*, we stopped to bargain for some. Imagine our surprise when he would not part with them under a rupee each. Expostulation was in vain—one of the gentlemen who had left the day before had paid him that price for one; that was the value, and no less would be taken for one. Cabbage-growing in the Shan States must be a lucrative business. In the gardens about the town I noticed cocoa-nut and Palmyra palms, custard-apple, guava, orange, citron, pummelo, plantains, and mango-trees and sugar-cane, tobacco, turmeric, chillies, onions, pumpkins, and other ordinary plants seen in gardens. A woman was cutting up green tobacco-leaves for use by forcing them through a hole in a plank at the end of a small table, and slicing the leaves at the other side of the orifice.

On returning to the *sala*, Ramasawmy, Dr Cushing's servant, came to interview him, and raised a bobbery. He was indignant. In the course of conversation with my boys, he had found out that each of them was receiving five rupees a-month more wages than he had bargained for. Here was fat in the fire. It was shameful; he would not be treated so; he would leave that moment and return to Maulmain. It was useless Dr Cushing's remarking that my boys were not in the same position as his boy, being only hired for the journey, whilst he had been with him for years, and had accompanied him on former journeys at the same wages. It was unjust. He would not stand it. He had told Portow and Loogalay, and they had laughed at him.

He would not stop. He would go at once. Blubbering with passion, he proceeded to pack up his pah, sleeping-mat, and blanket, and would have left the *sala* with them if Dr Cushing, who remained as cool as a cucumber, had not told Portow and Shway Wai to prevent him from moving the things, and despatched a note to the head-man asking that the boy might not be allowed to leave the village with the elephant-men whom I had just paid off. The boy was bound to give him a month's notice before leaving, and he must do what he was bound to do. The storm was merely a passing gust of temper, and Ramasawmy was at work again the next day as cheery as a lark and as brisk as a sparrow.

We were pleased to see our old acquaintances the sparrows and crows again. These birds are only seen in the neighbourhood of large villages and towns, where people most do congregate. I cannot better depict the strong sense of humour existing amongst the Shans than by relating their fable of the peacock and the crow, which runs as follows:—

STORY OF THE PEACOCK AND CROW.

In days of yore when time was young, and birds conversed as well as sung, the peacock and the crow were both grey birds. One day, at the suggestion of the peacock, they mutually agreed each to do its utmost to improve the personal appearance of the other. The crow, taking a paint-brush, some fine feathers, and beautiful colours, in an artistic manner performed his part of the bargain. Then handing the brush to the peacock, who was admiring himself in a placid pool, asked that bird to decorate him. The peacock, excited with admiration and conceit at his splendid appearance, for a long time turned a deaf ear to the remonstrances and pleadings of the crow. At length, taking the brush, he laid on the crow a layer of black as a ground-work for the other colours. Then strutting off to the pool he had another look at himself. Returning, he shrieked with laughter at the contrast, and dancing round the crow, displaying his lovely plumage, assured the justly incensed bird that he was such fun, he could not think of spoiling his appearance by further use of the brush.

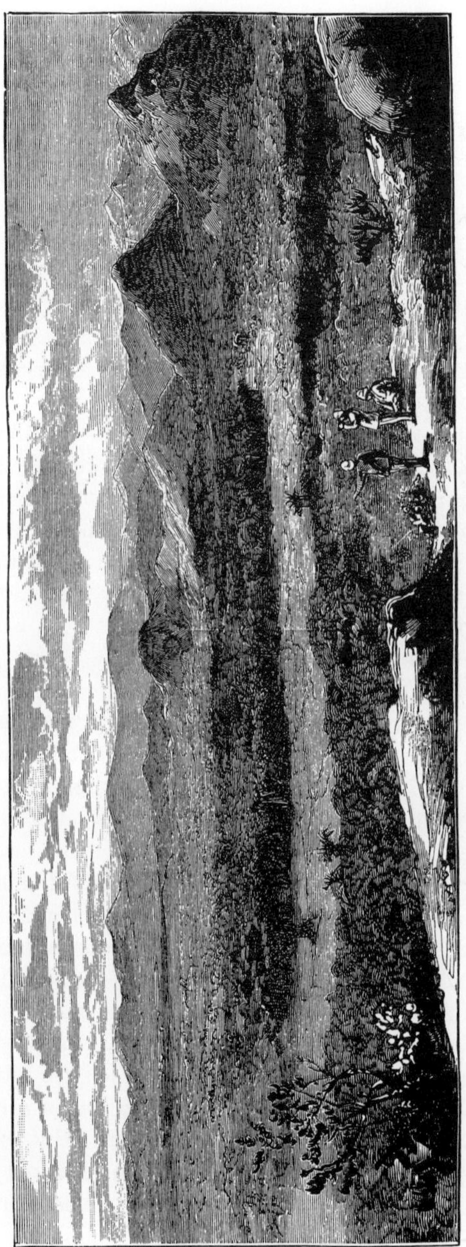

View to the south from a hillock behind Muang Haut.

Before dinner I clambered up the southern hillock at the back of the town, and sketched the country from the base of a pagoda. To the south, fourteen miles distant, appeared Loi Kern, the northern flank of the great bulwark of hills and table-land through which the Meh Ping tears its way in stupendous gorges to the plains of Siam. One of its eastern peaks is crested by a pagoda of much sanctity, to which pilgrims from all parts gather. Between us and Loi Kern lay a great forest-clad plain, with short spurs jutting into it from the Bau plateau. The narrow rice-plain of Muang Haut could be seen winding like a large river through the forest. Turning to the west, Loi Kom loomed above the spurs, and between it and Loi Kern stretched Loi Pang Ma, the eastern flank of the Bau plateau. The pagoda on the hillock to the north and west of the one that I was sketching from is called Tat Oo-kyow, or the pagoda of the gemmed offering-box. Another pagoda cresting a neighbouring peak at the end of a spur is named Tat Loi Som.

In the evening I was amused by watching Veyloo and Jewan having a long conversation with a Zimmé Shan about the prices of things in that place. Every day they had learned a few words and sentences of Shan from Portow, and now, with the aid of expressive signs and gestures, were prepared to do battle with the stall-keepers in the bazaars.

The next morning we sent for the head-man of the town to arrange for a fresh supply of elephants to take us to Zimmé, and to obtain what information we could from him. He came followed by several of the villagers, and ascending the stairs, crouched *shekoing* on the threshold. On our asking him to approach to our temporary table, he came half crawling and half hopping in on his hands and feet like a huge toad. This is the ordinary mode of courtesy shown by an inferior to a superior in the Shan States and Siam. Not only the common people and village head-men use this form of ceremony, but a prince visiting another of higher social rank either prostrates himself on the ground, or squats down, places the palms of his hands together, and raises them up to his face.

He said elephants were not procurable in the neighbourhood of Muang Haut, and to procure boats to convey us and our things to Zimmé might take him two or three days. The ordinary hire for an elephant from Zimmé to Muang Haut was 30 rupees. The hire of a boat, including a steersman and three polers, from Muang Haut to Zimmé was 60 rupees, and two boats would be required for our party.

The wages of each boatman to Bangkok varied between 70 and 80 rupees; to Raheng, from 24 to 25 rupees; to Paknam Po, 30 rupees; and to Zimmé, 15 rupees. The time taken by a boat in going to Bangkok averaged fifteen days in the rains, and thirty days in the dry season. From Bangkok to Muang Haut took forty-five days in the rains, and two months in the dry season. From Zimmé to Muang Haut took two days in the rains, and from four to five in the dry season. From Muang Haut to Zimmé, six days in the dry season; in the rains the journey was always done by elephant.

A caravan-man conducting eight to ten laden bullocks from Zimmé to Muang Haut and back received 10 rupees with food, or 15 rupees without food, the journey there taking him eight days. From Zimmé to Maulmain and back he got 20 rupees with food, or 30 rupees without food, the journey there taking thirty days. A good bullock carries 40 viss; a small one, 30 viss: no load is ever placed on a cow.

A porter carrying 20 viss—66⅔ lb.—receives 2 rupees a viss going to Maulmain, and the same returning to Zimmé, or at the rate of Rs. 1344 a ton carried either way. The journey for a quick travelling porter from Zimmé to Maulmain takes fifteen days, and the same back.

The rainfall at Muang Haut and Zimmé was less than at Maing Loongyee. Sometimes for a whole month in the rains it only drizzled now and then. The previous year the crops on the higher ground had suffered through deficient rainfall. The rice-fields yielded a hundred-fold on the best land, and from fifty-fold upwards on the poorest. The town contained fifty houses; its inhabitants were traders and cultivators, chiefly the former.

Having pumped the head-man dry, we wandered through the town and inspected the religious buildings. The temple was a fine building 54 feet long, varying in breadth from 17 feet at the porch, 21 feet at the two ends, to 24 feet in the central portion. The roofs were in two tiers, leaving a space of 2 or 3 feet between the tiers. The roof of the centre portion rose higher than that of each end, and the roof of the porch was lower. Leading up to the porch was a plastered brick staircase. The floor and walls were likewise of plastered brickwork, and stopped some distance from the roof, which was supported by teak posts, those on the outside being built into the wall. In the centre portion, and the end next the porch, wooden gratings were let into the walls to aid in lighting the buildings. The interior posts which supported the upper tiers of the central portion were painted black, with an ornamental band of gilding $4\frac{1}{2}$ feet from the ground. The two posts in the chancel were painted red, with a similar gilded band at the same height from the ground. Inside the chancel was a sitting image of Gaudama 10 feet high, and six others 4 feet high, besides a dozen smaller ones.

When at Maing Longyee some large images were being made, and in my walks I watched the process from day to day. A core of clay is first accurately carved into the required shape. It is then plastered over with a layer of cloth. Over this is spread a thick coating of *thyt-si* varnish mixed with sawdust. Other coatings are then added until the required stiffness is acquired. The casting is then removed from the core by slitting it up along the sides. It is then carried to the temple and erected on the pedestal that has been prepared for it. The halves being placed together, other coatings are applied which cause the halves to adhere. The whole is then perfected with a layer of gold-leaf. Some of the larger idols are made of bricks plastered over, others of stone, and some of bronze.

Under a shed in the temple grounds were several musical instruments—amongst them two large tapering drums, one 2 feet 9 inches long, 11 inches in diameter at the larger head, and 9 inches in diameter at the smaller head. The other drum was of the same size, but had only a single head; its tapered end was fixed in a hollowed-out pedestal of *padouk* wood, which was so resonant as to be nearly a drum in itself.

After visiting the abbot, who had a few novices with him in the monastery, and trying to bargain with him for some of his palm-leaf documents, we returned to the *sala*. On our way back we noticed two boats discharging their cargoes of rice, and at once hired them for our journey to Zimmé. They were flat-bottomed, and each about 40 feet long. When all the luggage and men were on board, we had only space enough to sit in a cramped position on a mat, the mat roof nearly touching our heads.

At 6 A.M. the temperature was 54° in the shade; at 2 P.M., 89° in the shade, and 118° in the sun; at 3 P.M., 92° in the shade; and at 8 P.M., 77° in the shade.

CHAPTER VII.

LEAVE MUANG HAUT—LEGEND OF THE RAPIDS—FOOTPRINTS OF BUDDHA —POWER OF ACCUMULATED MERIT — INDRA'S HEAVEN — RIVER SCENERY — FISHING - DAMS — LOI PAH KHOW—LARGE FISH—NAKED BOATMEN—A PLEASANT RETREAT—WARS BETWEEN THE BURMESE AND SHANS—A SUGAR-PRESS—SILVER-MINES—PATH FOR THE RAILWAY — WATER-WHEELS — THE TIGER-HEAD MOUNTAIN — PLEASANT MORNINGS—A RIVER SCENE—CHANTING PRAYERS—THE VALLEY OF THE MEH LI—COUNTRY-HOUSE OF THE CHIEF OF LAPOON—VIANG HTAU—VISIT TO A MONASTERY.

HAVING loaded the boats, we started from Muang Haut a little after 8 A.M. on the 20th of February for Zimmé. After passing through the fishing-dam at the north of the island which stretches for half a mile above the town, we turned a bend, and at the end of the next loop reached Pa-kin-soo, a celebrated sand-cliff which stands up like an old sandstone castle with towers and buttresses weather-worn and crumbling into ruins.

LEGEND OF THE RAPIDS.

The legend attached to this cliff has given rise to the names of the rapids in the gorges below Muang Haut, and runs as follows: In ancient days a Shan princess of Viang Soo or Kiang Soo, being crossed in love by her parents refusing their consent to her marriage with a nobleman of a hostile State, determined to levant with her lover. Accordingly, one moonlight night she mounted behind him on a pony and went galloping away towards his home. When nearing the river they heard her father with his followers clattering and clammering behind them. Reaching the bank, they found themselves on the crest of the cliff, with the river a sheer drop of 120 feet below. Her father being nearly at their heels, they had no time to dodge to the right hand or to the left; they must take the leap or be caught. The lover, eager for the safety of the princess, hesitated for a moment, when his lady-love, nothing daunted, sprang in front of him, struck the pony and forced it to the leap. From that time they lived only in story, and the places where their bodies, pony, whip, saddle, harness, and other equipment were stranded, were named acccordingly.

Proceeding two and a half miles farther, we halted for breakfast near a pagoda and visited the Phra Bat, a footprint of Gaudama, which is situated a quarter of a mile from the west bank of the river. The footprint is 5 feet 4½ inches long, and 2 feet broad, and is impressed on a huge granite boulder, and decorated in the usual manner. Although a place of pilgrimage, no monastery is attached to it, and the temple in which the Phra Bat lies is becoming a ruin. To account for the supernatural size of the footprints, which are found of various dimensions throughout the country, we must remember that virtuous men, the possessors of accumulated merit, have intellectual properties which, besides virtue (*dharma*), knowledge, calm self-control, include supernatural power (*aiswarya*), which enables its possessor to make his way into a solid rock, to sail to the sun on a sunbeam, touch the moon with the tip of his finger, expand so as to occupy all space, and swim, dive, or float upon the earth as readily as in water. Through merit, in fact, the intellect (Buddha) attains the "absolute subjugation of Nature," so that "whatever the will proposes, that it obtains." But merit, however vast the stock, is consumed like fuel: thus even those in Indra's heaven who "drink their fill of joys divine," fall again to earth after their accumulated stock of merit is spent, and have to continue their series of births and deaths until they are purified from desire, when they obtain Neiban, become as the winds are, or as if they had never been born.

Opposite our halting-place we noticed tobacco-gardens

belonging to a village invisible amongst the dense foliage. Our morning's journey had been delightful; the long bends of the river, and the slow movement of the boat as it was poled up-stream, rendered surveying a pastime after the continuous turns and twists, with the accompanying frequent observations, incurred on our land march—the more so after the pitching, rolling, and jolting I had undergone on the elephants.

It was most refreshing, after the leafless forest about Muang Haut, to see the magnificent foliage skirting the river. Large bamboos in bunch-like clumps, not the impenetrable thickets we had previously met; the lights and shades on the golden greens of their delicately coloured plumes; and the deep recesses between the clumps, in whose stately presence the scrub-jungle disappears; the cooing of doves; the gaily decked kingfisher watching for its opportunity to plunge on its prey; the *lep-pan* (silk-cotton trees) 120 feet high, with pegs driven into the trunks to serve as ladders for the cotton-pickers, their white trunks and bare horizontal branches looking like shipping with yards up as we rounded the bends; the flower of the *pouk* flaming out at intervals; low islands covered with scrub willows, whose leaves glistened in the sun; the mist driving along the face of the water, ascending in little twirls and vanishing; the bell-music of passing caravans; the plaintive cry of the gibbons; the *oo-kee-or* calling its own name; and little grey and buff-coloured squirrels springing about the trees,—all added a charm to the scene. Even without an Eve, one felt inclined to express one's pleasure in Adam's words:—

> "Sweet is the breath of morn, her rising sweet,
> With charm of earliest birds; pleasant the sun,
> When first on this delightful land he spreads
> His orient beams on herb, tree, fruit, and flower,
> Glist'ring with dew; fragrant the fertile earth
> After soft showers."

The silk-cotton of the *lep-pan* tree is too short and brittle to be made into yarn or cloth; the soft downy cotton is therefore solely used for stuffing cushions, pillows, and beds.

Resuming our journey, we passed Ta Nong Hluang—the

Ferry of the great Fishery or Lake—where several fishing-stake dams stretched across the river and had to be opened to allow our boats to pass. Some distant hills were now visible to the east, and occasional hillocks were seen in the same direction. A little beyond the 164th mile the Meh Kom, or Golden River, entered. The Meh Kom drains the gully in the hills to the north of Loi Kom. As we proceeded, the banks to the east were occasionally perpendicular bluffs of soil, sand, and gravel, remains of the old lake-bottom not yet washed away by the movements of the river. We halted for the night at Ban Hsope Kyem, a small village at the mouth of the Meh Kyem, which enters from the west after draining the hills in the vicinity of Loi Pah Khow—the Mountain of the White Cloud—so called from its head generally being enshrouded in mist. Our camp for the night was 167 miles from Hlineboay, and was bounded on the west by beautiful and grand hill scenery.

View from near Ban Hsope Kyem

Loi Pah Khow, the great dome-shaped hill which we had

seen a little to the east of north soon after leaving Bau Hluang, now lay west-north-west 15 miles distant; and the intervening country to the south-west, to within five miles from the river, had the character of a plateau riven by great chasms or defiles through which the drainage passes. To the north-west the country was more broken up, some of the hills presenting evidence of past subsidence in the precipices which were visible on their slopes and faces. Loi Pah Khow dominates the Zimmé range of hills, and appears to rise to 8000 or perhaps 10,000 feet above sea-level.

The next morning we left at seven. The stream has worn its way not only through the old lake-bottom, but into the sandstone and laterite sub-surface, as these rocks are frequently exposed in the banks. After passing two small villages and through a reach bordered by Loi Kai Khee-a on the west and a sandstone cliff 50 feet high on the east, we halted for breakfast at the village of Ban Peh, where many men were fishing with nets in the river. Our boys purchased an excellent fish, 10 lb. in weight, and several smaller ones, for tenpence, which were a pleasant addition to our meal.

Our boatmen, in deference to us, wore white cotton jackets with short sleeves, and a handkerchief tied round their loins extending only half-way to their knees. Many of the men in boats on the river had not even this pretence at decency, but were as naked as Adam before the Fall. The river being shallow in places, the men were in and out of the water frequently to lug the boats over the shoals; and I presume this partly accounted for their primitive habits.

After breakfast we started again, and passing the Ta Pa, or "rock-ferry," named from the conglomerate and sandstone formation that outcrop in the banks, we reached Ban Meh Soi, in which was situated the first monastery we had seen since leaving Muang Haut. Over the water was a neat thatched-roofed building 12 feet long and 9 feet broad, with wooden posts, the sides planked for 3 feet in height, and a bamboo floor raised 3 or 4 feet above the top of the bank, with which it was connected by a foot-bridge. This little summer-house had been built for the use of the *Phra*, or abbot, when repeating at the time of full and new moon the ritual appointed for cleansing himself from his sins.

From the village we saw the high plateau or great table-topped hill from which Loi Hsope Kang springs; the crest, which extended for some miles, was peakless and as flat as a board. Two miles farther we passed two islands situated in a deep reach of the river called Wung Hoo-a Kwai, "the pool of the buffalo's head." Thence for five miles to the place where we halted for the night there was not a vestige of a habitation or a garden seen from the river. If there were any in the vicinity, they were effectually screened by the fringes of bamboos which lined the banks.

Leaving early the next morning, we noticed a low range of hills four miles to the south-east, and soon afterwards passed the end of a low, straight, and level spur from this range looking like a great embankment, and known as Loi Ta Khan Lai, "the hill of the passage of the hundred steps." Two miles farther, we reached Ban Nong Long, "the village of the lake of monk's coffin." This village formed the refuge of Phya Cha Ban, the chief of Zimmé, when he fled from the Burmese in 1777.

From Ban Nong Long northwards the country becomes more populous. After passing the mouth of the Meh Kang, where a large caravan of laden Shans was crossing the river, we halted at a suburb of Wung Pan for breakfast. Here we noticed a simple press for extracting sugar from the sugar-cane. It was driven by a buffalo yoked to a long bamboo lever, which worked a central wooden shaft, which had part of its length cogged, and its lower portion smooth but notched with grooves. The cogs worked into two similar cogged shafts. The three shafts fitted into an upright frame, thus completing the press. The syrup is boiled in pans 2 feet 9 inches broad and 6 inches deep, set in holes on inclined ground, fuel being fed under them through short tunnels, and the flues consist of shorter ones with their exit up-hill. The buffalo being scared by the sight of two invaders of his country, had to be replaced by two men, a woman, and a boy whilst I sketched the machine.

Leaving Wung Pan, we proceeded through several straggling villages and reached the southern mouth of the Meh Li, which enters from the east.

The Meh Li flows from the south through a very picturesque and well-wooded country. Near its source, not far from the silver-mines, is a gorge or gap in the hills leading into the valley of the Meh Phit. Through this gorge a branch railway might be constructed to connect Raheng with Lapoon and Zimmé. The branch might be continued from Zimmé past Muang Ken and Kiang Dow *viâ* the Meh Pam into the valley of the Meh Fang, whence it could be carried across the Meh Khoke through Muang Ngam into the Meh Chun valley, where it would again join the main line in the plain of Kiang Hsen. The best caravan route between Raheng and Zimmé passes through the gap.

Nearly opposite the mouth of the Meh Li is a fine monastery called Wat Ta Sala, after the *sala*, "traveller's rest-house," that has been erected a little higher up the river, and a little beyond, at the village of Fang Min, we passed three large spider undershot water-wheels.

The axle or boss of each wheel was of hard wood, about 3 feet long and 5 inches in diameter. From this radiated two rows, about 2 feet apart, of spokes from 10 to 12 feet long. The two rows were joined together at the top by paddles made of bamboo matting, 2 feet broad by 1 foot deep. The spokes, each formed of one-third of a split bamboo, were connected together at the periphery of the wheel by a light lattice-work formed of strips of bamboo, on the under side of which were fastened joints of bamboo about 1 foot long to serve as buckets to bring up the water. The lower part of the wheel was immersed for 3 feet in the current, and the water was emptied into a trough near the top, from whence it was conveyed to the gardens and fields. The boss of the wheel worked upon two light trestles made of wood. The wheel was so light that it required little current to set it in motion. I passed 220 of these spider-web wheels between Ta Sala and Zimmé. Similar water-wheels are found in the Chinese provinces of

Kweichau and Ssuchuan, as well as in Upper Burmah and the Shan States. They are used for pounding and grinding rice as well as for irrigation, and lifting water for household purposes. It is a singular spectacle to watch several of these wheels, placed within a few feet of each other, in ceaseless motion, their shafts humming loudly, and the water splashing and sparkling all over them.

Just above Fang Min, between it and the monastery of Ban Dong, which lies on the east of the river, favoured by a long stretch of the river which enabled me to see over the tops of the trees lining the banks, I caught sight of the Loi Hoo-a Soo-a, "the mountain of the tiger's head," so called from the aspect of a precipice on its western extremity. Beyond it, twenty miles distant to the north-west, lay Loi Pah Kung, an undulating hill or plateau of great height, a monarch among the mountains, forming part of the main range of the Zimmé hills.

After passing three villages and another fine monastery, we reached the northern mouth of the Meh Li and halted for the night. The banks in the neighbourhood are very low, frequently not more than five and a half feet in height, and must at times be subject to inundation.

The early morning is the most enjoyable part of the day in the Shan States, and is delightful during a boat journey. As the sun pours its rays through the trees, a flood of light is shed upon the thickets on the opposite bank of the river, displaying, amongst glistening dewdrops, a wonderful variety of beautiful hues and colours. The birds are singing their morning orisons; the doves are cooing from the tall cotton-trees, which are shedding showers of scarlet lily-shaped blossoms; the jungle-fowl crowing from their bamboo fastnesses; blue jays flop along from tree to tree, croaking as they fly; gaudy woodpeckers tap at the old tree-trunks in search of their morning's meal; divers, springing from the water, speed for a few yards and dart in again; snipe, plover, and snippets are strutting on the sand-banks, and kingfishers flash in the sunlight like living gems. The whole scene teems with music, life, and light. The breeze rustling in the tree-tops, the deliciously cold morning air bathing one's face, and the universal enjoyment around us, wafts care away, renews our youth for the time, and we enjoy the pleasures of paradise.

Starting soon after six, we passed through Loi Law, a village which nestles in gardens of graceful palms and fruit-trees, and lines both sides of the river. The air was scented with the fragrance of orange and pummelo blossoms; bells tolled by the breeze tinkled from the pagoda, and the sound of children's voices, joined with the deeper tones of men chanting their morning's devotions, were wafted to us from the monastery. Girls tripped gaily along the banks with their water-jars balanced on their heads; children who could barely walk dragged great buffaloes along by their nose-rings; pariah dogs barked at us; and the impudent crows scolded us from the banks for breaking into the harmony of the scene.

Loi Hoo-a Soo-a with Loi Pah Kung in the background.

Ten minutes after leaving the village, I halted to sketch Loi Hoo-a Soo-a and Loi Pah Kung; and a mile farther on ascended Loi Noi, a small granite knoll on the west bank that is crested by a pagoda, in order to settle the position and make a drawing of the hills in the valley of the Meh Li. Between us and Loi Ta Mau and Loi Chang Moo, "the mountain of the crouching elephant," so called from its appearance, the whole plain for a distance of thirty miles appeared to be one great forest with a few small isolated hills cropping up here and there, the area under cultivation being entirely hidden by dense fringes of trees. The Zimmé plain is at its broadest at Loi Noi, and feathers off thence to both ends. Its total length from the gorge beyond the Meh Teng to Loi Chang Moo is seventy miles.

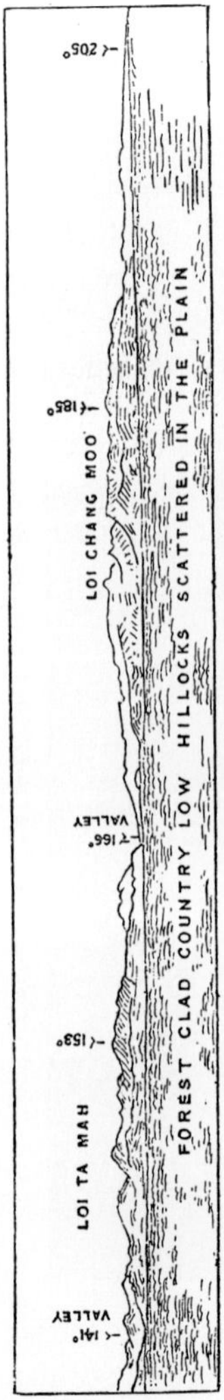

View from the top of Loi Noi at 8 A.M. 23d February.

Leaving Loi Noi, we passed, on the east bank, the country-house of the Chow Hluang, or chief, of Lapoon, near which a landing-stage of bamboos and a flight of steps had been erected for the use of the chief. Two miles farther we passed Ban Ta Pee, the village to which lepers are banished. The bamboo clumps fringing the river now became more scarce, and were replaced by fruit-trees and tobacco and other gardens.

Hsong Kweh, or Htone Htau, the village where we breakfasted, is on the site of the ancient city of Viang Htau. On visiting the religious buildings, which consisted of a pagoda, two temples, and a monastery, I picked up a fragment of an ancient tile, on which were raised three figures — the first a man clothed in a flowing raiment, then an unclad man with a ring or fetter on each ankle, followed by a naked woman with a bracelet or fetter upon each wrist. The portion of the tile containing the heads of the figures had been broken off and lost. The smaller temple had a handsome staircase, the sides of which were formed of twisted snakes and dragons adorned with scales of gold and green tinsel. The plaster scroll-work which embellished the doorway was admirably designed and of excellent cement. Both Burmese and Shans have developed a great talent for architecture and ornamental tracery.

The old monk and his acolytes were evidently pleased at our visit, and had no objection to being photographed. I therefore took two excellent groups, which unfortunately came to nothing, as the plates were blotched, like all the others I had wasted my time in using. Before reaching the monastery, a party of young men and women forded the river in front of our boat, laughing at each other's endeavour to join decency with the attempt to keep their garments from the water, which was nearly waist-deep—a nearly impossible feat.

CHAPTER VIII.

DESCRIPTION OF SHAN HOUSES—CABALISTIC CHARMS—SUPERSTITION—ANCESTRAL AND DEMON WORSHIP—SHAN DYNASTIES IN BURMAH—ZIMMÉ UNDER THE BURMESE—RULES FOR HOUSE-BUILDING—POSSESSING A GHOUL—THE SHADOW SPIRIT—KISSING WITH THE NOSE—FURNITURE—MEALS—CHINESE CHOP-STICKS—SPINSTERS—WEAVING AND EMBROIDERY—DYES—CHINESE HONGS—FISHING—REVOLT AGAINST BURMAH—ZIMMÉ AND LAPOON DESERTED—A REST-HOUSE—SHAN DIALECTS—ENTRANCE OF THE MEH HKUANG—MUSICAL WATER-WHEELS—BRICK AND TILE WORKS—HOUSES FOR THE DEMONS—HOUSES IMBEDDED IN GARDENS—LIGHT-COLOURED BUFFALOES—MY FIRST HUNT IN BURMAH—A FINE PAGODA—APPROACH TO THE CITY—ARRIVE AT ZIMMÉ—AMERICAN PRESBYTERIAN MISSIONS IN SIAM AND ZIMMÉ.

THE houses in the Shan villages along the river-banks are situated in orchards of fine fruit-trees, separated from each other by palisades. The people, like the Burmese, are very fond of flowers, and rear them in their gardens, and in wooden boxes and earthenware pots placed on the balustrade of their verandahs. Young children encircle the top-knot on the head with orchids and sweet-smelling flowers. Girls wear roses, magnolias, bauhinias, jessamine, and orchids in their hair; and net flowers, seeds, and buds into fragrant and beautiful hanging ornaments of various designs. Young men are seen with flowers in the holes in their ear-lobes, which likewise serve as holders for their half-smoked cheroots. Even coolies at work in the fields have flowers in their ears to regale themselves at intervals.

The houses of the peasantry are generally built solely of bamboo, with roofs thatched with grass or the leaves of teak and *eng* trees. The walls are roughly constructed of bamboo matting; and bamboos slit open and spread out by gashing them on the inner side form floor planks a foot and more in width. Not a nail is used in the structure; slips of bamboo twisted into string form the only fastenings when cane is not procurable. In a country where fires are frequent, and bamboos spring up like grass, these houses are eminently adapted to the requirements of the people, as they are cheaply constructed and can easily be replaced.

Passing through the gateway in the bamboo palisading, you enter the garden where the house stands with its floor raised six or eight feet from the ground. Under the house is a space where elephant howdahs, gardening implements, and materials are kept, and where cattle can be tethered for the night. Ascending the steps, you reach a platform or verandah, which is usually partly or wholly roofed. The houses are invariably built with the gable-ends facing north and south; the verandah being generally at the southern extremity.

The east side of the verandah has a wall continuous with that of the house. Along this wall is a shelf on which are placed offerings of flowers for Buddha and for the beneficent spirits. On the western side of the verandah stands a covered settle for the earthen water-pots, which hold water for drinking and cooking purposes. The outer posts of this verandah, when only partially covered in, rise high enough to support the balustrade, on which pot-herbs, onions, chillies, garlic, flowers, and orchids are grown for family use.

The floor of the uncovered portion of the verandah serves in the daytime as a drying-place for betel-nuts and fruit, and at night, after the heat of the day, furnishes a resort for a quiet lounge under the fast cooling sky. If the family is religiously disposed, it is to the verandah that the monks are invited to conduct a merit-making service for the prosperity and health of the household; and it is to the verandah that witch-finders, medicine-men, and sorcerers, as well as monks, are received to render their services for a small consideration in cases of sickness.

Look on the tops of the house-posts, under the rafters, and you will find cabalistic charms inscribed on fragments of cloth, which have been placed there to prevent the intrusion of malignant spirits who bring calamity, disease, and death.

The belief in the spirits of the earth, found in all the dark corners of the world, and at one time nearly universal, fetters its victims with the bonds of superstition. Superstition saps all manliness from them, makes them live in constant dread of their surroundings, and consider themselves akin in soul to spirits inhabiting the lower grades of creation and the vegetable and mineral kingdom.

The spirits in the unseen world, although considered to have previously inhabited human forms, according to the people are as malicious as monkeys, and can only be kept in good humour by constant coaxing. The very best—the spirits of their ancestors, and the spirits of deceased monks, the teachers of their youth—will certainly take vengeance if provoked by neglect.

Knowing that Shan dynasties reigned in Upper Burmah from A.D. 1298 to 1554, and in Lower Burmah from A.D. 1287 to 1540, and again from 1740 to 1746; that the people of Zimmé were tributary to, and at times directly ruled by Burmah, between A.D. 1558 and 1774; and that Talaings, the people of Lower Burmah, flocked to Zimmé and Siam, and settled there in the latter half of last century and in the first half of this century,—it is not surprising to find that many superstitions held by the Talaings and Burmese are common to the people of Zimmé. Thus the instructions given in the Burmese Dehttohn upon house-building, and choosing the site and materials, and also as to the lucky day for the commencement of the house, are generally applicable to Zimmé as well as to Burmah. Superstition takes under its guidance almost every detail; and when the house is completed, it still directs as to the day and the manner of moving in to take possession, and even as to the direction the people are to repose in at night. No door or windows are allowed in the eastern wall, and the family sleep with their heads to the east.

The flooring of the house is supported by posts forked at the top to carry the floor beams on which rest the bamboo joints for supporting the planking. The walls and roof of the house are supported by other posts let two feet into the ground, and reaching to the wall-plates or to the ridge of the house, according to their position. A peculiar feature in most of the Zimmé houses is the general practice of inclining the walls slightly outwards from the floor to the roof.

The posts of the walls are arranged in sets of threes, fives, sevens, &c., as odd numbers bring luck. The spaces between each set of posts have specific names. The door of the house and the verandah or platform in front of it are almost always at the south end. The post that is occupied by the spirits, "Pee," is on the east side next to the corner post nearest the door. The guardian spirits of the house are supposed to occupy the portion of this post above the floor, and malignant or evil spirits the portion below it.

The Pee Hpōng, or ghoul spirit, who resides in the lower region of the earth, possesses people in the following manner: A person in communion with this spirit rises quietly from sleep at night, and stealing down-stairs, tips his (or her) nose thrice against the spirit post. This action makes the face lustrous, and by its light, as by a lamp, the possessed person seeks the vile food that he craves. When satisfied, he re-tips his nose, the ghoul vanishes, and he returns to bed. The ghoul, I presume, is inhaled when first tipping the nose, and exhaled when re-tipping it. Kissing amongst the Shans and Burmese is performed by inhaling through the nose, and not as with us through the lips. Another spirit rising from the centre of the earth is Phya Ma-choo Lat, the shadow spirit, that renders people prematurely careworn and old.

The house has its floor raised a few inches above that of the verandah, and the interior is divided into one, two, or more apartments, according to its size and the wants of its owner. The furniture of the houses is very simple. Mats and cushions are piled in a corner ready for use; the handsomest cushions being triangular in section and embroidered at each end. Simple mats made of fine strips of bamboos or of a species of rush, often worked into patterns, serve as mattresses in summer, and are replaced by home-made cotton mattresses in the colder months. The mattress is rolled up during the day, and placed on the floor at night, and over it is suspended a thick cotton mosquito-curtain, through which one would think it scarcely possible to breathe. Curtains made of book muslin would be much more conducive to health, and would be equally serviceable, as they would keep out the sand-flies as well as the mosquitoes, which an ordinary mosquito-net does not do, as I found out before I had been many days in Burmah.

The fireplace consists of a wooden frame about four feet square and six inches deep, filled with earth or sand. On this is placed a light iron tripod, or what equally serves the purpose, three pieces of brick or stone to rest the pot on when the fire is kindled. In the dry season cooking is carried on in the garden, but in the rains in a compartment of the house, the smoke finding its way out through the door, windows, interstices in the mat walls, and through the roof. The utensils consist, besides the water-jars, of a few pots, pans, baskets made waterproof by coatings of *thyt-si* or wood-oil to serve as buckets, dippers to scoop the water from the jars made of half a cocoa-nut shell fitted with a carved wooden handle, spoons, and a few china bowls.

At meal-times, which occur about seven in the morning and towards sunset, the table, about a foot and a half in diameter and six inches high, is taken down from a shelf and placed on the floor, and by its side is put the tall slender basket of steamed glutinous rice. A lacquer or brass tray holding little bowls of fish, pork, beef, bamboo-shoots, vegetables, and curry, all cut up fine before being put in the pot, and fruit, or perhaps only a bowl of curry, a dish of pickled or dried fish, vegetables and some fruit, are then laid on the table. After the family circle has gathered round, the steamed rice is served separately to each person in a small basket. The members squatting like tailors round the tray in a circle, take up the rice in lumps with their fingers, and dip it into the common bowl of curry, and pick out tit-bits from the other bowls as it suits their fancy. When soup or gravy is served, a common spoon is used; each takes a spoonful and then passes the spoon to his neighbour. After meals it is customary to wash your own bowl, as well as your mouth and fingers.

Whatever one may think of the habit of eating with one's fingers, it is much more seemly than the Chinese custom of

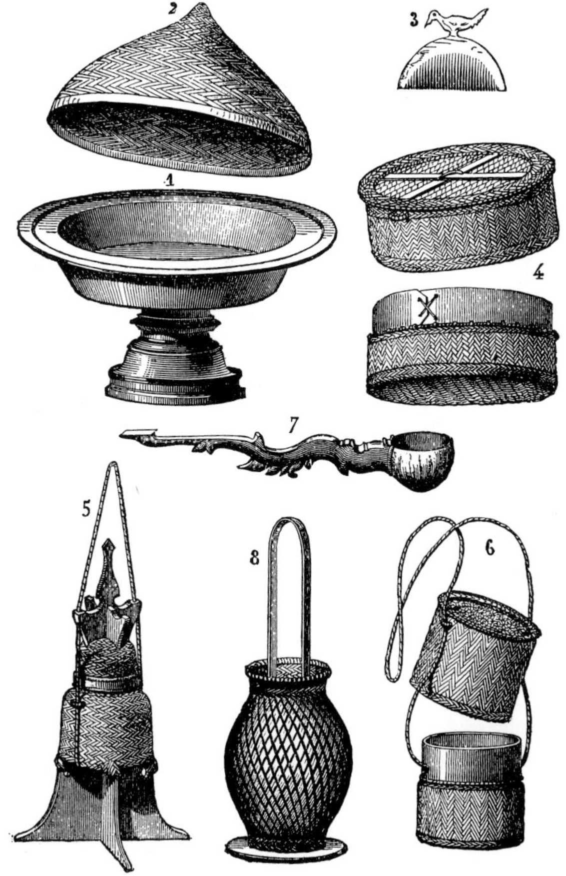

1, 2, *Lacquered bamboo dish with plaited cover.* 3, *Wooden comb.* 4, 5, 6, *Baskets for carrying cooked rice.* 7, *Ladle for water.* 8, *Bamboo lantern.*

feeding with chop-sticks. It is simply disgusting to watch a Chinaman shovelling in his food, and attempting to convey it neatly to his mouth, with these curious and most unsuitable implements.

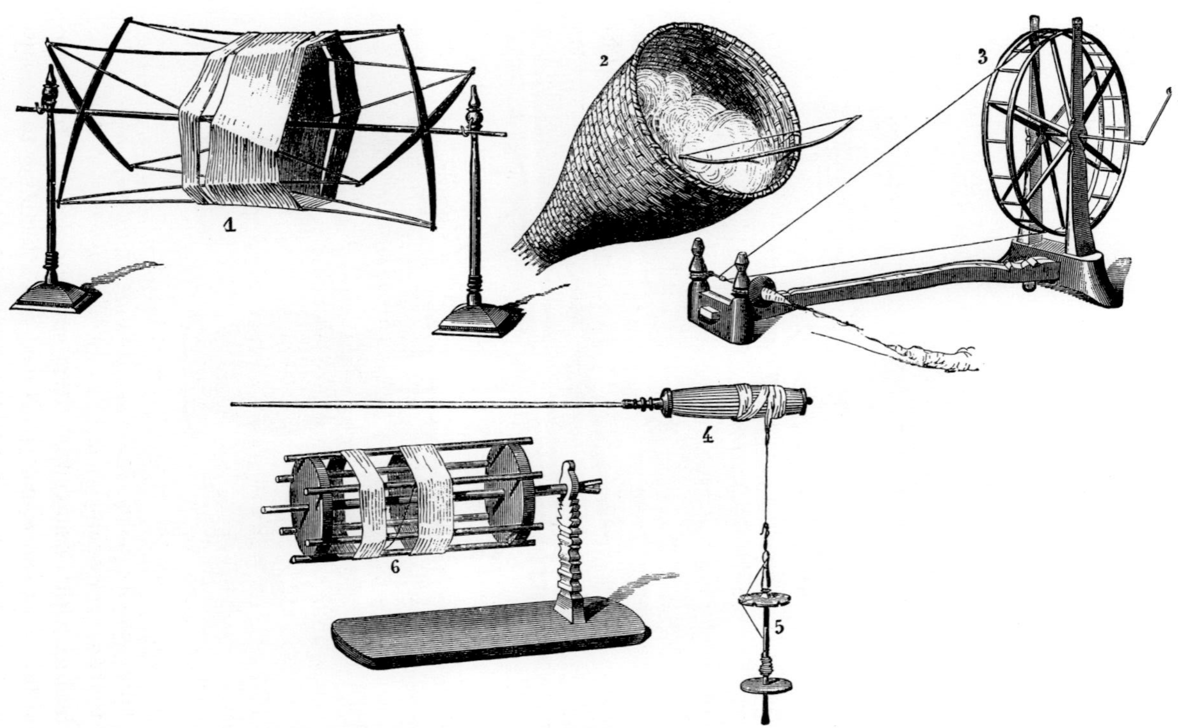

1, *Divider for cotton.* 2, *Basket and bow for carding cotton.* 3, *Wheel to spin cotton.* 4, 5, *Spinner for silk.* 6, *Divider for silk.*

As in olden time in England, so now in the Shan States, every unmarried woman is a spinster, and makes homespun garments for the household. Each house has its native loom and spinning implements, and the women, rich and poor, spend much of their time in providing clothes for the monasteries and for their home-folk. Many are skilled in embroidery, working beautiful patterns in gold and silver thread, and in worsted, cotton, and silk. Both cotton and silk fabrics are woven at the looms, and many of the embroidered goods are taken to Burmah, where they fetch a high price.

The cotton is grown in the gardens surrounding the house, or purchased in the neighbourhood. Some of the silk is produced from the cocoons of the local silk-worms, and the rest is brought by the Chinese from China. The dyes used by the people to within the last few years were solely vegetable; but these, and pity 'tis so, are being displaced by German aniline dyes. The favourite colours are indigo, orange, maroon, and a reddish brown. Many of the Muhseurs and Upper Shans use a black dye made from the berries of the ebony tree. Turmeric and safflower give a yellow dye; soapacacia, green; tamarind-fruit a deep-red colour, approaching purple; and sapan and *thyt-si* wood, red.

After breakfast we left Htong Htau, the monk and his acolytes coming to the bank to see us off. Half a mile farther the Meh Khan, a river 150 feet broad, enters from the west. In the village at its mouth is a large teak-built house in an extensive stockade belonging to a Chinese *hong* or merchant company. We soon afterwards reached Wang Hluang Pow—the Wang Pow where Phya Cha Ban removed his court after deserting Zimmé in 1775.

The houses about here are thatched under the gable-ends as well as on the roofs. The village extends for over two miles, chiefly along the east bank of the river. Rows of women, approaching each other in lines extending from bank to bank, were fishing with drop-nets, formed of a wire frame 2 feet 6 inches square, to which the net is attached. The frame of the net is suspended from four pieces of bamboo string, one at each corner, tied together to form a handle.

On the west bank of the river is a fine temple and monastery; and a little above Wang Pow a large rest-house stands boldly out from the trees, and is called Nong Doo Sakan by the Zimmé Shans, and Nong Loo Sakan by the Shans in the British Shan States. In the same way *Loi*, "a mountain," in British Shan turns to *Doi* in Zimmé, and in Kampti Shan is *Noi*. The dialectic differences amongst the various tribes of Shans chiefly lie in a change of the first letter of words and in the occasional dropping of the second letter of a double consonant at the commencement of a word. *Ruen*, a house, and *pla*, a fish, in Siamese, become *huen* and *pa* in Zimmé and Kampti Shan; *ban*, a village in Siamese and Zimmé dialects, becomes *man* in Kampti; *chang*, an elephant in Siamese and Zimmé, becomes *tsang* in British Shan and Kampti; and *ny* changes into *y*, *kl* to *kr*, *kh* to *k*, *k* to *ch*, and *ch* into *s* and *ts* in various dialects. Most of the Zimmé Shans call Zimmé "Kiang Mai"; the Siamese term it "Chieng Mai." The Zimmé and British Shans talk of "Kiang Hai"; the Siamese call that place "Chieng Rai."

Nong Doo Sakan was erected at the expense of the villagers, as a work of merit, for the accommodation of travellers journeying along the main road to Muang Haut. It is built entirely of bamboo and thatched with *thek-keh* grass. Over a stream on the opposite side of the river was a wooden bridge—the first I had seen since leaving Burmah.

Continuing our journey through the village of Kweh Chow, we reached the southern mouth of the Meh Hkuang, which enters from the east. Between it and the northern mouth lies Pak Bong, a revenue station of the Shan State of Lapoon.

The Meh Hkuang rises in the hills to the north-east of Zimmé, close to the sources of the Meh Low, and by means of canals and irrigating channels irrigates the Zimmé and Lapoon plain nearly to the bank of the Meh Ping. A short distance from its mouth it is joined by the Meh Ta, on which lies the large village of Pa Sang, where Chow Ka Wi La, the successor of Phya Cha Ban, established his court for the fifteen years previous to the reoccupation of Zimmé in 1796. Owing to the rebellion of the Zimmé Shans against the Burmese in 1774, when they threw off the Burman yoke and accepted the protection of Siam, a period of warfare ensued. The Burmese besieged Zimmé in 1775. When relieved by the approach of a Siamese force, the Zimmé Shans scattered to the north and south, and the chief, Phya Cha Ban, removed his court to Ta Wang Pow, and, on the approach of a Burmese force, fled to Raheng. The Burmese entered Siam, but were repulsed after they had taken several Siamese cities. The Zimmé chief then returned with his people to Wang Pow. In 1777, owing to a fresh advance of the Burmese, he removed his court to Nong Long, but the following year, owing to the retirement of the Burmese, fixed it at Lapoon, where he was attacked by the chiefs of Kiang Hai and Kiang Hsen. He then fled southwards and set up his court at Wang Sa Kang. Zimmé was deserted for twenty years, 1776-1796, and Lapoon for forty-one years, 1779-1820.

Two miles beyond Pa Sang we halted for the night at a village on the eastern bank, where ten great spider-web wheels in continuous motion watered the gardens and neighbouring fields. The music made by the axles of these wheels working on the trestles which supported them, resembled the tones of an organ, and at night lulled us to sleep.

Next morning we passed a brick-field where seven small clamps, each ten feet square and five feet high, were being burned. Close by, on the opposite bank, a miniature Shan house, about the size of a large pigeon-house, had been built for the accommodation of a local demon. Many such houses, even in the grounds of temples, were subsequently seen along the route. The boatmen passing us in the various craft were now all clad, as the villages were numerous, and roads skirted the river. Several of them were wearing billy-cock felt hats, common amongst lower-class Chinamen.

We halted for a few minutes at the village of Nong Sang, or Nong Chang, "the elephant's lake," to inspect the tile-works. The men were puddling the clay on a buffalo's hide by pounding it with their feet. The roofing-tiles are a quarter of an inch thick, nine inches long, and four and a half inches broad, and are turned up at one end for three-quarters of an inch to enable them to hang on to the battens of the roof. They are moulded separately on a bench, across which the man sits astride. After sanding the mould, he plunges the clay into it, and cuts off the superfluous material with a string fastened to a fiddle-bow. The upper face of the tile is then smoothed with a three-sided stick, which has been previously cleansed by rubbing it against two cylindrical brushes made of cocoa-nut fibre, which lie in a little trough, raised on posts, and full of water. The front of the mould is movable. The tiles are taken out and dried under a thatched shed, and afterwards are placed on their side-edge in a kiln and burned. The tiles are used for roofing the temples and better class of Shan and Chinese houses.

Two miles farther we passed another village of tile-makers, and at the 220th mile came to Ban Hsope Long, above which is a series of long, cultivated islands. Both banks of the river as well as the islands are embanked to save the cultivation from being swamped in flood-time.

Above Hsope Long, which extends for about two miles, we passed through the village of Ta Kwai, "the buffalo's ford," and halted for breakfast. From here the banks of the river to some miles above the city of Zimmé are nearly continuously fringed with villages. The houses, temples, and monasteries are imbedded in, and often hidden by, beautiful orchards, containing palms, cocoa-nut, mango, tamarind, citron, orange, pummelo, and many other fruit and flowering trees, and the whole scene on land and water is one of bustling life.

In an hour we were off again, and after passing the temple and monastery of Koon Kong, came to a large *hong* belonging to some Chinese merchants of Raheng. A mile farther the Meh Kha entered from the west, and just above its mouth is the village of Pak Muang.

Opposite Pak Muang many buffaloes of a light colour were lying in the river, enjoying still contentment, with their nostrils only just above the water. If they had not been too indolent to scent us, they would have advanced with heads stretched out, horns laid back, and nostrils sniffing to satisfy their natural curiosity, and then have plunged back helter-skelter to the bank, and stood gazing at us from a respectful distance; or else, finding we were strangers of the hated white race, have lowered their heads, made lances of their horns, and charged full tilt at us. My first experience of hunting in Burmah was being hunted when on pony-back by a herd of buffaloes in full chase after me, and being saved by the herd boy, a lad of eleven or twelve years of age, who, happening to be between me and them, rushed forward and drove them in another direction. I would gladly have tipped that boy if I could have got at him without renewing my acquaintance with the buffaloes. At Ta Nong Pai, and later at Song Kare, a village at the mouth of the Meh Ka, which enters from the east, I got a good view of Loi Soo Tayp,

View of Loi Soo Tayp from Ban Meh Ka.

the great hill behind Zimmé, and made sketches, at the same time taking angles to the well-defined peaks. We halted for the night at the monastery of Chedi Lee-am, which is situated at the 233d mile to the east of the river.

Chedi Lee-am, the pagoda to which the monastery is attached, was the largest seen by me in the Shan States. A hole five feet in diameter had been broken into one side of it near the top, in order to rob the shrine; otherwise it was in good repair. This pagoda is peculiar in shape, and resembles a rectangular church-steeple rising in five great steps or tiers, cut off from the tower and placed on the ground. Its summit has not been provided with a *htee,* or umbrella.

Each side of each tier had three niches, and each niche

contained a statue of Gaudama larger than life, making sixty images in all. At each corner of each tier was a pedestal finished off with a flame-like ornament at the top. The pagoda was 60 feet square at the base, and 120 feet high. It is made of brick, and plastered over with excellent cement.

The next day, the 25th of February, we left early, being eager to arrive at Zimmé, which was distant less than two hours' journey. The night's rain had washed the face of Nature, burnished the trees, and brightened the whole landscape. The cool fresh morning air, that bathed one's hands and face, was scented with the fragrance of flowering shrubs and trees, and the panorama we were passing through was delightful.

Temples decorated with dark red and gold, and picturesque monasteries, were set like gems in the beautiful fringes of foliage that skirted the banks. Women and girls, gaily attired in a striped petticoat, or one of a small tartan, and a silk scarf thrown over the left shoulder, tripped along barefooted on their way to the city, with baskets of garden-produce and flowers. Here was a group of men and women squatting on the sands, and having a chat before crossing the ford; there men, women, and children, with their garments tucked up above their knees, laughing and joking as they waded the stream; children playing in the water, dashing it about and splashing each other; cattle lowing on the banks on their way to the fields; the sun lighting up the bald pates and yellow garments of the monks and acolytes who were passing in processions and carrying their begging-bowls through the suburbs, which now lined the banks; women and children heaping their little cups of rice and saucers of fish and condiments into the monks' bowls—whilst the monks,—at least the young ones, who have the reputation of being a jovial crew,—peeped over their fans, which were intended to veil fair women from their sight.

Half an hour before reaching the wooden bridge that spans the river, we came in sight of the walled city, which lies 430 yards inland from the west bank; then rowing between vegetable gardens, which had been planted on the numerous sand-banks, halted at the bridge to learn the position of the quarters of the American Presbyterian Mission, which had been established since 1867 in the suburbs of Zimmé, and since 1840 in Bangkok. The bridge lies 82¼ miles from Muang Haut and 236½ miles from Hlineboay, or about 300 miles from Maulmain. The height of the banks near the bridge is 1008 feet above sea-level.

CHAPTER IX.

OUR RECEPTION—THE MISSION-HOUSE—A BEAUTIFUL VIEW—A REPAST—REV. J. WILSON—ANCIENT BOUNDARIES OF ZIMMÉ—CITY OF ZIMMÉ—POPULATION—THE BRIDGE—AN HERMAPHRODITE—YOUTHFUL DIANAS—FEMALE DRESS—THE MARKET—SHOPS—THE PALACE—VISIT THE KING—DISCUSSION ABOUT THE RAILWAY—PRISONERS IN CHAINS—VISIT A PRINCESS—SHAN EMBROIDERY—A GREAT TRADER—AMOUNT OF CARAVAN TRAFFIC—NUMBER OF ELEPHANTS—BOAT TRAFFIC.

In the meantime Dr M'Gilvary, hearing that our boats had passed, had hurried off a servant to follow them and conduct us to his house. The house is built in a large palisaded garden, which is separated from the east bank of the river by a cart-road.

Entering the garden, where English roses were growing amongst the glorious flowers and flowering shrubs of the tropics, and the air was scented with the sweet blossoms of orange and pummelo trees, we were met by Dr and Mrs M'Gilvary and their little son, who gave us a hearty welcome, and insisted upon our enjoying their hospitality during our stay in Zimmé. Nothing could be more agreeable to us. Pleasant friendly faces, lovely flowers, beautiful fruit-trees, a fine, large, commodious house, a splendid view of Loi Soo Tayp, and the best possible position for collecting information—what more could be desired? The house was constructed for the accommodation of two families of missionaries. One-half was unoccupied, as the Rev. Mr Martin and his wife were on their way from Bangkok, so no one would be cramped by our taking up our quarters there; besides which, Drs M'Gilvary and Cushing were old friends. We therefore gladly accepted the offer.

The Mission-house is built of teak with a shingle roof, in the ordinary style of bungalows in Burmah. A staircase leads up to a broad verandah, from which the front bedrooms and sitting-rooms are entered. At the back are the bath-rooms and another verandah, with a flight of steps leading to the garden and kitchen. The orchard contains fine shady clumps of bamboos, cocoa-nut, mango, tamarind, pomegranate, custard-apple, pummelo, guava, orange, citron, papaw, and coffee trees. The passion-flower grows in great luxuriance, and affords a luscious fruit, which can either be eaten as a vegetable, or like a papaw or a melon.

After the constant strain upon my attention during the journey, I greatly enjoyed reclining in a long-armed chair in the front verandah of the house, and watching, whilst I lazily puffed at my cigar, the ever-changing expression of the great mountain at the back of the city. The lights and shades swiftly flitting across its forest-clad slopes, as the clouds coursed betwixt it and the sun; the beautiful *bijou* views in the early morning, as the mist opened out and closed in when dissolving under the influence of the sun; the foreground formed by suburbs on the other side of the river, embosomed in orchards, amongst which the areca-nut, palmyra, and cocoa-nut palms reared their graceful stems and beautiful plumes; the stream of ever-varying and ever-picturesque life moving along the road and river; the music formed of the murmur of distant voices; the clearer notes of those that were near, and the clash and clatter that proceeds from the busy haunts of men,—the whole was like a pleasant dream, such a one as Ole Luk Oi, in Andersen's 'Fairy Tales,' showed the good little boy when he had thrown dust in his eyes and led him into Dreamland.

Having been shown our rooms, we had the luggage carried up and the necessary things unpacked, adding some of our stores to Mrs M'Gilvary's *cuisine* for the forthcoming banquet.

What a banquet that was! Never in my life, since or before, have I so enjoyed a repast. A nice white tablecloth and napkin once more under one's nose, and European food, with American dainties, and dessert, where fresh strawberries, gathered in the Mission garden, made their appearance, and violets were placed in glasses by our side. I felt more inclined to feast my eyes and my sense of smell than to eat—everything was so tempting and so tasteful. Then the fragrance of a well-cooked dinner; and fresh vegetables, and plenty of them; and that pumpkin-pie, the first I had ever tasted,—it was a feast for the gods! A *gourmet* who wishes to revel in the highest pitch of epicurean enjoyment, could not do better than take a trip into the jungle, and after recouping his jaded appetite, suffering from six weeks' privation and frugal fare, taste the relish of such a feast.

After dinner was over, we received a visit from the Rev. Jonathan Wilson, who had been with the Mission at Zimmé since 1868, the year after it had been established there by the Rev. Daniel M'Gilvary. After giving me a hearty shake of the hand, he asked what he could do for me, and was delighted at the prospect of a railway being carried from Burmah through Siam and the Shan States. Railways were the grandest civilisers in the world, and would do wonders in ameliorating the wretched condition of the people and in spreading Christianity through the land. "Don't be afraid of troubling me," he said; "I shall be only too delighted to aid in your good work." He then asked me to come and talk matters over with him at his diggings. He lived next door, all by himself. His wife was recruiting her health in America, and the two young ladies, who resided in one-half of the house and taught in the Mission schools, were away in the district. We accordingly strolled through the gardens to his house, where, after talking over matters, he promised to have my gold-leaf changed into silver; to collect all the information he could about trade and prices from the people; to inquire about the manners, customs, spirit-lore, and superstitions of the people; and give me a written memorandum about them. I was certainly most fortunate in securing the aid of missionaries who had been so long in the country as Mr Wilson and Dr M'Gilvary, particularly when they manifested such interest in gathering information for me.

The ancient kingdom of Zimmé, or Kiang Mai, according to M'Leod, "comprised fifty-seven cities, mentioned in the Burmese books as fifty-seven *Kraings* (corruption of *Kiang*, a fortified or walled city), many of which at present exist, or their ruins can be traced. Muang Nan and Muang Phé (Peh) were included in the number, and the capital was both Kiang Mai and Kiang Hai, a place to the northward on the Mé Khók (Meh Khoke). It extended from the Mé Khong (Cambodia river) to the Mé Khóng (the Salween river) east and west. To the northward it was bounded by the territories of Kiang Tsen (Hsen) and Kiang Tung, which extended to the Mé Khók; to the southward to the territories of Kampeng, belonging to Siam." The kingdom, according to the Siamese history, was known as Sawakamala, and its capital as Krung (Kiang) see Satanahkanahut, probably Pali names, and not used colloquially, but merely in religious and State documents.

The city of Zimmé, which lies 430 yards to the west of the river, is divided into two parts, the one embracing the other, like a letter L, on the south and east sides. The inner city faces the cardinal points, and is walled and moated all round. The walls are of brick, 22 feet high, and crenelated at the top, where they are 3½ feet broad. The moat surrounding the walls is 30 feet wide and 7 feet deep. The outer city is more than half a mile broad, and is partly walled and partly palisaded on its exterior sides. Both cities are entered by gates leading in and out of a fortified courtyard.

The inner city contains the palace of the head king, the residences of many of the nobility and wealthy men, and numerous religious buildings. In the outer city, which is peopled chiefly by the descendants of captives, the houses are packed closer together than in the inner one, the gardens are smaller, the religious buildings are fewer, and the population is more dense. The roads in both cities are laid out at right angles to each other; no rubbish is allowed to be placed outside the gardens of the houses, which are palisaded; water is led into the town from a stream flowing from Loi Soo Tayp; the floors of the houses are all raised

6 or 8 feet from the ground; and the whole place has an air of trim neatness about it.

The suburbs of the city extend for a great distance, straggling along both banks of the river, and it is therefore difficult to fix the line where they may be said to cease. Dr Cheek, a son-in-law of Dr M'Gilvary, had an extensive practice among the princes and people of Zimmé, and endeavoured to arrive at an approximate estimate of its population. Taking a length of 9 miles and a breadth of 2 miles, or 18 square miles, as the area covered by the city and its suburbs, he arrived at the conclusion that its population could not be less than 100,000 souls. I do not think the double-city by itself can contain more than 30,000 or less than 20,000 inhabitants.

Another estimate formed by Dr Cheek concerned the population of the State of Zimmé. This was based upon an incomplete list of the houses upon which a levy was to be made for feeding the Yaks, or local deities, at the yearly sacrifice. The list included 97,000 houses at the time Dr Cheek saw it; and as seven people on an average live in each house, the population of these houses could not be less than 600,000 souls. Allowing for the other houses not then noted, and for the houses of Lawa, Karen, Muhseu, and other hill-people who are not enumerated in the subscription lists, the gross population of the Zimmé State—including Zimmé, Kiang Hai, Kiang Hsen, Muang Pow, Muang Houngson, Muang Fang, Muang Ken, and its other sub-provinces—must be about 700,000 people.

The following day, accompanied by Drs Cushing and M'Gilvary, I made a round of visits to the king and members of the Court at Zimmé. Leaving the house, we followed the bank of the river to the timber bridge, and crossed it to the western suburbs. The centre span is removable, so as to allow the royal boats of the chiefs to pass through, and is raised about a foot above the rest of the flooring, thus being a great hindrance to the passage of carts and carriages. When driving over the bridge, our carriage had to be lifted on and off this raised portion. No nails or bolts were used in the structure; consequently the planks moved up and down like the keys of a piano as we passed over it.

Following the road through the western suburb, I entered one of the shops to purchase some Chinese umbrellas, as mine were the worse for wear, and was served by a person dressed in ordinary female costume, who seemed to be very masculine in appearance, and considerably above 4 feet 10 inches in height—a height few Zimmé Shan women attain to. On telling Dr M'Gilvary, he informed me that the individual was an hermaphrodite; that this peculiar form of Nature's freaks was by no means uncommon in the country; and that all such people were obliged to dress in female costume.

It is a pretty sight in the early morning to watch the women and girls from the neighbouring villages streaming over the bridge on their way to the market, passing along in single file, with their baskets dangling from each end of a shoulder-bamboo, or accurately poised on their heads. The younger women move like youthful Dianas, with a quick, firm, and elastic tread, and in symmetry of form resemble the ideal models of Grecian art.

The ordinary costume of these graceful maidens consists of flowers in their hair, which shines like a raven's wing, and is combed back and arranged in a neat and beautiful knot; a petticoat or skirt, frequently embroidered near the bottom with silk, worsted, cotton, or gold and silver thread; and at times a pretty silk or gauze scarf cast carelessly over their bosom and one shoulder. Of late years, moreover, the missionaries have persuaded their female converts and the girls in their schools to wear a neat white jacket, and the custom is gradually spreading through the city and into the neighbouring villages.

The elder women wear a dark-blue cotton scarf, which is sometimes replaced by a white cotton spencer, similar to that worn by married ladies in Burmah, and have an extra width added to the top of the skirt, which can be raised and tucked in at the level of the armpit.

On gala occasions it is the fashion to twine gold chains round the knot of their hair, and likewise adorn it with a handsome gold pin. The Shans are famous for their gold and silver chased work; and beautifully designed gold and silver ornaments, bracelets, necklaces, and jewel-headed cylinders in thëir ear-laps, are occasionally worn by the wealthier classes.

After passing through the gates of the outer city we entered the market, which extends for more than half a mile to the gates of the inner city, and beyond them for some distance towards the palace. On either side of the main road little covered booths or stalls are set up; but most of the women spread a mat on the ground to sit upon, and placing their baskets by their side, expose their provisions upon wicker-work trays or freshly cut plantain-leaves.

The variety of vegetables exposed for sale is not very great, and consists chiefly of sweet-potatoes, yams, onions, mushrooms, cucumbers, pumpkins, gourds, sword-beans, onions, garlic, Indian corn, young bamboo-shoots, chillies, and seri-leaf for chewing with tobacco, areca-nut, and lime.

Some of the market-women bring ducks and fowls, others tobacco, areca-nuts, native confectionery, jaggery, rice, wax, and flowers; besides oranges, citrons, pummeloes, mangoes, tamarinds, plantains, cocoa-nuts, and melons, and any other fruit that may be in season.

In the meat-market—which is served only by men—pork, fish, and frogs, and sometimes venison, are sold, and occasionally beef can be had. Cattle may not be killed without an order from the Court, and whoever kills a beast must expose its head and feet to ensure that it has not been stolen. Before this rule was made, cattle-theft is said to have been frequent. The market generally lasts about three hours, but some of the unsuccessful linger a little longer in the hope of selling their wares.

In the shops adjoining the market, some of which are kept by Chinamen and Burmese, the occupiers are general dealers. In them are kept for sale umbrellas and fans, lacquered brass, and crockery-ware, native embroideries, English cotton piece-goods, broadcloths, velvets, velveteens, satins, silks, muslins, Chinese silks and crapes, silk jackets and trousers, silk jackets lined with fur, German aniline dyes and needles, Swedish and English matches, tinned salmon, sardines, milk, butter, jam, swords, knives, nails, gongs, hoes, large shallow iron pans, iron tripods for setting over the fire, brimstone, bluestone, arsenic, native and patent medicines, pestles and mortars for elderly toothless people to crush their betel-nut in, vegetable-wax tapers for burning in the temples, Chinese perfumery, and pictorial paper scrolls; kerosene oil and lamps, glass basins, decanters and mantelpiece vases, and a selection of earthenware jars, pots and pans; in fact, all that a native purchaser has learned to desire.

Passing from the outer into the inner town, we continued along the main road until we came to the enclosure wall of the palace grounds. The gate of the palace lies 1140 yards from the entrance of the inner town, and leads into an extensive court containing several buildings. The palace faces the gate, and is a substantial one-storeyed building, slightly Chinese in aspect, with brick walls, plastered over with an excellent cement, and a tiled roof.

Ascending a flight of steps, paved with black tiles, we entered the audience-hall, which occupied the whole front of the building. The floor of the hall is inlaid with various woods, several chandeliers hung from the ceiling, and the walls were papered like an English drawing-room, and adorned with long, narrow, gilt-framed mirrors. The remainder of the furniture consisted of a lounge, an easy-chair, a dozen drawing-room chairs, upholstered in green rep, and a small tea-table. Through the doors leading into the private apartments some elegantly designed carved lattice-work partitions were seen, which served as screens to the interior of the palace.

A few minutes after we were seated, the king, dressed in a green silk *loongyee* or skirt, and a white cotton jacket with gold buttons, entered the hall, and after shaking hands, welcomed us in a quiet and dignified manner. Tea was then brought in, and we seated ourselves round the table. After a few preliminary remarks, Dr M'Gilvary told him the object of my visit, and the great boon to his country that the construction of a railway to connect it with Burmah and China would be. He was rather thick-skulled, and had never been remarkable for intelligence. He could not understand how trains could move faster than ponies, or how they could move at all without being drawn by some animal. Anyhow, they could not ascend the hills, for they would slide down unless they were pulled up.

I explained to him that I had made three railways in England, and therefore he might rely upon what I said. Railways were made in various parts of the world over much more difficult hills than those lying between Zimmé and Maulmain; that even along the route I had taken it would not be very expensive to carry a railway, and that it would be still easier to carry one from Maulmain to Raheng. As to the possibility of trains being moved without being drawn by animals, he could ask any of his people who had been to Rangoon; all of them would tell him that locomotives, although on wheels, dragged the train along.

He seemed quite stupefied by the revelation. It might be so—it must be so, as I had seen it—but he could not understand how it could be. He was very old; he could not live much longer; he hoped we would be quick in setting about and constructing the line, as otherwise he would not have the pleasure of seeing it.

I then asked him to aid me in collecting information, and in choosing the best route through his territories by having me provided with the best guides, and by issuing instructions to the governors of the provinces to assist me by every means in their power. This he promised to do; and after a little general conversation, we shook hands with him, thanked him for his kindness, and departed.

We next visited Chow Oo-boon-la-wa-na, the only sister of the queen, and the daughter of the late king of Zimmé. On entering her grounds we noticed several prisoners in chains sawing timber. An iron collar was riveted round their necks, and from this a string supported their leg-irons and enabled them to work more easily.

There being no Government allowance for their food, the prisoners are dependent upon the charity of the market-women and their own relations for their victuals. The term of their imprisonment depends greatly upon the ability of their relations or friends to pay the fines which are imposed for all crimes but murder. The prisoners, when not at work, are allowed to roam about the city in their chains, and their relations are held responsible if they should escape.

Ascending the steps of the house we entered a broad verandah, where several of the princess's women were engaged on fancy needlework, and in weaving. Some were embroidering triangular - shaped velvet ends for Shan pillows; others were embroidering silken skirts, and showing great skill and taste in the designs and workmanship. The audience-hall was raised about 15 inches above the verandah, and at its back was a large stand of arms containing old Tower muskets marked with G. R., swords, cross-bows, and lances, many of the last being imitations made out of wood and painted red. The muskets are sold in Bangkok for 7 or 8 rupees each, and fetch from 10 to 12 rupees in Zimmé. It must be about equally dangerous to fire with such a weapon as to be fired at.

After being introduced to the princess and her little daughter by Dr M'Gilvary, and admiring the embroidery which was worked in coloured silks and gold and silver threads, I broached the subject of my visit by telling her about the proposed railway, and saying that the missionaries had told me that she was the best person to apply to about the trade of the country, and that I should be deeply obliged if she would give me what information she could upon the subject.

In reply she said that she was delighted to hear about the railway. She was one of the largest traders in the country, and would do what she could to further the project. A railway, she knew, would bring wealth to the country, and carry the produce cheaply away. Every one, nobles and people, would be glad if a railway was made to connect their country with Burmah and China.

She went on to say that she had long taken an interest in the currents of trade that passed through Zimmé; and, in her own interests, had endeavoured to arrive at the number of men and animals employed in the caravan trade.

No accurate statistics had been made, but she would gladly give me the outcome of her inquiries.

Then, after a little consideration, she told me that from 700 to 1000 laden mules and ponies came yearly from Yunnan, and from 7000 to 8000 from Kiang Tung, Kiang Hung, and other places in the British Shan States; 1000 elephants are employed in carrying goods to and from Kiang Hsen, chiefly for transhipment to Luang Prabang and elsewhere; 5000 porters travel into Lower Burmah, and 4000 to the neighbouring States, and to the British Shan States lying to the north; 3000 laden oxen ply between Zimmé and Lakon, and from 500 to 600 to Lower Burmah. The movement of unladen animals for sale, she said, was as follows: Between 5000 and 6000 buffaloes were brought yearly to Zimmé from Luang Prabang, and numerous oxen from Lapoon and Lakon; and from 200 to 300 elephants were yearly taken into Burmah. The porters travelled throughout the year, and the Chinese caravans proceeded as far south as Ootaradit, a Siamese town at the head of the navigation of the Meh Nam.

According to her, elephants were very numerous in the country; there were fully 8000 both in Zimmé and Lakon, even more in Nan, and about half that number in Peh. A considerable boat traffic existed on the river, particularly in the rainy season. One thousand boats plied between Zimmé and Raheng, many of them proceeding to Bangkok.

When taking leave, the princess promised to aid me in getting elephants for continuing my journey, and said she hoped we would give her the pleasure of our company at dinner before we left. We then returned to our house, as it was about breakfast-time, and Mrs M'Gilvary would be expecting us.

CHAPTER X.

CHOW OO-BOON, A SPIRIT-MEDIUM—CONSULTING ANCESTRAL SPIRITS—AN EXORCIST—SPIRIT OF WITCHCRAFT—ILL-TREATING A PATIENT—TREATMENT OF WITCHES—FALSE CHARGES—MISSIONARY DESTROYS AN IMAGE—EXECUTION OF CHRISTIANS—PROCLAMATION IN FAVOUR OF CHRISTIANS—MISSIONARIES PROTECT WITCHES—UNDERMINE SUPERSTITION—GHOSTS PERCHING ON TREES—A MISSIONARY GHOST—HEADLESS DEMONS—A DEMONIAC.

AFTER breakfast I went next door to have another chat with Mr Wilson. He told me that Chow Oo-boon had great power with the members of the Government, who were all connected with the royal family; because, besides being the queen's sister, she was the spirit-medium of the family. As an instance of her power, he stated that when called in to consult the spirits after the late *Chow Hona*, or second-king, was struck down with sickness, she boldly told him that the spirits were displeased at his oppression of the people, and advised him at once to abolish certain vexatious taxes, particularly the monopoly of arrack, or rice-spirit.

The method practised when consulting the beneficent spirits—who, like mortals, are fond of retaliating when provoked—is as follows: When the physician's skill has been found incapable of mastering a disease, a spirit-medium—a woman who claims to be in communion with the spirits—is called in. After arraying herself fantastically, the medium sits on a mat that has been spread for her in the front verandah, and is attended to with respect, and plied with arrack by the people of the house, and generally accompanied in her performance by a band of village musicians with modulated music.

Between her tipplings she chants an improvised doggerel, which includes frequent incantations, till at length, in the excitement of her potations, and worked on by her song, her body begins to sway about, and she becomes frantic, and seemingly inspired. The spirits are then believed to have taken possession of her body, and all her utterances from that time are regarded as those of the spirits.

On showing signs of being willing to answer questions, the relations or friends of the sick person beseech the spirits to tell them what medicines and food should be given to the invalid to restore him or her to health; what they have been offended at; and how their just wrath may be appeased. Her knowledge of the family affairs and misdemeanours generally enables her to give shrewd and brief answers to the latter questions. She states that the *Pee*—in this case the ancestral, or, perhaps, village spirits—are offended by such an action or actions, and that to propitiate them such-and-such offerings should be made. In case the spirits have not been offended, her answers are merely a prescription; after which, if only a neighbour, she is dismissed with a fee of two or three rupees, and, being more or less intoxicated, is helped home.

In case the spirit-medium's prescription proves ineffective and the person gets worse, witchcraft is sometimes suspected, and an exorcist is called in. The charge of witchcraft means ruin to the person accused, and to his or her family. It arises as follows: The ghost or spirit of witchcraft is called Pee-Kah. No one professes to have seen it, but it is said to have the form of a horse, from the sound of its passage through the forest resembling the clatter of a horse's hoofs when at full gallop. These spirits are said to be reinforced by the deaths of very poor people, whose spirits were so disgusted with those who refused them food or shelter that they determined to return and place themselves at the disposal of their descendants to haunt their stingy and hard-hearted neighbours. Should any one rave in delirium, a Pee-Kah is supposed to have passed by.

Every class of spirits—even the ancestral spirits, and those that guard the streets and villages—are afraid of the Pee-

Kah. At its approach the household spirits take instant flight; nor will they return until it has worked its will and retired, or been exorcised. Yet the Pee-Kah, as I have shown, is itself an ancestral spirit, and follows as their shadow the son and daughter, as it followed their parents through their lives. It is not ubiquitous, but at one time may attend the parent and at another the child, when both are living. Its food is the entrails of its living victim, and its feast continues until its appetite is satisfied, or the feast is cut short by the incantations of the spirit-doctor or exorcist. Very often the result is the death of its victim.

When the exorcist, spirit-doctor, or witch-finder is called in and asked whether he considers the patient is suffering from a Pee-Kah, he puts on a knowing look, and after a cursory examination of the person, generally declares it to be so. His task is then to find out whose Pee-Kah is devouring the sick person. After calling the officer of the village and a few head-men as witnesses, he commences questioning the invalid. He first asks, "Whose spirit has bewitched you?" The person may be in a stupor, half unconscious, half delirious from the severity of the disease, and therefore does not reply. A pinch or a stroke of a cane may restore consciousness. If so, the question is repeated; if not, another pinch or stroke is administered. A cry of pain may be the result. That is one step towards the disclosure; for it is a curious fact that, after the case has been pronounced one of witchcraft, each reply to the question, pinch, or stroke is considered as being uttered by the Pee-Kah through the mouth of the bewitched person.

A person pinched or caned into consciousness cannot long endure the torture, especially if reduced by a long illness. Those who have not the wish nor the heart to injure any one often refuse to name the wizard or witch until they have been unmercifully beaten.

On the sick person naming an individual as the owner of the spirit, other questions are asked—such as, "How many buffaloes has he?" "How many pigs?" "How many chickens?" "How much money?" &c. The answers to the questions are taken down by a scribe. A time is then appointed to meet at the house of the accused, and the same questions as to his possessions are put to him. If his answers agree with those of the sick person, he is condemned and held responsible for the acts of his ghost.

The case is then laid before the judge of the court, the verdict is confirmed, and a sentence of banishment is passed on the person and his or her family. The condemned person is barely given time to sell or remove his property. His house is wrecked or burnt, and the trees in the garden cut down, unless it happens to be sufficiently valuable for a purchaser to employ an exorcist, who for a small fee will render the house safe for the buyer; but it never fetches half its cost, and must be removed from the haunted ground. If the condemned person lingers beyond the time that has been granted to him, his house is set on fire, and, if he still delays, he is whipped out of the place with a cane. If he still refuses to go, or returns, he is put to death.

The late King of Zimmé, on hearing from the villagers of the Karen village of Ban Hta, that their head-man was bewitching them and would not leave the village, allowed the people to club him to death. About three years before my visit another case came to the knowledge of the missionaries, where two Karens were brought to the city by some of their neighbours, charged with causing the death of a young man by witchcraft. The case was a clear one against the accused. The young man had been possessed of a musical instrument, and had refused to sell it to the accused, who wished to purchase it. Shortly afterwards he became ill, and died in fourteen days. At his cremation, a portion of his body would not burn, and was of a shape similar to the musical instrument. It was clear that the wizards had put the form of the coveted musical instrument into his body to kill him. The Karens were beheaded, notwithstanding that they protested their innocence, and threatened that their spirits should return and wreak vengeance for their unjust punishment. Witches and wizards in the Shan States are free agents and have made no compact with the devil. The old Burman custom for the trial of witches was similar to that practised in former times in England: the thumbs and toes being tied together, the suspected person was thrown into the water, and sinking was a proof of innocence, floating of guilt.

In Mr Wilson's opinion, the charge of witchcraft often arises from envy, or from spite; and sickness for the purposes of revenge is sometimes simulated. A neighbour wants a house or garden, and the owner either requires more than he wishes to pay, or refuses to sell it at all. Covetousness consumes his heart, and the witch-ghost is brought into action. Then the covetous person, or his child, or a neighbour, falls ill, or feigns illness; the ailment baffles the skill of the physician, and the witch-finder is called in. Then all is smooth sailing and little is left to chance.

In the early days of the Mission at Zimmé, Christians were very unfavourably looked on by the officials. This may partly have arisen from what I consider to have been, under the circumstances, an injudicious act of a missionary. An old temple-ground was handed over to the missionaries as a compound for their houses and schools. The temple was in ruins, but a sandstone image of Buddha, five feet in height, was intact, and was much reverenced by the people, who placed offerings of fruit and flowers before it. The missionaries used the ruins of the temple for levelling the ground, and buried the image under the *débris*. One day during some alterations it was dug up, and the people swarmed into the compound to pay their respects to it, although it had lost its head. The missionary then took an axe and knocked it to pieces before the people, who were naturally horrified and offended at the, to them, sacrilegious deed. The people were still more disgusted by seeing the pedestal upon which the image had been seated turned into a garden seat, and the fragments of the image made into a rockery.

Another cause of friction arose in 1869 from two new converts neglecting to aid in repairing the palisading round the outer city when instructed to do so by the officials. The missionaries believed that the affair arose merely from a misunderstanding. Anyhow, the two converts were seized, and fastened with ropes passed through the holes in their ear-laps to the upper beams of a house, and next day clubbed to death. The missionaries complained to the King of Siam, and a Siamese official was sent up to inquire into the case. The King of Zimmé, being bound to Siam only so far as tribute and his foreign relations were concerned, answered the commissioner by stating that it was his affair and not Siam's, and that he intended to kill as many of his own people as he chose. It was not till nine years afterwards, in the present king's reign, five years after the appointment of the Siamese commissioner at Zimmé, that a proclamation, issued by the Siamese Government, declaring that any of the Siamese Shans might change their religion with impunity, was allowed to be placarded up in the Court of Zimmé. At the time of my visit, the missionaries had made nearly two hundred converts and were much respected by the princes and the people.

Besides converting the people and opening schools for their education, the missionaries have been doing their utmost to conquer the belief of the people in witchcraft; and I was glad to hear that it had become a custom with several of the princes of Zimmé and the neighbouring States, as well as other intelligent people, to call in the aid of the physician attached to the Mission in cases of serious illness in their families. Another blow has been given to superstition by the missionaries sheltering those who lie under the accusation of witchcraft. At the time of my visit sixteen accused families were residing in the Mission grounds, some of whom had been converted to Christianity; and most of the children were attending the schools.

The people account for no harm having happened to the missionaries through their harbouring witches by saying that the Pee-Kah are afraid of Europeans, and clamber up the tamarind-trees near the gate of the Mission when the witches go in, and wait until they leave the yard to enter them again.

One of the trees outside the compound was much dreaded by people who had to pass near it. The cries of the spirits were often heard from its branches at night. At times the spirits descended to the ground and confronted passers-by. One of them resembled a child about a year old; then, in a second, its form would expand and grow until it was taller than the tree, when it would vanish after forcing a scream of horror from the affrighted beholder. This ghost for some reason assumed the appearance of a missionary.

One day Mr Wilson saw a fire built close to the tree, and two men squatting near it. On approaching them he noticed that one was holding two small chickens over the flames, whose feathers were already half consumed. The other had a bundle of bamboo splints, which he was sticking into the ground to support a platform, upon which the fowls, when roasted, were to be offered to the spirits. This was too much for the embodied missionary, who, much to their dismay, insisted upon their taking their offerings out of his compound.

A Shan ghost.

When visiting Dr Peoples, the physician attached to the Mission, he told me of a strange case of hysteria which arose from the belief of the Shans in evil spirits. There was a man living in the northern quarter of the city who possessed a garden of areca palms and plantains. In the garden was a well, the abode of a Pee-Hong, or headless spirit: all deceased murderers, adulterers, and other people who have been executed become Pee-Hong. In its way to and from this well the Pee-Hong passed through a grove of trees, which the owner, against the wishes of his neighbours, who feared the wrath of the demon, determined to cut down. A short time after the trees had been destroyed he became very uneasy and unwell; and whenever thinking or talking on the subject, figures appeared on his limbs and body, in the form of regular welts, shaped like leaves and trunks and whole trees—sometimes resembling plantain-trees, at others areca palms. Having tried every form of exorcism, he applied to Dr Peoples for help through his medical assistant, but refused to display the spirit manifestations before him, saying that they would not appear before Christians. The doctor prescribed for the man, and went to visit him the next day at his house, but he had left his family and started for a famous shrine. Many months had passed since then, but nothing further had been heard of the demoniac.

The belief in the transmigration of the soul into the bodies of animals is apt to give rise to a peculiar form of hallucination. In one of the Siamese books a tale is told of a wife plotting the death of her affectionate husband with her paramour, and, on the success of the plot, marrying the latter. Soon afterwards the woman noticed a snake in the house, which she thought must be her late husband, as she imagined it looked lovingly upon her. After killing the snake she had a cow which she killed for the same reason. Then she had a dog which followed her everywhere with affectionate watchfulness, and she, thinking her husband's soul must be in it, killed it. After the dog's death a child was born, who, because it looked at her with loving eyes, she thought must be her husband. Not daring to cut short its life, and unable to bear the sight of it, she gave it out to be nursed. When the child grew up, it is said to have remembered the various migrations of its soul from the time that it was the husband of its own mother, and to have told the story to its grandmother.

CHAPTER XI.

VISIT THE SIAMESE COMMISSIONER—DESCRIPTION AND DRESS OF SIAMESE — DECEITFUL OFFICIALS—PRINCE PRISDANG'S LETTER — PIE-CRUST PROMISES—A MOUNTEBANK—CALL ON THE PRINCESS—TREATY OF 1874—SIAM'S RELATION TO SHAN STATES—FORMER OBSTACLES TO TRADE REMOVED—VISIT FROM CHOW OO-BOON — ASSASSINATING A LOVER — SHAN QUEEN IN ENGLISH DRESS — FAST AND EASY-GOING ELEPHANTS PRIZED — KIAN YUEN, AN OLD CAPITAL—A CHINESE PAGODA — CITY OF THE FLOWER-GARDEN — MUANG LA MAING, THE SITE OF THE FIRST ZIMMÉ SHAN CITY—ASCENT OF LOI SOO TAYP—THE PAGODA OF THE EMERALD RICE-BOWL — PAGODA SLAVES — DR M'GILVARY JOINS MY PARTY — VISITING BURMESE FORESTERS — RELIGIOUS BUILDINGS ERECTED BY THE BURMESE.

In the afternoon Dr M'Gilvary went with me to call on the Siamese commissioner, who resides in a large, two-storeyed, whitewashed brick house, near the west bank of the river. We were shown into an airy upper room, which serves as an audience-chamber, and is furnished with a large round table surrounded by a number of chairs. On our entry we were welcomed by Chow Don, the junior Siamese assistant-commissioner, a bright, gentlemanly-looking young man about twenty-four years of age. A few minutes later the Siamese commissioner, an iron-grey-haired, well-built man above the average height of Siamese, and very plausible and courteous in behaviour, came in, and after shaking hands, offered us cigars and tea.

Amongst the Siamese the dress of the two sexes is exactly alike, but the women are shorter and more brazen-faced than the men, and wear a love-lock above each ear. Both have their hair cut short at the back and sides of the head, and wear it either swept back from the forehead or parted in the middle. It is very thick, coarse, and intensely black.

Their dress consists of a *panung* or waist-cloth, and a jacket. The *panung* is a plaid-shaped cloth about 7 feet long and 2½ feet broad, and made of cotton or of silk. It is passed round the body, held together tight in front, where a twist in the top is made, and tucked in. The two trailing ends are then picked up, passed under the legs, and tucked in at the small of the back. The upper classes wear stockings, often of gay colours, and elastic-sided boots or shoes, and girdle themselves with a cricketing belt, or with one fastened by a buckle set with precious stones.

The average height of the Siamese men is 5 feet 3 inches, or 3 or 4 inches less than that of the Zimmé Shans. The women seldom exceed 4 feet 9 inches in height. They seemed to me to be a cross between the Khas and the Shans, made more repulsive by a dash of the Malay and Chinese. They have broad, flat, lozenge-shaped faces; high cheek-bones; small bridgeless noses; low foreheads; small, black, pig-eyes; wide mouths; thick, non-protruding lips; a yellowish-brown complexion; and, generally, a sullen expression.

I had been warned before leaving Burmah that Siamese officials are deceitful above all things, and that I must not rely upon a single atom of information I got from them. From personal intercourse, I found that the gentleman who warned me was strictly correct in his judgment. In answer to your questions, they tell you the most plausible lie that trips to their tongue, and if you chance to test their accuracy by reverting to the subject in the same or a future conversation, contradict themselves most flatly. If you trouble yourself to point out the inconsistency of their statements, they are ashamed — but only of not having played their game better.

After a little preliminary conversation, I told the commissioner that Prince Prisdang, the Siamese ambassador in London, had promised about seven months before to write to the King of Siam about my mission, and had written to Mr Colquhoun as follows: "I have no hesitation in informing you that any well-digested scheme which has for its object the improvement of the commercial position of Siam, and the consolidation of the kingdom, will receive the attentive consideration of his Majesty and my Government; and that his Majesty will allow all facilities to be given for any purposes of exploration, or of gaining accurate knowledge, by properly qualified persons, of the nature of the country proposed to be traversed by the railway."

He told me that he had received no instructions whatever on the subject from the king, but no doubt he would receive them in a few days; in the meantime he would gladly do all he could to aid me in my project.

I then asked him to aid me in gathering information about the trade and population of the country, and to give me a letter to the various princes in the district, asking them to aid me to the utmost in their power. This he promised to do, and the conversation became general. When I received the letter, it proved to be so milk-and-watery that it was worse than worthless, and Dr M'Gilvary advised me to keep it as a curiosity, and not to show it. All his other promises were merely pie-crust—made to be broken.

Just as we were preparing to go, Phra Udon, the senior assistant-commissioner, came bounding in like a clown at a circus, greeting us all boisterously with "How do you all do? So glad you've come. All well, I hope?" Then he hurried round from one to the other, and shook hands in an affectionately jovial manner. I had heard about this individual before I came, and was therefore more amused than surprised at his manner. There was no ceremony about him. We were jolly companions every one, and he would be delighted to be the tomfool of the party. It is surprising how such a mountebank could have got even into the Siamese service. From subsequent inquiry, I learnt that he was a native of Ceylon, who, with other monks, had come over to Siam many years ago at the invitation of the king, and who, managing to curry favour at Court, threw off the yellow robe and entered the Government service.

Conversation now passed into a shower of questions from Phra Udon, amid which our answers could barely be squeezed edgewise; this moment Siamese, the next English, and every now and then the two combined. After a time, I grew weary of the assumed joviality, and was glad to say good-bye and retreat from the scene.

Our next call was upon Chow Boo-re Rak, the Chow Hoo-a Muang Kyow, or head of the Gem City—a man of fine stature, with a keen eye and intelligent mind. We did not detain him long, because he was hearing cases in his house, but went to see the king's eldest son by a former marriage, who holds the post of Chow Racha Boot; and afterwards Chow Oo-ta-ra-kan, who, if primogeniture ruled the accession to the throne in the Shan States, would have been King of Zimmé. To prevent disturbances the King of Siam kept Noi Maha Prome, his father and the eldest son of a former king, at Bangkok, until the day of his death.

Having finished our calls we strolled homewards, chatting about the various people we had seen.

The Siamese judge, or commissioner, was appointed under the Anglo-Siamese treaty of 1874, whereby we recognised the control of Siam over the Shan States of Chiengmai, Lakon, and Lampoonchi (Zimmé, Lakon, and Lapoon). This treaty arranged for the policing of the frontier, the extradition of dacoits, and the appointment of Siamese judges at Zimmé. The judges were to decide between British subjects having passports and Siamese subjects; but a proviso was made that in case the British subject did not consent to the jurisdiction of the court, his or her case should be tried by the British consul at Bangkok, or the British officer in the Yoonzaleen district of Lower Burmah.

Previous to this treaty the Siamese authority in the Shan States was confined to the regulation of their foreign affairs and sanctioning the appointments of their elected chiefs, Siam protecting the Shan States of Chiengmai, or Zimmé; Lamphang Lakhon, or Lakon; Lampoonchi, or Lapoon; Muang Nan, or Nan; Muang Phrë, or Peh, or Prai, or Phray (these four States were comprised in the ancient kingdom of Zimmé, and Lakon and Lapoon still look up to Zimmé as their parent State, and in a vague manner are controlled by it); and Luang Prabang, or Hluang Prabang.

In return for Siam's protection against foreign invaders, these six States agreed to send triennial tribute to Siam in the form of gold and silver boxes, vases, and jewelled necklaces, together with curious gold and silver trees valued at from £15 to £35 each.

Trade between British Burmah and Siam and its Shan States may be said to date from the Anglo-Siamese treaty of 1855-56. Up to that time Europeans, descendants of Europeans, Burmese, and Peguans from British Burmah, were not allowed to enter the Siamese dominions for purposes of trade, although our native of India subjects were permitted to do so. Siam's policy was simply that of perfect seclusion from her neighbours.

Next day Chow Oo-boon, accompanied by her eldest son Chow Sook Ka Same and her niece, the only child of the queen, returned our call, and were followed by a long train of attendants bearing silver-handled umbrellas, and gold betel-boxes, water-jars, and cigarette-platters. The son looked thirteen years of age, and the niece about two years younger. The missionaries said the children when grown up would make an excellent match, but they were doubtful whether the queen would consent to the union, as the father of the boy was not of royal blood. They were both very well behaved, and were evidently fond of Dr and Mrs M'Gilvary. Chow Oo-boon had been the steady friend of the missionaries at Zimmé ever since the Mission had been founded.

This princess was no ordinary person, and her life was a romance. Highly intelligent, and a capital woman of business, a great trader, and the owner of large tracts of land, extensive teak-forests, and numerous elephants, serfs, and slaves, love was yet to her "the summer's sun, nature gay adorning." She was very amorously inclined, and during many years had given the queen great anxiety and trouble in controlling her headstrong fancies. Her first husband was the eldest son of the eldest son of a former King of Zimmé, and would have been on the throne had the rule of succession been the same as in Europe. Their only child, a daughter, is married to Chow Sing Kam, the eldest son of Chow Racha Boot, and therefore the grandson of the present king.

Since her first widowhood the princess had made several *mésalliances* with people not of the royal family, much to the annoyance of the queen, who not only refused to acknowledge the marriages, but removed the objects of her affection beyond her reach. At length Chow Oo-boon sought to foil her sister by selecting a wealthy Burmese timber-trader, over whom she thought the queen dare not exercise authority, as he was a British subject. Here she was mistaken. The queen had him apprehended and escorted to the frontier, where he was told that it would be well for him to keep away from Zimmé for the future. Not to be balked, as soon as this Burmese was over the border, she selected another, and began philandering with him.

The queen was now quite out of patience, so one dark night, when the Burman was on his way to the princess's residence, he was waylaid and clubbed to death. Greatly enraged at this assassination, Chow Oo-boon is said to have done her utmost to have the matter brought to trial by the British authorities, who, however, considered it politic to pass it over. Years had passed since then, the sisters were reconciled, and Chow Oo-boon gave no more cause for anxiety, but expended her love and care upon the education of her children.

After chatting for a little while, the princess invited us to dinner on the following Saturday, March 1st, and said that, as we should be detained waiting for elephants for two, or perhaps three days, she had arranged for two of hers to be at our house the next morning to take us to the pagoda on Loi Soo Tayp; it would be a pleasant excursion for us, and I could get a fine view of the country from the enclosure.

Whilst we were talking, two of her ladies-in-waiting were crouched at her feet ready to hand her cigarettes or her betel-box, whilst others were seated on the staircase near the edge of the verandah, and a few were following the children, who with young M'Gilvary were racing about the house and enjoying themselves. Before the princess left, I brought out some Maltese jewellery, and said I should be much pleased if she would accept it as a present. She admired the filigree-work, and was evidently much gratified, and asked me if I had a sister or a wife, as she would like to have embroidered shirts made for them if I thought they would be pleased with them. I said that my sister would be delighted to accept one, as she was very fond of beautiful things; and Shan embroideries, particularly the specimens seen at her house, were certainly exquisite in their design and workmanship.

When our visitors had gone, Mrs M'Gilvary told me that the queen as well as the princess frequently visited her, and that her daughter, Mrs Cheek, at their request had made them full suits of European dress, and that they looked very well in them. I should think, however, that their handsome native costumes suit them much better, and it would be a pity to hide their feet in shoes or boots, for, like their hands, they are delicately formed—small and narrow, and decidedly pretty.

Next morning two male elephants with silver trappings, and roofed howdahs with beautifully carved frames, were led up to the verandah for us to mount. Mine was a very large one, measuring fully ten feet from the top of the shoulder to the ground, but rather awkward in its gait, which made it unpleasant to ride; Dr Cushing's was slightly smaller, and more agreeable for riding. Ease in gait is one of the great considerations when hiring or purchasing an elephant to ride, for there is as much difference in their gait as there is in that of horses. One with pleasant paces and a swift walk always fetches a high price, and should walk fully four miles an hour, or double the pace of an ordinary elephant. Females are very often easier for riding than the males, but it is considered derogatory for a noble to be seen on one.

Having comfortably settled ourselves in our howdahs, with a tin of gingerbread nuts, a Chinese cosey-covered teapot, and an enamelled iron cup and saucer on each of our seats, and our lunch packed away under them, we started, and after crossing the river above the bridge, followed the road which skirts the northern moat of the city. In half an hour we passed the White Elephant Gate, the chief entrance to the city; and after traversing rice-fields for about an hour, we reached the foot of the hill, and commenced to ascend the spur by a path which runs between the aqueduct that supplies Zimmé with water, and Huay Kao, the parent stream. The foot of the hill lies four miles from the east end of the bridge.

To the north of the city, immediately bordering the road we had traversed, lay the remains of the ancient city of Kiang Yuen, which has perhaps given rise to the Zimmé Shans being known as Yuen Shans by the Burmese. I had no time to inspect the ruins, but noticed several large temples and pagodas. One of the latter, known as the Chinese pagoda, is peculiar in shape, being formed of five flattened balls of brick masonry, each diminishing at the top, and placed one above the other. It has no umbrella, or *htee*, at the top, and is said to have been erected by a Chinese general named Utau, when besieging the city some centuries ago.

Some distance beyond the city the road crosses the ramparts and moats of a large fort, which had been erected by the Burmese when they last besieged the city in 1776. This fort is now known as Muang Soon Dok, the town of the flower-garden. To the south of the fort, and between the city and Loi Soo Tayp, are the ruins of Muang La Maing, the ancient capital of the Lawas, of which nothing but the ramparts and ditches remain. It is upon the site of this city that Kun Ngu, the third son of Kun Lung, the chief of Muang Mau, is said to have built his capital. Kun Lung, according to the story of Muang Mau, which was translated by Mr Ney Elias, descended from heaven by a golden ladder into the Shweli valley, near Bhamo, in A.D. 568.

The ascent of the hill as far as the waterfall, which lies about a mile and a half from the foot of the hill, was easy, and from thence onwards the slope became rather steep. The aqueduct takes its water from the Huay Kao just above where the stream plunges over a ledge forming the crest of the fall, and a shelter for many small images that have been placed under it by pious pilgrims. A small temple containing a solitary image of Gaudama has been erected near the head of the fall.

Continuing the ascent along the bank of the torrent, which rushed, glistening and foaming, down its channel of bare granite rock, at eleven o'clock we reached the rest-houses at the foot of the knoll on whose crest the Mya Sapeet *chedi*, or pagoda of the Emerald Rice-bowl, is erected. The journey from the east end of the bridge had taken us four and a half hours, the distance being a little over eight miles.

Weary with the incessant rolling and jolting we had suffered from our long-legged, cumbersome beasts, we felt relieved from suffering as we stepped off the elephant's head on to the verandah railing of one of the rest-houses, and threw ourselves down on the floor for a stretch whilst our breakfast was being prepared.

After our meal we ascended a long flight of steps, bordered by fine large pine-trees, to the enclosure containing the religious buildings. The avenue of pines was most likely planted by the Burmese when they built, repaired, or added to the pagoda in 1760. We found an inscription giving this date for the erection of the pagoda on a board in a corner of one of the buildings. The Shan history of Zimmé gives the date of the pagoda as 1790, but this evidently refers only to further additions or repairs.

The enclosure on the summit of the knoll is square, and surrounded by a roofed shed which faces inwards, and has an entrance-gate in the centre of each side. The pagoda is Burmese in design, about 50 feet high, covered with copper plates heavily gilded, and surrounded by a copper-sheathed iron railing. The pedestals at the four corners of the basement of the pagoda are coated with a glass mosaic of various colours, and facing each side of the pagoda is a temple containing an image of Gaudama. The walls and posts of the temples are richly decorated with designs in gold and vermilion. The platform of the enclosure is 1993 feet above the plain, and 3001 feet above mean sea-level. The summit of Loi Soo Tayp appeared to be about 3000 feet higher than the crest of the knoll.

From the entrances facing the plain, on a clear day the view must be magnificent; but at the time of our visit the hills on the other side of the plain were shrouded in haze, and we could only see the country for two or three miles beyond the town. The city and villages were hidden by the foliage, and the whole plain as far as we could see looked one great orchard of palm and fruit trees, with here and there a narrow slip of rice-plain. Nothing can be more deceptive than travelling through such a country, the great hedges of fruit-trees and clumps of handsome bamboos that fringe the fields continually hiding the extent of the cultivation. In the fringes surrounding the fields, and in the beautiful groves that are scattered about, lie the houses of the villagers, making it simply impossible without a census to arrive, or even make a near guess, at the population.

Seeing one of the *Ka-wat*, or pagoda slaves, sweeping up some fallen leaves, Dr Cushing asked him to relate the legend of the pagoda, and the origin of its name. In reply, he told us that, long, long ago, a company of *Pee*, or spirits, brought five of the bowls which are used for begging by the monks, and offered them at the shrine. These were each of different colours—red, yellow, white, blue, and green—cut out of precious gems, and fitted one within the other; the green, or emerald bowl, containing the rest. The pagoda is therefore named "The Pagoda of the Emerald Rice-bowl." He further assured us that the right name for Loi Soo Tayp was Loi Soo Tee, its name having originated from a white elephant that ascended the mountain, bearing sacred relics, exclaiming as he reached the top, "Soo Tee," or "the place ends."

The pagoda slaves are looked upon as outcasts by the remainder of the people, and are either the descendants of pagoda slaves, or have been dedicated to the service of the pagoda by their master on account of the merit accruing to the deed, or have been so dedicated as a punishment for crimes they have committed. Not even a king dare free a pagoda slave; for if he did so, he would after this life infallibly have to descend to the bottom of the most fearful hell. They are not only pagoda slaves and outcasts, but their posterity must remain so during the dispensation of Gaudama Buddha, embracing a period of 5000 years after his death, which is said to have occurred B.C. 543. Pagoda slaves may not be employed in any other work than keeping the shrine in order, and are obliged to present tithes of all they produce for the use and maintenance of the pagoda and its monks. On our return the journey took only three hours and a half, as the elephants went quickly down the hill, and were in a hurry to get home for their evening's feed.

In the evening I besieged Dr M'Gilvary, endeavouring to persuade him to accompany us to Kiang Hsen. I assured him that the journey should be no expense to his Mission, either for food or for elephants; that he would be of very great use in collecting information from the people; and that it would be delightful both for Dr Cushing and myself to have his company. He said that he was really unable to go with us on that journey, as his year's supply of boots were on their way from Bangkok, and the ones he had would fall to pieces before he returned. I replied that I had two pairs of Walkingphast's boots, which were quite new, and I should be so pleased if he would try them on; that they were spare ones; and that I should certainly not need more than one pair besides those I had in use; that his doing so would be an actual relief to me, as I felt that I was carrying about useless baggage. He was very shy of the offer at first; but I succeeded in talking his wife over, and she managed to persuade him not to disappoint us, and that the trip was exactly what his health required. I shall ever remember this good lady and her husband with pleasure, admiration, and gratitude. They were utterly unselfish in all their thoughts and actions, and quite untiring in heaping kindness upon us.

The following days I strolled about the place, and visited several of the Burmese foresters with Loogalay, who had been having a high time amongst them, but found they knew very little about any part of the country except in the regions where they worked their forests. They all lived in large substantial teak-built houses, and appeared to be well off, if one might judge by the liquors and other refreshments they placed on their table.

I learnt from them the Shan and Burmese names of many of the trees, which afterwards enabled me to record them in

Burmese when only the Shan names were given me. Nothing strikes a traveller in Indo-China more than the extensive knowledge of the flora of the country possessed by the people. Not only can an ordinary villager tell you the names of the various plants and trees that you meet, but also their uses, whether as dyes, drugs, oils, or resins.

On expressing my surprise at there being so many temples and monasteries in the city and neighbourhood, they said that, although many had of late years been repaired by the Shans, nearly all of them had been built by the Burmese when governing the country from A.D. 1564 to 1774.

CHAPTER XII.

DINNER AT THE PRINCESS'S—ARRANGEMENTS FOR START COMPLETED—A PASSPORT—OUR PAVILION—THE ZIMMÉ PLAIN—LEAVE ZIMMÉ—CANAL IRRIGATION — HALT AT MUANG DOO — THE CHOWS ASTRAY—CAMP-DINNERS AND COOKERY—EXCELLENT MADRAS SERVANTS—ALTERATION IN JEWAN — COURTSHIP, MARRIAGE, AND DIVORCE — KUMLUNG, OR FAMILY PATRIARCH AND PRIEST—PRICE OF SLAVES—SLAVE-BONDAGE—FOREIGN MARRIAGES — SERFDOM IN ZIMMÉ—FORMATION OF CLANS — GOVERNMENT MASTERS IN SIAM — CROWN COMMONERS.

CHOW OO-BOON made great preparations for her dinner, which she had served in European style, on a table beautifully decorated with flowers. Mrs M'Gilvary furnished the crockery, cutlery, and table-linen, and our Madras servants superintended the cookery. Among the guests were the daughters of the queen and princess, three princes, and Phra Udon and Chow Don, the two Siamese assistant-commissioners. Fingers, for the nonce, gave way to knives and forks, and even Phra Udon, the Singhalese buffoon, showed that he could behave himself before ladies.

There was no apparent anxiety on the part of the hostess as to whether or not the dinner would turn out a success. All were affable, courteous, and pleasant, and appeared bent upon adding to the general enjoyment.

The princess informed me that arrangements had been made for our starting early on Monday, as, to prevent further delay, she and some of the princes had agreed to supply us with elephants, and a letter had been signed by the Court calling upon the governors of the various provinces to afford us their aid.

A similar passport issued for one of my later journeys

was translated for me by Dr M'Gilvary, and ran as follows: "The Proclamation of Chao Phya San Luang and Chao Phya Saw Lan, and all the officers, old and young, at the Court, to Tow Rat of Chiang Dow (Kiang Dow), and Phya Khenan Phek of Chiang Ngai, and Phya Kuan of Muang Pow, and Phya Soo Ree Ya Yot of Muang Fang, greeting. You are informed that now there has been a Royal Order that Nai Hallett and the teachers M'Gilvary and Martin, the three Nais and their servants and personal attendants, nineteen persons, twenty-two persons in all, with six elephants and one horse and eight guns, may go to Chiang Hsen, Muang Ngai, Muang Pow, and Muang Fang. When the foreign Nais have arrived and wish to go in any direction at any time, you are ordered to levy good and reliable men that are conversant with the roads, the brooks, and the mountains to escort them, according to the custom of the country, from one city and province to another, to whatever place or village the foreign Nais shall wish to go. Again, if the foreign Nais are in need of provisions of any kind, you are ordered to provide supplies and look after them. Let them not be destitute of anything whatever. This is given by the Royal Order on the thirteenth day of the waxing moon of the eighth month of the year twelve hundred and twenty-six" (7th May 1884).

This passport, as is usual, was scratched with a stile upon a narrow strip of palm-leaf which coils up into a ring and has a stamp embossed on it at each end. This stamp determines the real authority of the document, and is examined before reading the document. These strips of leaves are tough and unaffected by water, and are therefore, for the purpose, superior to paper. When the writing grows dim it is easily made legible by wetting the finger and rubbing it over the leaf, thus cleansing the smooth surface and filling the scratches with the dirt so removed.

On Monday, the 3d March, we had everything packed early in the morning, but were delayed until nearly one o'clock before the last elephant came in. We were to be conducted to Kiang Hai by Chow Nan Kyow Wong, the eldest son of Chow Hoo-a Muang Kyow, the fourth of the joint rulers of the Zimmé State. Chow Nan Kyow Wong had left the city the night before, accompanied by his six followers and his young son, in order to prepare the first encampment for us. He took with him four large elephants, one of which was loaded with our baggage, and a small one, and eight elephant-drivers and attendants.

The party with me, besides the Chow and his company, comprised forty-one persons—viz., Dr Cushing, Dr M'Gilvary, two Shan interpreters, three Shan servants, three Madras servants, Moung Loogalay, eight Shan elephant-men, and twenty Shan porters with four large elephants. As a shelter from the night-dews we carried a tent, so capacious and so convenient for carriage that it reminded me of the one in the 'Arabian Nights' which would shelter an army and yet could be put in one's pocket. Ours was formed of a roll of long-cloth, 30 feet long and 15 feet wide, that packed into a roll 21 inches long and 7 inches in diameter.

The great Zimmé rice-plain is divided into more or less extensive fields by orchards containing beautiful clumps of bamboos and mango, tamarind, palmyra, cocoa-nut, areca-nut, and other trees; and in these orchards, and in pretty groves scattered about the plain, nestle numerous villages and detached houses. Until the hills are reached the country is one ceaseless succession of orchards and rice-fields, all of which, nearly up to the east bank of the Meh Ping, are irrigated by canals and channels drawing their water from the Meh Hkuang, the river on which the capital city of the Shan State of Lapoon lies.

Starting from the bridge a little before one o'clock, we proceeded in a north-easterly direction, and halted for the night in the fields of Muang Doo, having passed within view of nineteen villages in the seven and a half miles' march. We were disappointed at finding that the Chow and his son had not passed through the village, and that nothing was known there of his movements. As soon as the elephants were unloaded some of the Shans commenced cutting bamboos for the erection of our pavilion, and before we had finished bathing, it was completed and our dinner was ready.

Our dinner-table consisted of a cane-covered howdah-seat placed on the top of two wooden spirit-cases set on end and some distance apart. A couple more cases, set one on the other, served as my seat, and my companions were enthroned on their folding camp-chairs. The long arms of my chair, although adding greatly to my comfort, and being handy for writing, prevented it from being drawn up to our improvised table.

The rapidity with which a hot dinner was served by our Madras servants would astonish stay-at-home people. Soup being in tins, takes very little time to cook, as it has only to be heated; bacon takes but a minute or two; and vegetables, curry, chickens, tapioca, and rice-puddings having been prepared and more than half cooked at our last halting-place, are quickly served. But even so, the boys deserved great credit for their readiness and good management.

Whilst the cooking things and things to be cooked were being unloaded, men were despatched in search of water and firewood, and the boys were preparing their fireplace; and however tired they might be after a long tramp, they always prided themselves upon their cookery, and the celerity with which our meals were served. All this they did merrily and with light hearts; and hardly once during the journey, even when they were suffering from frequent attacks of fever, have I seen them out of temper. They knew that we all had our work to do, and they took a pride in doing theirs to the best of their ability.

It was pleasant to watch the continuous improvement in Jewan's *physique*. When hired for me by Go Paul, a Madras boy who had been with me for many years, he looked a mere stripling, with legs little better than broomsticks in appearance, and a chest that spoke very little for his capacity for travel. Every day his calves were getting bigger, his chest was expanding, and he seemed to become more vigorous. Travel was certainly rapidly making a man of him.

In the evening Dr M'Gilvary called up some of the most intelligent of the Shans to give me information about their customs, commencing with courtship and marriage. They told us that a youth was allowed to visit a girl either in private or in the family circle, and that courting-time is known as *Bŏw ow-ha sow* (*Bow*, a bachelor; *ow-ha*, to visit; *sow*, a virgin or maid). A lad, when courting without witnesses, places himself entirely in the power of the girl, as it is the custom to take a woman's word as conclusive proof of any alleged breach of delicacy, and for such breaches the spirit-fine required by the ancestral spirits of the family can be levied.

The amount of the spirit-fine varies, according to the custom of the family, from a bunch of flowers to nine rupees. Such fines are due, not merely as a solatium for indelicate acts towards the females of the family, but for accidentally coming into contact with them. Even in general company, if a woman is touched to call her attention, and she reports the fact to the *kumlung*, the patriarch and priest of her family, the fine can be levied. If the girl neglects to report the occurrence at once, and sickness, caused by the anger of the unappeased ancestral spirits, happens subsequently in her family, her word is still taken, and the fine is levied.

The practice of the patriarch or head of the family being the priest, is a survival from ancient times, and was customary amongst Aryan tribes, as is evidenced by the Vedas. Mr Kingsmill, in his 'Ethnological Sketches from the Dawn of History,' says that the Djow, or Chau, who founded the first historical empire in China, B.C. 1122, were an Aryan race, and their ruler, "the Djow Wang," was not so much supreme ruler as supreme priest. He alone could perform sacrifices to the memory of the mystical ancestors of the house. In each State a similar position of affairs was to be noticed. The Emperor of China is the high priest of the State religion as well as the ruler of the empire.

At times a youth serenades a girl alone, accompanying himself upon a peculiarly shaped two-stringed banjo; at other times he is accompanied by the village band. If the lad considers that he has won the lady's affection, he asks his parents, or the *kumlung* of his family, to obtain the consent of her relations, and to arrange for the marriage.

If an illegitimate child is born, twenty-four rupees as well as the spirit-fine has to be paid to the *kumlung* of the girl's family, and the man must likewise provide a sacrifice of an ox, or pig, or fowl, according to the requirement of the spirit of the woman's family. No other claim can be made on the man, and the woman has to support the child.

According to Dr M'Gilvary, the custom of levying the spirit-fine is strictly adhered to amongst the nobility as well as amongst the people. As an instance, he told me that on sickness occurring in the palace at Zimmé inquiry is at once made, and if any breach of delicacy has occurred, the male culprit is fined, and the spirits of the royal family are appeased. In case of the act having been a breach of the seventh commandment and the act has been between a serf and a slave of the palace, the man must either pay the spirit-fine and seventy-two rupees, the legal redemption price of the woman, or marry her and become a slave. The culprit, if a noble, is merely mulcted in the spirit-fine required by the spirits of the family, and is free from other charge. In cases of adultery, forty rupees has to be paid to the injured husband, as well as the spirit-fine. If the husband refuses to receive his wife back after her misconduct, he must hand the forty rupees received by him to her family, who must receive her. The Zimmé Shans, as a rule, are a chaste people, and the few soiled doves in Zimmé have flown there from Siam.

The marriage ceremony consists of paying the spirit-fee in the presence of the *kumlung* of both families, and drawing out an agreement for the payment of the *ngeun kŭn soo*, the sum a man has to forfeit if he divorces his wife. Both women and men amongst the Shans can divorce each other at will; but divorces without ample cause are looked upon with disapproval by the people, and the ease with which the marriage-tie can be broken has not led to experimental marriages as it did amongst the ancient Romans. If a woman divorces her husband, she has first to purchase the *soo-han*, or right of divorce, which seldom costs more than fourteen rupees; and in case of a divorce, the children pertain to the woman, except in the case where the husband is a slave, when the master has a right to one male child, or, in the absence of male children, to one of the other sex.

In the case of a woman marrying a slave, the master has

a right to one male child, or, if there is no male, a daughter. If the slave of one man marries the slave of another, it is the custom for the master of the wife to purchase the husband. If the husband's master refuses to part with him he can claim his freedom.

The judicial price of a man slave is fifty-four rupees, and of a female slave seventy-two rupees. Amongst the warlike races of the hills the opposite rules, the value of the male being greater than that of the female; but in the Shan States, where the woman does most of the work, the woman is decidedly as a worker worth more than the man.

In cases of debt, a man can either pay the debt, the interest of the debt, or serve his creditor in lieu of the interest. It is optional for a man to serve or pay the interest, unless a special agreement has been made. If a man owes more than he, his family, and possessions are worth, or having sufficient, will not pay, the creditor informs the court, which enforces the claim by putting the debtor in chains until the debt and court fees are paid. Men often linger out their existence in slave-bondage.

Any person may settle in and cultivate land in the Shan States that is not already under cultivation, and does not become a serf to the chiefs unless he marries a woman of the State; and even then he can remain free, with his wife, and any family that may be born to them, if he pays seventy-two rupees for her redemption. Unless this redemption money is paid, no woman is allowed to remove from the country.

All the Zimmé Shans, except the nobles, are serfs, but have the right to change their allegiance from one lord to another. This right is a great check against oppression, as the more serfs a prince has, the more powerful he is, and the more chance he has of becoming the future king of the State. On his marriage a male serf changes his allegiance to the lord of his wife's parents, and resides near the wife's family. Thus in the old days clans were formed, patriarchs became chiefs, and relations serfs. Captives likewise strengthened the community, for although they themselves were treated as slaves, their descendants would in time merge into the body of serfs. Slaves taken as wives must tend to influence the breed of the people, otherwise it is difficult to account for the difference in type between the Burmese Shans and the Siamese.

In Siam the right of changing their lord has been taken away from the people, the majority of whom are classed as *prai-luangs*, or Crown commoners, and all of whom, outside the Chinese and subjects of foreign Powers, are serfs of the Government, and are placed in classified gangs under grinding Government masters. A *prai-luang* must either serve for a month thrice in a year, or pay an exemption tax of ten dollars and eighty cents each year. The hardship and oppression that accrue to the people under this rule is thus referred to by the Rev. S. J. Smith in the preface to his translation of the Siamese 'Laws on Slavery':—

"The present system of requiring annually the personal services of the common people, without reward or provision for food and home during service or exposure, making them the helpless victims of the too often merciless, heartless, and exorbitant exactions of unscrupulous and tyrannical Government masters, is a crying evil that demands beneficent legislation."

CHAPTER XIII.

PAYING FOR SUPPLIES—LAND AND TEAK-FORESTS BELONG TO CHIEFS—LAND RENT — LIGHT TAXATION—LEAVE MUANG DOO — UPPER MEH HKUANG—ASCEND A PLATEAU—A SURPRISE—LUONG HKORT—THE MEH HKORT—PASS BETWEEN THE DRAINAGE OF THE MEH PING AND MEH KONG—PRECAUTION AGAINST DEMONS—SHANS WILL NOT TRAVEL ALONE—A SCARE FOR TIGERS—HEAD-DRESSING AND TATTOOING OF ZIMMÉ SHANS — CHARMS LET IN THE FLESH — A QUIET RACE—VILLAGERS RESPONSIBLE FOR LOSS AND CRIME IN NEIGHBOURHOOD—MUST NOT LEAVE VILLAGE WITHOUT PERMISSION—SURVEYING UNDER DIFFICULTIES—THE LITTLE ELEPHANT'S FUN — THE MEH WUNG AND MEH PING—A VAST PLAIN DEPOPULATED—TIMIDITY OF ELEPHANTS —RESIDENCE FOR DEMONS—REACH VIANG PA POW.

THE next day we waited in vain for the Chows, and for another elephant with the things that we had left behind. I whiled away the time by sketching one of the houses and the hills to the east of the plain, and in taking observations for the daily curve of the aneroid readings, and for temperature. The house was thatched with leaves of the *eng* tree, and the thatching was continued under the south gable-end and over part of the verandah platform. In the garden was a pond with a good many ducks on it, and one of the usual granaries, which are roofed, and formed of large barrel-shaped bamboo baskets, well raised from the ground, and plastered over to keep out rats, mice, and insects.

During the afternoon I was much amused by watching Dr Cushing, who appeared to be both puzzled and annoyed. We had made it a rule to pay for everything that we received from the people, and the Chow Phya, or judge, who accompanied us, had ordered the head-man of the village to bring in the usual provisions of rice, chickens, and ducks that are presented to officers when travelling through a district. There they were all at the Doctor's feet; but how could he pay for them? The rice had been collected in cupfuls, a cup from each house. No coin was small enough to pay for a cupful, and it would be absurd, if not impossible, to attempt to pay for it. Then the fowls and ducks were unaccompanied by their owners, and if he gave the money to the head-man, that functionary would have simply pocketed it, and the villagers would have been still unpaid. Here was a fix. We required the poultry, and must have the rice. At lâst he settled it with his conscience by accepting

A Shan house.

the rice as a present, and sending the head-man back to fetch the owners of the birds. Whether the right men were paid or not, even then, was a source of perplexity to him. This little scene was reacted at nearly every village we halted at throughout the journey, and the qualms of our consciences were eased at the cost of much worry, and at the expense of our being considered fools by the Shan officials, who could not understand our objection to preying on the people, and our departing from the customs of the land.

The whole country belongs nominally to the five supreme chiefs, who form the Government. These grant certain districts to other princes and nobles, who receive a bucket of rice for every bucket that is planted by the people, as land-tax or rent for the land occupied by them. The teak-forests give a large revenue to the chiefs. Taxation is light, and, outside the monopolies on pigs, spirits, and opium, is made up chiefly of not very burdensome import and export duties. From all I could learn, the people were much better off and infinitely better treated than the people in Siam.

Early the next day, the elephant with the remainder of our baggage arrived from Zimmé, and I received a letter telling me that Dr Paul Neis, of the French navy, who had been surveying the country to the north and east of Luang Prabang, had arrived at Zimmé *viâ* Kiang Hai. We soon afterwards heard that the two Chows were camped about five miles ahead, waiting for us, and we therefore determined to start.

Leaving Muang Doo at half-past ten, we followed the Meh Kok, a canal 30 feet broad and 4 feet deep, to the village of Tone Kow Tau, and soon afterwards left the rice-plain and entered a pass, with the crests of the hills half a mile distant on either side of us. Through this short gap the Meh Hkuang flows on its way to join the Meh Ping. After leaving the pass, we crossed a bend of the river, which is here 80 feet wide and 7 feet deep, and halted on its banks, close to the camp of the Chows. The prince appeared very glad to see us, and said that the mistake through which we had not met earlier had arisen from our having started from Zimmé in the afternoon instead of in the morning.

After a good night's rest, we were awakened by the shrill cry of peacocks, which seemed to be challenging each other from all directions, and by half-past seven had everything packed and had left the camp. We were in high glee at again being under way, and felt like schoolboys off for a holiday. The morning was simply delightful, the air was delicious, and although most of the trees were leafless, the temperature at starting was only 55°. Turning northwards, we followed the Meh Kang, a stream 30 feet wide and 6 feet deep, to the village of Ban Hai, and shortly afterwards crossed it, and commenced to ascend, amidst outcrops of trap-rock, the steep slope of Loi Pa Chāu.

The ascent, although only 500 feet, was tedious, and took us an hour and a half, as the elephants had to crawl up, resting after every footfall, before they raised their huge bodies up for another step. The slope was clad with teak-trees, and the village at the crest of the ascent is known as Ban Pa Sak, the village of the teak-forest. This village and its surroundings was a great surprise for us—like what the Giant's country must have been to Jack after mounting his bean-stalk. What we had taken for an ordinary unoccupied range of hills when we were crossing the Zimmé plain, was an extensive undulating plateau; and here on its very edge was a village, beautifully situated amid gardens of palms and fruit-trees, with a pleasant little brook of icy-cold water meandering through it from some springs near at hand. The village is 251½ miles from Hlineboay, and 1820 feet above the sea.

After crossing the plateau, we descended along the Meh Ka Lah to the Meh Hkort, and halted for the night at the village of Luong Hkort, which is situated in a broad part of the valley. A small monastery, temple, and pagoda adorn the crest of a low flat-topped spur, about a mile to the north-east of the village.

Leaving a little before seven the next morning, and turning east, we ascended the narrow valley of the Meh Hkort, and the following morning reached the crest of the pass. The incline of the valley had been easy throughout, and the deep shade of the forest had made the journey from Luong Hkort very pleasant.

The water-parting which separates the streams draining into the Meh Ping from those flowing to the Meh Kong, was 276 miles from Hlineboay and 4235 feet above the sea. The rise in the fifteen miles from the village had been 2656 feet. This was the highest point reached by me upon any of my journeys. The thermometer at 10.15 A.M. read 71°, or 9° less than it had been at the same time at Muang Doo.

Following the Meh Chay Dee down-stream, we reached a

halting-space, and found the place so pretty and the flowers of the bauhinea-trees in its neighbourhood so fragrant, that we settled to spend the next day, Sunday, there. We had descended 1003 feet in six miles from the crest of the pass, and I was astonished to find teak-trees interspersed through the forest at a height of 3089 feet above the sea.

I noticed that the elephant-drivers placed *ta-lay-ows*, or small pieces of lattice-work, on tall sticks stuck in the ground, on the paths leading to and from the camp; and on inquiry, I learned that they were intended to entangle any evil spirits that might wish to injure our party. The Shans consider such precautions fully sufficient to ward off their malignant foes. The spirits, in their opinion, have as little intelligence as the birds of the air, and any scarecrow device will keep them at a distance. You cannot send a man alone even with a letter, because a Zimmé Shan will not travel without a companion; and on our asking the reason, we were told that ill would certainly come to the man who drew the water if he likewise made the fire. It gave one quite an eerie feeling to be with a people who believed the land to be full

A ta-lay-ow.

> "Of calling shapes, and beck'ning shadows dire,
> And airy tongues, that syllable men's names
> On sands, and shores, and desert wildernesses."[1]

Another device that one notices at the cattle-camps is an array of pegs rising about eighteen inches from the ground, joined together by a creeper, or a cane if it be handy, and enclosing the space within which the cattle are tethered. The people believe that tigers, trying to steal into the camp, come with their breasts against the cane, and finding it yield, retreat for fear that it may be a trap. Travellers shun camps that have been used for cattle, as they are generally infested with gad-flies and other disagreeable insects.

The Zimmé Shans, unlike the British Shans, do not wear a chignon, nor twine a silk handkerchief round their head,

[1] Milton, "Comus," act i.

but have their hair dressed either in the ancient or modern Siamese styles. The modern style much resembles the European fashion; the ancient style consists in shaving the sides and back of the head, and merely leaving a tuft like a clothes-brush at the crown. Their bodies are tattooed from the waist downwards, sometimes as far as the ankle. This custom does not now extend either to the Siamese or to the Lao Shans, who occupy Luang Prabang and the portion of the Meh Kong valley that lies to the south of it, although tattooing is known to have been general among their ancestors in the country to the north and south of the Yangtsze Kiang long before our era commenced. It is not unlikely that the Burmese acquired the habit from the Shans. The tattooing generally consists of figures of birds and beasts and mythical monsters, including dragons and ogres. Men who prize the reputation of being dare-devils have charms in the form of cabalistic signs, arrangements of numbers and words, contained in squares tattooed in red on their chest, back, and arms.

The tattooing instrument is a single split needle set in a heavy brass socket. Having filled the needle with a preparation of indigo, the operator pricks the pattern by a series of small punctures into the skin. Vermilion is used when tattooing the upper part of the body.

Some dacoits let in talismans under the flesh, and precious stones are carried about in the same manner. The talismans are mystical incantations inscribed on gold, silver, lead, pebbles, pieces of tortoise-shell, or even horn. It is not at all uncommon to meet a Shan with several knobs on his chest, concealing the talismans that he has inserted as charms to render him proof against bullet and sword. There is perhaps not a man in the country who does not carry about with him one or more charms; some string them like beads and wear them as necklaces.

As a rule, the Zimmé Shans are a very quiet and tractable people, and have a strong sense of what is just and right. Very few crimes occur among them: this may be partly due to the people not being allowed to leave their neighbourhood without the permission of their local head-men, and to villagers being held responsible for any loss or crime that may occur in their district, unless they can prove that the loss was accidental, or can trace the crime to the culprit.

Having enjoyed our Sunday's rest, we left early the next morning, and continued skirting, and frequently crossing, the stream. The deep forest through which we passed was scented by the fragrance of bauhinea-blossoms, and decked with the flowers of the *pinleh kathyt* and *poukbin*. The covering of my howdah was soon nearly destroyed by the bamboo-bushes, which in places had partly overgrown the path. The mahouts were lopping off the overhanging branches and sprays that were likely to interfere with the howdahs; the elephants were tugging down saplings and crushing them under foot; and I had to be constantly on the alert to guard against the spear-points of the lopped bamboos that pierced through the roof and threatened to poke out my eyes. Surveying the constant twists of the path under such circumstances is both difficult and dangerous.

The valley became wider as we proceeded, and little plains from 400 to 800 feet across were of frequent occurrence. The procession of elephants frequently closed up, owing to our having to cut our way, and I was able to see the pranks the little elephant accompanying the prince played with the men: he was making little rushes and hustling them over, and at times giving a sudden lurch as he trotted by them, which, unless they were ready and nimble, had the same effect. Every one was laughing at each other's discomfiture, and Ramasawmy, Dr Cushing's boy, was crowning Portow's great straw hat, unbeknown to him, with a garland of leaves.

The granite boulders ceased near the 288th mile, where pine-trees still crowned the low spurs on either side of us. Shortly afterwards we passed a caravan of thirty-one laden cattle. Soon great glades appeared in the forest, which gradually assumed a park-like appearance, and it became apparent that we were on a great rolling and formerly cultivated plain which extended as far as the eye could reach. Through the vast plateau now spread before us, the Meh Low, flowing north, passes on its way to the Meh Kong, and to the east of it the Meh Wung, flowing south, proceeds to join the Meh Ping. The dip to the Meh Low was not perceptible, and the rise in the plateau dividing that river from the Meh Wung seemed one with that which we were descending. Loi Mun Moo, the range to the east of the Meh Wung, was 18 miles distant, and not perceptible, being hidden by the haze. The water-parting between the two rivers, I found on a subsequent journey, was only 2148 feet above the sea, or 181 feet lower than the camp we had breakfasted at.

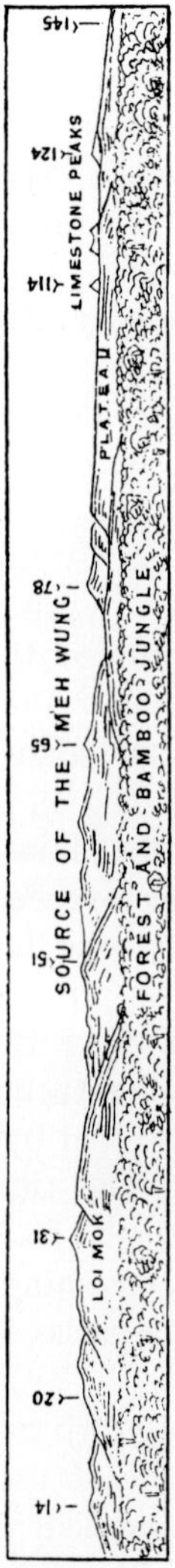

View of Loi Mok and the head of the Meh Wung at 4.42 P.M. 10th March.

The plain had evidently been at one time under cultivation, as very few trees had been left standing: the population had doubtless been swept away in the wars of last century, and was still too sparse to cultivate one-twentieth of the splendid plain. The scrub-jungle and grass on the slope of the high plateau to the north-west was in a blaze as we turned to the north and approached it; the elephants began trumpeting with fear, and we were forced to make a slight detour in order to prevent them from becoming panic-stricken. Elephants, although immense in size, are very timid, and easily startled. We had to take them off the path and turn their heads away into the jungles whenever we heard the tinkling bells of an approaching caravan; and they will turn tail and run at the sight of any audacious little dog that thinks fit to bark at them. I have been told that their eyes slightly magnify objects, and they imagine the little dogs are much larger than they really are. This may be so, but one requires to be very cautious in accepting such statements from gentlemen who, on meeting a stranger, are glad to take him in.

Near the 295th mile I entered the rice-fields of Ban Fu-ee Hai, and after crossing the Meh Low, 30 feet broad, 8 feet deep, with 1½ foot of water, halted near Viang Pa Pow to sketch the hills in which the Meh Wung takes its rise. We camped for the night at three rest-houses lying to the north-west of the palisade and moat of the city. Another rest-house in palisaded grounds at the south-west of the city has been set apart for the residence of the local demons, and their offerings are frequently made to appease them and keep them in good temper. Our camp was 300¼ miles from Hlineboay, and 1721 feet above the sea.

CHAPTER XIV.

A CHINESE FORTIFICATION—CHINESE ARMY DESTROYED BY FAMINE—VIANG PA POW—KIANG TUNG LAWAS—WITCH VILLAGES—AN INTELLIGENT PRINCE—BEST DIRECTION FOR RAILWAY—PURCHASE AN OX FOR FOOD—AN ANCIENT LAKE—LEAVE PA POW—UPPER GORGE OF THE MEH LOW—KIANG TUNG LAWAS A JUNG TRIBE, AND DISTINCT FROM BAU LAWAS—BURMESE SHANS—CATTLE WITH NOSE-BAGS AND MASKS—EFFECT OF SOIL ON FOLIAGE—SURPRISES IN THE JUNGLE—TEMPLE AT BAU MEH PIK—OFFERINGS TO DECEASED ANCESTORS—THE VALLEY OF THE MEH SOOAY A GAME-PRESERVE—INDICATIONS OF GOLD—ROAD TO VIANG POW—LOWER GORGE OF THE MEH LOW—PORTOW, THE LITTLE ELEPHANT'S PLAYMATE—LOI KOOK—LOI CHANG SHANS RETURNING FROM FRONTIER DUTY—UNWARRANTABLE ACTION OF CHINESE GENERAL—KIANG HUNG SHANS BURMESE SUBJECTS IN 1886—REMOVAL OF CAPITAL—KIANG HUNG ANNEXED BY BRITISH IN 1888—SHANS DREAD ENTERING DESERTED TEMPLES—DECEASED MONKS CLASSED AS DEMONS—WORSHIPPING DECEASED MONKS—SUICIDE OF A PRINCESS AND TWO OF HER MAIDS—SOUSED BY AN ELEPHANT—COURTESY OF THE CHOW HONA OF KIANG HAI—AN IMMENSE PLAIN.

VIANG PA POW—the City of the Croton Forest—is a Viang Hau or Yunnan-Chinese city, which was fortified and stockaded by the Chinese when they sent four armies to attack Burmah (A.D. 1765-69), and was unoccupied when M'Leod passed it in 1837. The Chinese forces are said to have been much harassed by the Lawas and other hill tribes, and being entirely cut off from their supplies, had to kill their ponies for food, and ultimately to retreat. Famine proved their chief enemy, and very few lived to reach Yunnan.

The city is surrounded by a double moat and an inner rampart, the latter palisaded on the top with teak-logs standing 12 feet high from the ground. It is 1700 feet long, 1073 feet broad, and contains seventy houses. The *muang*, or district, has 322 houses scattered amongst the Shan villages, and about 2250 Shan inhabitants. The valley of the Meh Low is, however, chiefly occupied by the Kiang Tung Lawas, whose houses are far more numerous than those of the Shans. These Lawa gain their livelihood by cultivating rice, cotton, sugar-cane, and indigo, and by mining iron, and making muskets, dahs, spears, ploughs, chains, and other articles. We passed by many of their villages between the city and Ban Meh Pik, and later on between Kiang Hai and Muang Hpan.

The Shan villages in the Muang have been set apart for the habitation of reputed wizards and witches. These people have the choice of settling here or in Muang Ngai, Muang Pai, and in Kiang Hsen—all of which regions are deficient in population. Dr M'Gilvary told me that many of the people accused of witchcraft are so foolish as actually to believe in the truth of the accusation, and that there is more superstition and consequent fear, hatred, and malice in the witch villages than elsewhere in the country.

Soon after camping I had a visit from Chow Chaum Muang, a first cousin of the Queen of Zimmé, the most intelligent native met by me during my journeys. With the aid of a box of matches, he took great pains in explaining to me the general features and lie of the country. He said there was no range of hills between Viang Pa Pow and the valley of the Meh Wung, and that the best direction for the railway from Raheng would be from Kiang Hsen *viâ* Kiang Hai, Muang Hpan, Penyow, Ngow, and Lakon. As he arranged the matches according to the lie of the hills and streams, I sketched the plan on paper. I found his information extremely correct. The Shan nobles are certainly much more truthful and reliable than the governors and officials in Siam, who pride themselves upon their duplicity, and do as little as they can to aid a visitor to their country, and all they can to deceive him.

Early the next morning our Chow ordered in a fresh supply of rice, ducks, and fowls, and asked us if we would like to purchase an ox for food. Of course we gladly consented, and handed him the money. The owner seemed loath to part with the animal, and we more than fancied that the prince had taken heavy toll of the money before it passed from his hands. Anyhow, all of our party had a pleasant addition to our diet for some days. Most of the meat was subsequently smoked and jerked, and therefore kept well.

North-east of the city, about five miles distant, Loi Mok—a range of hills twenty miles long—commences. In this range the Meh Wung takes its rise, and we are about to skirt these hills until we leave the Meh Low for Kiang Hai. The range forms the eastern flank of an ancient lake-basin, which is now drained by the Meh Low. The basin in which Muang Pa Pow lies was formerly severed from the lake by Loi Pa Tyoo, and apparently forms part of the previous drainage-area of a former lake on the Meh Wung.

We had to wait till 1 P.M. for ten fresh coolies and two elephants to replace the twenty coolies we had brought from Zimmé. When these arrived, we left the camp and proceeded due north down the valley of the Meh Low. After passing through the rice-fields of three Shan villages, great spurs from the ranges on either side began to close in; and at the 303d mile we entered the forest, and soon afterwards crossed a flat-topped spur about 70 feet high which proceeded from Loi Mok.

A mile farther we crossed a bend of the Meh Low where the stream was 80 feet wide, 6 feet deep, and had 1 foot of water, and entered the gorge where the river had broken through the hills. Here we met a large company of Kiang Tung Lawas returning from fishing, and carrying fishing-nets which were weighted at the bottom with chains. The women, young and old, were bare to the waist, and the men were dressed, like our Zimmé Shan followers, in garments of cotton dyed with indigo.

There could be no mistaking this race for the Bau Lawa: like the La-hu, whom I met in Kiang Hai, they are akin in language to the Lolo tribes of the Jung race in Yunnan. This is evidenced by comparing the Lolo vocabularies given by Mr Bourne in the report of his journey in South-western

China (Blue-book, China, No. 1 of 1888) with the vocabularies given by me in the account of my exploration.

For the next three miles we were amongst the hills. Great spurs covered with teak and other valuable trees sloped up from the river, in whose bed shales and flagstones cropped up. The grass and scrub-jungle on some of the spurs was on fire, and my elephant, from fear, was playing a scale sounding like one played on a child's tin trumpet, and by no means resembling the ordinary roar of the beast. After crossing two bends of the river, we reached the Kiang Tung Lawa village of Ban Ta Kau, which is situated beyond the gorge, and halted for the night.

After dinner we called up the head-men of the village, and took their vocabulary. To show the utter difference between their language and that of the Bau Lawas, I may mention that fire, water, fish, and pig in Bau Lawa are—*ngau*, *raowm*, *ka*, and *layt*; whilst in Kiang Tung Lawa they are—*bee*, *hlang*, *laung-teh*, and *wa*. The Lawas said that nearly every year some of their kinsmen from the neighbourhood of Kiang Tung paid them a visit, and that their forefathers were immigrants from the north, and not natives of the Zimmé State. These people have not such pronounced oval faces as the Lolos in Ssuchuan (although probably of the same race) or the La-hu near Kiang Hai, and at first sight I took them for Burmese Shans. They have, however, better developed noses than the Shans, and some of their women might be taken for handsome gipsies.

Next day we started before the morning mist had been dissipated, and passed through the fields of Ban Pa Bong. The spurs on either side of us were rapidly retreating, and we were now well into the old lake-basin. At the village the plain was three miles broad, and it quickly expanded to six and seven miles, the hills on either side being frequently lost in the haze. The small trees and bushes were spangled with the large pale-blue flowers of a creeper; and white convolvulus, jessamine, and the yellow blossoms of a vine-leaved creeper were frequently seen.

Near Pa Bong we met fifty-three laden cattle, accompanied by a party of Burmese Shans wearing blue trousers and jackets, and great straw hats atop of the silk handkerchiefs which were twined round their top-knots. All the oxen wore nose-bags made of rattan-cane, to prevent them from browsing by the way; and the leaders wore a mask in front of their faces, fancifully worked with cowrie-shells, and topped by a beautiful peacock's tail. This, of course, was to make the animals hideous, in order to frighten the demons away. Besides the ordinary brass sleigh-bells that are hung round the necks of the oxen, a large bell was suspended from a frame above the leader's head. The bells are useful for letting the elephant-drivers and other caravans know of their approach, and to enable the caravan-men to track the animals when they are grazing at a halting-place.

The morning was pleasant, and the country very beautiful, and made even more so by the mist rising and falling as it lifted from the plain and was swept from the valleys by the morning breeze. The great variety of trees in the portions of the plain that were not under cultivation, and the constant recurrence of trees out of and in leaf, was a source of continual surprise. The same class of trees were in full leaf in one place where the soil was rich, and had dropped their leaves at a place close by where the soil indicated a laterite formation.

The elephants amused themselves as they went along by showering down bamboo seeds upon the men as they passed among the clumps, and seemed not to care at all for the mahout's whip with the lump of lead attached to the end of its thong. The climate in the basin of the Meh Low being moister than in the Zimmé plain, the verdure is more luxuriant. I noticed a bamboo 60 feet high growing without soil, rooted in the arm of a tree four feet above the ground.

At times, on stretching my neck out of the howdah in order to get a further glimpse of something we had passed, I would see a group of white-turbaned Shans squatting in a bamboo bower, looking, in their great peaked hats and their blankets wrapped round them, like gnomes in the Black Forest. Here would be a party of villagers who had scuttled out of sight as they heard us approach. There a group of porters, with their burdens by their side, chatting and resting in the shade. In a jungle-clad country, nothing could be easier than to surprise an enemy.

After passing several Lawa villages we reached the large Shan village of Meh Pik, or the Pepper river, and halted for ten minutes to visit a temple, which was handsomely decorated with gold-leaf and vermilion, and occupied by a very ugly image of Gaudama, about which stood many smaller and less hideous images. The offerings, which consisted of flowers, food, dolls' houses, and toy elephants and ponies, were indications of what the votaries wished forwarded to the spirits of their deceased relations and friends. Written instructions frequently accompany such emblems, stating for whom they are intended, and at the tag end the writer curses any one that steals them, and hopes that that individual may be punished in the four hells.

Leaving the village we entered a large grazing-plain, in which many buffaloes with their usual attendants, white paddy-birds and mynahs, were feeding in the plain, crossed the Meh Low and the large rice-plain of Ban Pong, and halted for the night on the bank of the Meh Soo-ay, near the large village of the same name, which is situated 323½ miles from Hlineboay and 1566 feet above the sea. Ban Meh Soo-ay is the headquarters of the governor of this district, who called on us as soon as he heard of our arrival. He told me that the valley of the Meh Soo-ay is the private game-preserve of the King of Zimmé, and that no one is allowed to hunt there, or even enter the valley without the royal permission. It is therefore uninhabited, except by deer, tiger, rhinoceros, elephant, wild cattle, and other large game. From slate and quartz being the only pebbles in the stream-bed, it is not at all unlikely that gold may exist in the hills stretching into this valley, as it does in the same geological formation in other parts of the Shan States.

From the village of Meh Pik, which we had passed, he said a path led westward across the hills to Viang Pow, which was reached by caravans in three days. The descent on the Viang Pow side of the hills was very gradual, but part of the ascent from the Meh Low side was difficult.

His village contained sixty houses, but he could not tell, without referring to his books, the number in the other villages under his jurisdiction. In the village I noticed peach-trees, the first I had seen.

The next day we left early, and a mile and a half from our camp entered the gorge through which the Meh Low escapes between the spurs from Loi Kook Loi Chang on the west and Loi Mok on the east. These two ranges form the north and east flanks of the old lake-basin, which is now

The little elephant's fun.

drained by the Meh Low. For five miles, spurs from either side occasionally approached near the stream, which we had frequently to cross in order to shorten our route, as the river is very serpentine in its course. Whilst passing through this gorge, Ramasawmy was playing "God bless the Prince of Wales" on a reed flute; and the little elephant was taking every chance he could to hustle the men over as they crossed the river, and souse them with water from his trunk. If there is truth in transmigration of souls, that little rogue must have been a monkey in a former existence, and had not lost his zest for malicious pranks.

Portow, who had an overweening opinion of his own dignity, and was bent on setting up as an oracle, was unfortunately not only the butt of the boys, but likewise the sport of the baby-elephant. Many a time have I seen him hustled over by the youngster, who seemed to have picked him out as his playmate. Slily and softly stealing up behind, he would suddenly increase his pace, and with a quick shuffle or a sudden lurch shoulder him sprawling to the ground. Portow during this part of the journey behaved like a hunted or haunted man, ever looking behind to see whether the dreadful infant was near.

The large spurs on our left were called Loi Pa Kuang, the hill of the deer-forest; Loi Wung Ngoo, the hill of the snake pool: between which rose Huay Pak Chang, the brook of the elephant's mouth; and Loi Kee-Wo Hay, the hill where the cattle scatter their dung, so called because the cattle caravans that cross it on their way by a short cut to Kiang Hai, are much distressed whilst ascending its steep sides. There were several plains in the gorge, the spurs being at times half a mile and a mile apart.

At the 330th mile, the river, then 1500 feet above sea-level, takes a sudden bend to the east, and passing betwixt an isolated hill and the last spur from Loi Mok, enters the Kiang Hai plain. At the end of the spur is the small village of Ban Tsen Tau, and in front of the isolated hill were three deserted houses in old patches of cultivation, which had been occupied by witches on their way to settle at Kiang Hsen. After leaving the river, we commenced crossing the small spurs which stretch into the Kiang Hai plain from Loi Kook Loi Chang, and halted for the night at a pretty mountain-stream, the Huay Wai, the brook of bamboos. Shortly after our arrival we met 200 Shans on their way back to Zimmé from Kiang Hsen, carrying their things on light bamboo shoulder-trestles, somewhat similar in shape to the frames of the pack-saddles used for caravan cattle and mules. The men rest the trestle first on one shoulder, and when tired on the other. The Shans were returning from doing frontier duty; some disturbance having arisen in the Burmese Shan States to the north.

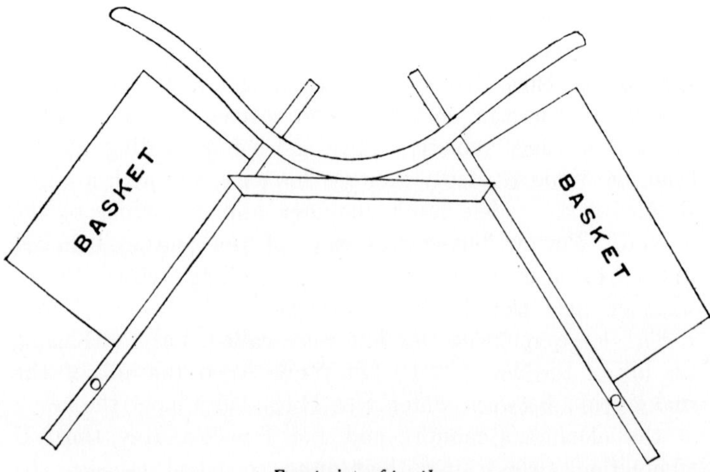

Front view of trestle.

These disturbances are alluded to by Mr Bourne of our Chinese Consular Service in his report (Blue-book, China, No. 1, 1888), where he notes that when at Ssumao in January 1886, he heard that "in 1884 the Chinese asserted their authority through Ma Chung, the General at Puerh, in a rather questionable manner, by the removal of the Hsuan-wei Ssu, and also of the officer (Pa-tsung) of the Liu-kun district." The Hsuan-wei Ssu is the chief of Kiang Hung, and the district named is the one nearest to Ssumao belonging to Kiang Hung.

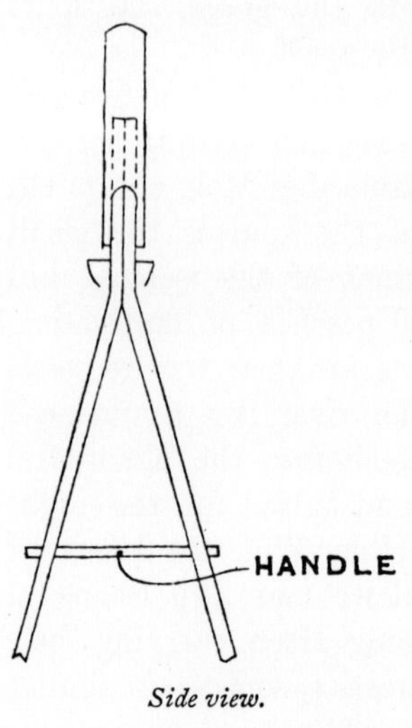

Side view.

On Mr Bourne sending his writer "to visit a Burmese temple (Mien Ssu) situated four miles south of Ssumao, and forming part of a castle belonging to the Liu-kun Tu-ssu,

. . . they (the priests) described themselves as Burmese subjects, but said they bore a heavy yoke, having to pay taxes both to Ssumao (the Chinese frontier-post) and to Che-Li (the Chinese name for Kiang Hung). My writer, who has been in Burmah, described the castle as quite Burmese in construction."

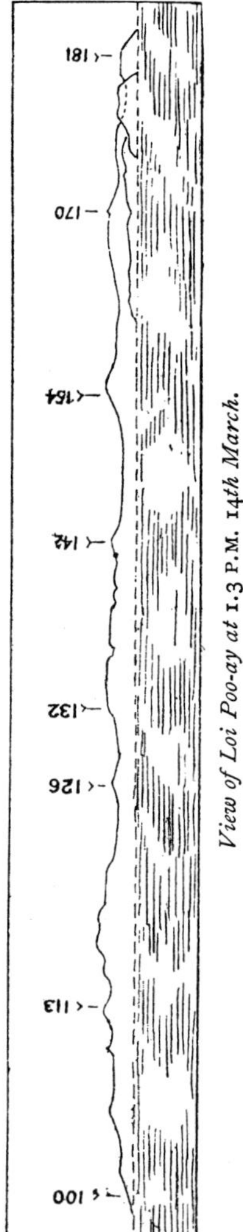

View of Loi Poo-ay at 1.3 P.M. 14*th March.*

The fact that the Shans within four miles of Ssumao considered themselves to be subject to Burmah in January 1886, a year after we had annexed that country, is most important. It thus becomes evident that the "Upper Burmah Notification, No. 75, of 1888," by which "all of the territories east of the Salween river which on the 27th November 1885 owed allegiance directly or indirectly to the King of Burmah" are included in our dominions, includes the portion of the Burmese Shan States that lies to the east as well as to the west of the Meh Kong river, and therefore the whole of the country through which the Burmah-Siam-China Railway will run from Kiang Hsen right up to the Chinese frontier-post at Ssumao. If we had not annexed the Shan States of Kiang Tung and Kiang Hung, they would inevitably have fallen sooner or later to the French, and our only practicable road for a British railway to China would have been foolishly relinquished, together with the trade of the people of Western China.

When talking about the temple we had visited at Ban Meh Pik, Dr M'Gilvary told me that the Shans are afraid to visit a deserted temple, for the reason that the images of Gaudama are inhabited by Pee Soo-a Wat, the spirits of deceased Buddhist monks, who are the protecting spirits of the temple.

If neglected, having nothing to live on, they become savage, and sit like Giant Despair, gnawing their nails; being thenceforth classed amongst demons, or malignant spirits. If a temple is not totally abandoned, and offerings are made to only one image by a worshipper, the envious spirit of another is apt to avenge himself by startling the votary; and should the person afterwards become ill, or should accident or other misfortune happen to him, the image is thenceforth regarded by the people as the embodiment of a malign spirit. Ancestral spirits and those of a family clan, if not worshipped and fed every three years, likewise become malignant in their inclinations.

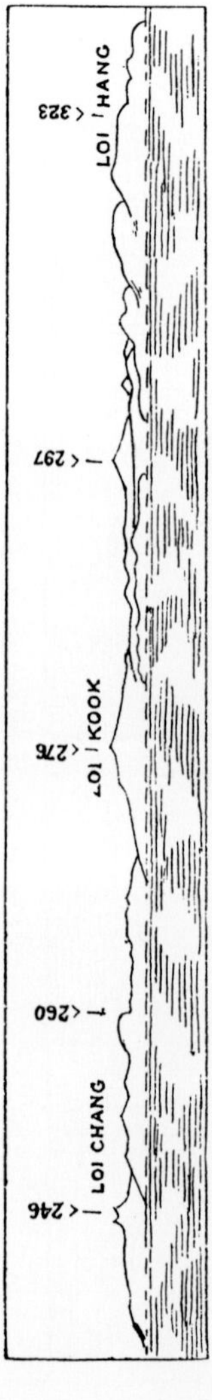

View of Loi Kook Loi Chang at 1.3 P.M. *14th March.*

When an abbot, celebrated for his learning and virtue, dies, it is the custom for those who have spent their monastic life under his instruction, to prepare a shrine for him in some part of their house, or, if still in the monastery, in their dormitory, where flowers and food are placed for the acceptance of the spirit of their deceased teacher. If he is treated with neglect or disrespect, he may become a spirit of evil towards his former pupils. Apparitions may be caused by good or evil spirits.

With reference to his having told me that the Shans were a romantic people, Dr M'Gilvary said that suicide amongst them was by no means unusual. If a man considered that he had been slighted or ill-used in any way, he was apt to brood over the fact, and work himself into a state—when he would take his own life. Only a year or two ago one of the princesses being crossed in love, hung herself from a branch of a tree; and two of her maids, finding her suspended, in sorrowful despair at having lost their sweet mistress, sought to accompany her in death by dangling from the same branch.

Starting early the next morning, we crossed a few low spurs and then descended to the great plain of Kiang Hai. As we passed near the first village, my elephant, which had taken a trunkful of water at the last brook, made a bad shot, and sent it flying over me and my survey-book. This feat made Portow, who was walking by the elephant to translate for me, nearly die of laughter; his sense of fun for once becoming greater than his sense of his own dignity. We halted for the night at the large village of Don Chi. The villages in the neighbourhood belonged to three *Kwangs*, or sub-districts, and contained 600 houses. In one of the villages I noticed several papaw-trees in the orchards. The juice of the fruit of this tree renders any tough meat tender, and has been successfully employed in the removal of the false membrane in diphtheria.

We put up for the night in the hunting residence of the Chow Hona, or second chief, of Kiang Hai, who arrived in the evening, but courteously insisting that we should remain, put up elsewhere. From the large plain near the village we could see Loi Poo-ay eleven miles to the east, stretching away to the south, and giving rise to the small hillocks that separate the sources of the Meh Low from those of the Meh Ing; and to the west were Loi Kook Loi Chang, and some smaller hills on the south of the Meh Khoke.

CHAPTER XV.

PRINCES IN THEIR BEST CLOTHES—A PROCESSION—REACH KIANG HAI—DILAPIDATED HOUSES—THE MEH KHOKE—NGIOS FROM MONÉ—KIANG HAI—FORMER SIAMESE CAPITAL—EARLY HISTORY OF SIAM—VISIT THE CHIEF—POPULATION—RUINED CITIES—ARRANGEMENT BETWEEN BRITISH SHANS AND SIAMESE SHANS—RECENT ENCROACHMENT OF SIAMESE—NAME ENTERED AS BENEFACTOR IN ROYAL ANNALS—VISIT FROM LA-HU—OVAL FACES—KNOWN BY THEIR PETTICOATS—MONOSYLLABIC LANGUAGES DIFFICULT TO TRANSLATE—LA-HU A LOLO TRIBE—COMPARISON OF VOCABULARIES.

THE following morning I noticed that Chow Nan and his son had cast their travelling attire, and were gorgeously arrayed, looking like gay butterflies. The prince was resplendent in a new red silk *panung*, a blue jacket with gold buttons, and, for the first time since we left Zimmé, in shoes and white stockings. His son, similarly shod, was adorned with a green satin jacket and a yellow silk *panung*.

Dr Cushing with the help of the Chow, who had set his heart upon entering Kiang Hai in state, marshalled the procession. Ten armed men led the way, and were followed by the prince's elephant, some attendants, Dr Cushing's elephant, some attendants, Dr M'Gilvary's elephant, some attendants, my elephant, five loaded elephants and the baby-elephant, and a long train of servants, porters, and elephant grooms. I could not help laughing as we went along, as we appeared so like a travelling circus advertising itself in a provincial town.

Leaving the Chow Hona's house at half-past six, we marched through the plain, passing several laterite hillocks, and crossing one to avoid a swamp—and skirting five villages, until at the village of Sun Kong we came in sight of the crenelated walls of Kiang Hai. Thence we traversed the graveyard of the governors of the city, and shortly afterwards that of the abbots of the monasteries, entered and crossed the city, and halted at the rest-house lying between it and the Meh Khoke. The rest-house is situated 352¼ miles from Hlineboay, and 1320 feet above the sea.

One of the tomb pillars in the cemetery of the governors was six feet in height, and had a pyramidal cap ending in a flame-like ornament. For one foot from the ground the pillar was six feet square. Five steps, or offsets, occurred in the next foot in height, reducing the sides of the square for the following foot to four feet; then three offsets, together measuring three and a half inches in height, supported a cap five feet square, upon which the pyramid rose in offsets of two inches. In front of the pillar was an altar, on which flowers and vegetable-wax tapers had been freshly laid.

The rest-house in which we put up was in a very leaky condition, owing to the thatch not having been renewed, and to the devastation wrought in the leaves and rafters by the bamboo-beetles. The Chow's rest-house, which was next to ours, was in a still worse condition, as many of the floor-planks and girders were rotten, and the floor was thus a succession of man-traps. This was soon remedied, for as soon as the Chow Hluang heard of our arrival he despatched men with new bamboos and thatch to render our habitations more secure and comfortable.

Kiang Hai, whose Pali name is Pantoowadi, is picturesquely situated on the south bank of the Meh Khoke. From the crest of the small hillocks near the city, when the air is free from haze, the eye can range 20 miles westward up the river valley; 18 miles eastward to Loi Tone Yang; the same distance to the south, or farther if there was anything high enough to see; and to the north as far as the low hillocks, 15 miles distant, which divide the Kiang Hsen plain from the valley of the Meh Khoke.

A series of low laterite hillocks spring up from the plain to the west of the city. This plain, and that to the north of the river, is inundated in places for a depth of two feet in the rains for eight and nine days at a time. Two of the hillocks serve as portions of the ramparts on the north and west sides of the city.

The river rises in a plateau two days' journey to the south-west of Kiang Tung, and its sources are separated from the Kiang Tung plain, which is 2500 feet above the sea, by Loi Kum, the Loi Peh Muang which divides the Kiang Tung State from that of Moné, a State lying to the west of the Salween.

The Meh Sim, which enters the Salween, rises near the sources of the Meh Khoke; and the head of the pass, crossed by Dr Cushing in 1870, between Kiang Tung and the head-waters of the Meh Sim, is 6500 feet above the sea, or 4000 feet above the Kiang Tung plain.

At the sources of the Meh Khoke, according to some Ngio Shans whom I interrogated, is the district of Muang Khon, which comprises several villages. Two days farther from Kiang Tung, down the Meh Khoke, is Muang Khoke, from which the river takes its name. Six days from Kiang Tung, still down the river, lies Muang Sat, or Muang Hsat, and a day farther Muang Khine and Wang Hung. Still lower down is Muang Tat Pow, then Muang Nyon and Ta Taung. The latter is distant four days by water from Kiang Hai, and five or six miles above the entrance of the Meh Fang into the Meh Khoke. The above Muangs, or provincial States, are situated in extensive plains, and Muang Sat has frequently formed the base of Burmese operations against Siam. As Muang Sat has been incorporated by us in the dominions of the chief of Muang Pan, one of our Shan States lying to the west of the Salween, it will be seen that we have already carried our protection over the hills which divide the waters of the Salween from those of the Meh Kong into the valley of the Meh Khoke.

Above Ta Taung the valley of the Meh Khoke lies in the British Shan States. From thence eastwards, half-way to Kiang Hai, the Meh Khoke forms the Anglo-Siamese boundary; the frontier then turns in a north-eastern direction to the Meh Kong, which it reaches a few miles above Kiang

Hsen. To the east of Loi Peh Muang[1] the people are known to the Zimmé Shans as Tai Ngio, and pertain to the Shan States west of the Salween. The chief of Moné had rebelled against the Burmese in 1882, and taken refuge with the chief of Kiang Tung: this may account for so many Ngios having recently occupied the deserted country lying to the north of Kiang Hsen. The chief of Moné has since been reappointed to his State by the British.

The Meh Khoke at the ford above the rest-houses is 600 feet broad, but narrows to 350 feet just below the town. At the time of our visit it was 13 feet deep from the top of the banks, and had 3 feet of water in the channel. Loi Pong Pra Bat, the hill of Buddha's footprint, the southern extremity of Loi Peh Muang, ends about nine miles to the north of the city.

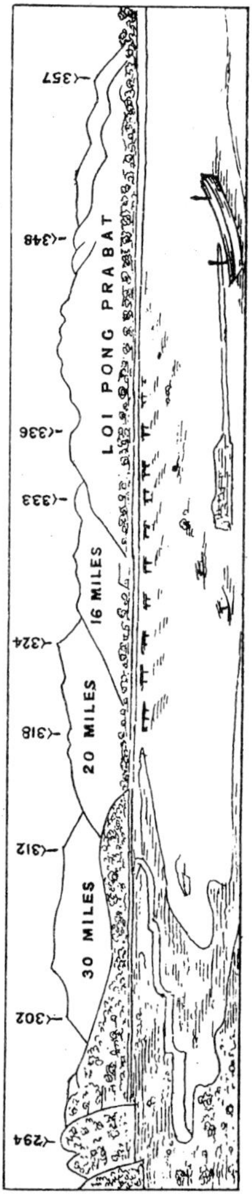

View up the Meh Khoke from the Sala at Kiang Hai.

Kiang Hai, which is called Chieng Rai by the Siamese, like all Shan cities is neatly laid out, and the roads are straight, ditched, and neatly kept. The gardens of the houses are palisaded with bamboos, pointed at the top, and have strong teak entrance-gates, which are closed at night. Water is led into the town from a neighbouring stream by an aqueduct entering near the western gate. There are twelve entrances into the city, eight of which are larger than the others. The Siamese, or Chau Tai, claim Kiang Hai (Chieng Rai) as their early capital.

[1] Peh Muang merely means the division or boundary of the States, and is applied to all ranges that form boundaries.

After breakfast we went into the city to call on the Chow Hluang, who was an old acquaintance of Drs M'Gilvary and Cushing. He resided in a large temporary house built of bamboo and thatched, whilst a large teak-house was being erected for him on the site of the house of a witch that had been burnt after the ejectment of the family in 1870.

The chief—whose head was shaved in the ancient Shan style in South-eastern China, still practised amongst the Lau Yuen or Lao in the Meh Kong valley and by a few Ping Shans, which leaves only a cock's-comb of hair—received us without his jacket, bare to the waist. He was about sixty-five years of age, and most courteous in his manner; and, like the other chiefs we called upon, did all he could to assist us and give me the best information in his power.

In answer to my questions, he said that there were 300 houses in the town and 1700 in the district, making 2000 in all. On an average the houses contained seven inhabitants. This seems to be the usual number throughout the Zimmé States. He gave us a great deal of information about the country, said that the river was full of weeds near its exit to the Meh Kong, and that the land for some distance above its mouth was inundated during the rains.

The country abounded in ruined cities, and must have been very populous at one time, but the wars at the end of last century and at the beginning of this had left it very destitute of inhabitants; and those who had not been killed had partly fled to Mokmai and Moné, Shan States, to the west of the Salween; while the rest had been taken captive to Zimmé, Lakon, Lapoon, and Nan.

The Burmese Shans had endeavoured to occupy Kiang Hsen in 1873, but Zimmé remonstrated with them, and sent 500 men to prevent them from settling there.

An arrangement had since been made, in 1881, under which the Ngio, or Moné Shans, built their large villages about the Meh Khum, and the Zimmé Shans were allowed to occupy Kiang Hsen, and the plain to the south of the Upper (British) Shan villages. As the Zimmé Shans have since encroached, and built a fort to the north of the Ngio villages, disturbances are certain to occur unless we insist upon the Siamese retiring within their proper boundary. The fort is simply a provocation to the Ngio Shans.

The wife of the chief, a very homely lady, made kind inquiries after Dr Cushing's wife, who was with him on his former journey, and said that she had often thought of them since they had left. On my presenting the chief with a watch, he was so gratified that he called for the royal annals and recorded my name in them, together with the fact of my being the donor of it. The chief was full of the late visit of Dr Paul Neis, and expressed his amusement and surprise that a European should wander about the country in native garb and accustom himself to native habits.

When we got back to our house, we found a group of La-hu (called by the Shans Mu-hseu or Moo-sur) squatting near the steps, and evidently much interested in our surroundings and the cooking of our Madras boys. The men, besides the ordinary Burmese Shan trousers, and jackets with loose sleeves, dyed with indigo, wore black turbans twisted about their hair, which was done up in a knot on the top of the back of their head. Their faces were a distinct oval, like that of their kinsfolk the Lolos of Ssu-chuan and Yunnan. Their eyes were well opened, but had a slight tendency to the Mongoloid droop of the inner corner of the eyelid, but less than amongst the average Chinese.

The La-hu women were dressed in a petticoat, and a blue spencer folded across the chest, with tight sleeves reaching to the wrist. Like the men, they wore a black turban, one end of which hung down behind over their chignon. Their hair was drawn back from the face, in the Burmese fashion, but the chignon was placed higher up on the back of the head. Their forehead was higher than it was broad, their cheek-bones high, their nose and mouth well formed, the nose slightly expanding at the nostrils, and their face was a decided oval. Thin silver hoops, about three inches in diameter, hung from the lobe of each ear, and round their necks they wore finely plaited cane necklaces.

The clan to which the hill tribes belong is generally denoted by the pattern of the petticoat of the women. It may therefore be as well, for the information of future travellers, to describe that of the La-hu. The upper portion of the petticoat is worked with horizontal red stripes, having interwoven lines of gold-thread; then comes an inch of plain red, followed by an inch and a half of blue, one inch of red, four inches of black, two and a half inches of blue, and a turning of a quarter of an inch of red at the bottom. Both men and women carried tobacco-pipes made of the root and part of the stem of a bamboo. One of the men had some Shan writing and numbers tattooed in vermilion on his arm as a charm. None of the others were tattooed.

The La-hu had very active figures, well set up, and, like all mountaineers, great freedom in their gait. There was

Front-face.

Side-face.

A La-hu youth.

not the slightest sign of timidity or shyness about them; the women were even more at ease than the men, did most of the talking, and were evidently the cocks of the walk. All came up into the *sala* as soon as they were invited, and at once squatted round us, like children round a Christmas-tree, bent on seeing and handling everything, and joyously receiving anything that might be presented. It was amusing to watch the signs of curiosity and eagerness in their eyes, as I showed them the bead necklaces and other trifles that they would receive after giving me their vocabulary and the information I required.

They all understood Shan as well as their own language; but even so, these monosyllabic languages have so many tones and inflections, that great caution and care have to be taken when translating, to prevent all chance of error. Professor Forchhamer gives an instance of this in the Shan word *kan*, which, although written with only two letters, *k* and *n*, "is capable of conveying sixteen totally distinct meanings, according as the vowel is pronounced with the high, low, middle, or rising tone; with teeth and lips either widely or but slightly opened; with full or restrained expiration of breath." Luckily, I had with me two exceedingly capable and careful Shan scholars, Drs Cushing and M'Gilvary; and even then we had at times the greatest trouble to agree upon the true sound that was uttered in a strange language; many of the consonants might be taken for one or another, as the sound was strangely between the two—*W* running into *V*, *H* into *R*, *L* into *D*, aspirates into non-aspirates, and single consonants into double ones. How the men and women did laugh as they tried to put us right by pronouncing a word dozens of times over. To see Dr Cushing leaning over, with his hand up to imply the request for perfect silence, and then eagerly become as if all ear for the sound of the word, was better than a play. I was of little use, except in taking the letters down whilst they were being haggled over by my two companions, and stating the words and sentences I wished to be translated.

To show that the La-hu are a Lolo tribe, I will compare a few of the words in the La-hu vocabulary with words taken by Mr Bourne from the Lolo tribes in Yunnan. In Lolo, father, fire, foot, gold, hand, head, iron, and moon, are *ha-pa, um-to* and *mi, t'u chieh, shi, la, ê-ku, shu, la-pa*; in La-hu they are, *nga-pa, am-mee, keu-sheh, shee, la-sheh, o-ku, shō, ha-pa.* The resemblances would be still greater if the same person had taken down the two vocabularies—as *mee* and *mi*, *chieh* and *sheh*, *am* and *um*, and perhaps other syllables, would have been similar.

Having given us their vocabulary, the La-hu said good-bye, as they wanted to return home; took up their presents, smilingly accepted the rupee offered to each of them, and promised to return the next day. More could be got out of us, and perhaps out of them, in two visits than in one.

CHAPTER XVI.

A STATE VISIT FROM CHIEF—INSIGNIA OF OFFICE—PLENTIFUL RAINFALL —RAIN-CLOUDS FROM THE NORTH—ONLY SILVER COINS—INDIAN MONEY—FRONTIER DUES—FERRY TOLL—FISHING AS A LIVELIHOOD —SALT AND COWRIES AS SMALL CHANGE—TRICKS WITH THE CURRENCY IN SIAM—ROBBING THE POOR—A FOOTPRINT OF BUDDH—A MONK SPOÏLT BY THE LADIES—RUINED TEMPLES STREWN WITH BRONZE IMAGES—CARL BOCK'S LOOT—THE EMERALD BUDDH—A TATTOOED LAOS SHAN—MADRAS BOYS TAKEN FOR OGRES—MARCHING IN SINGLE FILE—SCENE AT THE FORD—CHEAP PROVISIONS—CHINESE CARAVANS—COST OF CARRIAGE—OPINION OF DR CHEEK AS TO THE PROSPECTS FOR A BURMAH-CHINA RAILWAY—POPULATION OF SIAMESE SHAN STATES—PROTECTION OF CARAVAN—BIRDS AND MONKEYS DYING OF GRIEF—SECOND VISIT FROM THE LA-HU—MARRIAGE CUSTOMS—DIVORCE—GOLD IN THE KIANG TUNG LAWA COUNTRY—FISHING BY TORCHLIGHT.

In the afternoon the Chow Hluang came in state to return our visit. He was dressed in a pith helmet, a plum-coloured silk *panung*, a white cotton jacket with gold buttons, a white sash round his waist, and sandals which he kicked off at the door. He was accompanied by a train of followers holding a large umbrella over him and bearing some of the insignia of his office. The full list of these is given in the chronicle of the governors as follows: Two gold cup-stands, two gold boxes with conical covers, a gold stand for a water-goblet, a gold utensil for siri-leaf, which is chewed with betel-nut, a gold box for lip-salve, a gold-handled sword and scabbard, a silver coronet set with rubies, two helmets and sets of weapons, as well as two elephants.

He told me that the people of Kiang Hai never suffered from drought; the rainfall was plentiful, greatly exceeding that of Zimmé and Lakon, and the rain-clouds came from the north, not from the south-west as in Burmah. On expressing my surprise, Dr M'Gilvary informed me that the statement was correct, for he had often noticed the fact in Zimmé. This of course would account for Kiang Hai and Kiang Hsen being much more favoured with rain than Lakon, Zimmé, and Lapoon, which lie to the south of the great hills forming the water-parting of the Meh Ping and the Meh Kong. Tea grows wild on the hills to the north of the Meh Khoke, and is cultivated by the hill tribes.

He said that no copper coins were in use in the city, and that the coinage consisted of Indian rupees, and two and four anna bits. The smaller coins are scarce, and are used for buttons and other ornaments. Small purchases are made by barter.

The frontier-duty station is at Muang Doo, a village to the north of the Meh Khoke, where 3 rupees are levied on every ten laden porters, 4 annas on a laden ox, 3 annas on an unladen ox, and 8 annas on a laden pony or mule. Two ponies in every ten are allowed to pass free. Similar frontier import duties are levied in the Siamese Shan States of Lakon, Lapoon, Peh, and Nan. No frontier duties exist in the Burmese Shan States.

At the ferry over the Meh Khoke, near Kiang Hai, a toll is taken which covers the ferry hire, but is charged whether the animals are ferried across or wade the river. The toll amounts to 4 annas for a laden mule, pony, or ox, and 2 annas for a laden porter. No other duties or tolls are levied in the Zimmé State from people entering it from the north.

The only other taxes raised in Kiang Hai are upon the sale of animals. Both the buyer and seller of an elephant have to pay 5 rupees; the purchaser of a buffalo, 8 annas; of cattle, 4 annas; and of a pony, 8 annas. The land tax goes to the feudal lord, and may be considered as land rent. Comparing it with the tax of one-fourth of the produce, which by the Code of Menu should go to the king, this tax is very light, being only one basket of paddy for each basket that is sown. The out-turn in the Zimmé States varies from 40-fold to 250-fold the amount sown.

The people of Kiang Hai gain their livelihood chiefly by catching and drying fish, which are very plentiful in the streams and lakes. They export the fish to Zimmé, Ngow, Lakon, and Lapoon, in exchange for areca-nuts, cloth, salt, and other necessaries. English salt from Bangkok sells at Kiang Hai for 16 rupees a *sen* (266⅔ lb.), or about a penny a pound. Salt from Muang Nan fetches only 14 rupees for the same weight. The salt-mines in Muang Nan are situated in the hills above the capital, at Muang Mang, Bau Soo-ek, Bau Hsow, and Bau Wa.

Dr M'Gilvary said that up to 1874 salt was used as currency for purchases in the Zimmé market; and that up to 1865, *bee-a*, or cowries, were in use in Siam: the value of these were so small that from 800 to 1500 went to a *fuang* (7½ cents). The cowries were imported from Bombay.

The late King of Siam determined to stop the use of cowries as currency, and floated a token money of lead. As he could place what value he liked upon the lead coins, he resolved that 64 large stamped pieces, or 128 small stamped pieces, should go to a *tical* of silver, although the lead in them would cost less than half that amount. At the same time he issued a new flat silver *tical* (60 cents), a trifle less heavy than the bullet-shaped *ticals* that had been issued in the previous reign.

The monetary transaction in lead would bring 100 per cent profit to his treasury, and likewise—which he does not seem to have counted on—to the treasury of any one who thought fit to forge the coins. For some time the Government made a splendid profit, but soon domestic and foreign forgers filled the market with their bogus issue. A great panic ensued among the people: the lead pieces were generally refused, and the Government had to stop coining them.

Before the collapse of the lead coinage, the king determined further to replenish his treasury by another device. He issued copper coins, two of which were to be valued at a *fuang* (7½ cents), and to weigh together a trifle over half an ounce. To ensure their being taken by the people, he declared cowries to be no longer current. As he did not call the cowries in, and exchange them for the lead or copper coins, they became worthless to their possessors.

This was a sad stroke of fortune for the poor people, but worse was to come. When the present King of Siam came to the throne, finding that forgery of the debased coinage was naturally prevalent, he reduced the currency value of the old lead coins by declaring 40 of them equal to a *fuang*, or 320 to a *tical*,—considerably less than the actual value of the lead contained in them. The copper pieces he reduced in value to 8 for a *fuang*, or to a fourth of the value that they had been issued at. The people thus lost the gross value of their cowries, and were robbed of half the value of their lead coins, and three-fourths the value of their copper ones.

The only parallel that I can find for such vexatious proceedings on the part of a Government, is that of Turkey, which repudiated its paper currency in 1877-79, and in the latter year demonetised its debased coinage. But Turkey had the excuse that it had become bankrupt in 1875. It is well for the Siamese Shan States that their currency is that of British India and not that of Siam, or the people would have suffered with the Siamese. The only Siamese currency seen by me to the north of Kampheng Phet were copper coins used for small change.

After the chief had gone, we strolled about the ruins in the city. The chief of these are at Wat Pa Sing, and Wat Ngam Muang, "the beautiful temple of the city." In the former was a Pra Bat, or footprint of Gaudama, 6½ feet long, 3 feet broad, and 4 inches deep, impressed on a stone slab, and heavily gilded; a Chinese image of Buddha; one of Maha Ka Sat; besides the ordinary images.

Maha Ka Sat, if one may judge from his likenesses, must have been a very Falstaff in the flesh. Portow accounted for his plumpness, by telling us that this individual, although very religiously disposed, was so handsome, that when he put on the yellow robe and became a monk, all the women doted on him; and as the monks and *nanes* with their pupils went round in the morning collecting food for the day, they piled up all the tit-bits into his bowl. From over-indulgence he grew enormously fat, and lost all chance of becoming a Buddh in his next existence.

The ruins both within and without the city were strewn with valuable bronze images. The people objected to these being taken away, as they contained the spirits of deceased monks, who would certainly wreak vengeance on them if their domiciles were removed from the sacred precincts. All of the trouble experienced by Carl Bock in the Zimmé States arose from his robbing the ruined temples of their images, and snapping his fingers in the faces of the chiefs and people when they remonstrated with him. How he escaped from the country with his plunder, and why he was not murdered, is an enigma to me.

A crowned Buddha.

On the north end of a hillock which protrudes from the north-west corner of the city, where the old palace was situated, and near the river, are the walled grounds of a temple and pagoda, trimly kept, and in good repair. From these grounds the view of the country to the north and west is superb: the great spurs of Loi Pong Pra Bat in the distance look like isolated mountains, the spurs rising considerably higher than the crest of the range linking them together. This peculiar arrangement is noticeable in all the great hill-ranges that I saw in the Shan States, the spurs seeming to have been carved out of a great uneven plateau. Between the great spurs and the river several low hillocks, seemingly the remains of a low-lying plateau, are seen, and amongst these the river winds its way amidst limestone bluffs.

In A.D. 1436 one of the pagodas in the city was rent by lightning, and the celebrated "Emerald Buddh," cut out of green jasper, was exposed in the shrine in its breast. This image is now enthroned under a seven-tiered white umbrella in Wat Pra Kao, at Bangkok. When discovered it was removed to Zimmé, then being rebuilt after its destruction by the Siamese in 1430. Afterwards it was removed to Vieng Chang, probably early in the sixteenth century, when the successor of the Laos king who ruled at Zimmé moved the capital to Vieng Chang; and ultimately to Bangkok in 1779, two years after the Siamese had made Vieng Chang a province of their empire.

The Lao, with heads shaven with the exception of a blacking-brush tuft at the top, have an absurd resemblance to the wooden monkeys on a draw-stick, formerly sold in the Lowther Arcade. One seen at Kiang Hai was decorated with a peculiar form of tattooing consisting of a mass of blue dots free from any design, with the exception of ornamental edging along the waist and below the knees. This style of tattooing may be a specimen of an ancient type once current amongst the eastern branch of the Shans. At a little distance it resembles a pair of knee-breeches. I have never seen it elsewhere, except in the case of one of the princes of Muang Nan.

The next morning I watched the people streaming over the ford on their way to market, and was amused to see the terror expressed in the faces of the women as they passed our *sala*, and were horrified at the sight of our Madras boys. Group after group screamed with fright, and scurried by as fast as they could go. Those who looked back were further scared by the hideous grimaces the three scamps made at them. The women must have taken the boys for *yaks*, or ogres: they had evidently never seen black men before.

It is the habit of every one in the Shan States to proceed in single file, and the same rule is followed by the elephants and caravan animals. For some time in the early morning the procession of people and animals on their way to the city was continuous. Gaily dressed Burmese Shans, carrying their goods on shoulder-bamboos, passed by, and were often accompanied by their women, who were dressed in beautiful embroidered skirts, loose blue spencers, and steeple-

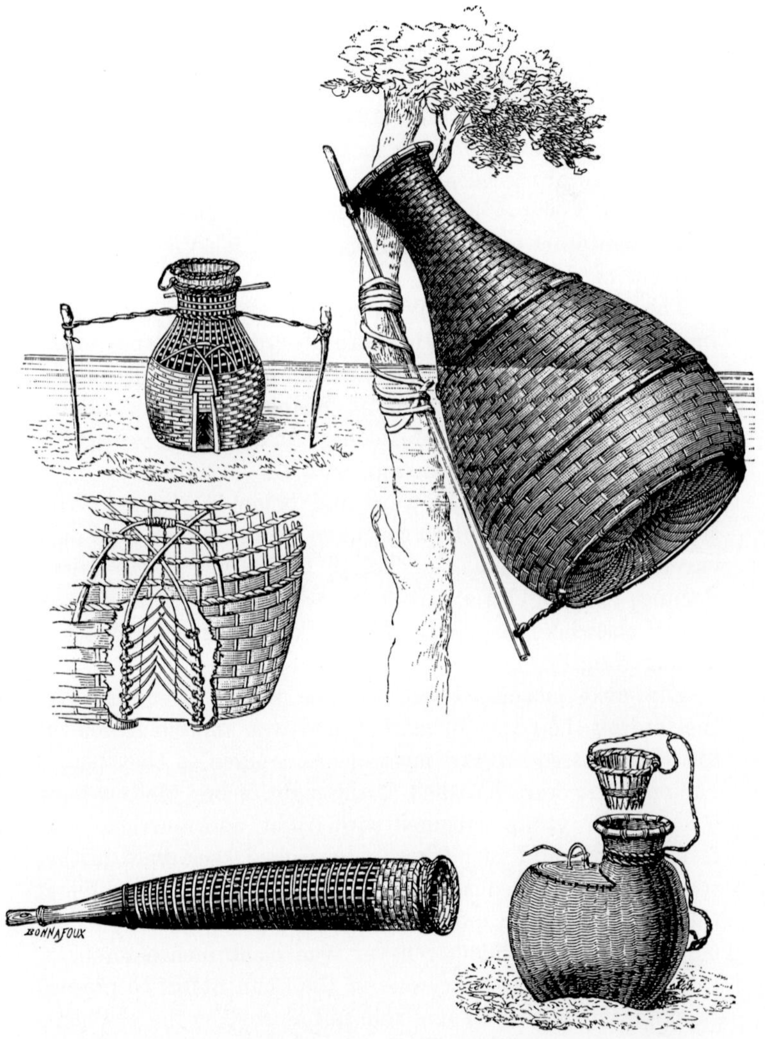

Fishing implements used in Siam.

crowned broad-brimmed hats of plaited straw, or else of palm-leaf, similar to those worn by the men, and separated from the crown of their head by a pad, and fastened under the chin by a string. Then would come a string of fisher

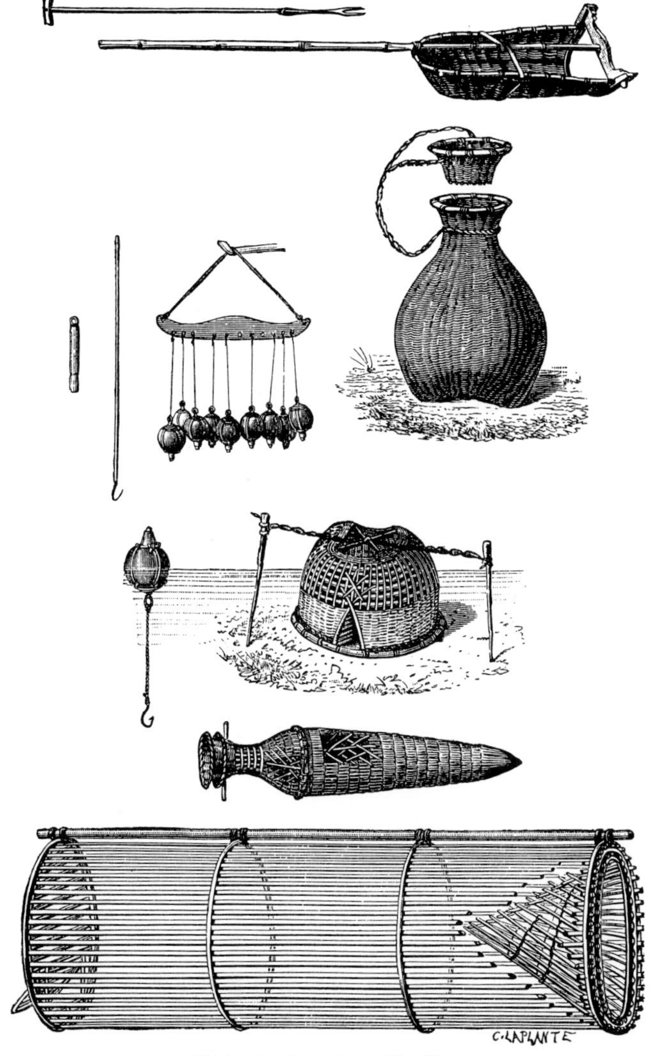

Fishing implements used in Siam.

men and women from the great staked fishing-dam that has been erected across the river a little above the ford.

These would be followed by market-women, long caravans of laden oxen, mules, and ponies; and lastly, by some elephants. The market-women, having just crossed the ford, were short-kilted, and, as is usual with the Zimmé Shans, the unmarried women were guiltless of clothing above the waist.

The prices in the market would make the mouths of our stay-at-home people water: large fowls, twopence each; large ducks, fourpence; rice, three pounds a penny; fresh fish, a halfpenny a pound; and sugar, a penny a pound.

A company of Yunnan Chinese with a caravan of twenty-six ponies camped close to our rest-house. The head-man told me that they had brought with them silk thread, straw hats, and copper pans, and had come from Nah Hseh (Yunnan Fu). Altogether, they would be six months absent, but two months of that time would be spent in selling their goods, in purchasing salt, betel-nut, &c., for sale and barter amongst the Karens, and in bartering for and purchasing the cotton they intended to carry back with them. The journey from Kiang Hai to Yunnan Fu takes them six weeks.

The cotton costs them 5 rupees a *muen* (25 lb.), and fetches 20 rupees at Yunnan Fu. The cost of carriage, including collection for each *muen*, is therefore 15 rupees, or (with exchange at sixteen pence for a rupee) £89, 12s. a ton. Assuming Lakon as the centre of their collecting ground, the average distance a ton would have to be conveyed to Yunnan Fu if carried by railway, would be 665 miles; and the cost for the journey, at a penny a mile, would be £2, 15s. 5d., or—if we allow £9, 12s. a ton for the cost of collection, and £80 as the present cost of carriage—nearly twenty-nine times as cheap as the cost by caravan.

Dr Cheek, a son-in-law of Dr M'Gilvary, who was for some years stationed at Zimmé as medical officer attached to the American Presbyterian Mission, interested himself in collecting information concerning the country, and caravan traffic. In a book termed 'Siam and Laos,' recently published by the American Presbyterian Mission Board, he states, in an article written before I explored the country, that—

"Sir Arthur Phayre represents the Laos (Shan) 'traders as industrious, energetic, possessing a marvellous capacity for travelling as petty merchants, and longing for free trade.' My own knowledge, after a residence of several years in Cheung Mai (Zimmé), confirms this official statement.

"The agricultural richness of the plain is known. The forests of valuable timber clothing the hills and mountains are another source of wealth. A large proportion of the teak timber shipped from Maulmain comes from the Zimmé forests. The mineral resources of this Laos country are varied and extensive: deposits of many of the useful and precious metals are known to exist; iron, copper, zinc, lead, silver, antimony, nickel, and gold are found in greater or less abundance. Coal has been found along the river (Meh Ping) after heavy rains, and petroleum has also been discovered.

"The importance of Zimmé is not, however, sufficiently indicated by a statement of the productions and population of the province. Its resources can never be fully developed if it is in the future to remain so cut off from the rest of the world as it always has been. The problem of a direct trade-route connecting China with the British possessions in India, is at the present time attracting much interest. The route across northern Yunnan, *viâ* Bhamo, into Burmah, has been sufficiently investigated to ascertain that for overland commerce to any considerable amount it is impracticable. It remains to discover the best route possible through the Laos (Zimmé Shan) country.

"To one who is aware of the extent of the trade that exists and has been carried on for many generations between Zimmé and Yunnan, and of the ready access to Zimmé from Maulmain, the discussion of *the possibility of discovering a trade-route* connecting South-western China and British Burmah seems superfluous. The caravan of Yunnan traders coming yearly to Zimmé clearly demonstrates the existence of *a* trade-route, and this native track is probably available for a much more extensive overland transportation of merchandise than at present exists.

"The Yunnan caravans bring silk and opium, iron and copper utensils, and other articles, which they exchange principally for cotton. This caravan trade has materially increased within the past few years, though I have been informed that years ago it was much more extensive than it is now. The gradual recuperation of Yunnan, consequent upon the restoration of order there, probably explains this recent increase of trade.

"The fact that a party of ten or twelve men with a caravan of sixty or seventy mules makes this journey from Tali in Yunnan, *viâ* Kiang Hung and Kiang Tung, to Zimmé, is a sufficient indication of the safety of the route. A caravan of sixty mules will ordinarily carry merchandise to the value of 12,000 to 15,000 dollars, occasionally a larger amount. Most of the Yunnan traders who come to Zimmé come from the neighbourhood of Tali."

Such is the opinion of an exceptionally intelligent and scientific observer, who has traversed the Zimmé States in various directions, has studied the capabilities of the country, and has lived amongst the people for many years. In another place he gives the population as follows: "The entire population of the five Laos (Siamese Shan) provinces tributary to Siam is estimated at about 2,000,000;" and he states that "a recent census of the houses throughout the province of Cheung Mai (Zimmé) gave the number of 97,000, and the census was not at that time (the time Dr Cheek saw it) complete; the population of the entire province is not under 600,000."[1]

Another Chinese caravan, consisting of eleven men with thirty-seven laden mules, passed by without stopping, on their way to Maulmain. The head-man told me that a bundle of the straw hats contained 120; that he had purchased them for 250 rupees in China; and had sold some for 450 rupees a bundle in Kiang Tung. The best kinds cost from 280 to 290 rupees, and fetch 500 rupees. The hats are two feet in diameter, with a six-inch peaked dome for the top-knot of the hair. The price includes the oilskin covers. Only the head-man was armed. He carried two

[1] Siam and Laos, p. 544.

horse-pistols and a trident. Their only other protection was a savage Tartar dog.

A crane, four feet three inches high, known to the Burmese as a Jo-Jah, slate-coloured, with a red band round the top of its long neck reaching to its eyes, was a fund of amusement to the boys, as it was quite tame, and boldly foraged amongst them for any scraps that they chose to fling it. These birds are seldom seen except in couples. The Burmese say that it is cruel to kill one, unless you likewise slay the other, for the remaining bird would become broken-hearted and pine away. I should not be surprised if this were so, for when living in Maulmain I had an instance under my own observation of an animal starving itself to death after losing its companion. I generally had some birds and other animals—parrots, paroquets, lemurs, tiger-cats, monkeys, &c.—about the house, which had been brought in from the jungle; amongst these was a gibbon, and a small long-tailed monkey that used to sleep at night cuddled up in the gibbon's arms. The little monkey fell ill and died; the gibbon was inconsolable, refused food and water, and followed its companion in two or three days.

After breakfast the La-hu who had visited us the previous day came according to their promise, and brought with them two of their children, who were as fearless as their parents, and gladly accepted and ate the biscuits and jam that we gave them, although they had never been accustomed to such luxuries. The jam was especially appreciated; the men and women tasting some from their finger, smacking their lips after it, and then letting the children finish it up. They were evidently delighted with the upshot of their former interview, and sat beaming round us in a half-circle, waiting to be questioned.

Their villages near Kiang Hai were Ban Meh Sang Noi, Ban Meh Sang Hluang, Ban Meh Kong, Ban Huay Sang, and Ban Poo Hong, containing in all fifty-six houses. In the Kiang Tung hills their villages were numerous, and contained on an average ninety houses. Many La-hu villages existed in the hills between Kiang Hai and Kiang Tung. Their weapons are bows and poisoned arrows. Their cultivation consists of glutinous rice, tobacco, cotton, and chillies; and as they cultivate more than they need, they barter the balance with the Shans for any articles they require.

I then inquired about their marriage customs, and learnt that a young man, after gaining the permission of his lady-love, seeks her parents' consent. If they are agreeable to his suit, they request the patriarchs of the village to marry the couple. On the appointed day the youth brings a present of tea and torches, and, sitting by the side of the girl, offers the present to the patriarchs, whilst he and his intended make obeisance with their hands uplifted and pressed together.

The youth is then asked whether he intends to perform all the duties of a husband towards the maiden, and on his answering in the affirmative, the elders give them their blessing. Afterwards the people assemble, and sit down at a banquet provided at the expense of the youth, where rice-spirit is poured out like water, and which includes various kinds of meat, amongst which are rats and mice, but not dogs, cats, or snakes; and, 'mid women and wine, mirth and laughter, all goes right merrily.

After the marriage feast is concluded, the couple reside in the house of the wife's parents for two years, and then for the same period in that of the husband's parents. If they are childless, they continue at the latter abode. A La-hu may only have one wife at a time.

Divorce on either side is at will, but must be accompanied by a payment of 40 rupees to the divorced party. The sons become the property of the man, and the daughters belong to the woman. The goods are divided equally, but two-thirds of the money and one-third of the clothing go to the man; and the remainder of the money and clothing, as well as the house, to the woman. Even if the wife is an adulteress, the husband must leave as soon as the division and settlements are made.

According to the La-hu, the chief seat of their race is on the east of the Salween river, about 30 days' journey north-west of Kiang Tung, where their chief town, Koo-lie Muang Kha, is situated at the head of the Meh Kha, a river which empties into the Salween.

In connection with the existence of gold to the east of the Salween, they told me that at Nong Sen, a place in the Lawa country to the north of Koo-lie Muang Kha, there was a very great quantity, but the people who live near the *Nong* (lake) dare not touch it for fear lest the *Pee*, or guardian spirit, of the locality should destroy them. Thirty Shans once persuaded a Lawa to guide them to the lake, under the promise that they would not remove any of the gold. On reaching it the Shans, under pretence of bathing, took off their clothes, and, whilst bathing, grubbed up the gold and swallowed as much as they could hold, and thus carried it away. One of them swallowed fully 30 rupees' weight, and others even more.

In the history of the Shan empire of Mung Mau, which has been translated by Mr Ney Elias, is shown the tribute payable to Mung Mau (a Shan State on the Shweli river that enters the Irrawaddi below Bhamo) by its tributary States about the close of the thirteenth century of our era, which likewise betokens wealth of gold in the country to the north of Kiang Hai. Monyin had to send a yearly tribute of a million horses (a large number is probably meant); La-mung (La-Maing, the ancient city of Zimmé), 300 elephants; Yung-Lung or Muang Yong (the Burmese Shan State to the east of the Salween to the north of Kiang Hsen, which most likely included Kiang Hsen and the rest of the Burmese Shan States lying to the east of the river), a quantity of gold; Muang Kula, or Kalei, water from the Chindwin; and Ava (which then included the ruby-mine district), 2 *viss* ($6\frac{2}{3}$ lb.) of rubies. The history of Loi Htong likewise refers to gold nuggets being found in the country.

The La-hu bury their dead in a coffin, and place the clothes of the deceased, together with food, on the top of the grave, so that the ghost may not trouble them for neglecting it.

In the evening, and in fact every night during our stay,

men and women were fishing together in lines by torchlight. The light of the torches attracts the fish, and brings them blindly dashing into the nets. Many were using drop-nets; others, cane baskets. Dr M'Gilvary told me that the men were very cautious not to chance coming into contact with the women whilst fishing, for should one chance even to tread on a woman's foot in the water, and sickness subsequently occur in her family, the ailment would be traced by a spirit-doctor to that act, and a fine would at once be levied upon the man by the *Kum-lung*, or elder, of the woman's family.

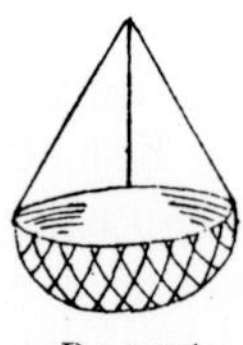

Drop-net.

CHAPTER XVII.

LEAVE KIANG HAI—A HOT SPRING—ELEPHANTS WITHOUT TUSKS—ELEPHANT-DRIVING—DANGER WHEN DRIVER IS CARELESS—A LARGE RICE-PLAIN—BARGAINING WITH THE ABBOT AT MUANG DOO—BLOODTHIRSTY FLIES—ELEPHANTS AS TOOL-USERS—INHOSPITABLE ANCESTRAL SPIRITS—GAME PLENTIFUL—UTTERANCES OF TIGERS—A MAGNIFICENT FOREST—A STINK-WOOD—WATER-PARTING BETWEEN THE KIANG HAI AND KIANG HSEN PLAINS—BRAVE BUTTERFLIES—A FIELD FOR AN ENTOMOLOGIST—PSYCHE IN BURMAH—A CENTRAL ASIAN BELIEF—THREE SACRED HILLS—BUDDHA AND CONFUCIUS—LEGEND OF LOI HTONG—VALLEY OF THE MEH CHAN—PASS TO MUANG FANG—KIANG HSEN PLAIN—SIAMESE AGGRESSION—DESERTED CITIES OF MANOLA—TIGERS—ATTACK ON KIANG HSEN IN 1794—WILD ANIMALS—LEGEND OF MUANG NŎNG—THUNDERSTORM—FLOODED COUNTRY—LEANING PAGODA—REACH KIANG HSEN.

On the morning of the 18th of March we said good-bye to Chow Nan and his son, and accompanied by the large crane as far as the ford, set off again on our journey. After crossing the river we struck north, and continued through low ground to the fields of Pan Pa Teun, the village of the *eng* forest, inhabited by witches who have been banished from other places. Near the village is a ruined pagoda; and from thence onward teak-trees are scattered through the forest. At 356 miles we crossed the Nong Ko Kheh, or lake of the Chinese bridge, and halted for breakfast. The lake is merely a straggling swamp, about 50 feet broad and 3 feet deep, which serves as a breeding-ground for fish. While the boys were getting breakfast I sketched Loi Pong Pra Bat, the hill of the hot spring from Buddha's footprint.

The large male elephant I was riding had no tusks, and was called by the driver Ko-dau, which I learnt was the ordinary term for tuskless males. Those with one tusk are known as Nga-aik. For the last half-mile we had been passing amongst bamboos and tall grass, and my mahout was guiding the elephants by knocks on the head. A knock on the left temple signified turn to the right; one on the right temple, go to the left; one on the forehead, go slowly; and the animal was warned to look about by the sharp utterance of his name. Unless a driver keeps his eyes to the front there is always a chance of the roof of the howdah being stripped of its covering, and of the occupant having his eyes thrust out, or being otherwise injured. Several times I have had the insecurely fastened howdah unbalanced by an awkwardly swaying animal bringing it into contact with trees. Then it is a case of saving self and things how one can, unless the mahout can support the howdah until further assistance arrives.

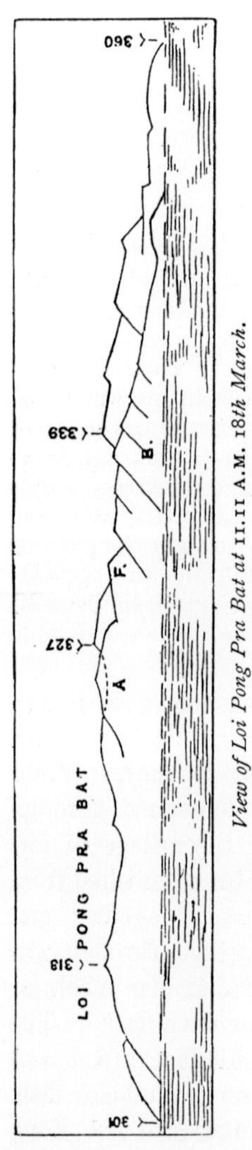

View of Loi Pong Pra Bat at 11.11 A.M. *18th March.*

Note.—A and B in a line < 300 at 1.55 P.M. A and F in a line < 294 at 2.58 P.M.

On leaving the camp we entered a rice-plain five miles long, at times more than a mile and a half broad, and fringed with beautiful orchards which contained splendid clumps of bamboos, and nestled several large villages. The foliage, although chiefly evergreen, had an autumnal aspect, owing to the bamboos shedding their leaves, and the buff-coloured young leaves of the mangoes, which had recently sprouted, aiding the delusion.

A mile from the camp we passed through Ban Doo, the village where import duties are levied. Here, on my return, I purchased from the abbot of the monastery several books concerning astrology, alchemy, sorcery, cabalistical science, and medicine. Seeing two silver images of Gaudama, with resin cores, I haggled with him for a long time over their price. At first he pretended that it was impossible for him to part with these images, as offerings had been made to them; but at the sight of many two-anna and four-anna bits his compunctions gave way, and I carried them off in triumph. They cost me dear, however, for on my sending them home, with other things, to my sister, our canny custom-house officials charged the resin as solid silver.

Large herds of cattle and buffaloes were feeding in the plain, and waging ceaseless war with their tails against myriads of bloodthirsty gad and elephant flies. The elephants were likewise greatly annoyed by these flying leeches, and carried leafy branches in their trunks to switch them off their bodies. No one who has seen elephants fanning themselves with great palmyra-leaves, switching at the flies, or scratching themselves with twigs, could consider man the sole tool-using animal.

On leaving the rice-fields at Done Ban Kwang, we crossed the Meh Khow Tome, near a village of the same name, and halted for the night. The Meh Khow Tome is 12 feet broad, 5 feet deep, and had 9 inches of water in its bed. Its name implies the "river of cooked rice," and is said to be derived from Gaudama having cooked rice on its banks when proceeding to impress his footprint on Loi Pong Pra Bat.

On reaching the camp I noticed rain-clouds gathering overhead, and asked the Chow Phya to arrange for our occupation of a large vacant house that had just been completed. On the arrival of the village head-man, he told us that owing to the spirits not having been propitiated, if any one slept under the roof misfortunes would certainly happen; and he begged us to refrain from doing so. He said game was exceedingly plentiful in the neighbourhood, and that wild elephant, rhinoceros, wild cattle, and pigs were often seen by the hunters; and deer, hare, pea-fowl, jungle-fowl, and quail were abundant.

Tigers, and, I believe, leopards, were prowling round the camp after nightfall; the clear "peet, peet" of the tiger and the "myow" came from different directions. The Shans, however, declared that they were both the cries of tigers—one when they were angry or in search of food, and the other when they were satisfied.

Early the next morning we recrossed the stream, and followed it up for four miles, the plain gradually rising as we proceeded. Teak-trees were sprinkled through the forest which neighboured the plain, and numerous yellow-flowered orchids hung in clusters from the branches of the trees. The forest gradually closed in, leaving a grass plain three-quarters of a mile wide, which we edged on the west, occasionally startling an elk-deer. A low hillock fringed the east of the plain, backed by a higher one three-quarters of a mile beyond it.

The forest was one of the most magnificent and varied I have ever seen. Padouk, thyngan, thytkado, wild mango, kanyin, banian, and many other fine trees whose names I do not know, grew to an enormous size. One looked for giants to match the trees, everything was so huge. The forest was a fit home for elephants and rhinoceroses. A kanyin-tree that I measured was 20 feet in girth 5 feet from the ground, and over 200 feet in height.

One of the men brought Dr M'Gilvary a piece of bark off a large tree, and after smelling it, he sent it to Dr Cushing, who, after doing likewise, forwarded it to me. It nearly knocked me down. Of all the horrible odours I ever met with, that was the worst. Bracken and other ferns, as well as screw-pines, flourished in the deep shade of the forest.

At 367 miles we crossed the Huay Pa Au, the last stream that enters the Meh Khow Tome, and fifteen minutes later, without any perceptible rise, reached the Huay Leuk, which is said to enter the Meh Chun. We had crossed the water-parting between the Kiang Hai and Kiang Hsen plains without being aware of it.

Half a mile farther we crossed the toe of a spur, and then passed amidst low hillocks until we reached a dry brook 6 feet wide and 5 feet deep, where we halted for breakfast. The hills had ceased, and we were in the Kiang Hsen plain. The height of the water-parting between it and the plain of

Kiang Hai was 1471 feet above the sea, and only 151 feet above Kiang Hai. Our camp was 369½ miles from Hlineboay, and 1447 feet above the sea.

Whilst inking the notes in my field-book, butterflies settled on my hand, and were as brave and persistent as house-flies. No sooner had I shaken them off than they were back again, being rocked on my hand as I wrote. The jungle, particularly in the neighbourhood of water, simply swarms with insect-life. An entomologist could fill a case in a morning's walk. He would have but to shake his net under the leaves of a few bushes for walking-leaves, stick-insects, ant-cows, lady-birds, and a variety of remarkable beetles, to drop into it.

Tiger-beetles, ground-beetles, bombardier-beetles, whirling water-beetles, mimic-beetles, stag-beetles, chaffer-beetles, click-beetles, scavenger-beetles, rove-beetles, sexton-beetles, chameleon-green beetles, glowworms, fireflies, floral-beetles, blister-flies, long-snouted beetles, capricorn-beetles, tortoise-beetles, ladybird-beetles—all are found in the jungle. Dr Mason, in his work 'Burmah,' states that Captain Smith collected specimens of nearly 300 species in Toungoo, a town in Burmah, on the Sittang river.

In connection with butterflies, Dr Mason remarks that "when a person dies, the Burmese say the soul, or sentient principle, leaves the body in the form of a butterfly. This too was the faith of the Greeks more than 2000 years ago. Among the ancients, when a man expired, a butterfly appeared fluttering above, as if rising from the mouth of the deceased. The coincidence is the more remarkable the closer it is examined. The *psyche* or soul of the Greeks, represented by the butterfly, was the life, the perceptive principle, and not the *pneuma* or spiritual nature. So the Burmans regard the butterfly in man as that principle of his nature which perceives, but not that of which moral actions are predicated. If a person is startled or frightened so as to be astounded for the moment, they say 'his butterfly has departed.' When a person is unconscious of all that is passing around him in sleep, the butterfly is supposed to be absent, but on its return the person awakes, and what the butterfly has seen constitutes dreams.

"The Greeks and Burmese undoubtedly derived these ideas from a common origin. In the Buddhist legends of the creation of man, which originated in Central Asia, it is stated that when man was formed, a caterpillar, or worm, was introduced into the body, which, after remaining ten lunar months, brought forth the living man; and hence the reason why a butterfly is supposed to leave the body at death."

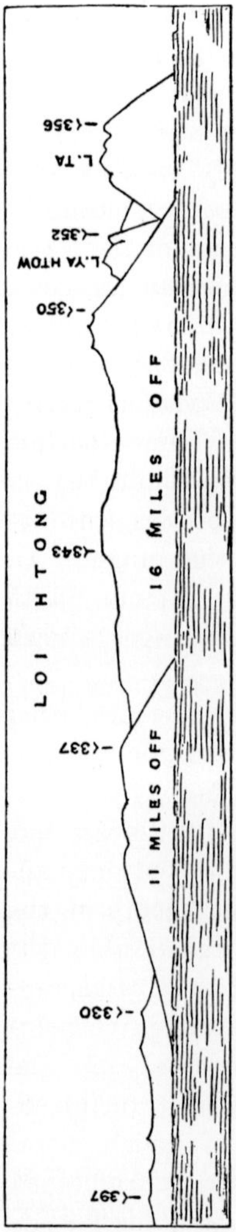

View of Loi Htong, Loi Ya Tow, and Loi Ta, at 2.34 P.M. 19th March.

Leaving the brook, I skirted some granite boulders, and halted for an hour in a grassy plain, a mile from the camp, to sketch Loi Htong, Loi Ta, and Loi Ya Tow. Where these hills come together, the end of each is precipitous, the precipices confronting each other. The villagers say that Loi Htong and Loi Ta were about to fight when Loi Ya Tow (Ya Tow, an honorific term given the grandmother on the father's side) stepped in between and stopped them. These hills, or rather the shrines on them, are held in high esteem by the people, and pilgrimages are made to them by pilgrims from great distances, as it is believed that many sacred relics of Gaudama, and of the three previous Buddhs, are enshrined there.

According to "The History of the Shrine of Loi Htong," which I borrowed from the pagoda slave who had charge of it, the shrine, which is situated in a cave on the summit of the hill, contains 566 relics of Gaudama, the last Buddh. These relics consist of his collar-bones, the hair of his head and body, his teeth, and the little stones, as large as mustard-seed, found in the ashes after the body was burned: 500 of them were deposited there shortly after the Buddh's death by Phya A-soot-a, the king of Kiang Hsen; 50 by the king of Muang Yong, the State to the north of Kiang Hsen, a hundred years after the death of the Buddh; and 16 by a *russi*, or hermit, 1980 years later, or in A.D. 1437.

Further to attract pilgrims to the shrine, the history relates that all the four Buddhs of the present *lawka* [1] visited the shrine, and that the third Buddh called twelve celestial fountains into existence in its neighbourhood. Worshippers bathing in one would be healed of all their diseases, and have every desire fulfilled. Another conferred wisdom. Another enabled a person to see the spirits, who are shrouded from mortal vision by a white veil. Another dispelled all angry passions. Another renewed youth and youthful desires. Another was for the Yaks, or ogres, to bathe in. One of the fountains on the east of the shrine is guarded by a serpent that lives in the heart of the mountain. The shrine is said to be guarded by two monkeys who were placed there by Gaudama Buddh at the time of his visit, when he ordained that offerings of fruit, flowers, and rice should be made to the monkeys and their descendants by the people, and that all making the offerings should prosper greatly.

Another part of the history relates that three hundred years after the last Buddh's death a Tay-wa-boot,[2] or male angel, brought a young banian-tree from Himapan, and planted it to the north of the shrine. Whoever wished to obtain sons or daughters had only to place a prop under the eastern branch. One placed under the northern branch would ensure the attainment of all earthly blessings. One placed under the western branch would cure all bodily ail-

[1] During the present *lawka*, or existence of the world, four Buddhas are said to have appeared. The dispensation of each lasts 5000 years. Gaudama Buddha was the last of the four, and his death, according to the Ceylon histories, occurred B.C. 543, but according to Professor Muller, B.C. 477, or a year after that of Confucius. A *lawka* is a whole revolution of nature. The world, according to Buddhists, is continuously destroyed and reproduced, but each *lawka* lasts an incalculable length of years.

[2] A Dewah, or inhabitant of Indra's heaven.

ments. A person placing a prop under the southern branch would attain Neiban, the state of peaceful restfulness, the highest bliss desired by a Buddhist.

The history likewise contains a few particulars about the early relations of the Shans with the Lawas, and the foundation and dynasties of Kiang Hsen.

During my halt a jungle-fire sprang up in the long grass, and the elephants became restless. My companions, therefore, went on to the place where we were to camp for the night, and my mahout took his elephant out of sight of the fire. I was so bent on sketching and taking angles, that I woke up from my work surprised to find myself alone. Loogalay, with the heedlessness of a Burman, had loafed off with the other servants, when he ought to have been in attendance upon me. Following the track for about half a mile, I found my elephant waiting for me, and continued through the grassy plain, where the trees were still in leaf, and soon afterwards crossed the Meh Chan, or Meh Tsan as it is called by the Burmese Shans. The Meh Chan is a stream 30 feet broad, 7 feet deep, with 2 feet of water in the channel. It flows from the west, but turns north-east at our crossing, and enters the Meh Khum near Kiang Hsen.

After passing some distance through the straggling village of Ban Meh Chan, a suburb of Ban Meh Kee, I halted to sketch the hills, which stretch for 25 miles to the west, and enclose the valleys of the Meh Chan and Meh Khum. Mr Archer, of our Siam consular service, who crossed from Muang Fang into the valley of the Meh Chan in 1887, reported that the pass between the source of the Meh Chan and the Meh Khoke (Meh Khok) was some 2650 feet above the sea. As the Meh Khoke, where crossed by him, must have been at least 1500 feet above the sea, the rise in the 18 miles from the Meh Khoke to the top of the pass would have been only about 1150 feet, and the fall in the 32 miles from the pass to Ban Meh Kee (Më Khi) only 1200 feet. There would therefore be very little difficulty in connecting Muang Fang with Kiang Hsen by a railway.

The Kiang Hsen plain extends for 12 miles to the west

of Ban Meh Chan, the hills forming an irregular amphitheatre, with a diameter of 17 miles. To the south the plain is fringed by low isolated hills and hillocks; to the north-east it stretches for 18 miles to the Meh Kong; and it continues northwards for 43 miles up the valley of the Nam Hu-uk (Më Huok), or for 20 miles beyond the fort that has recently been built by the Siamese at Viang Hpan (Wieng Phan), on the Meh Sai. If we include the Kiang Hsen, Kiang Hai, and Penyow plains, which are conterminous, the total length of this vast plain is over 115 miles. Assuming its average breadth as 10 miles, there is ample room in it for a million people to earn their living by agriculture. Viang Hpan lies 23 miles north of Ban Meh Chan.

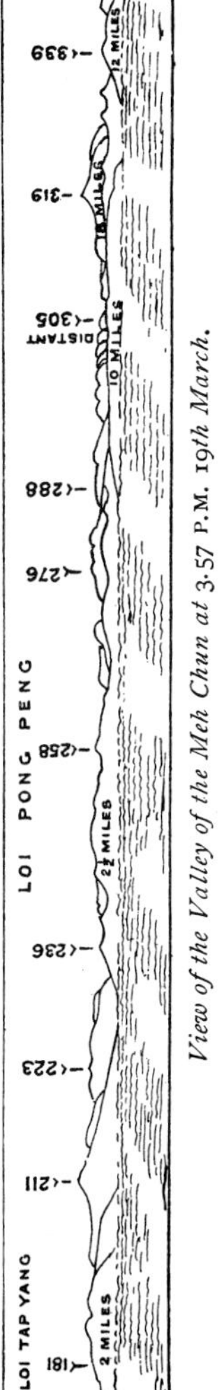

View of the Valley of the Meh Chun at 3.57 P.M. 19th March.

At the time of my visit, the Siamo-Burmese frontier passed between Ban Meh Kee, the northernmost Siamese Shan village, and Ban Meh Puen, the southernmost Burmese Shan village, the two villages being distant some 1950 feet. At the time of Mr Archer's visit the Siamese had encroached 22 miles within our frontier, by building their fort on the Meh Sai. Unless this is rectified, disturbances will certainly occur between the Ngio Shans, our subjects, and the Siamese. Even as it is, our subjects consider that the Meh Khoke to its mouth forms their proper boundary, and that the Siamese had no right to encroach beyond that river.

After an hour's halt, I again started, and passing through the village, crossed the stream, and traversed a teak-forest for the next ten minutes. Most of the small hillocks that are scattered about the plain are covered with teak-trees. Leaving the forest, I again entered the plain, which was covered with thatching-grass, and crossed to where my party was encamped on the banks of the Meh Chan. The camp was situated 376 miles from Hlineboay.

Leaving early the next morning, we continued through the plain, which was much cut up by irrigation-channels, and had evidently at one time been under cultivation, and halted for breakfast on the outer fortifications of the centre one of the three ancient cities of Manola, which lay on our left.

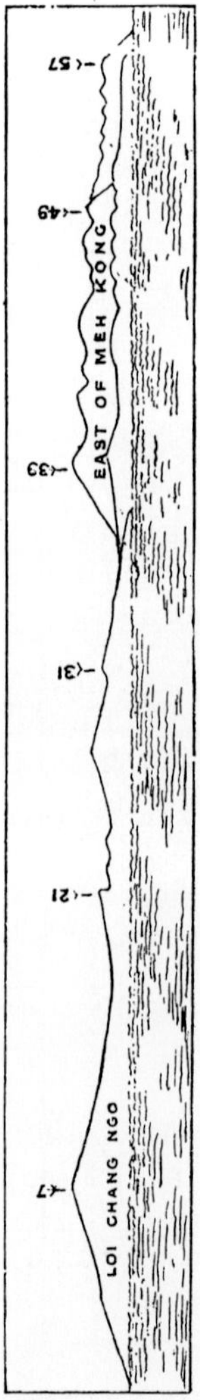

View of Loi Chang Ngo at 4.49 P.M. 20th March.

The three cities of Manola, "the silver mountains," are said to have been built by the Tay-wa-boot, or male angels. They are each about half a mile in diameter, and are erected on separate knolls. The ditch of the one visited by me was 100 feet wide, and 40 feet deep from the top of the inner rampart. Great trees, some over 100 feet high, growing on the fortifications, indicated that the city must have been deserted for two or three hundred years. Close to the city, at the eastern suburb of Ban Kyoo Pow, a tiger had seized a cow the previous night, on the banks of the Meh Chun, and both had rolled into the river; the tiger was so surprised that it allowed the cow to escape. The owner, hearing the noise, fired off his gun to scare the tiger.

The people of the neighbouring village complained of the ravages committed by wild pigs; thirty of these animals had rooted up part of their crops the previous year. According to the villagers, the enormous plain we were passing through was entirely under cultivation previous to A.D. 1794-97, when Viang Chang and Luang Prabang besieged Kiang Hsen; but now the greater part of it is covered with elephant-grass, and forms the haunt of vast herds of deer, black cattle larger than buffaloes, rhinoceroses, and other wild animals. Wild elephants are at times seen in the unsettled parts of the plain, but none had been captured recently.

There were no ruins in the city; but after leaving it I noticed in a teak-forest, near the village of Ban Pa Sak, the remains of a pagoda and temple. A mile and a half to the right of the village is a hillock called Loi Koo, or the hill of the royal sepulchre. Continuing through the plain, we came to the village of Meh Tsun Tsoor, where a tiger had endeavoured to carry off cattle the previous night, but had been frightened away by the villagers. We halted for the night at Pang Mau Pong, or the camp of Dr Pong, a celebrated hunter.

Phya In or Indra.

Loi Chang Ngo (the hill where the elephant became drowsy) commences about four miles north of the camp, from which there is a fine view of it, as well as of Loi Saun ka-tee (the hillock to the north of Kiang Hsen), and some distant precipitous hills lying to the east of the Meh Kong. Loi Chang Ngo derives its name from the following legend: Before the destruction of Muang Nŏng by Phya Then, or Indra, the sacred white elephant left the city, and went trumpeting to Chang Hsen; hence its name (Chang, an elephant; Hsen, trumpeting). From Kiang Hsen it proceeded to Loi Chang Ngo, and disappeared. It is supposed to be slumbering there still.

The legend of Muang Nŏng relates that Phya Then was incensed at the inhabitants of the city eating white eels—most white animals, except white men and white cats, are considered sacred by the Shans—and submerged the city, turning the site into a lake. Only a hunter's house, which was built on the outskirts, remained. He had asked the people for some of the fish, but had been refused. The name Phya In, used by the Zimmé Shans for Indra, seems to be a compromise between the Phya Then of the Burmese Shans (which is doubtless derived from the Tien of the Chinese) and the Indra of the natives of India.

The Koo Tow.

During the evening (20th March) we had a heavy downpour of rain, accompanied by thunder and lightning.

The next morning, after leaving the village fields, and crossing the Meh Chan for the last time, we passed between a newly raised footpath and a ditch for about half a mile. The footpath had been raised, because, when the Meh Kong is in high flood, the ground about here and between this and Kiang Hsen is occasionally inundated by the Meh Khum. At 389 miles we skirted a hillock, called Loi Ngome, on our right, and soon afterwards came to the village and fields of Hsan Hsoom Hpee. Many low hillocks were now seen at distances varying from 800 feet to four miles to our right. A short distance from Kiang Hsen I halted near an irrigation-canal, 100 feet wide and 6 feet deep, to visit the Koo Tow, a celebrated leaning pagoda, which, unlike any other pagoda that I have seen in Indo-China, has been built in the Chinese style. The figures of the Tay-wa-boot or male angels, which are executed in bas-relief in excellent plaster, are Burmese in design. The pagoda is circular, and about 75 feet high; the upper 60 feet rising in three storeys, like a drawn-out telescope. Each storey is divided into two by an ornamental band, above which are Tay-wa-boot with hands upraised and palms pressed together in adoration, and below which are similar Tay-wa-boot with hands pressed together in front of their chest. Before the pagoda a Burmese image of Gaudama has been erected, which was still in good condition with the exception of the loss of a hand and an arm.

On remounting the elephant, a deer sprang up from the long grass close by and crossed the track. Six minutes later I crossed the Meh Khum, or golden river, 80 feet broad and 9 feet deep, with 3½ feet of water; and three-quarters of a mile from the pagoda, entered the fortifications which enclose the west central gate of Kiang Hsen. The gate opens on to one of the main streets of the city, along which we passed amidst numerous ruins of religious buildings, and a few clusters of recently built houses, to the *sala* or rest-house, which we occupied during our stay. The *sala* is situated 1274 feet to the west of the Meh Kong, or Cambodia river, 393 miles from Hlineboay, 1097 feet above the sea, and only 89 feet higher than Zimmé.

CHAPTER XVIII.

THE MEH KONG AT KIANG HSEN—RINGWORM—EXTENSIVE RUINS—DESCRIPTION OF CITY—IMPORTANCE OF SITUATION FOR TRADE—CHINESE SETTLERS FROM SSUCHUAN, KWEICHAU, AND YUNNAN—PROJECTED RAILWAY—SURVEYS BEING MADE BY KING OF SIAM—EXCURSIONS FROM KIANG HSEN—TEAK-FORESTS—ROBBING AN IMAGE—LEGEND OF KIANG MEE-ANG—ANCIENT CITIES—COMPARISON BETWEEN ANCIENT BRITONS AND SHANS—ANCIENT PRINCIPALITY OF TSEN—KIANG HUNG—DESTRUCTION OF KIANG HSEN—CARRIED AWAY CAPTIVES—TREACHERY IN WAR—POPULATION OF ZIMMÉ CHIEFLY SLAVES—KIANG HSEN REOCCUPIED IN 1881—RESETTLING IT—ACTION OF KING OF SIAM—FRIENDLY FOOTING OF MISSIONARIES—VIEW ACROSS THE KIANG HSEN PLAIN—FLOODED COUNTRY—LEAVE FOR KIANG HAI—A WHITE ELEPHANT—BRANCHES AS SUNSHADES—ELEPHANT-FLIES—EMIGRANTS FROM LAPOON—BEAUTIFUL SCENERY—MR ARCHER'S DESCRIPTION OF TRAFFIC ALONG THE ROUTE.

WHILST the elephants were being unloaded and the servants were preparing breakfast, the Chow Phya, or district officer of Kiang Hai, who had been deputed to accompany us to Kiang Hsen, went to the Chow Hluang's to inform him of our arrival, and we strolled to the bank of the Meh Kong, the Cambodia river of the French, to see the view.

We found ourselves a few miles above the entrance of the Meh Khoke, which is here separated from the Meh Khum by a long hillock, called Loi Chan (the steep hill). Just below the mouth of the Meh Khoke, the Meh Kong commences its great eastern bend, which stretches through two degrees of latitude to Luang Prabang.

The distance between Kiang Hsen and Luang Prabang by boat is about 200 miles, and the journey was performed by Dr M'Gilvary in six days. The first day's journey took him to Kiang Khong, a city of two or three thousand inhabitants, and the capital of a district under Muang Nan. In describing the river between Kiang Khong and Luang Prabang he says: "The river is a mile wide in places, and where the channel is narrowed it rushes along with frightful rapidity. Mountains rise from either bank to the height of three or four thousand feet. The river fills the bottom of a long winding valley, and as we glided swiftly down it there seemed to move by us the panorama of two half-erect, ever-changing landscapes of woodland verdure and blossom. Only as we neared the city did we see rough and craggy mountain-peaks and barren towering precipices."

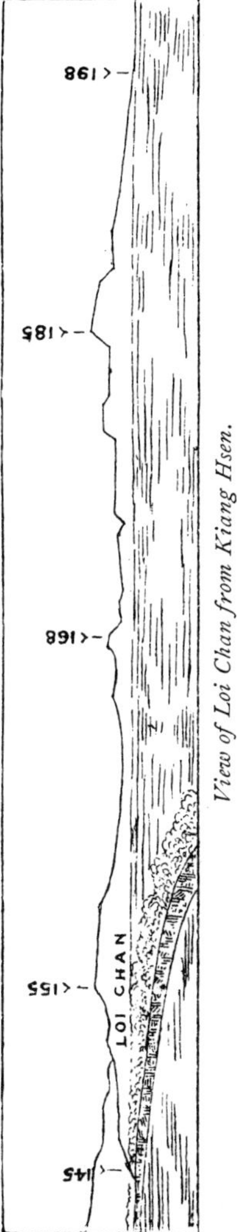

View of Loi Chan from Kiang Hsen.

The scenery from the bank of the river at Kiang Hsen was magnificent. The great river flowing in its deep channel, partially restricted by sandbanks, was a mile wide, 21 feet below its banks, and unfordable. To the east, about 40 miles distant, a mass of mountains about 30 miles in length, and perhaps forming part of the long winding valley spoken of by Dr M'Gilvary, showed boldly against the sky; to the north-east, nearer the river, rose the precipitous hills we had previously seen from Pang Mau Pong; and between the mountains and the river, the country appeared to be a vast forest-covered plain, in which low hills were visible at 4 and 20 miles' distance.

To the south, beyond Lāun Ten (the island of the embankment), a tree-clad island, containing the ruins of many religious buildings, which is said to have been the site of an extensive city, and to have been joined on to the mainland, is the mouth of the Meh Khoke; and beyond it, on the same bank of the river, Loi Meh Yap closes in the view, and separates the valley of the Meh Khoke from that of the Meh Yap.

On our return to the *sala,* the Chow Phya of Kiang Hai informed us that the Chow Hluang was away on a fishing excursion, and that the Chow Hona, the second chief, was absent at Zimmé. The son of the Chow Hluang and the chief Chow Phya of Kiang Hsen had returned with him to pay us a visit, and see how they might add to our comfort. They said that doubtless the chief would return by the day after the morrow, as although some distance away, he would certainly hasten back as soon as the messengers they had already despatched reached him.

View of hills east of the Meh Kong river.

The son of the chief was sorry his father was not there to welcome us, and still more so that, owing to smallpox raging in his own family, he was himself unable to offer us hospitality. He thought we would be more comfortable in the court-house, which was a new and capacious building; but on visiting it with him, we found it in an unfinished condition, and only partially floored, so determined to remain in our smaller but more cosy quarters.

Seeing the Chow Phya covered with ringworm, I gave him some Goa powder, and told him how to apply it. I afterwards learnt that it worked a perfect cure, for the Chow Phya showed his gratitude by writing to Dr M'Gilvary, and forwarding me a copy of the history of Kiang Hsen, which I had expressed a wish to obtain. The work, however, proved to be valueless, except as a curiosity. Mrs M'Gilvary, who kindly offered to translate it for me, finding it utterly unreliable—indeed, merely an olio of Buddhist legends and improbable events—soon threw the manuscript aside, considering it useless to waste further time upon it.

After breakfast we rambled through the city, about half of which was covered with the remains of fifty-three temples, and of monasteries and pagodas in their grounds. The seeds of the pipal tree, *Ficus religiosa*, had been dropped

The great bend of the Meh Kong from Kiang Hsen.

by birds into the interstices of the brick masonry of the pagodas, and grown into large trees. The roots of the trees, after shattering the masonry, had prevented it from falling, by clasping it in their strangling embrace. Splendid bronze images of Gaudama, generally in a good state of preservation, were scattered about in every direction, and often half buried in the *débris* of the fallen buildings.

The images varied from 6 inches to 7 feet in height, and one known as Taung-lan-ten is an object of pilgrimage to hundreds of worshippers from the British and Siamese Shan States. This image, which is about 5 feet in height, has a legend attached to it, which relates that, when the great bronze image, now at Ava, known as the Aracan Buddha, was cast, a fabulous bird, called a galoon, alighted at the site, and fanned the furnace with its wings; and a *naga*, or dragon, came and blew the fire up with its breath. As their reward for these meritorious acts, Gaudama resolved that in their next birth they should be born men, and the galoon should cast a similar image at Kiang Hsen, and the *naga* one at Zimmé. A bamboo and thatched shed had recently been erected over the image as a temporary shelter,

Ruins at Kiang Hsen.

in place of the handsome building, with pillars and tiled roof, whose remains lay shattered around it.

What struck me most in the ruins of the temples was the vast number of the images, the excellence of the plaster which still adhered to the remains of the massive brick walls and pillars, and the beauty of the ornamental decorations. The people of the city in olden times must have been numerous, wealthy, and highly skilled in the arts, to account for the number of the monasteries, and the workmanship displayed in the images and buildings.

Kiang Hsen is built in the form of an irregular parallelogram, with its sides facing the cardinal points. The city, which is about 11,057 feet long, and 3900 feet wide, is protected on three sides by double ramparts and a ditch. The eastern side is unprotected; the fortifications, together with about a quarter of a mile in width of the city, having been swept away by the encroachment of the river. The outer rampart, having a base of 70 feet, is 12 feet wide at the top, and 14 feet high; its outer slope is much flatter than the inner one. The inner rampart has a base of 75 feet, and is 18 feet in height. In its centre is a wall 2½ feet wide, from which the earthen slopes extend for 30 feet within the city, and for 43 feet outside. The crenelated

Plaster decoration on pillars.

top of the wall having been destroyed, a strong teak palisade 6 feet high has been erected against its inner side as a protection. The ramparts are 97 feet apart from the centre of their crests, and the bottom of the ditch is 30 feet wide, and has silted up to the level of the ground inside and outside the city. The entrances to the city are fortified by double courtyards, defended by brick walls and palisading, and by an outside ditch, as shown on the sketch. There is a large gap in the southern ramparts, which is said to have been made when the Lao Shans attacked the city in 1797.

Kiang Hsen is admirably situated for purposes of trade, at the intersection of routes leading from China, Burmah, Karenni, the Shan States, Siam, Tonquin, and Annam. It forms, in fact, a centre of intercourse between all the Indo-Chinese races, and the point of dispersion for caravans along the diverging trade-routes. When the country is opened up by railways, and peace is assured to the Shan States to the north by our taking them fully under our protection, the great trade that will spring up between Burmah, Siam, the Shan States, and China, will make the city of great importance. Its position as a commercial centre in the midst of the vast plains which extend on both sides of the river; its bountiful climate and productive soil; the wealth in teak and other timber, as well as in minerals of the surrounding regions; and the fact, brought out by Mr Bourne in his report, that Chinese from Ssuchuan (Szechuen), Kweichau, and Yunnan, are settling in the Shan States to the north of it, will soon tempt immigrants to take up the now vacant land, and ensure the city and district a large and prosperous population.

The King of Siam is fully aware of the great value of the region, and has been doing his utmost for several years to increase its population, by resettling the country with the descendants of its inhabitants that were taken captive, or else had fled from the Burmese into the Siamese Shan States. The king is likewise having surveys made by English engineers for the portions of the Burmah-Siam-China Railway lying within his territories, and has likewise instituted surveys for branches to connect Zimmé, Luang Prabang, and Korat with the railway. These surveys, together with estimates for the construction of the lines, are to be completed in three years from March 1888.

During our stay at Kiang Hsen, I spent my time in sketching, taking observations, and in collecting information about the country. I was thus unable to accompany my companions upon some of their rambles. One of their excursions led them to Muang Hit, the site of a city on the east of the river, about three miles to the north of Kiang Hsen. No remains were found, with the exception of the old moat, an inscription on the bronze cap of a pagoda, giving A.D. 1732 as the date of its erection, and a house and clearing that had recently been deserted. Iron-mines exist near the ruins, but the neighbouring country was uninhabited except by deer, tigers, leopards, wild cattle, and other wild animals.

View of western hills.

Three Burmese Shan villages, containing 130 houses between them, had recently been built a mile or two above Muang Hit. The boundary between the Burmese and

British Shan States would therefore cross the river about this city.

Teak is the principal tree in the forests on both sides of the river, and even the ruins in Kiang Hsen were partially hidden by teak-trees that had sprung up since its desertion. From Kiang Hsen to Kiang Hai, teak is found on most of the hillocks.

Another day they visited the site of the ancient city of Kiang Mee-ang, which is situated on the west bank of the river, five or six miles above Kiang Hsen, at the point where the Meh Kee-ang joins the Meh Kong. It had lately been colonised by the Ping Shans, and about forty houses had been built there at the time of Dr Cushing's and Dr M'Gilvary's visit. The path to the ruins led along the bank of the river, and was thickly wooded with excellent teak-trees. No remains were found, with the exception of the moat, and the ruins of a shrine which had been erected on the summit of a hill.

The principal image in the temple had been executed in plastered brickwork, covered with the ordinary coatings of *damma* and gold-leaf, and some sacrilegious plunderer had knocked its head off in order to obtain any treasure that might be contained inside. According to Dr Cushing, it is the custom of the Shans, when constructing a brick image, to make a square cavity running down from the neck to the vicinity of the heart, to be used as a receptacle for pieces of silver, which are generally put in to represent that organ.

On asking the chief, on his return to Kiang Hsen, about Kiang Mee-ang, he said there was a remarkable legend attached to it, which ran as follows: The chief of Kiang Mee-ang (who died three years before the destruction of Kiang Hsen), owing to his abundant merit, had the power of calling up armed allies from any direction to which he turned his face. During his lifetime his State was at peace. When the Ping Shans conquered the country, they sent his body, which was covered with a complete mask of gold-leaf (also an ancient Egyptian custom), to the Siamese king at Bangkok. The King of Siam, knowing the merit of the deceased ruler, and fearing that his power might adhere to his corpse, had it buried face downwards, as no army could invade Siam from that direction.

The chief told us that many other cities were scattered about the country, but owing to their having been depopulated during the wars of last and the beginning of this century, most of their names had been forgotten. There are, according to him, many ruins at Peuk Sa (a consultation), which is otherwise known as Kiang Hsen Noi, and lies between the city and the Meh Khoke. Muang Poo Kah (the city of the kine-grass troops) lay to the north; Muang Ko, about two days' journey above the city; Kiang Hpan, near Loi Ta; Muang Nong (the submerged city), to the south near the Meh Khoke; Viang Wai (the bamboo city), to the west of Ban Meh Kee; Muang Loi (the city of the hills), a mile to the north of Kiang Hsen, and Kiang Mak Nau.

Some of the cities whose names are lost are known as Chinese cities, and are said to be the remains of fortified camps erected by the Chinese in bygone ages, during their various invasions of the country. Others are said to have been built by the Lawas when they held sway in the country. Some were erected by angels, *nyaks* (serpents or dragons), and genii; and those of later construction, by the Shans.

Many of the cities bore a strong resemblance to the ancient Celtic fortresses found by Cæsar in Britain, which are described as fastnesses in the woods, surrounded by a mound and trench, calculated to afford the people a retreat and protection during hostile invasion of their territory. The Venerable Bede, who was born in the seventh century of our era, described the mode of erecting fortified Celtic camps as follows: "A vallum, or rampart, by which camps are fortified for repelling the attack of enemies, is made of turf cut regularly out of the earth and built high above the ground like a wall, having a ditch before it, out of which the turf has been dug, above which stakes made of very strong timbers are fixed." This exactly describes many of the fortified cities and camps in the Shan States.

There is likewise a resemblance between the appearance,

customs, and habits of the Shan tribes, and those of the earliest known inhabitants of Britain, who are said to have belonged to the tawny, black-haired section of mankind. Both were divided into numerous petty tribes and sections of tribes, often at war with one another, and generally devoid of everything like unity or cohesion, even under pressure of foreign invasion; both were given to offering up human sacrifices in order to appease the wrath of local deities; and both races tattooed their bodies. The Shan house-architecture likewise resembles that of the ancient Britons, whose houses and cattle-sheds were formed with reeds and logs, surrounded by stockades constructed of felled trees. Houses built of bamboo matting and logs, with palisaded enclosures, are the ordinary type of architecture in the Shan States.

At one time the principality of Hsen or Tsen (some Shans aspirate the initial, and some do not) was far more extensive than it is at present. From B.C. 330 to B.C. 221, when the kingdom of Tsoo was conquered by the Emperor of Ts'in, Tsen was tributary to Tsoo; and at the time the Chinese conquered South-western Yunnan (B.C. 108), Tsen, then a state of Ma Mo (a Shan kingdom in the upper part of the Irrawaddi valley) confederation, extended southwards from the Yunnan lake, and eastwards to Nanning. It probably comprised the Shan States of Tsen-i-fa or Kiang Hüng, Tsen-i or Theinni, and Kiang Tsen amongst its *muangs*, which became feudatory to Burmah between A.D. 1522-1615.

The upper part of the old principality of Tsen, when formed into a separate State, was known to the Chinese as Chan Li (Chang Li), and later as Che-li. This principality was broken up by the Chinese in A.D. 1730, when they forced the chief to pay tribute for the six *pannas* (or districts) lying to the south of Ssumao and to the east of the Meh Kong, and annexed the portion of his territory lying to the east of the Meh Kong, that extended as far north as half-way between Puerh and Chen Yuan Fu, and as far south as and comprising Ssumao. Thus the chief of Che-li (the Kiang Hung of the Shans, and the Kaing Yung-gyi of the Burmese) became tributary to China, as well as feudatory to Burmah.

In conversation with the Chow Hluang of Kiang Hsen, he told us that he was descended from the ancient line of Kiang Hsen, as well as from the ruling line of Zimmé. The present capital, according to him, was built in 1699, and destroyed by the Ping Shans in 1804. In giving the history of its destruction, he said that in 1778, four years after the Ping Shans had thrown off their allegiance to Burmah and become feudatory to Siam, the Lao Shans of Vieng Chang and Luang Prabang became tributary to Siam, and, urged on by Siam, besieged Kiang Hsen from 1794 to 1797.

During the siege the Lao forces were commanded by Phya Anoo, the chief of Vieng Chang, who, enraged at the long resistance, issued a proclamation declaring that every male found in the city should be put to death on its capture. This made the resistance of the besieged desperate. The Lao finally succeeded in undermining and breaching the middle of the southern wall, when a storming-party under Phya Tap Lik made an entrance; but so fiercely were they met by the defenders, that they were not only driven back, but their leader was captured, and subsequently drowned in the Meh Kong. A month later the Lao forces gave up the siege, being unaware of the fact that famine was raging in the city, and would, if the siege had continued, soon have forced its inhabitants to surrender.

Between 1779 and 1803, according to the history of Zimmé, Kiang Hsen was attacked six times by the Ping Shans, and only taken by them in 1804. During the siege by the Lao in 1797, a body of 300 Ping Shans established themselves as an army of observation near the city, but did not take part in the operations. An agreement is said to have been made with their commander, that if he would return with 3000 troops, the inhabitants would kill the Burmese troops and open the gates.

Previous to its fall in 1804, the commander of the Ping troops, which included the joint forces of Zimmé, Lakon, Nan, and Pheh, secretly informed the chief of Kiang Hsen that they had only come to accede to his former proposal, and merely wished Kiang Hsen to throw off the Burmese yoke and become feudatory to Siam, as the Ping Shans had already done; and he promised that, if the inhabitants of Kiang Hsen would massacre the Burmese governor and his troops and open the gates, the Ping Shans would form a defensive and offensive alliance with them. The inhabitants of Kiang Hsen accordingly slew the Burmese governor and the 300 Burmese soldiers who were within the walls, and opened the gates to the Ping Shans. They soon found to their cost that they had been treacherously dealt with. The city was destroyed; some of the people escaped across the Salween and settled in Mokmai and Monay, and the rest were taken captive to the Ping States, and distributed amongst them. With the Shans treachery is an ordinary occurrence in warfare: the persons deluded are ashamed at having been taken in; the successful party chuckles and crows over his cleverness.

From the time when Kiang Hsen was captured till 1810, Ping Shan armies frequently raided into the Burmese Shan States—proceeding as far west as the Salween, and as far north as the border of China—sacked the towns, and carried away the inhabitants into captivity. The late General M'Leod, when at Zimmé in 1837, states in his journal that "the greater part of the inhabitants of Zimmé are people from Kiang Tung, Muang Niong (Yong), Kiang Then (Tsen or Hsen), and many other places to the northward. They were originally subjects of Ava (Burmah)." In another passage he says: "They, with the Talaings (Peguan Burmese), comprise more than two-thirds of the population of the country."

The Chow Hluang told me that before he left Lapoon to take up the government of Kiang Hsen, when it was reoccupied in 1881, his retainers numbered fully 30,000 souls, amongst whom were 2500 fighting men. Every man from eighteen to seventy years of age, who is not a slave, is reckoned as a fighting man; and allowing one grown man to every five souls, there must have been fully 6000 grown men amongst his dependants. This proportion between full-grown slaves and fighting men shows that there were about 17,500 slaves amongst his 30,000 retainers. The descendants of Burmese refugees and captives in war are classed as slaves by the Siamese and the Ping Shans, and are parcelled out amongst the ruling classes. His statement must be taken with a grain or two of salt, as the chiefs are apt to give Falstaffian accounts of the numbers of their retainers.

In order to repopulate Kiang Hsen, which had been deserted for seventy-seven years, the King of Siam ordered a list to be made of the descendants of captives that had been taken from that State, so that they might be sent

A Shan house in Kiang Hsen.

there. This list, when forwarded to Bangkok, included 500 full-grown men in Lapoon, 1000 men in Lakon, and only 370 men in Zimmé. The chief of Nan, although there were over 1000 full-grown men in his State descended from Kiang Hsen captives, refused to comply with the order, on the plea that Nan had lately repopulated the country to the north of the great bend of the Meh Kong. He further stated that he would on no account form a joint settlement with people from the Shan States of Zimmé, Lakon, and Lapoon; but if they failed in being able to settle Kiang Hsen, Nan by itself would settle it. The chief of Lakon likewise remonstrated against the order, urging, as an excuse for not obeying it, that, as his State had established and repopulated Penyow and Ngow, it was but just that the other States should have the glory of establishing Kiang Hsen.

The King of Siam, having but a small hold upon Nan, thought fit to admit its excuse, but ordered that Lakon must send 1000 full-grown men; Zimmé, 1000; Pheh, 300; and Lapoon the whole of the dependants of the prince who had been appointed ruler of Kiang Hsen. Lakon absolutely refused to comply with this order, and it was only after he was charged with rebellion by the king that he consented to send between 500 and 600 men with their families to Kiang Hsen. Up to the time of my visit the people had been merely arriving in dribblets, and only 607 houses had been erected in the State, of which 139 were in the city. The Chow Hluang said many immigrants from Lakon, Zimmé, and Lapoon were then on their way to Kiang Hsen, as the King of Siam was determined that the full tally ordered by him should be completed. Many of these immigrants were met by me when returning to Kiang Hai. On the Burmese side of the frontier the Moné Shans, the Ngio, had erected 641 houses.

The Chow Hluang appeared to be very angry with the chief of Lapoon, his former suzerain, for preventing some of the 2500 serfs, who had offered to follow him as their liege lord, from leaving Lapoon. It is the custom among the Ping Shans for a serf to have the right of changing his allegiance from one lord to another if he wishes to do so, and this right has always acted as a great check to the growth of oppression. On the Chow Hluang being appointed to Kiang Hsen, 2500 serfs placed their names on his list, and offered to accompany him with their families and slaves.

The rainfall is not nearly as plentiful in Lapoon as it is in Kiang Hsen, and the plains of Kiang Hsen are renowned for their fruitfulness: thus the people would greatly improve their prospects by the change; besides which, there are always fewer Government monopolies in the frontier districts. Kiang Hsen, being made into a separate State, would not be dependent upon Lapoon. The Chow Hluang of the latter State was therefore naturally averse to losing a large body of his people, and had consequently obstructed the emigration by all the means in his power. The chief of Kiang Hsen, tired of remonstrating with the chief of Lapoon, had appealed to Zimmé and Bangkok to have him compelled to send his adherents to Kiang Hsen.

The chief of Kiang Hsen was an old acquaintance and friend of Dr M'Gilvary, and seemed well pleased to see him. Nothing struck me more during my journeys than the high estimation in which the American missionaries were held by the chiefs. Not only were they on a kindly and friendly footing with them, but by their bold strictures upon acts of injustice, and by exposing and expostulating against the wickedness and senselessness of certain of the reigning superstitions, they had become a beneficent power in the country.

During our stay the chief did all he could to make us comfortable; sent us the best fruit, fowls, and vegetables at his disposal, and allowed an ox to be killed for us, although there were at that time not more than sixty oxen amongst the settlers in the whole region. After the animal was slaughtered, cut up, and removed, its late companions, attracted by the scent, gathered round the spot in the most pathetic manner, sniffing at the ground, and time after time, when driven away, returning, and wandering uneasily about, as if aware that some ill fate had befallen their comrade.

The day before we left Kiang Hsen, I took a walk to the pagoda on Loi Saun-ka-tee, the hill to the north of the city, in order to sketch the hills to the west of the plain, and, as far as possible, fix their position. The air was clear, and I got a splendid view. Loi Htong, Loi Ya Tow, and Loi Ta, which I had previously sketched on entering the Kiang Hsen plain, now lay a little to the north of west, at a distance of about seventeen miles. Farther to the north, Loi Pa Hem loomed up in the distance, and seemed not to belong to the same system of hills: this hill was passed by M'Leod when on his way to Kiang Tung in 1837. The great plain we were looking at, in which a few hillocks outcropped, extended to the foot of the mountains, but its northern and southern extensions were hidden by the low hills on which we were standing, and the hillocks which we had skirted on our way to the city.

On calling to say good-bye, before leaving on March 24th, I asked the chief about the floods that occasionally happened in the plain to the south of the Meh Khum. These, he said, were chiefly caused by the flood-waters of the Meh Kong backing up the water of the Meh Khum. When the Meh Kong was at its highest, the inundation sometimes rose two and a half feet over the bank, but the flood never extended north of the Meh Khum, nor farther inland than Loi Champa and Hong Seu-a Teng (the fishery where the tiger leapt); and even in this strip of plain there was a space between the Meh Chun and the Meh Khum, extending to Ban Nan Hta, which was never overflowed. The land near the mouth of the Meh Khoke, and for some distance up-stream, was also subject to inundation, the flow of the water in that river being impeded by water-weeds. Having finished my calls, and made presents to the chief and officials, and thanked them for their hospitality, we had the elephants loaded, and a little after one o'clock in the afternoon left the city.

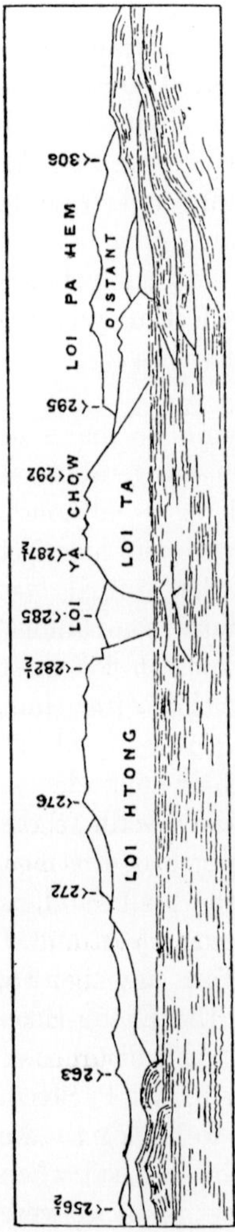

View of hills west of Kiang Hsen Plain from pagoda on hill.

The first night we halted at Pang Mau Pong, where we had stayed on our way to Kiang Hsen. I chose a different elephant for the return journey, much against the wish of the Chow Phya, who was accompanying us; it being considered *infra dig.* for a gentleman to ride any but a male beast. But I preferred ease to dignity; my former long-legged elephant having jolted me with its jerking pace, and the one I chose, although a female, moving with an exceptionally easy gait. The elephant-driver, on my noticing that its head was salmon-coloured speckled with darker spots, assured me that if it had been a male, it would have been honoured as a white elephant, and presented to the King of Siam. My eyes had become so inflamed with the constant glare from the white paths, and from peering at the small figures on the silver rim of the prismatic compass, that I was obliged to give up night-work as far as possible, and on my return to England I had to commence wearing spectacles.

The next morning we started at 6 A.M., all feeling much better for our long halt at Kiang Hsen. The boys were

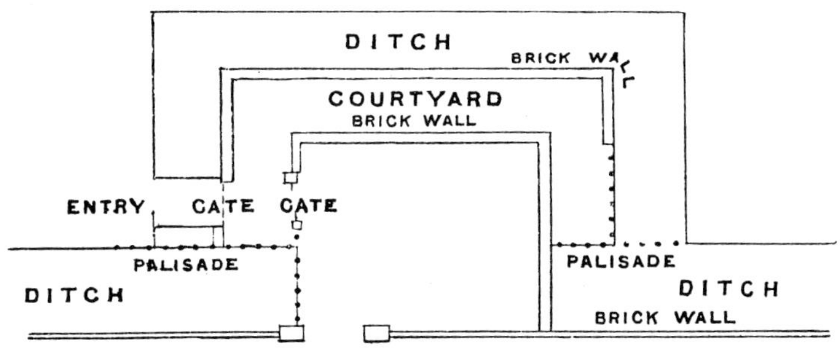

City enclosure. Sketch of an entrance to Kiang Hsen.

quite rejuvenated, and walked along briskly under their umbrellas in the fresh morning air, singing scraps of songs as they went, joking with each other, and with all whom they met. When tired by a long journey they become jaded, and walk as if they have tar on their feet. After passing two caravans of laden cattle conveying the goods of some immigrants from Zimmé, we halted at a village to purchase fresh vegetables, but could only procure a few onions. Some of the trees had sprouted after the rain on the 21st, and everything was looking fresher than before.

Starting again, we passed some men carrying eel-spears, and stopped for breakfast at Kyoo Pow on the banks of the Meh Chun, where we bought some bringals and mustard-leaves. Many doves were cooing in the trees, and did not go into a pie, as I refused to let the boys have the gun to shoot them. We likewise saw a few green paroquets.

After breakfast we were off again, the elephant-men carrying leafy branches to shelter their eyes, as we were proceeding due west. We passed another caravan of laden cattle, and halted for the night at Ban Meh Kee. I had thoroughly enjoyed the journey—being mounted on an easier beast, and having a complete holiday, as I had previously surveyed the route.

Next day we woke up with the thermometer marking 57°, and were off before 6 A.M. An hour later we met a caravan of sixty-three laden oxen conducted by Burmese Shans on their way to Kiang Tung. The leading oxen had masks, embroidered with beads, on their faces, surmounted by peacocks' tails. We then entered the evergreen forest—where the gibbons were wailing, and doing wondrous feats of agility, outleaping Leotard at every spring—and halted for breakfast amongst some gigantic *kanyin* and *thyngan* trees.

In the afternoon we made a short march to our former halting-place at Meh Khow Tone. The gadflies in the forest were nearly an insupportable nuisance. These vampires were so intent upon drawing blood, that they never moved as my hand slowly approached to crunch them. They are noiseless on the wing, and painless in their surgery. One is unaware of their presence until a ruddy streak appears on one's clothing. The elephants constantly scraped up the dust with their trunks to blow at the flies, where they could not reach them with the leafy branches that they carried. Our boys hurried along, armed like the elephants, slashing at the flies on their shoulders and backs. We were all glad to reach the camp.

Shortly before halting we passed several hundred emigrants from Lapoon, squatting down and enjoying their mid-day rest, with their packs by their side, and their oxen grazing close by. A great part of their baggage was borne by the men on shoulder-bamboos.

We were off before six the next morning, and after passing fifteen Kiang Tung Shans on their way back from Maulmain with their purchases, a Chinaman carrying three huge iron pots for distilling, and caravans of forty cattle carrying the goods of some of the Lapoon emigrants, we entered the Yung Leh rice-fields. Rain had evidently fallen since we passed through them on our way to Kiang Hsen; the scene was changed as by an enchanter's wand, and had now the aspect of spring. Young leaves were sprouting on the trees, even the evergreens were decked with them, while the leaf-dropping bamboos looked quite fresh, the rain having freed them from their coatings of dust. Paddy-birds had arrived, and were perched in flocks upon some of the trees, making them in the morning mist look a mass of white blossoms. Five great *jo-jas* (slate-coloured cranes) strutted through the plain, companies of caravan Shans were dotted about, under temporary mat shelters, with their packs stacked by their sides, and large herds of cattle were grazing in the distance. The mist rising and falling as it cleared off the valley, gave us beautiful peeps at houses nestled in the orchards, which framed either side of the plain. The whole scene formed an ideal landscape, the realisation of an artist's dream—a scene to which one would fain recur.

After halting for a quarter of an hour at the monastery in Ban Doo, to bargain with the abbot for some magical and medicinal books, we hurried along to the ford of the Meh Khoke, crossed the river, and were welcomed by our old friend the *jo-ja*, who still acted as sentinel to the rest-house outside Kiang Hai.

In the account of his journey from Kiang Hsen to Kiang Hai in February 1887, Mr Archer, our consul at Zimmé, brings out the importance of the trade converging at Kiang Hai, and passing over the portion of the route we had traversed to the Burmese Shan States and China, along which we propose the railway to China should be carried. He states that "the road from Ban Me Khi (Meh Kee) to Chienghai (Kiang Hai) is probably the greatest and most important thoroughfare in the whole of the north of Siam, and the traffic here is comparatively very considerable: in the course of a day I passed many caravans of pack-animals, some consisting of a long file of over a hundred bullocks.

The greater proportion of the traders were Ngios (Burmese Shans) from Chiengtung (Kiang Tung), who came to purchase goods in Chiengmai and Lakhon (Zimmé and Lakon), chiefly cotton goods, iron, and salt. Very few of the Laos (Ping Shans) seem to venture into Chiengtung territory for trading purposes; in fact, it is apparent that the Laos cannot compete with the Ngio and Toungthoo traders and pedlars. This, again, is the route taken by the Ho, or Yunnanese traders, on their yearly trading expeditions to Moulmein (Maulmain)."

In another report Mr Archer gives the route now taken by Chinese caravans from Yunnan to Ootaradit (Utaradit), the city at the head of navigation for large boats on the Meh Nam. He says: "The route followed by this caravan was from Yunnan (Fu) to Puerh, Ssumao, Kiang Hung, Muang Long, Muang Lim, Kiang Hsen, Kiang Hai, Peh, and Utaradit or Tha-It. These caravans come down to Tha-It every year, but the greater part go eastward towards Chieng Mai (Zimmé), and some as far as British Burmah. These traders are pure Yunnanese, and are called Hō by the Siamese." It is interesting to know that this direct route from Yunnan Fu to Penyow, which lies between Kiang Hai and Peh, passes through the same places as our proposed railway from Maulmain, and will therefore greatly facilitate its survey.

CHAPTER XIX.

AT KIANG HAI—FEROCIOUS DOG—CHINESE PACK-SADDLES AND MULES—ROUTES FROM CHINA—ARTICLES OF MERCHANDISE—RICHNESS OF KIANG HSEN PLAIN—VISIT THE CHOW HONA—MAN KILLED BY WILD ELEPHANT—CHIEFS WISH FOR RAILWAY—WOULD HELP BY GRANTING WOOD FOR BRIDGES AND SLEEPERS—KAMOOKS FOR LABOURERS—CHINESE SHANS AND CHINESE WOULD FLOCK IN FOR HIRE—EASIEST ROUTE FOR LOOP-LINE TO ZIMMÉ—TREES LADEN WITH WOMEN AND CHILDREN—DR M'GILVARY PURCHASES AN ELEPHANT—RECEIVES PRESENT FROM CHOW HONA—SUNDAY SERVICE—UNSELFISHNESS OF DR M'GILVARY—LAPOON IMMIGRANTS—DEATH-RATE OF IMMIGRANTS—BOXING—A WOMAN IN CHAINS—LEAVE KIANG HAI—YOUNG ELEPHANTS A NUISANCE—A YELLOW-TURBANED MONK—FIREWORKS—WHISTLING ROCKETS—GIGANTIC ROCKETS AT FUNERALS—A LOVELY LOLO-LAWA WOMAN—SPRING BLOSSOMS—CROSS THE WATER-PARTING BETWEEN THE MEH LOW AND THE MEH ING—HOT SPRINGS—HOUSES ERECTED FOR US—FISHERIES—ARRIVE AT MUANG HPAN—FORMATION OF A SETTLEMENT—EMIGRANTS TO KIANG HSEN IN 1887—PROSPERITY OF COUNTRY—MR ARCHER'S OPINION—THE FATHER OF THE STATE—LIKE A HIGHLANDER—DESERTED CITIES—AN ANCIENT CHRISTIAN—VIANG POO KEN—RAPID DECAY OF BUILDINGS IN A MOIST CLIMATE—ANTS AT WORK—DAMMING STREAMS FOR FISHERIES—INJURY TO DRAINAGE—THE MEH ING A SLUGGISH STREAM—A HARE—OPPRESSIVE ATMOSPHERE—SEARCHING FOR WATER—BOILING MUD TO MAKE TEA—A DISTRESSING MARCH—CITY OF CHAWM TAUNG—A CELEBRATED TEMPLE—BUDDHIST LEGEND—A GOLDEN IMAGE SIXTY FEET HIGH—LEGEND OF PENYOW—A BUDDH FORTY-FIVE FEET HIGH—GAUDAMA EXISTING FORMERLY AS INDRA—A SHAN RACHEL—REACH PENYOW.

WHILST the elephants were being unpacked, I approached the mule-loads of a large Chinese caravan encamped near our *sala*, to take the dimensions of a pack-saddle. The Yunnanese muleteers were some distance away, squatting on the banks of the river, enjoying their pipes and a chat, having left their goods in charge of a fierce Tartar dog, somewhat like a Pomeranian, or rather a cross between a Pomeranian and a wolf. On seeing me touch one of the saddles the dog rushed forward, snapping from all directións. I did not like to strike the dog for doing its duty; I was therefore greatly relieved when the head-man, seeing my dilemma, ran up and called him off. After greeting me, he unloosed the packs from one of the saddles so that I might examine it. It was ingeniously suited to its purpose, and consisted of a light wooden frame formed to the curve of a mule's back, and had a raised arch in the centre to prevent it from resting on the animal's spine and thus giving it a sore back. Saddles and packs are securely fastened to each other, and are loaded and unloaded together.

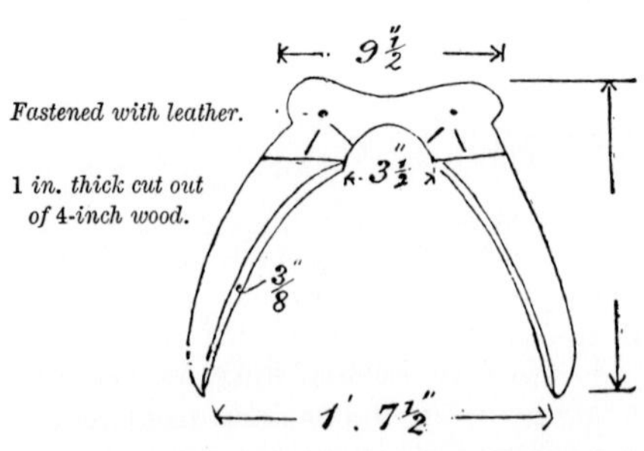

CHINESE PACK-SADDLE—FRONT VIEW.

The animals are sagacious and well trained, and come when called. At the time of loading, a saddlecloth is placed on the mule's back, the saddle with the packs attached is lifted by two men, the animal passes underneath, and the saddle is placed on its back and kept in place by a crupper, and harness embracing the chest and rump. No belly-band is used, and the whole is quickly adjusted. Many small brass bells are placed on the trappings, and the leaders sometimes have a bell shaped out of resonant

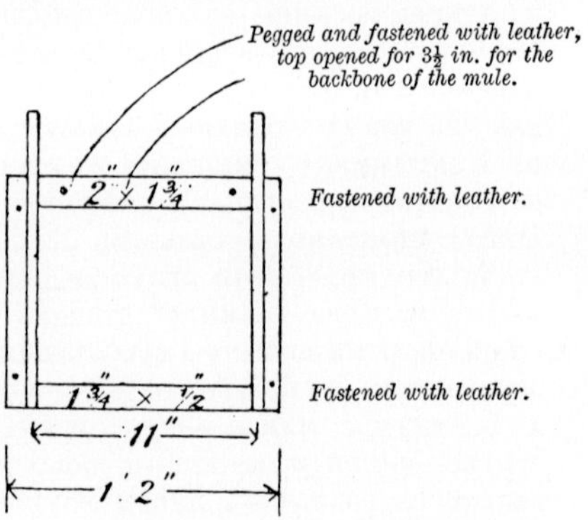

CHINESE PACK-SADDLE—SIDE VIEW.

wood, fitted with a clapper, and hung over their heads. The tinkling of the small bells and the clatter of the large ones enable the men to trace their beasts if they stray during a halt, and give warning of their approach to elephant-drivers, so that they may back the elephants from the path, and thus save them from being scared. The only arms carried by this company of Chinese consisted of a couple of ancient horse-pistols and a large iron trident.

The traders from Yunnan generally proceed *viâ* Ssumao, Kiang Hung, Muang Long, and Muang Lim—places neighbouring the Meh Kong—to Kiang Hai, whence they find their way *viâ* Zimmé to Maulmain; *viâ* Penyow and Peh to Ootaradit, or Tha-It, in Siam; and spread by various routes over the Ping Shan States, to purchase raw cotton to carry back on their return journey. Some of the caravans returning from Maulmain sell their European goods at Kiang Tung, proceeding to it along the route traversed in 1837 by M'Leod. A few of the caravans coming south likewise use this route, in order to dispose of some of the broad-brimmed straw hats they purchase in Yunnan. These hats are supplied with oilskin covers, and sell at Lakon, according to quality, at three rupees and six rupees each. They likewise bring from Yunnan opium, bee's-wax, walnuts, brass pots, ox bells, silk piece-goods, silk jackets—some of which are lined with fur—silk trousers, figured cloth, and tea. From Kiang Tung they carry lead, *dahs* or swords, steel in ingots, lacquer-boxes, tea, and opium.

Noticing that the head-man wore a skull-cap of horse-hair worked into a handsome lace, which he had bought for a rupee and a half, I purchased it from him for two rupees. On my showing him some black and white kinds of tailor's thread, he tried their strength, and said that he had never seen any like them before, and when their virtues were known in Yunnan they would have a good sale, as they were much stronger than ordinary cotton-thread.

After breakfast one of the Christians from Ban Meh Kee, who happened to be in Kiang Hai, hearing of our arrival, came to see Dr M'Gilvary. He said the land in the Kiang Hsen plain was exceedingly fruitful, and that last season he received a return of fully 250 baskets of paddy for each basket sown.

Learning that the Chow Hona, or second chief, had returned, we went to call on him. On approaching his house we noticed four ladies winding silk in the verandah, one of whom at once went to call him. After welcoming us warmly, he said a wild elephant had just killed a man close to the city. The man's companions, on seeing the elephant approach, had clambered up trees, and shouted to him to do likewise. He refused, saying the elephant would not hurt him. After the elephant had passed, they again called to the man, and receiving no answer, searched the jungle, and found his remains quite mashed up. The prince said this elephant was so fearless that it was in the habit of crossing the rice-fields close to the city in broad daylight. The Chow Hluang had issued an order against its destruction, as it was of enormous size, and served as a stallion for his female elephants. His feet, as measured from his footprints, were two feet broad; and therefore, as the height of an elephant equals double the circumference of his feet, his height would be 12 feet and 3 inches, or greater than that of any of the King of Siam's elephants. There is a general belief amongst the Burmese and Shans that the spirits of human beings who have been slain by an elephant ride on the animal's head, warning him of his approach to pitfalls and hunters, and guiding him to where he may kill people, so as to add to their own company. It is therefore considered hopeless to even fire at one which has destroyed many men. Tracking a wild elephant on foot is always dangerous, as it is liable to return on its path and attack its pursuers.

We had a long chat with the prince about the proposed railway. He appeared to be a very intelligent man, and although gaunt and ungainly in build, with an awkward gait, possessed great strength, and was evidently very active. His temperament was high-strung, and his black bead-like eyes wandered in every direction with a vigilance that nothing could escape. He seemed much interested in the extension of trade with Burmah, Siam, and China, and said the chiefs and people would be delighted if the railway was put in hand. Every help they could give would be gladly rendered; that teak was plentiful in the country, and free permission would certainly be granted to cut it for the sleepers and bridges. As for labour, as many Kamooks as would be required could be hired from Luang Prabang. Their wages for working in the teak-forests were fifty rupees a-year and food, and the latter did not cost more than three rupees a-month. Gangs of Chinese Shans from the Shan States to the east of Bhamo come every year to work in the Ping Shan States, and could be employed on the railway. Other Shans would doubtless stream in from Yunnan when once it was known that more labour was required, and that good wages would be paid. A great part of the labour in Kiang Tung is carried out by Chinese from Yunnan.

The following day the Chow Hona breakfasted with us. In answer to our inquiries, he said the easiest route from Zimmé to Kiang Hsen was *viâ* Viang Pow and Muang Fang, crossing the Meh Khoke at Ta Taung, and thence over Loi Kee-o Sa Tai (2650 feet above the sea) to the Meh Chun, and along that river to Ban Meh Kee, where the route joins that which we had taken. A better route we afterwards found would be from Zimmé *viâ* Muang Ngai; thence up the Meh Pam, and over the Pe Pau Nam (water-parting) into the valley of the Meh Fang. The pass over the water-parting is only 2158 feet above the sea. From Muang Fang this route would follow that indicated by the prince, which was traversed by Mr Archer in 1887. The loop-line could be completed by joining Zimmé with the main line again at Lakon, or, *viâ* Muang Li, near the mouth of the Meh Wung.

On our returning his call, we found some of the fruit-trees in his garden absolutely laden with women and children picking the fruit, and teeming with laughter and merriment. Dr M'Gilvary, being very much pleased with the paces of the female elephant I had been riding from Kiang Hsen, had arranged on the journey to purchase it from the mahout, who was its owner, for 500 rupees, and had just learnt that the Chow Hluang, whose serf the owner was, had decided to purchase it for 400 rupees, and that the man dare not say him nay. On his telling the Chow Hona of his disappointment, he said he would at once go and expostulate with the chief about it. It was only right that Dr M'Gilvary should have the animal, as he had made the first and highest offer, and it was not fair that the man should be robbed of 100 rupees. He asked us to stop, and said he would be back in a few minutes. On his return he told us he had been successful; and that the Chow Hluang, who had not previously heard of Dr M'Gilvary's offer, had at once given up his claim. As a mark of his friendship for the Doctor, the Chow Hona insisted upon presenting him with a handsome covered howdah for the elephant, and would not hear of payment being made for it. I noticed many similar instances of friendship on the part of the nobles I met on my journeys towards Dr M'Gilvary, who seems by his utter unselfishness and frank cordiality, and great tact and kindness, to have won the esteem of the people of the country.

On the 30th March, being Sunday, he held a service in the town, and had a large audience of Shans. His delivery is very simple and unaffected. The man is a thorough gentleman at heart, as well as an earnest enthusiast in his mission. The more I saw of him, the more I liked him. I never, during our long journeys together, saw him do a selfish action. When tired, and nearly worn out with insomnia and fever, he sat up late, night after night, to translate for me, because otherwise I could not procure the information I required, as everything had to be packed and the elephants off by daybreak.

Many hundreds of Lapoon immigrants on their way to Kiang Hsen were encamped near our *sala*, and one morning fully 1000 others crossed the river on their way to Kiang Hsen. It is pitiful to learn from Mr Archer that he was told by the Chow Hluang of Kiang Hsen in 1887, that about a third of the immigrants had died since the foundation of the colony in 1881. In Mr Archer's words, "The privations the early settlers had to suffer probably increased the mortality; but fever was doubtless engendered by clearing the rank vegetation, and will lose much of its virulence when the country is better occupied."

One morning the mist lifted from the valley of the Meh Khoke, and I was able to sketch the hills stretching thirty miles to the west, or as far as the eye could reach. It was evident that the great rib spurs jutting towards the river from the northern range were very much higher than the backbone from which they sprang: this seems frequently to be the case in the hills between the Meh Kong and the Salween.

View up the Meh Khoke from Kiang Hai.

Whilst watching a couple of the elephant-drivers boxing with regular boxing-gloves, our old acquaintances the Moosurs came to pay us a visit, and again brought their children with them. It was merely a case of "How-do-you-do?" and "Good-bye," as we had to go to the Chow-Hluang's to complain about two of the promised elephants not having arrived. On reaching his house he told us that the wife of the owner of the elephants had sent word that the elephants had been scared by a jungle-fire, and had stampeded; that her husband was away after them, and had not yet returned. On our telling the Chow Hona the cause of the delay, he ordered the woman to be brought to the Court-house and put in chains. The elephants were at once brought in, and we were able to start on the morrow.

Next morning, the 31st March, the Chow Hona and Chow Nan Kyow Wong, our companion from Zimmé, came to see us off, and were accompanied by the Chow Phya, or head judge of Kiang Hai, who had been told off to conduct us to Penyow. Six large elephants, two of which had babies with them, had been hired for us, and Dr M'Gilvary rode the elephant he had purchased. I once more chose an easy-going female elephant for myself, and had the amusement of watching the pranks of its big baby during the march. These young elephants were the source of immense fun, but were an intolerable nuisance to the men on foot, whom they delighted to playfully tumble over like ninepins when the opportunity, for which they were always on the alert, occurred. By half-past six we had said good-bye and left Kiang Hai, which is 183 miles distant from Zimmé by the road we were to take. The mileage on this journey implies the distance from that place, and therefore gets less as we proceed.

Leaving the city by the south gate, we journeyed for ten miles through the plain to the village of Yang Tone, situated on the Meh Low, where we halted for breakfast. Our march led us through or near eleven villages, all of which were embosomed in orchards fringed with beautiful feathery bamboos. On our way we met a caravan of thirty laden cattle, a company of eight Burmese Shans, and a Buddhist monk wearing a huge yellow turban, similar to those worn by the monks in the Chinese Shan States.

Ban Yang Tone is a large village stretching along the banks of the Meh Low, and contains a fine temple and monastery. On entering the latter, we found the monks and their acolytes making fireworks, amongst which were rockets to be used at an approaching festival. These rockets were formed of a tube of bamboo, 14 inches long and 2 inches in diameter, tied to a light bamboo 15 feet long, the head of which had been turned into a whistle. Ten other whistles, of various lengths and notes, were fastened round the head of the rocket. When fired, the rocket ascends to a great height, and is accompanied by music made by the air rushing through the whistles. Other rockets of great size are made for setting fire to the funeral pyre on which the bodies of monks are burned. According to Mr Scott (Shwé Yoe), in his admirable work 'The Burman,' some of these rockets "are of huge size, constructed of the stems of trees hollowed out, and crammed full of combustibles, in which sulphur largely predominates. Many are 8 or 9 feet long and 4 or 5 in circumference, and secured by iron hoops and rattan lashings. Up in Mandalay some are very much larger. These are let off at the funeral pile from a distance of 40 or 50 yards, the largest being mounted on go-carts, and many others guided by a rope fastened to the *pyathat*, the rocket sliding along by means of twisted cane loops."

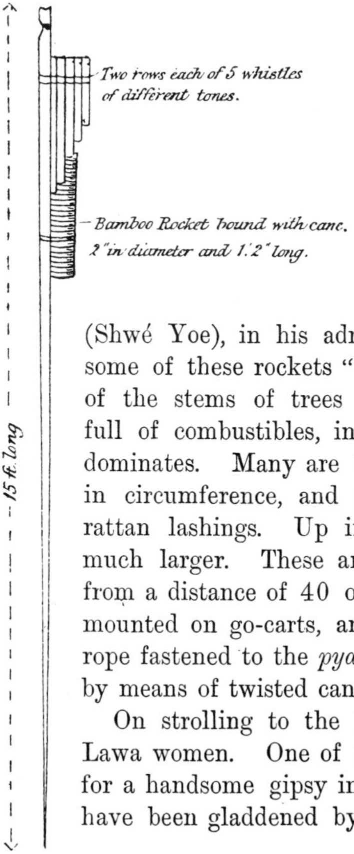

Rocket-stick of bamboo, formed into a whistle at the top.

On strolling to the Meh Low, I met two Lolo-Lawa women. One of these would have been taken for a handsome gipsy in England. An artist would have been gladdened by the chance of securing such perfection for his model. The grace of her pose, the faultless symmetry of her person, her fearless aspect, and perfect self-possession, her pleasant voice, and the courteous unconstrained manner in which she answered my questions, bespoke her one of nature's fairest works. Unluckily I had only the bumptious village elder Portow with me to catechise the woman;

and a crowd of village boobies soon gathered round, who looked upon the whole matter as a joke, and jeered at the woman and her friend. She soon became justly and proudly irate, and refusing to impart further information, walked disdainfully away. The few words of her vocabulary that I procured, placed it beyond doubt that she was of the same race of Lawas whose villages I had passed in the upper portion of the valley of the Meh Low after leaving Muang Pa Pow. She said that she resided in one of the five Lawa villages that are situated in the basin of the lower portion of the Meh Low, which together contained about a hundred houses.

Leaving the village, we traversed a great rice-plain, and entered a forest of bamboo, in which many teak-trees were scattered. We soon afterwards crossed the Huay Wai, upon which is situated, three hours' journey up-stream, the ancient city of Viang Wai (the rattan-cane city). Some of our men who made a detour through the city, reported that one of its gateways was still erect, and there were ruins of a temple inside the walls. The forest we now entered was brightened by yellow, orange, and red blossoms, and some of the trees were decked with tender spring foliage. After passing many teak-trees and another village, we crossed the Meh Low, here 300 feet wide and 12 feet deep, with 2 feet of water, and halted for the night at the pretty village of Ban Long Ha. We had travelled 15 miles during the day, and had risen 120 feet since we left Kiang Hai.

The next morning we were off by half-past five, and after skirting an old cut-off bend of the Meh Low (the *ow* in Low is pronounced as in " cow " in English), crossed the saddles of three small hillocks which mark the water-parting between the Meh Low and Meh Ing. The aneroid marked a fall from our camp to the crest of the saddles; but as there must have been a rise, I have assumed it to be 10 feet. The valleys between the hillocks are inundated to the depth of 3 feet in the rainy season.

Continuing through the vast plain, which, as near as I could judge, averages between 25 and 30 miles in breadth, we halted for the night not far from Ban Poo-ken, the headquarters of the governor of the district, which is known as Muang Hpan or Muang Phan.

Referring to this small province in 1887, Mr Archer writes: "Muang Phan, a cluster of villages half-way between Chienghai[1] (Kiang Hai) and Phayao (Penyow), forms an agreeable contrast to the new settlements farther north. The plain, laid out in rice-fields interspersed with fruit-gardens and villages, is bounded on the west by gently sloping mountains (an isolated hill); the scenery is picturesque, and the general appearance of cultivation and prosperity is most refreshing.

"The former capital of Muang Phan is said to be situated at the foot of the low range of hills which bound the plain on the east, and a new town is now being founded on its site.

"The history of this small province is interesting, as showing in what manner colonies are effected, and how confusing are the boundaries of the different States. The country was evidently deserted during the early part of this century; later, a part of it was occupied by people from Lakhon (Lakon), who, however, afterwards withdrew farther south. About fifty years ago a settlement was made by people from Lamphun (Lapoon), who have since gradually brought the country to its present prosperous condition. Muang Phan is therefore governed by the State of Lamphun, though not adjacent to it; but both Lakhon on the south and Chienghai on the north lay claim to at least a portion of the little province.

"Whilst at Muang Phan, I witnessed another phase in the formation of settlements in this country. The chief of Chiengsen (Kiang Hsen) having received permission to establish in his province a number of the inhabitants of Muang Phan, proceeded, in the language of the country, to drive the people into the new colony. However sound may be this policy of migration, it was impossible not to commiserate the unfortunate people who were thus driven from a comfortable home into a bare, uncultivated country, where

[1] Mr Archer gives the Siamese pronunciation of the names; I give that of my Burmese-Shan interpreters.

it would cost them many years of struggle to recover only a portion of their former prosperity. Unable to dispose at so short a notice of their houses, their gardens, and fertile rice-fields, they were compelled to abandon everything that could not be easily transported. I met many of these families, some carrying their children, or perhaps the domestic fowl, in their arms; and some, such few household goods as they were able to remove.

"Muang Phan, as well as the district under Phayao (Penyow) directly to the south, is populous, and appears, indeed, to enjoy greater prosperity than most of the surrounding country. It is well irrigated, and the crops are generally good, while many of the other common necessaries of life are here abundant and cheap. Fish is indeed very plentiful in the extensive lake, or rather marsh, that occupies the centre of the plain, and it forms an important article of export, giving rise to a considerable trade with all the neighbouring States."

Our proposed railway passes through both Muang Phan (Muang Hpan) and Phayao (Penyow) on its way to Kiang Hsen.

Having erected our tent with the aid of a few bamboos borrowed from the villagers, we sent a messenger to inform the Pau Muang (father of the State), or governor, of our arrival. Soon afterwards he came in and welcomed us, and sat down with us to dinner. He was a powerfully built, grey-haired, massive-headed old gentleman, about 5 feet 10 inches high; and had it not been for his costume and language, might have been taken for a fine old Scotch Highlander.

On receiving notice of our intention to pass through his province, he had set to work collecting transport for us; but only three elephants had as yet been brought in from the district, which, with sixty porters, he hoped would be sufficient to carry us and our baggage. After thanking him for making these arrangements, we said perhaps it would be better that the elephants with us should continue as far as Penyow, in which case we should not require additional means of conveyance. To this our elephant-men were agreeable, and thus a burden was taken off the governor's mind.

He told us many deserted cities existed in his neighbourhood. Viang Poo Ken lay about half a mile west of our camp; Viang How, on the Meh Hsan; another Viang How, on the Meh Ing; Viang Teung (the city of teak-trees), on the Meng Loi; Viang Hsen Kong; and Viang Lau (Viang Law), on the Meh Ing, three days' journey above Kiang Khong. He then drew a map on the ground with pieces of bamboo and matches, and explained to us the features and lie of the country.

The next day a Christian, eighty years of age, came to visit Dr M'Gilvary; and Dr Cushing rambled with me through the villages, and strolled under the shade of noble trees, through splendid park-like scenery, to Viang Poo Ken. This deserted city is about half a mile square, and is divided into three compartments. Its outer rampart was 10 feet high, and its ditches 50 feet wide and 10 feet deep. Another fortress, circular, and 400 feet in diameter, crested the top of the hill. No ruins were found in the city and fortress. Buildings built of wood or bamboos, if vacated in a moist climate like that of the Shan States, rot away in a few years, and leave no trace behind them. Even brick and stone buildings, when deserted, are rapidly destroyed by pipal-trees, and crumbling down, are covered with turf in the course of centuries. Those navvies the ants are ever throwing earth over the masonry records of past generations. These workers are nowhere more numerous, and their work is nowhere more speedily accomplished, than in Indo-China.

We left Muang Hpan in the afternoon, and made a short journey of 4½ miles to the Huay Kok Moo (the stream of the hog pens), where we halted for the night—having crossed several small streams and canals all flowing eastward into the Meh Hang, or into the fisheries through which that stream passes on its way to the Meh Poong. Huay Kok Moo itself, however, flows into a large lake-like marsh which serves as a fishery, and forms one of the principal sources of the Meh Ing. A cutting from the latter fishery into the Meh Poong, which enters the Meh Ing, would shorten the course of the Mêh Ing by 30 miles, and save the Penyow plain from inundation, thus enabling a vast tract of country to be cultivated.

The population being sparse in the State, and not even a tenth of the available land having been taken up for agriculture, the people have thrown dams across some of the streams to turn them and the low-lying country into fisheries, into which shoals of *plasoi*, or young fish, ascend from the Meh Kong. This river commences to rise in April with the melting of the snow, and is in high flood in July or August. When at its highest, it inundates large tracts of country which serve as breeding-grounds for the fish. As the waters subside, the young fish enter the streams, and appear in dense lines fringing the banks on their way up-stream. The dams are partially removed at the close of the fishing season, to allow fresh fish to enter when they come up-stream to breed. Incalculable harm is being done to the drainage of the country by the fisheries, as the upper courses of the dammed streams will in time silt up, when great expense will be required to relieve the water-logged country. Streams should not be bunded until the end of the rains, and all dams should be removed before they commence.

The haze of the atmosphere, aided by the fires occurring amongst the long grass of the plains, had obscured our view since leaving Kiang Hai; and the plain, except where broken by occasional hillocks, seemed interminable on all sides. The soil was rich, and it was evident that only more inhabitants were required to turn the plain into a vast rice-field.

Leaving camp soon after dawn, we continued for three miles through the grassy plain, crossing the beds of several dry streams and canals, and then entered the extensive rice-fields of Ban Meh Chai, the northern border village of Penyow, which contains 100 houses and a well-kept temple and monastery. According to the head-man of the village, owing to the land having been under cultivation for years, paddy only yields eighty-fold the amount sown in his fields, or less than one-third its yield in the newly taken-up land in the Kiang Hsen plain. Eighty-fold, however, is fully double the average yield in Burmah.

After crossing the Meh Chai, in the centre of the village, we skirted the fields for another mile, and crossed the Nong Hang near the site of a witch's house, which had lately been pulled down, after the occupants had been driven from the village. Two miles farther, we came to and crossed the Meh Ing flowing to the right, close to the village of Ban Mai. This river was here 25 feet wide and 9 feet deep, and had only 1½ foot of water in its bed. It had a barely perceptible current, and flows south as far as Penyow, then doubles round Loi Loo-en and turns north-east on its way to join the Meh Kong. Turning to the east, we followed the plain for two miles to the foot of Loi Loo-en, along which the track continues to Penyow. Loi Loo-en is a pleasantly wooded hill about nine miles long, running nearly north and south, and has formed the site of several cities, some of which I subsequently visited during my stay at Penyow.

A fire was raging in the plain, and a terrified hare, the first I had seen during the journey, raced across the path in front of my elephant. The atmosphere had grown oppressive, and although scarcely eleven o'clock, the thermometer marked 91° in the shade. All were parched with thirst; the boys lagged one foot behind the other, and the men scratched holes in the dry stream-beds, seeking in vain for water. About one o'clock we reached a dry brook having a few muddy puddles in the bed, and determined to halt for breakfast. Half a mile farther would have taken us to the village of Pang Ngao, where we might have got better water, but we were all-unconscious of its existence.

Getting off our elephants, we flung ourselves down under the shade of a great tree, where the temperature was 96°, and waited whilst the men dug holes in the ground in search of pure water. None was to be found, so at length the boys set to work to boil some liquid mud to make our tea. Such tea, when made, we had not the stomach to drink, and could therefore only rinse our mouths.

The march had been very distressing both to the elephants

and men, and it was well that Penyow, where we were to rest, was only three miles distant. We started again, continuing to skirt the hill, and about three-quarters of a mile from Penyow passed the site of the ancient city of Chaum Taung, which is divided into three compartments by the usual ramparts and ditches. A little farther we came to one of the most sacred places of pilgrimage in the Shan States, Wat Phra Chow Toon Hluang (the temple of the great sitting Buddha), and scrambled down from our elephants to inspect it.

The walls were of plastered brickwork, and the beautiful roof rose in five graceful tiers to a great height. On entering the temple, we saw a colossal image of Gaudama 60 feet high, measuring 26¼ feet across the hips, with hands 6½ feet long. Great pieces of yellow cloth, interwoven with tinsel, covered the chest, and many tawdry banners were suspended over and around the image, which is said to be of pure gold, but doubtless has been formed of brick, and overlaid with the usual plaster and gold-leaf.

LEGEND OF CHAUM TAUNG.

The legend of the temple runs as follows: At the time when Gaudama Buddha was proceeding from Kiang Hai to Penyow, he arrived at Loi Loo-en, where he met a *yak* or ogre, who attacked and wished to devour him. Avoiding the attack, the Buddh stamped on the ground, impressing a *Phra Bat* or Buddha's footprint, and revealed himself to the *yak*. At the foot of the mountain he saw an old couple, husband and wife, clearing the trees to form a garden. These people, having nothing better to offer, reverently presented the Buddh with the stone mortar in which they crushed their betel-nut. Buddh therefore foretold that the country in future should be noted for its stone utensils.

On his reaching the site of Viang Chaum Taung, a goldsmith, seeing the Buddh, came forward with an offering of rice, and poured it into the Buddh's begging-bowl. Wishing to quench his thirst whilst eating the rice, Gaudama sent An-nōn (Ananda, his favourite disciple) to the pond, which included the site of the temple. Phya Nyak, the king of the dragons, would not allow the water to be taken. On learning this, Buddh exclaimed, " The three last Buddhs, Ka-Koo Senta (Kaukasan), Ko-Na Kamana (Gaunagone), and Kakapa (Kathabah), have visited this place and eaten rice." He then became gigantic, swelling to the size of Ko-Na Kamana, and stepping on the head of Phya Nyak, pressed him down into the water, and thus made him aware that he was a Buddh. The king of the dragons at once procured a stone for Buddh to sit on whilst bathing and drinking. Incensed at water having been refused to him, Buddh prophesied that the country should be without river-water in the hot season. He then ordered Phya In (Indra) and Phya Nyak, that after his entering Neiban (the state of eternal rest), and half of his dispensation of 5000 years had elapsed, they should take gold, and offer it to the old people who had made offerings to him, and who would be reborn on the same spot), and instruct them to make an image of him with the gold in the middle of the pond: the image to be of the size of Ko-Na Kamana. Having finished prophesying, he left Penyow.

Phya Nyak, the king of serpents and dragons.

The old people, it is believed, after passing through three existences, were reborn at Penyow, and made the image in Wat Phra Chow Toon Hluang. The ditches round the three cities of Viang Chaum Taung are said to have been dug by *yaks*, or ogres, whilst Buddh was resting in it eating the rice and waiting for Ananda to bring him water.

On reaching Penyow (Panyow or Phayao), Buddh summoned the people to listen to his preaching. The men, who were clearing the fields with long knives, at once hurried to him with their implements in their hands. Buddh, looking at them with astonishment, exclaimed, "Pahn Yow!" (what long knives!); thence the place is known as Pahn Yow or Penyow.

Another city, called Viang Moo Boon, situated two days' journey to the south-east of Penyow, is said to have had its trenches and ramparts marked out by a sacred dog, and executed by *nyaks* or dragons. According to some Buddhist books which give histories of twenty-four Buddhs who preceded Gaudama (Sakya Muni), who is the only Buddh known to history, the twenty-third Buddh lived as a layman for 3000 years, and was 45 feet high; the twenty-fourth Buddh lived 20,000 years, and was 30 feet high; and Gaudama, the twenty-fifth Buddh, had existed for 100,000 ages when he was retranslated to the earth. For 36,500 years he existed as Indra, the great king of the Dewas, after which time, being desirous to save mankind, he passed through a course of existences on this world, the history of which is given in the 510 Zahts or Jatakas.

A quarter of an hour after leaving the temple, we were gladdened by the sight of a Shan Rachel drawing water from a well close to the city walls. How often she drew water for the men, and willingly and laughingly offered it to the thirsty souls, who seemed as if they would never be satisfied, I cannot tell. She did so as long as it was required, and then, after letting them draw some for the elephants, walked jauntily off with her bamboo buckets swinging in either hand.

We then entered the city, and halted at the court-house, under a magnificent tarapeuk tree, covered with great dangling blossoms, which from a distance looked like cat-tail orchids. Although half-past five when we halted, the temperature was still 91°. This was by far the hottest march we had made; and the glare and dust, joined with thirst, and constant peering at my instrument, made my eyes and head ache so that I could hardly keep to my work. It was getting dark when we arrived.

Muang Penyow is situated in the great elbow-curve made by the Meh Ing, and lies 130 miles from Zimmé, at a height of 1266 feet above the sea.

CHAPTER XX.

SETTLED BY LAKON — POPULATION — SMALLPOX — TUTELARY SPIRITS— ANCIENT CITIES — TRADE - ROUTES AND COST OF TRANSPORT — THE CENTRE OF PING STATES — A LAKON PRINCE — VIEWS ABOUT RAILWAY—SMALLPOX RAGING—CALLOUSNESS OF NATIVES—DR CUSHING INFECTED — DESERTED CITIES — FAMOUS FOR POTTERY — GAMBLING CURRENCY—GAMBLING GAMES IN SIAM—FIGHTING CRICKETS, FISH, AND COCKS—COCK-CROWING IN INDO-CHINA—VARIATION IN TIMES OF NEW YEAR—GAMBLING MONOPOLY IN SIAM—PROCLAMATION OF THE KING—GAMBLING CHIEF CAUSE OF SLAVERY—PARENTS SELLING CHILDREN INTO SLAVERY—SLAVERY NOT ABOLISHED—PROCLAMATION ISSUED TO DELUDE FOREIGNERS—POSITION OF PEOPLE DAILY GROWING WORSE—A MONEY-LENDER BUYING INJUSTICE FROM PRINCES AND NOBLES—ENCOURAGING GAMBLING—GAMBLING-HOUSE JAILS—STATE OF SIAMESE GOVERNMENT MONOPOLIES—EFFECT OF CORVÉE LABOUR—BURDENSOME TAXATION—NO JUSTICE—GENERAL DEMORALISATION—SHAN STATES BETTER GOVERNED.

On our reaching Penyow, the Chow Phya, who was conducting us, went to the governor to announce our arrival, and we were assigned the court-house for our habitation; but as it was far from waterproof, we put up at a *sala* near the south wall. It would have been better to have camped near the temple outside the city, for during our stay our water had to be fetched from the well we had passed near the entrance-gate. The water drawn from the only well inside the city was nauseous and undrinkable, and the Meh Ing, which winds round three sides of the town, looked like a foul sewer, black with mud and filth held in solution. The current in the stream was barely perceptible.

In the morning we called on the governor, who has the title of Chow Hluang, or Great Prince—a pleasant old gentleman, who received us most courteously, and kept us in conversation for about an hour. He told us his Muang was resettled by Lakon, and is a sub-State of that principality. It contained 4820 houses, 300 of which were in the city. Each house on an average contained eight inhabitants: this average would give the Muang a population of 38,560 souls. Paddy, he said, yielded in his district a hundred-fold on well-irrigated land, and eighty-fold on land subject to drought or inundation.

After the chief had recounted the Buddhist legends, previously given, Dr Cushing was so disgusted at seeing him fondling his young son, who was covered with smallpox scabs, that he bade adieu. On passing me, he whispered that there were four cases of smallpox in the family. Dr M'Gilvary kindly stopped on to the end of the interview, as I wished to learn about the trade-routes and geography of the country.

The *Pee*, or tutelary god, of the Muang,[1] is Chow Kam Doeng, the spirit of an ancient Lawa king who formerly ruled in Penyow: his predecessor is said to have been Phya Choo-ang.

The ancient cities whose names are known, situated in the chief's jurisdiction, include Viang Tum, Viang Tom, Viang Muang, Viang Heang, Viang Chaum Taung, Viang Poo Lam, and Viang Meh Ta Lat. Besides these, the following lie outside the district: Muang Teung to the west of Loi Mun Moo, between it and the Meh Wung; and Viang Moo Boon and Viang Kyow, two days' journey to the south-east. The journey over Loi Mun Moo to the Meh Wung, and thence along the valley of the Meh Wung to Lakon, takes eight and a half days; the journey to Zimmé by the Loi Sa-ket pass, takes five days; and the journey to Kiang Khong, on the Meh Ing near its junction with the Meh Kong, is done by elephants in six days.

With reference to the export of rice from Penyow to Lakon, which was suffering from drought, the chief told me

[1] Most Chinese and Indo-Chinese cities are under tutelary deities, as the cities in Egypt and Babylonia were in ancient times. The same custom prevails in India, where many cities are presided over by incarnations of one or other of the gods.

that the cost of carriage for an elephant load of 266 lb. over the distance of 71 miles, was 13 rupees and 8 annas, which, at an exchange of 1s. 5d. to the rupee, is equivalent to a charge of 2s. 3d. a ton per mile. As rice is carried by train in Burmah for a halfpenny a ton per mile, the cost of elephant carriage is fifty-four times as expensive. Dried fish taken to Zimmé fetch double the Penyow price.

In Mr Archer's report, he notes the importance of Penyow as the seat of a large fishing industry, and as a station "on the important route from Chienghai (Kiang Hai) to the southern Lao provinces. This town may well be called the centre of the Lao (Ping Shan) country, for it is situated at an equal distance of six days' march from nearly all the important places in the five States: Chiengmai (Zimmé), Chiengsen (Kiang Hsen), Nan, Phrë (Peh), and Lakhon (Lakon)."

On returning to our *sala*, we found Chow Rat, one of the princes of Lakon, who with his attendants was encamped outside the city, had come to pay us a visit. He, like all the princes of the Ping States whom I met, was free from awkwardness and affectation, courteous and well-mannered, and seemed anxious to oblige us by all the means in his power. He was evidently a highly intelligent man, and became much interested in the proposed railroad. After going fully into the matter, he said that the Ping princes would certainly do all in their power to facilitate its construction. Trade was as life-blood to the chiefs and people, and such a line would greatly increase the trade and wealth of the country. I had many talks with Chow Rat before we left for Zimmé, and he gave me a good deal of information about the country.

At the time of our arrival, smallpox had been raging in the city for twelve days, and had caused the death of seventy people. We visited house after house, and the disease seemed to be everywhere. Five and six deaths occurred each day during our stay: the pitiful screaming of the children suffering from the fell disease was heartrending. The deep boom of the chief's gong, the finest-toned one that I ever heard, sounded nightly at about eleven o'clock, when the bodies were taken from the city for interment.

Our servants and followers were utterly callous of the possibility of contagion—they had most likely all had the disease; and notwithstanding our injunctions to the contrary, ate and slept in infected houses. Had I been aware of the state of the city, I would have camped near the well at the entrance-gate. I have little doubt that Dr Cushing was infected with the disease whilst being shampooed by one of the interpreters, who had been sleeping and taking his meals at a house in which there were two or three cases of the disease.

One day we strolled through the remains of two deserted cities, situated in a park-like forest neighbouring Penyow. Viang Meh Ta Lat lies adjacent to the town, and was built in two or three compartments. It contains ruins of temples and pagodas, and is upwards of a mile long. Viang Poo Lam, which lies to the north-east of Viang Meh Ta Lat, is surrounded by double ramparts, with a ditch separating them. The ditch is 60 feet in width at the top, 15 feet at the bottom, and 20 feet deep from the crest of the inner rampart, which is 5 feet high, and 15 feet from the outer rampart, which is 10 feet high.

Terra-cotta pedestal.

Amongst the ruins we came across several fine images of Buddha cut out of stone; and near one of the pagodas, saw some octagonal tiles, which measured 2 feet across, and were 2 inches thick—the largest I have seen in Indo-China. The neighbourhood must have been famous at one time for its pottery, for besides the tiles, I found the remains of a large and handsomely executed terra-cotta image and pedestal in the grounds of one of the monasteries in the city. The mutilated supporters to the pedestal are elephants and eagles, the latter representing "Garuda," the sacred bird of Vishnu, in the Hindoo Pantheon, which was the mortal foe of the *nagas* or dragons, and all the snake race. Whilst rambling about these cities I became nearly clothed with caterpillars—whether of the silk-worm or not I do not know—which were dangling in myriads by long threads from the branches of the trees.

Phya Khrut or Garuda, the king of eagles.

On our return, Jewan came to me with a long face, complaining that the people in the town had given him some pieces of pottery instead of change, and asked what he should do. On looking at them I found they were octagonal in shape, and stamped on one side with Chinese letters. After showing them to Dr M'Gilvary, he said they were the ordinary gambling currency of the place, and represented two-anna and four-anna pieces. It appears that the gambling monopolist has the right to float them, and they are in general use amongst the people as small change. They remain current as long as the Chinese monopolist is solvent or has the monopoly. If he loses it, he calls the tokens in by sending a crier round, beating a gong and informing the people that he is ready to change the tokens for money. Dr M'Gilvary said that such tokens formed the sole small change at Zimmé before the Bangkok copper currency supplanted them.

In every village throughout Siam may be found common gambling-houses. These houses are usually built of bamboo; the entire front being of unsplit bamboo placed perpendicularly, every other one extending not more than four feet from the ground. This plan enables those passing to see what is going on inside, and is evidently intended as a bait. Everything is done to attract people to the den. Musicians and play-actors are hired and separated from the gamblers by a paper screen, with lamplight on the side of the performers, behind which a man is employed making shadow puppet-shows for the amusement of the spectators. A great gong is beaten, men utter unearthly sounds through horns, and the discord is made more complete by the grating notes of various stringed instruments and unmusical human voices. Play usually begins late in the afternoon, and lasts far into the night. At one end of a Chinese gambling-saloon is often an altar, and on it a figure of the god of luck. When weary with gambling or temporarily dispirited, the Siamese retire to watch the musicians and play-actors. The gambling in Siam consists, besides lotteries, of the mat game, the brass-cup game, the fish, shrimp, and crab game, and games at cards, which are conducted as follows:—

The Mat Game.—The gambling is conducted on one general plan, which is subject to certain modifications, probably for the sake of variety, lest the gamblers should weary of the monotony of a single method. A large mat, twelve or fifteen feet square, is placed on the floor. On this mat are two lines forming a rectangular cross. The four angles made by the two lines are marked respectively 1, 2, 3, 4. The proprietor sits on the mat in the angle marked 4, and has near him a pile of cowries (small shells formerly used as money in Siam). From this pile he takes a double handful. The gamblers place their money on any one of the numbers they choose. We will suppose there are but four playing, and that each places a *tical* on a different number.

After the players have put down their stakes, the proprietor counts out his double handful of shells into fours, and notes the remainder. If there is a remainder of two, the man who placed his money on No. 2 doubles his money. No. 4 loses his, while Nos. 1 and 3 neither lose nor win. If there is a remainder of 1, No. 1 doubles his money, No. 3

loses, Nos. 2 and 4 neither lose nor win. But there may be twenty or thirty playing. The principle is the same. All whose money is on the number representing the remainder, after counting out the fours, double their money; while all on the opposite numbers lose, and the other two numbers neither lose nor win. If the shells amount to even fours, No. 4 wins.

There is one modification of this game. The gamblers may place their money on the diagonal line between 2 and 3: then if there is a remainder of 2 or 3, that money is doubled; while if there is a remainder of 1 or 4, it is lost. In this case the chances both of gaining and losing are doubled.

In many of the gambling-houses smaller mats are used, and there are then several modifications of the game, according to the position of the money laid down. But the principle of the game is the same as that already described. The proprietors of these gambling-houses issue the porcelain money that we see in the market, which, when they are unable to redeem it, becomes absolutely worthless.

The Brass-cup Game.—In this game the proprietor has a square brass cup, in which he places a cube of wood. One half of one face of the cube is white and the other half red. The cube is put into the cup, which is then inverted on the mat or table, and gamblers place their money opposite any one of the four sides they choose. The cup is then removed, the cube remaining with the painted face uppermost. The money opposite the white wins, three for one, and the other three sides lose.

The Fish, Shrimp, and Crab Game.—While passing along the street one often sees an old man with a crowd of boys about him. He has a board before him, in size about 18 by 20 inches, and divided by lines into six equal oblong squares. In one of these squares is the picture of a fish, in another of a shrimp, in another of a crab, &c. The man has a cocoa-nut shell, in which are three large wooden dice, on the faces of which are pictures corresponding to those on the board. The boys place their pieces of money on any picture they choose. The proprietor rattles his dice in the shell, and then inverts it on the board. All who have money on the pictures corresponding to the upper faces of the dice, win ; all the rest lose.

Card Games.—The cards used in gambling are about one inch by three. These are marked to represent kings, governors, officers, soldiers, &c. A full pack contains 116 cards, and the principle of the game seems to be similar to that of games of cards in more enlightened countries.

The alphabet of gambling is learned by Siamese children nearly as soon as they can run alone. They are seen pitching their coppers in the street, according to rules they seem to understand, and their parents are often among the most interested spectators. The appetite for gambling is likewise fostered by the universal custom of fighting crickets, fish, and cocks, and the Government allows all classes to gamble without a licence during the three days the festivities of the New Year last.

Siamese children have few pets, and those they have are used for fighting. Just at sunset the boys may be seen searching for crickets. These little creatures are put into small clay cages, closed at the top by bars of little sticks, which let in the light and air. When they have collected a good number, the boys gather together in the evening and put all their crickets into a large box. Then commences a general scrimmage. Cricket meets cricket, as Greek met Greek, and the excited boys bet every copper in their possession on the one they think likely to win.

Small fish, called needle-fish, are also used for this sport. Two fish are put into separate bottles. The moment the bottles are brought together, the fish begin snapping, but of course cannot reach each other. Sometimes a looking-glass is held before one, and it is amusing to see how angry it will become. This passion for mimic fights grows in the boys ; and when they become young men, they spend most of their time at cock-pits, where nearly all their betting is done. The cocks in Indo-China resemble small game-cocks, and crow four times in the twenty-four hours—at midnight, dawn, noon, and sundown,—and thus serve to note the time.

In Siam, not including the Ping and Lao Shan States upwards of £100,000 is paid by the Chinese gambling monopolists for their licences. Five-ninths of this amount comes from the lottery-holders, and four-ninths from the gambling-houses. Nine-tenths of the monopolists sublet their farms, making from 15 to 20 per cent profit: 2 per cent of the money paid by the monopolists is said to be a private perquisite of the King of Siam.

In his proclamation, "concerning the limitation of the ages of the children of slaves and of free people," issued in 1874, the King of Siam declared: "With reference to gambling and all games of chance, where money is lost and won, it is a prolific source of slavery. These subjects have his Majesty's best thoughts as to their eventual termination. They now yield a revenue of 11,000 catties (528,000 dollars), which is regularly expended in defraying the expenses of the Government. If gambling were completely abolished, there would not be enough at the command for Government and military purposes to meet the deficit that would be occasioned by such abolition. This subject, however, his Majesty has presented for the deliberation of the council, and when definite conclusions have been arrived at they will be made known to the public." Fourteen years have elapsed since this proclamation was issued, during which time no further action has been taken in the matter. The king still draws revenue from the monopolists. The monopolists can still force the Prai-luangs, who form the majority of the inhabitants of Siam, to sell themselves, together with their wives and families; can still force freemen to sell their children, without the children's consent up to the age of fifteen, and with the children's consent up to the time that they reach their twenty-first year.

To explain this clearly, and to show the present state of slavery in Siam, I will here quote Articles 6, 7, 8, and 11 of the law passed by the king in 1874, which has not been rescinded:—

"*Art.* 6. If any of the people who are now free, having had no trouble necessitating their becoming slaves, should subsequently become involved, and the father, mother, the paternal grandfather, grandmother, the maternal grandfather, grandmother, uncles, aunts, elder brothers or sisters, be inclined to sell their children or relatives that were born in the year of the Major Dragon, tenth of the decade (A.D. 1868), (as the starting-point)—if less than fifteen years old, they may do so only temporarily (until they reach their twenty-first year)—and allow their services to the purchaser in lieu of interest, inserting their names in the bill of sale of the purchaser, with or without the knowledge of the person sold, the sale is valid according to the laws of the land, because the father, mother, and elder relatives are paramount, &c.

"*Art.* 7. If a child or a relative that has been born since the year of the Major Dragon, tenth of the decade (A.D. 1868), has attained any age between the fifteenth and twentieth year—that is, knows the difference between right and wrong—and the parents or elder relatives wish to sell and give their services to the purchaser in lieu of interest, and the seller places that person's name in a bill of sale, the party so doing must inform the person to be sold, that he may know and see the transaction, and attach his name to the instrument in confirmation thereof, to give it validity, and make it available to the purchaser: his valuation, however, shall be according to the rates of the present laws. If the person sold neither knows of nor saw the transaction, and has not appended, nor hired, nor asked others to write his name to the instrument, he cannot be regarded as a slave.

"*Art.* 8. If the child of a slave or of a free person born in the year of the Major Dragon, as the starting-point, has reached the twenty-first year of his or her age, should the parents or the relatives or the persons themselves become embarrassed and involved, and apply to sell such persons, offering their personal services in lieu of interest on the purchase-money, all moneyed people and property holders are hereby absolutely forbidden to purchase them as slaves, &c.

"*Art.* 11. All persons under obligation to the Government known as Prai-luangs,[1] soldiers, artisans, labourers, miners, provincials, attamahts; those whose freedom has been forfeited to the State for crimes against the laws,[2] royal domestics, labourers at the

[1] The great masses of the common people are marked and designated as Prai-luang. These are scattered all over the country. The provincial or the city authorities can demand of those thus marked three months' personal services each year, and there may be extra demands if there is a seeming need. The usual mode is to require service one month, and then allow them three months to carry on their own pursuits. The only derangement to this plan is the extra service. No pay is allowed for this service. For failure to perform the service he must pay $3.60 each month.—Extract from 'The Siam Repository.'

[2] Committed by themselves or by their relations. The law frequently ad-

Government rice-mills, Government weavers, silk manufacturers, female guards of the inner apartments of the palace, and the distributors and objects of royal charities; all people under obligation to the Government, and known as Kon-hluangs, who clandestinely and fraudulently allow their names to be entered into bills of sale, pledging their personal services in lieu of interest to the purchaser, if they have children born to them in the house of the money-master from and since the year of the Major Dragon, tenth of the decade, and those children have attained the twenty-first year of their age,—in all these cases let the money-master make known the circumstances to the Krom Pra Surasadee, that the real Government master may have him tattooed and designated to his proper group, the group to which his father and mother belonged, so that when off required (Government) duty he may serve his money-master, and when on required duty he may serve his Government master, according to the original laws."

As the majority of the non-Chinese inhabitants of Siam are included among the above-mentioned classes, and there is no penalty for their selling themselves and their children *clandestinely and fraudulently* as slaves; and as the money-masters are told that they can keep them as slaves, and the original laws will apply to them and their children so long as they are permitted by their money-masters to serve the Government for three months in the year as Government slaves,—the law affords no protection to these people, and was evidently not meant to be a protection to them. The law was, in fact, merely enacted and published by the king in order to throw dust into the eyes of foreign nations, so that they might imagine him to be an enlightened and civilised monarch. I was only lately assured by gentlemen residing in Bangkok that slavery was never more prevalent in Siam than it is at the present time.

Instead of improving the position of the majority of the people, the law of 1874 makes it considerably worse; for the former law of A.D. 1787 states—"It is well known that registered slaves are exempt from monthly service to the Government. Government can demand their services only

judges, besides punishment to the man, that his family and descendants shall for the future be slaves of the Government. The descendants of captives in war are classed and treated as Government slaves.

when there is war." For the future, the Government will be able to demand their services for three months in the year, during which time they will have to provide their own lodging and food, and during the remaining nine months they will have to serve their money-masters, and their children will have to bear the same burdens and servitude.

The usual method employed by money-masters in Siam wishing to retain bond-slaves who wish to pay off their debts and regain their freedom, is fully explained by a proclamation that was issued by the late king in 1867, which runs as follows:—

"Proclamation of his Majesty Somdetch Pra Shaum Klow, the 4th of the present Dynasty. About the Merchant Bahng Mew.

"His Majesty issued a royal mandate to be proclaimed and published to all the princes and Government officials without and within, and to the people of the capital and of the provinces, north and south, for general information, about the merchant Bahng Mew, whose official title is Kun Penit Wohahn.

"He is truly a rich man, but he is tortuous. He is tricky in words and in litigation. His Majesty has really detected his artifice, his tortuousness, and lack of honesty. He has no compassion on the common people, who are his debtors and slaves, who are desirous of paying their indebtedness and the moneys advanced in purchasing them.

"When money is offered to him, he will not receive it, and contends about the necessities of the seasons. 'Waters are worked for fish, and fields for grain.' If it happens to be the 4th or 5th lunation, he is invisible, cannot be seen. If it happens to be the 10th or 11th lunation, he offers sundry excuses, and for three years he has evaded receiving proffered payments.

"The slaves have poured out their complaints and deposited their payments at the courts. He makes interest with the legal officers, and has evaded receiving his money for more than three and four years. A number of other persons also have poured forth their complaints of wrongs received from his Satee (Chetty, a banker and money-lender) Bahng Mew, and because he is wealthy he has confused the legal officers.

"He has access also to princes and nobles, who support him in his wrongs. This royal mandate is issued to be made known to the princes, nobles, and Government officials within and without, forbidding all to give him any further support in his practices.

If they persist in backing him up, they will no longer be objects of royal favour. Given, Saturday, 1st of the waxing, 6th lunation, year of the Rabbit, 8th of the decade, Siamese civil era, 1229 (May 4, 1867)."

Returning to the subject of gambling. The latest law dealing with it was issued in 1794. In the previous reign an Act had been passed whereby the gambling-house keepers were not allowed to advance money for gambling purposes to the people. This caused a great falling off in the amounts paid to Government for the monopolies. The law of 1794 states that—

"When his Majesty ascended the throne, having quelled all commotions, he was graciously pleased to revise the laws. What it was befitting should be retained, were left as before. What was not fitting, was abrogated; but this (former) proclamation on gambling was not repealed, because his Majesty was graciously disposed towards the common people, who were biassed by avaricious desires, because the managers of the gambling establishments trusted them and allowed them to get into debt, even though they had not at their homes the means of meeting their liabilities—still the managers trusted them; but they did not think of their children and wives, but borrowed from the managers, played, and were trusted. When their losses increased, and the managers arrested them and enforced payment, they were obliged to borrow, run in debt, sell their wives and children, and submit to many hardships.

"With these facts in view that proclamation was allowed to stand, that the players might play only to the extent of their means. At the present time, however, the players have greatly diminished, have been impoverished more than in former times, and the royal revenue has diminished withal. The holders of the royal patents and the managers of the gambling establishments perceive that there are no players, and they fear they will not be able to meet their Government liabilities."

Further on the Act goes on to state—

"The former law cannot longer be retained, and is therefore abolished. Henceforth if players enter a gambling establishment to play, and are in want of wherewith to play, and wish to borrow the money, or the current pieces of crockery belonging to the gambling establishment, to stake as wagers, let the gambling farmer or his agents in charge of the establishment form an approximate estimate of the ability of the player, and lend him accordingly, and only allow him to play within his approximate ability, and the power of the gambling establishment to collect, as in the last reign."

After indicating the amounts that may be safely lent, which includes six dollars to a female who comes without ornaments or attendants, it continues—

"Again, players come to play at a gambling establishment who have no money of their own: they do not at first borrow from the manager, but take part in a play and lose, and having the money obstruct the interest of the game in the height of their excitement, and cause a delay of the fees: in such cases let the manager and his collectors remove the difficulty and make the necessary advances, remove the loser who does not pay, bind and fetter and enforce payment, according to the power granted to the gambling establishment. If the money is not obtainable from the party, make him or her over to the general farmer, and let him enforce payment to the particular manager."

The farmer has his own jails, where he can keep debtors in fetters, until they *clandestinely and fraudulently* pay their debt, by selling themselves and their children to him as slaves.

If it were not for slavery, serfdom, vexatious taxation, and for the vices of the people, the Siamese might be a happy race. Living as they do chiefly upon vegetables and fish; in a country where every article of food is cheap; where a labourer's wages are such as to enable him to subsist upon a fourth of his earnings; where a few mats and bamboos will supply him with materials for a house sufficient to keep out the rays of the tropical sun and the showers in the rainy season; where little clothing is needed, and that of a cheap and simple kind; where nine-tenths of the land in the country is vacant, without owners or inhabitants,—surely such a people might be contented and happy. The land is so fertile and the climate is so humid, that every cereal and fruit of the tropics grows there to perfection. Yet among the common people it is seldom a man or woman can be found who is not the slave of the wealthy or the noble.

The Government battens on the vices of the people

by granting monopolies for gambling, opium, and spirits. Government places the people under unscrupulous and tyrannical Government masters—merciless, heartless, and exorbitant leeches—who, unless heavily bribed, force the peasantry to do their three months' *corvée* labour at times and seasons that necessarily break up all habits of industry, and ruin all plans to engage in successful business.[1]

Government imposes taxes upon everything grown for human requirements in the country; fishing-nets, stakes, boats, spears, and lines are all taxed. The Government net is so small that even charcoal and bamboos are taxed to the extent of one in ten, and firewood one in five, in kind. Fancy the feelings of an old woman, after trudging for miles to market with a hundred sticks of firewood, when twenty of the sticks are seized by the tax-gatherer as his perquisite! There is a land-tax for each crop of annuals sown, and paddy and rice are both subject to tax; so that three taxes can thus be reaped from one cereal. The burdensome taxation is levied in the most vexatious manner that can be conceived; for the taxes are let out to unscrupulous Chinamen, who are thus able to squeeze, cheat, and rob the people mercilessly. It is no use appealing from the tax-gatherer to the officials. Money wins its way, and justice is unknown in Siam. Every one who has not a friend at Court is preyed upon by the governors and their rapacious underlings.

Such being the present state of Siam, one is not surprised to learn that the majority of its inhabitants, besides being slaves and selling their children, are libertines, gamblers, opium smokers or eaters, and given to intoxicating beverages. No amount of earnings will bear these heavy strains upon their industry and their purse. The effect of over-taxation

[1] "The abolition of the system of *corvée*, which weighs very heavily on the people, would be a boon of infinite benefit to the country. It is not only that the service lawfully due is heavy, but the opportunity for imposing vexatious and severe labour, with a view to receiving a bribe for dispensing with it, is eagerly taken advantage of by unscrupulous officials. A poll-tax of reasonable amount would probably bring in a greater sum to the Royal revenues, and would bear but lightly on the people."—Consular Report, Siam, No. 1, (1886).

has been showing itself of late years in the import of betel-nuts, bee's-wax, cocoa-nuts, molasses, and other articles, which were formerly exported. The effect of sapping the morals of the people by encouraging gambling, opium smoking and eating, and spirit-drinking, is displayed by their present state of degradation.

Nowhere in the Shan States is misgovernment and oppression of the people so rampant as in Siam. Taxation in the Shan States is exceedingly light; and the people are not placed under grinding Government masters, but have the power to change their lords at their will; they are not compelled to serve for three months in the year without receiving either wages or food; amongst them gamblers, opium-smokers, and drunkards are looked down upon and despised; and libertinism is nearly unknown. The only loose women seen by me in the Shan States were a few Siamese, who had taken up their quarters at Zimmé, the headquarters of the Siamese judge. Siam, in comparison with the Ping Shan States, is as pest-ridden Penyow, situated on its sluggish and fetid streams, to the healthy city of Muang Ngow, on its beautiful clear-flowing river, that we were about to visit.

CHAPTER XXI.

LEAVE PENYOW — WILD ROSES — AN INUNDATED COUNTRY — ROYAL FUNERAL BUILDINGS — POSTS TWO HUNDRED FEET LONG — COLLECTION AND USES OF WOOD-OIL —DESCRIPTION OF DAILY MEALS — WATER-PARTING BETWEEN THE MEH KONG AND MEH NAM — PATH FOR RAILWAY — A DEAD FOREST — REACH MUANG NGOW — SETTLED BY LAKON — KAREN VILLAGES — TEAK-FORESTS—FOUR THOUSAND BURMESE DESTROYED—A DISTRIBUTING CENTRE FOR MUANG NAN AND MUANG PEH — DEFICIENT RAINFALL — BURMESE PEDLARS — IMMIGRANTS FROM KIANG HUNG—A TERRIBLE DIN—THE ECLIPSE—BUDDHIST LEGEND — ELEPHANTS SHOULD REST AFTER NOON DURING HOT SEASON — LEAVE MUANG NGOW — RAILWAY FROM BANGKOK TO KIANG HUNG CROSSES NO HILL-RANGE — BATTLE-FIELD — THE STONE GATE — WATER-PARTING BETWEEN THE MEH NGOW AND MEH WUNG—A JOLTING ELEPHANT—BAN SA-DET—OFFERINGS FOR THE MONKS—PRESENTS FOR THE CHILDREN—THE BUDDHIST LENT—LIGHTS FOR EVIL SPIRITS—THE DEMON'S LENT—OFFERINGS TO THE NAIADS—ILLUMINATING THE RIVER—KING OF SIAM LIGHTING FIREWORKS—SCARING THE SPIRITS—OFFERINGS TO NAIADS AND DEMONS IN CASE OF SICKNESS—TRIAL BY WATER—SUPERSTITION AGAINST SAVING DROWNING FOLK—DESCENT OF THE RAIN-GOD INDRA—LIBATIONS—THE WATER-FEAST—BATHING THE IMAGES—SCENE IN THE TEMPLE—WAKING THE GODS WITH WATER—PROPITIATING THE LAWA GENII—THE WARMING OF BUDDH—A DOUSING—A COMPLIMENT—CALLING THE SPIRITS TO WITNESS—LEAVE BAN SA-DET—RUBY-MINES—REACH LAKON.

We were detained at Penyow from the 3d to the 8th of April, waiting the arrival of a fresh relay of elephants. The elephants had been turned out for the hot season to graze in the forests, and had to be tracked for long distances before they could be captured. At length, when four elephants had been brought in, Chow Rat, the Lakon prince, kindly lent us two of his own animals; and we thus, with

Dr M'Gilvary's elephant, and twenty porters, had as much transport as we required.

During our stay the Chow Hluang furnished us with rice and fowls, and the day before we left, to our great joy sent us the fore-quarters of a pig. Never was roast-pork more enjoyed by mortal beings.

Leaving Penyow the next morning about seven o'clock, we crossed the Meh Ing, which runs near the south gate of the city. The bed of the river at our ford was saucer-shaped, 80 feet wide, and 5 feet deep in the centre, and contained 1 foot of water, which was covered with a thick yellow slime, that emitted an unpleasant odour. After passing a great clump of rose-bushes, bearing ordinary tea-roses, we entered a plain covered with elephant grass and bamboo jungle, which is inundated to a depth of 5 or 6 feet in the rains.

Three-quarters of a mile from the city we left the low ground, and crossing the Meh Hong Sai, the brook of clear water, entered the rice-plain of Ban Meh Sai. This village is inhabited by people who have been turned out of other places in the district, under the accusation of witchcraft.

Near the village we noticed many padouk and pyngado logs, which had been dragged there for the purpose of building a temple and monastery.

Beyond the fields we entered a bamboo jungle, through which our elephants had to force their way by breaking down the bamboos and small trees, and snapping off such branches and twigs as would interfere with the howdah. It is surprising how docile these great animals are, and how sagaciously they obey the orders given them by their drivers. We halted for breakfast at a house that had been built for us in the pretty village of Meh Hong Khum, which is situated on a stream of the same name.

After breakfast, we visited the temple and monastery, where we found the priests busy making rockets for the approaching eclipse, and then continued through the forest to the village of Ban So. Thence proceeding through a slightly rolling country, where several small streams take their rise, we camped for the night under the shade of a great kanyin tree, near the Meh Na Poi, which enters the Meh Ing. We had risen 350 feet in 12 miles since leaving Penyow.

The kanyin (or oil-tree), under which we erected our tent, had it been on an affluent of the Meh Nam, might have been chosen for one of the main posts of a Pramene, or Royal Siamese cremation temple. When a king of Siam dies, his successor immediately begins making preparations for the construction of a Pramene, a splendid temporary building, under which the body, after sitting in state for several days on a throne glittering with silver, gold, and precious stones, is committed to the flames.

The late Dr Bradley thus described the erection of the posts in one of these buildings:—

"The building is intended to be in size and grandeur according to the estimation in which the deceased was held. Royal orders are forthwith sent to the governors of four different provinces far away to the north, in which large timber abounds, requiring each of these to furnish one of the four large logs for the centre pillars of the Pramene. These must be of the finest timber, usually the oil-tree (kanyin), very straight, 200 feet long, and proportionally large in circumference, which is not less than 12 feet. There are always twelve other pillars, a little smaller in size, demanded at the same time from the governors of other provinces, as also much other timber needed in the erection of the Pramene and the numerous buildings connected with it.

"The great difficulty of procuring these pillars is one main cause of the usual long delay of the funeral burning of a king. When brought to the city, they are dragged up to the place of the Pramene, chiefly by the muscular power of men working by means of a rude windlass and rollers under the logs. They are then hewed and planed a little—just enough to remove all cracks and other deformities—and finished off in a cylindrical form. Then they are planted in the ground 30 feet deep, one at each corner of a square not less than 160 feet in circumference. When in their proper place they stand leaning a little toward each other, so that they describe the form of a four-sided, truncated pyramid from 150 to 180 feet high. On the top of these is framed a pagoda-formed spire, adding from 50 to 60 feet more to the height of the structure. This upper part is octagonal, and so covered with yellow tin sheets and tinselled paper as to make a grand appearance at such a height."

The Ton Yang (or Ton Nyang), the Shan name for the kanyin tree, sometimes attains a height of 230 feet to the first branch. Its oil is procured in a similar way to the varnish of the Mai Hăk, or Thytsi tree. A large notch is cut in the tree two or three feet from the ground, and a basin is formed at the bottom of the notch, capable of containing three quarts of oil as it drops from the upper part of the notch. A fire is then built in the notches, and kept burning until all parts are well charred. A tree 12 feet in circumference often has three or more of these wounds, each giving from one to two quarts in twenty-four hours.

At first the oil appears milky and thin, but it gradually becomes brown and thicker by exposure to the air. A good deal of sediment collects in the jars into which the oil is put, which is mixed with rotten wood or other material, and formed into torches, from 15 to 18 inches long. These torches serve as candles and lanterns, and also for kindling fires. The oil is used for oiling boats, and, mixed with a finely pulverised resin, as a putty for filling the seams of the boats, and, with less resin, as a coating to protect their bottoms. In a few days it becomes quite hard and impervious to water.

Camping in the evergreen forest, under the great tree, with the air rapidly cooling after the heat of the day, was very enjoyable, and was rendered more so by recollections of our late stuffy quarters in the pest-ridden city. Then we had pork, roast-pork, for dinner! No one can realise what a luxury that is who has not existed mainly upon fowls for several weeks.

For the sake of future travellers in these parts, I may here note the particulars of our daily meals. Before dawn, whilst the elephant-men were bathing their charges in the neighbouring stream and we were having our morning dip, our boys were cooking our *chota haziri*, or early meal, which consisted of a tin of Kopp's soup mixed with a table-spoonful of Liebig's essence of beef, and some biscuits, with coffee, cocoa, or tea, and half cooking the fowls which would be required for our breakfast. By daybreak our meal was completed, and everything packed on the elephants, so that we might be away as soon as it was light. On each of our howdahs we carried a cosie-covered Chinese teapot, into which hot tea had been poured after having been brewed in another pot, and an enamelled teacup to drink out of when thirsty on the journey.

At breakfast, which was served during our mid-day halt, we had soup, chickens, sometimes a duck, curry, and rice, and vegetables when we could get them. The tender shoots of young bamboos, and certain fern-fronds when stripped of their stalks, form excellent substitutes for garden vegetables, and were frequently eaten by us when procurable. Our dinners were similar to our breakfasts, with the addition of fried plantains, tapioca, sago, or boiled rice and jam. Beef was a luxury seldom to be had, and to procure a beef-steak one had to purchase an ox.

The following morning we were off early, and two miles beyond our camp came to the water-parting that divides the streams flowing into the Meh Kong from those emptying into the Meh Nam. It was only 1643 feet above the level of the sea, or 377 feet above Penyow, which was here 14 miles distant.

Nothing could have been more surprising to us. Loi Kong Lome, the great range to our right that separates the Meh Ngow from the Meh Ing, was four or five miles distant, and dying down into the plain, while Loi Nam Lin, the main range on our left, was ten miles away, with its nearest spur two miles from us.

We were in a great gap between two ranges of mountains, and were merely crossing the undulating ground intervening between them. Here was a freak of nature to be taken advantage of for railway purposes. I had now proved that the water-parting of the Meh Kong and the Meh Nam could be crossed through a gap in the mountains, and that

Kiang Hung, at the foot of the Yunnan plateau, could be joined to Bangkok, the capital of Siam, by a railway passing through a series of valleys separated from each other by only undulating ground, which offered no physical obstruction to the carrying out of the work. It now remained to be seen whether an alternative line *viâ* the valley of the Meh Wung, which would bring Zimmé and Maulmain into nearer connection with the railway, was equally feasible.

Descending along the Meh Yu-ek, amongst hillocks and broken ground, we seemed to be passing through the valley of the shadow of death. The forest had a ghastly appearance. Dead bamboos lay like spellicans cast about in every direction, and many had been crushed down by others to the ground, which was carpeted with yellow silvery leaves. The light colour of the bark of the few trees scattered amongst the clumps was strangely in tone with the dead bamboos; and their yellow-green, fresh-sprouted foliage, added to the weird aspect of the scene. One could nearly believe that the pale-blue and yellow butterflies flitting over the path were the souls of human beings in the land of dreams, or on their pilgrimage to a new life.

After descending 363 feet in 4 miles, we reached Ban Hai, a hamlet in a forest of noble teak-trees. Near here, willows were growing in the stream-bed, and a caravan of thirty-five laden cattle passed on their way from Muang Peh to Kiang Hai.

We continued along the stream for another two miles, and then left it flowing to our right, and crossing a couple of low spurs, descended to and crossed the Meh Ngow. This river at our ford was 1073 feet above the sea, 60 feet broad, and 6 feet deep, with 6 inches of water in its bed. The fall from the crest of the pass to our crossing of the Meh Ngow was only 570 feet in a distance of 8 miles. Three-quarters of a mile farther we halted for breakfast at a house that had been erected for our use in the rice-plain of Ban Koi.

We were once again in a cultivated region, and from here to Muang Ngow our path led chiefly through rice-fields and tobacco-gardens.

Early the next morning we reached the beautifully wooded city of Muang Ngow, which is situated 93¾ miles from Zimmé, and 798 feet above the sea.

Muang Ngow is one of the smallest Muangs in the Ping States. It was resettled a few years ago by Lakon, and comprised at the time of my visit only 800 houses, which were scattered through the city and six villages. There were also a few Karen villages in the neighbouring hills, some of whose inhabitants had lately been converted by Dr Cushing's Mission, the American Baptist, that has done such good work amongst the Karens and other hill tribes in Burmah.

In reporting of this Muang in 1887, three years after my visit, Mr Archer states: "Muang Ngao (Muang Ngow) is an important sub-province of Lakhon (Lakon), and, besides its rich rice-fields, boasts of extensive teak-forests, which have recently been leased to a British company. The valley is broad and well cultivated, and the numerous and populous villages and the traffic on the roads showed greater prosperity and animation than I had yet seen, with a few exceptions, since leaving Chiengmai (Zimmé). Muang Ngao lies on the trade-route from Lakhon to the north, and the number of traders I met here proves it to be a trade station of some importance."

This Muang, which would be intersected by our proposed railroad, is 83 miles distant from Muang Nan, the capital of the Shan State of the same name, and three days and five hours' elephant journey, or about 60 miles, distant from Muang Peh, the capital of the State of that name. At the time when the Ping States threw off their allegiance to Burmah, Noi Atha, the governor of Muang Nan, which was then a principality of Zimmé, led a force of 4000 Burmese soldiers into the gorge of the Meh Si-phan, where they were crushed to death by rocks hurled down by the Shans from the overhanging heights. The Meh Si-phan, which enters the Meh Yom from the east, is skirted by the route from Muang Ngow to Muang Nan, and its name implies the "river of the 4000." Lakon and Muang Ngow would be equally well situated on the railway for tapping the trade of Muang Nan and Muang Peh.

On visiting the governor, who has the title of *Pau Muang*, or Father of the State, he received us with the usual frank courtesy of the Shan chiefs, and gave us what information he could about trade, trade-routes, and geography. Half of the people gain their livelihood by cultivating cotton, and the remainder by rice, tobacco, and other crops. The outcome of rice varies with the rainfall; and in good seasons the return is eighty to ninety fold, or about double the average in Burmah. The rainfall was insufficient in 1869 and 1883; though in other years their crops were good. The river does not inundate the land, but the hills being near, canals can easily be made to irrigate the fields.

Although there are many areca palms about the place, they do not fruit well; therefore betel-nuts, as well as seri-leaf, are brought from Zimmé. Dried fish come from Penyow and Kiang Hsen, and European goods from Bangkok *viâ* Lakon. Mr Archer met a number of Toungthoo and Burmese pedlars at the city; and the inhabitants exchange their cotton with the Chinese from Yunnan for salt, which the latter have purchased at Lakon for bartering in the district.

Immigrants from Kiang Hung, belonging to a branch of the Shans known as Lus, have formed settlements in the country between Muang Peh and Kiang Khong, as well as in the valley of the Meh Oo, a river that enters the Meh Kong from the north near the city of Luang Prabang.

The city of Muang Ngow is fringed with, and partially hidden by, fine fruit-trees; the gardens being rendered beautiful by handsome clumps of cocoa-nut and areca palms. The *sala* being in a filthy condition, and surrounded by a large caravan of laden cattle, we camped in the gardens.

In the evening we were startled by a terrible din which suddenly sprang up on all sides of us. Swarms of men, women, and children, seemingly maddened by excitement, were rushing about firing guns, horse-pistols, rockets, and crackers, in all directions; clashing together gongs, bells, brass basins, pots, bowls, bamboos, and anything within reach; and yelling, screeching, and hooting, made night horrible; while the discord was further increased by the barking and howling of frightened dogs. An eclipse was occurring—the *Naga* (or dragon) was swallowing the moon; and the people, naturally enraged, were determined that he should disgorge it. After the eclipse was over, clouds gathered over the sky and we had a sharp shower of rain.

The Buddhist legend that gives the origin of the name of this State is by no means complimentary to the people. It states that, when Gaudama Buddha arrived at Ngow and sent to the people announcing his arrival, they were engaged in fishing. Instead of returning home at once and putting on decent clothes, they stopped to finish their haul, and then presented themselves to him in their dripping clothes. On their approaching him, he exclaimed, "The people of this place are *ngow* (fools). The Buddha came to visit you, you did not hasten to him, and when at length you come, it is in this plight." This legend, I need hardly say, was not told me in Ngow, but by a *Chow Phya* of Lakon.

The temperature during the day varied between 69° at 5.30 A.M., 87° at 10 A.M., 92° at noon, 96° at 2.30 P.M., and 95° at 4.10 P.M. During the hot season it is desirable that the day's march with elephants should commence at daybreak and end by noon; afternoons are very oppressive, and the animals get jaded, particularly when travelling in an open plain or in a leafless forest.

We left Muang Ngow just as it was getting light, on April 11th, and crossed the plain to Ban Hoo-art, a village situated on the Meh Hoo-art, an affluent of the Meh Ngow. We then skirted the stream for five miles, and halted for breakfast on its bank, under a shady grove of trees. Many teak-logs had been dragged from the forest into the bed of the stream for floating to Bangkok during the rainy season. One of the teak-trees in the forest measured 16 feet in girth 6 feet from the ground. During our morning's march we passed two large villages, a party of Burmese Shans returning to Kiang Tung from Maulmain with their purchases, and a caravan of fifty laden cattle.

In the afternoon we journeyed through a teak-forest, and after crossing two low spurs, halted for the night on the bank of the Meh Lah. Our camp was 81½ miles from Zimmé, and we had risen 614 feet since leaving Muang Ngow.

A mile to the east of our crossing, the Meh Lah, which enters the Meh Ngow near the site of the ancient city of Muang Teep, is joined by the Meh Lah Noi, a tributary from the south, which drains a valley six and a half miles long, formed by a long low spur, which is connected at the head of the valley with the plateau on the west. This valley has the appearance of having been cut lengthways out of the former flat slope of the plateau, the spur seeming to be the lower continuation of the original slope. On ascending the plateau on the morrow, I noticed that in the space between the spur and the north end of the range of hills lying to the east, which commences some ten miles to the south-east, the only hill visible was a short precipitous mass of mural limestone, standing up several hundred feet in height, with its top looking like a great coronet.

It thus became apparent that a similar freak of nature to that already described in the water-parting between the Meh Ing and the Meh Ngow was present in that between the Meh Ngow and the Meh Wung. The ranges between the basins of the rivers are not continuous, and a railway can be constructed from Bangkok *viâ* Lakon, to Kiang Hung, which lies at the foot of the Yunnan plateau, through a series of great plains, which are only separated from each other by slightly undulating country.

Leaving the Meh Lah early the next morning, we ascended the slope of the plateau for two and a half miles by a good broad road, passing through a teak-forest to the Pah Took (Stone Tent), a pillar of limestone with a small cave in its western face. For the greater part of the way the ascent lay along a natural terrace 300 and 400 feet wide, bordered on the east by the slope of the plateau, and on the west by cliffs of mural limestone. In this neighbourhood a pitched battle is said to have been fought between a Zimmé army and one of Burmese Shans, but I could get no further particulars of the event.

At the Pah Took we turned west and ascended 90 feet to the Pah Too Pah (Stone Gate)—a gap 200 feet broad, in the line of limestone cliffs that fringe the eastern edge of the summit of the plateau. The cliffs on either side of the gap rose like the wall of a fortress to a height of 300 feet, and the ground at the gap was 1941 feet above the level of the sea.

Continuing along the eastern edge of the plateau, which sloped from north to south, we reached the base of Loi Pah Heeng. Leaving Loi Pah Heeng trending away to the south-west, we descended the eastern slope of the plateau—the same that we had previously mounted from the Meh Lah—and after marching a mile, reached the head of the Meh Lah Noi valley.

The crest of the spur at this point is 1564 feet above the sea, and I have assumed that elevation as the height that the railway would have to cross between the valleys of the Meh Wung and the Meh Ngow; but it is evident that a considerably lower pass might be found between the spur and the coronet-topped hill which still loomed above it in the distance.

Continuing our descent, we shortly afterwards came to the source of the Meh Mau, and skirting its channel until we found water in its bed, halted for breakfast and for the night — being hungry, thirsty, and weary with our long march. My long-legged male elephant had kept me in perpetual torment by plunging at every step, and nearly breaking my back. The voices of deer were heard in the vicinity of the camp after dark. These inquisitive animals were most likely attracted by the light of our fires.

Next morning we crossed the Meh Mau, and soon afterwards left it at the point where it turns south to enter the Meh Chang, which empties into the Meh Wung—seven and a half hours' journey to the south of Lakon. During the first three miles from the camp, we gradually ascended 171 feet to the source of the Huay Kyoo Lie, and then followed that brook down-stream for two miles to where its beautiful glen merges into the great plain of the Meh Wung.

After marching across the plain for three hours, we entered the rice-fields and suburbs of Ban Sa-det, and passing through the village, put up at the *sala*, or rest-house, which is situated on the banks of the Meh Wung. During the morning we met a party of Burmese Shans, accompanying 102 oxen laden with salt, which they were bartering for cotton to take back with them to Kiang Tung. Ban Sa-det is 60½ miles from Zimmé and 823 feet above the level of the sea.

The village was crowded with people from the neighbouring villages, who had come to join in the New Year festivities and to make their offerings at the temples and monasteries. Long strings of men, women, and children streamed past us in single file, all dressed in their best, on their way to the monasteries—some carrying baskets or brass trays on their heads, and others baskets dangling from both ends of a long flat shoulder-bamboo. Every conceivable want of the monks would certainly be satisfied. Pillows for their heads, handsomely worked three-cornered pillows to rest their elbows on, rugs to sit on, and mats for reclining; new yellow garments, lamps, palm-leaf manuscripts beautifully inscribed and covered with handsomely embroidered covers, fans and face-screens, luscious fruits and delicate viands,—what more could pious monks require, particularly when they were sheltered by such a beautiful and spacious building, situated in such a shady and well-kept garden, as had been erected for them by the people?

Women and children came crowding round the elephants whilst they were being unloaded; and as soon as our things were carried up the steps, followed closely in their wake to gaze at us and our doings and further satisfy their curiosity. Their natural politeness, however, forbade them to mount on to the verandah itself until they were invited to do so. Of course the invitation came as soon as we saw their heads above the level of the floor, and I ordered the boys to get out my packets of beads and bead necklaces so as to cheer the hearts of the little children with such inexpensive presents. How their eyes gloated on them! how their little hands clutched them when they were given! how the presents were passed round and separately admired! how this child wanted a necklace similar to what another child had got! how women who had no children with them urged that they had children at home, and pitifully besought me to give them beads for the absent ones! how there was no satisfying anybody! and those who could get no more were quickly replaced by others who had heard the glad tidings for the children. The whole formed a scene not easily forgotten, and I was sorry when I had to close my hoard in order to keep some of my wealth for distribution elsewhere.

The three days during which the festivities of the New Year last form the chief festival in Buddhist countries—except, perhaps, that ensuing at the end of the Buddhist Lent, which lasts from the day after the full moon of July to the full moon of October—when the merry season is ushered in by a great feasting of the monks, and fun waxes fast and furious. During Lent, marriages, feasts, and public amusements are forbidden to the pious. Some of the monks retire into the forest, or into caves in the hills far from the haunts of men, to devote themselves to religious meditation; and the people observe more strictly than usual the four duty-days which are prescribed in each lunar month, and in which all good Buddhists are expected to worship at the pagodas. Only the most pious of the monks turn into recluses during Lent. The remainder return each night to their monasteries, and are not free to roam through the country until that season is over. In the Ping States, throughout Lent, lanterns are hung aloft to guide the spirits through the air, and thus leave no excuse for them to descend into the streets. The observance of this custom is general, and probably arises from the fact that the close of the rains is an unhealthy season, and that certain spirits are believed to bring disease.

The malevolent and beneficent spirits—the belief in whom forms the earlier, and indeed the reigning, religion of the people—likewise have in the Shan States a Lent or season set apart for the stricter execution of religious duties towards them. This lasts from February to May, during which time the people very religiously observe the various rites and ceremonies of spirit-worship. One of these ceremonies consists in making offerings once in the eleventh month and once in the twelfth month to the spirits of the river, for having defiled the water by bathing and throwing refuse into it.

As soon as it is dark, the river becomes alive with joyous pleasure-seeking people hastening to the scene. Offerings, consisting of fairy skiffs and rafts of banana-stalks carrying flowers, betel-nut, seri-leaf, incense, and lighted tapers, are floated in myriads upon the river, and are replaced by others as they disappear in the distance. A similar ceremony occurs in Burmah and Siam at the close of Lent. Upon the toy rafts and boats floated in the river opposite Bangkok, and upon all the canals, are placed miniature temples, pagodas, and transparencies of birds and beasts, all brightly illuminated with wax candles. They are sent off one at a time, and float down with the tide, beautifully illuminating the river. When the miniature fleet has disappeared, the king applies a match to fireworks that have been arranged in boats; and then are seen trees of fire, green shrubbery, and a variety of flowers of ever-changing colours, with rockets and squibs in great profusion. Large and small guns are fired from the surrounding walls of Bangkok to scare away the evil spirits; and during the three days of the New Year festival, companies of priests are employed by the king on the top of the walls, going through certain ceremonies in concert, so as to drive the evil spirits from the city.

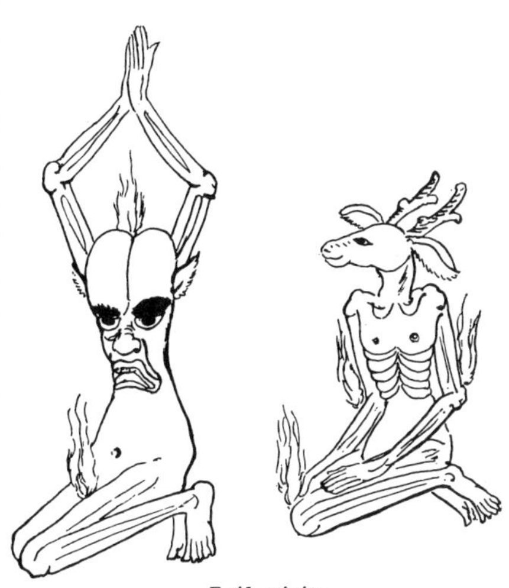

Evil spirits.

Offerings to the spirits of the land or rivers are frequently made in cases of sickness by the people. These consist of clay images, rice, vegetables, flesh, fruit, flowers, and wax tapers, set on toy boats or rafts and placed on the stream or in the street, whichever is the public highway. The spirits are supposed to find the food, &c., and become appeased.

Other superstitions are connected with these naiads. One seems to have given rise to the trial by water, which can still be claimed in the Ping States—both accuser and defendant having to enter the river and see which can keep his head longest under water without coming up for breath; and another, which accounts for the seeming heartlessness of the people towards drowning folk. The common belief is that the water-sprite will certainly resent the interference of one person in rescuing another, by at some future time claiming the rescuer as a substitute.

A dryad.

New Year's Day amongst the Shans and Burmese occurs at the time of the expected break of the south-west monsoons, and is held in honour of the great Indian rain-god Indra, who is invoked by the people to strike the great demon-shaped clouds (personified in India as the Demon Vritra) which bring the periodical rains, upon which the fertility of the ground depends. In the month of May, in India, the heat becomes intense: vegetation is dried up, the crops cannot be sown, the cattle droop, and milk and butter become scarce. Famine or plenty depends upon the expected rains, and the daily gathering of the clouds is watched with anxiety; but although the array of clouds is constantly enlarging, there is no rain until a rattling thunderstorm charges the ranks and the broken clouds let loose the impetuous showers. "This," according to the Sama Veda, "is Indra, who comes 'loud shouting' in his car, and hurls his thunderbolt at the demon Vritra."

Indra is represented in the Vedas as a young and handsome man, with a beautiful nose and chin, ever joyous, and delighting in the exhilarating draughts of Soma juice. When offering to Indra, the priest exclaims—"Thy inebriety is most intense; nevertheless, thy acts are most beneficent."

The evening of the next day, when we were at Lakon, the monsoon burst upon us. A great low-lying phalanx of black bellying clouds came up in battle array from the horizon, and, like a vast black curtain, quickly hid every star from our view. Then commenced the stupendous fight. Indra's bolts, dashing in every direction, rent the clouds, and the rain came pouring down in torrents upon the thirsty earth.

Amongst the Ping Shans, New Year's Day is the same as in Burmah, and is fixed by the position of the sun and not by that of the moon. It is the time of the great Water Festival, when for three days Phya In, or Indra—the rain-god and king of the Dewahs—is supposed to descend at midnight to the earth to stay for three or four days. On the signal of his arrival being given, a formal prayer is made, and jars full of water, which have been placed at the door of each house, their mouths stoppered with green leaves, have their contents poured on the ground as a libation to the god, in order to ensure the prosperity of the household; and every one who has a gun hastens to fire it off as a salute to the rain-god.

The first thing in the morning the people take fresh pots of water to the monasteries, and present them to the abbot and his monks; and in the afternoon the women proceed to the temples to wash the images, and later on freely douse their grandparents and other aged relatives. The scene of the image-washing is highly picturesque. Before leaving home for the temples, the women compound various perfumery from spices and flowers, which, when duly prepared, is cast into a metal basin—sometimes of silver—filled with fresh well-water. Newly cut flowers lie on the surface of the water, and likewise deck the hair of the women and girls, and even the top-knots of the little boys who accompany them.

Each woman, and even tiny little girl, bears a basin of perfumed water in her hands, and all trip along gaily, dressed in all the finery at their disposal, chatting and jesting merrily together, to the temple. As they enter its grounds, which are enclosed by low white-plastered brick walls, along two sides of which are erected sheds for the accommodation of pilgrims, the abbot and his monks, in their bright yellow garments, and with their bald pates glistening in the sun, may be seen strolling amongst the pleasant shady fruit-trees. Everything has been kept neat and trim by the pious villagers, not even a stray leaf is to be seen, and fresh sand has been scattered about the grounds as a finishing touch. The great white-walled temple, with its handsome many-tiered roof, and its floor raised some feet from the ground, stands with its door facing the entrance-gate, and a broad flight of steps, with handsome side walls surmounted by great plastered dragons embellished with coloured glass scales of various tints, and the bottoms of beer-bottles for eyes, leads up to the double entrance-door.

There are no windows in the building; and therefore the only light shed upon the great image, besides that glimmering from above, comes from the entrance-door, which faces the shrine, and from the rows of wax tapers which are placed on a stand before the image. On its pedestal are many smaller images covered with gold-leaf or silver, and all intended as resemblances of Gaudama Buddh; some depicting him in a sitting, others in a recumbent, and a few in a standing posture. As you enter the temple, leaving the sunshine for the dim religious light of the great hall, you notice about the altar wreaths and garlands of lovely flowers, fruit of various kinds, piles of newly made yellow robes which have been woven by the women, new mats, and various other offerings, that have been made to the temple and the monks.

The offerings not required, are supposed to be sold by the layman attached to the monastery, and the money given to the sick and needy. The monasteries, I may here remark, serve as refuges for poor travellers, who are welcome at all times to shelter and food as long as they conduct themselves properly.

The floor of the temple is generally of brick covered with a hard white cement, and the walls of the temples are frequently adorned with fresco paintings representing incidents in the lives of Gaudama Buddh, as related in the Zahts,—the favourite one being the Jataka of Naymee, where he is represented as a white ghostly figure in a chariot, passing through the eight hells and the six heavens of the Dewahs. The punishments depicted as happening to various evil-doers in the hells make one's flesh creep. Other pictures portraying the occupations of daily life, the different nationalities seen in the country, and even sepoys and British soldiers, besides

Punishments in the Buddhist hells.

civilians with great tall hats or enormous sola-topees, adorn the walls of some of the temples.

Groups of women and children are squatting about on the floor. Neighbours who have not met for a time are chatting together in an ordinary tone of voice. Youths and maidens are joking together, or having a quiet flirtation. Here an aged woman, telling her beads and mumbling her prayers, presses her hands together, and lifting them above her head, inclines her body in a low bow to the great image of Buddha, till her head and hands are pressing the floor. There a mother with her little child on her knee, closes its tiny palms on the stalk of a flower, and teaches the infant how to worship the great lawgiver Buddha.

Presently the abbot, or one of the elderly monks, commences in a monotonous tone to read one of the sacred books, which, being written in Pali, none of the women or children can understand. The service being over, the ceremony of bathing the images commences. All rise to their feet, and the men carry the smaller images into a miniature temple of bamboo, that has been erected in the grounds. When they are all arranged, the women gather around, and each one, taking her basin, dashes the water over the images, which are too sacred for a woman's hand to touch.

The missionaries told me that the images are likewise drenched with water in times of drought, when the rice crop is being injured for want of rain. Only the year before, the chief of Zimmé, accompanied by his retinue of princes and attendants, ascended to the temple of Loi Soo Tayp, and had the images removed from the building into the grounds of the pagoda. Then the pagoda and images were thoroughly doused with water, to awake the attention of the spirits of deceased monks that were domiciled in them, to the wants of the people. Another day a procession of a hundred monks visited the temple for the same purpose. Finding these spirits obdurate, or too somnolent to be of use, the execution of some convicts was hastened in order to propitiate Poo-Sa and Ya-Sa, the guardian, rain-producing genii of the hills, so that they might allow more water to flow down the streams for irrigating the fields. It is evident that the people believed that these tutelary spirits were hankering after their former diet, and had perhaps forgotten their promise to Gaudama when he visited their haunts.

Another peculiar ceremony occurs, according to Dr M'Gilvary, at the full moon of the fourth Ping Shan month, which usually falls in January. It is called by a name signifying "The warming of Buddh." About daylight, bonfires are kindled in the temple grounds, at which are assembled a larger number than usual of worshippers. It is the cool season of the year, when the mornings are uncomfortably cold; but no one dares to warm himself by the bonfires on that morning. They are sacred to the spirits of deceased monks inhabiting the images of Buddh, and are kindled for their especial benefit. When the fires are lighted, incense-tapers are taken by the priests, who go inside of the temple, prostrate themselves before the images, and invite them to come out and be warmed by the sacred fires. It is a sham invitation, however, so far as the images are concerned, as they are not carried out; but the spirits of the poor cold deceased monks are presumed to gladly accept it.

The greatest fun of the Water Festival at the New Year happens amongst the young people. Young men and maidens dash water over each other at every chance they have; little boys, with squirts and syringes, are in their glory; and every one is soon drenched to the skin. No one thinks of changing his clothes, and the fun continues day after day during the festival, amidst stifled screams and shouts of merriment. It is the hottest time of the year, and nobody catches cold; and no one would care to get through the three days with dry clothes! for the wetting is looked upon as a compliment.

Notwithstanding the great heat, the thermometer for three hours in the day marking 101° in the shade, we rambled about amongst the crowd, visited the monastery, pagoda, and temples, watched the fun and the fireworks, and thoroughly enjoyed ourselves. In the grounds of the pagoda were two fine bells, hanging in beautifully carved belfries. The bells had the usual pieces of stag-horn lying close to them. After completing their orisons, it is customary for the devotees to strike the bell thrice with the deer-horn, in order to awaken the attention of the guardian spirits, and every one else, to the fact of their having done so.

The next morning we were off early, and continued for nearly eight miles down the valley of the Meh Wung, through an extensive rice-plain, to the eastern entrance of the city of Lakon. On our way we passed near ten villages, and crossed a stream, which is known as Huay Bau Kyow (the Stream of the Ruby Mines). I therefore presume that rubies have been found near the source of this stream. Before reaching the city, we noticed a chain of high hills commencing to the east, each link either separated from the others or divided by merely undulating ground. They are certainly isolated from any other range, because the Meh Mau, which we had followed down from our last pass, after draining their eastern sides, enters the Meh Wung some miles below the city.

The eastern entrance of the city is distant 53 miles from Zimmé, and is protected by brick walls 15 feet high, which enclose a courtyard 40 feet long and 30 feet wide, entered by strong outer and inner gates. A brick wall of the same height extends round three sides of the city; while the western side is simply protected by a palisade—the former wall having been destroyed by the encroachment of the river, which skirts the north and west sides of the city.

After proceeding for three-quarters of a mile through the town, we left it by the western gate, and halted near the bank of the river at the house of Chow Don, the Siamese Assistant Judge, who had kindly placed it at our disposal.

CHAPTER XXII.

LAKON AND LAPOON DATE FROM THE SIXTH CENTURY—DESCRIPTION OF LAKON—A CHRISTIAN JUDGE—LAW AND JUSTICE—PUNISHMENTS COMMUTED TO FINES—LEGEND OF THE DIPPED PRINCE—LEGEND OF LAKON—A MODERN JOKE—LEGEND OF THE RING LAKE—THE GOD OF MEDICINE—THE ASWINS MENDING AN OLD MAN—ORIGIN OF QUACK-DOCTORS—A SIAMESE DOCTOR—THEORY OF DISEASE—MEDICINES—174 INGREDIENTS IN A DOSE—DRAUGHTS FOR THE POOR, PILLS FOR THE RICH—MEDICINES BY PAILFUL—EMPIRICS—BELIEF IN DEMONS AND WITCHES—MODE OF PAYMENT BY THE JOB—NO CURE, NO PAY—FEE TO THE GOD OF MEDICINE—PRIESTS TO THE DEMONS—SACRIFICES—CONTAMINATION FROM LEPERS—SMALLPOX AND VACCINATION—FILTHY DWELLINGS AND FURNITURE—NO PILLOW-CASES OR SHEETS—KILLING BUGS—VILLAGES ON THE MEH WUNG—DR NEIS'S SURVEY—KAREN CHRISTIANS—REV. D. WEBSTER—DR CUSHING ILL—EAGERNESS FOR WORK—MALARIOUS FEVERS—NUMEROUS KARENS IN BRITISH SHAN STATES—TRADE OF LAKON—VISIT THE CHIEF—CHEAP LABOUR FOR THE RAILWAY—GREAT HEAT—BURST OF THE MONSOON.

LAKON (Lakhon, Lakaung, Lagong, or Nakhon Lampang), the capital of a Shan State of the same name, is said to have been built on the site of an old Lawa city by Aindawa Raja, the younger son of Queen Zamma Dewah, who was raised to the throne at Lapoon A.D. 576. The queen is said to have been the daughter of the king of Vieng Chang, formerly a powerful kingdom in the basin of the Meh Kong, and the widow of a prince of Cambodia. It is a double city, part being built on either side of the river, and is the most important Ping Shan town to the south of Zimmé. The palace is in the section lying along the east bank; and the city with its suburbs is said to contain a population of about 20,000 souls, a hundred of whom are Chinese.

Like Lapoon (Labong or Lamphun), the State of Lakon

owes allegiance to Zimmé as well as to Bangkok, and formed part of the ancient kingdom of Zimmé. It contains 15 Muangs, or provinces. The chief's residence is of the usual type of double teak-framed houses, separated by a passage on the raised flooring, inhabited by Shan gentry, wealthy Burmese foresters, and Chinese merchants in the Ping States. Its compound, which contained two other buildings, is surrounded by a brick wall 10 feet high, much out of the perpendicular, on the south-west side, the foundations not having been carried low enough. On the opposite side of the road are several fine temples, resplendent with beautiful wood-carving and fresh gilding; and nearer the gate is the palace of the Chow Hona, or second chief.

The houses lining the streets are enclosed in large palisaded gardens, in which the dwellings for the demons, each two feet square, stuck upon posts, and looking like pigeon-houses, formed prominent features. Near the palace of the Chow Hluang are the court-house and jail. The latter is surrounded by a high plank fence. Looking through the chinks between the planks, we saw a few prisoners heavily loaded with chains squatting in the enclosure.

In the afternoon the head Chow Phya, Chow See Ha Nat, came to call on Dr M'Gilvary, and gave me much information. This nobleman had been for a long time the chief judge of the court, and some years before had been converted by Dr M'Gilvary. Since then he had been exemplary in his conduct as a Christian. I took the opportunity to question him as to the methods of conducting law and justice in the country. According to him, before the commencement of an action each party has to pay five rupees into court, the defendant having to borrow the money if he is not the owner of it. The charge is then written down by a court official, together with the evidence of the witnesses; frequently a *douceur* from either party weighs down the scales of justice, and gains the case for the richer or most unscrupulous party. Since he had become a Christian he had seldom been allowed to try a case.

Money in the Ping States, like charity, covers a multitude of sins; and for most crimes, in fact for all, at the will of the supreme chief the punishment of imprisonment, or even death, can be commuted to fines. As the salaries of the court officials, as well as some of the emoluments of the chiefs, depend upon bribery, fees, and fines, this is naturally the favourite mode of punishment. The higher the fine, the greater the fee, for 20 per cent is added to the fine as a fee for the officials of the court, and 10 per cent for the head judge. Fines for drunkenness are the perquisite of the supreme chief, whether Chow Che-wit (the Lord of Life, the title of the supreme chief of Zimmé and Muang Nan) or Chow Hluang (the title of the chiefs of Lakon, Lapoon, Peh, Luang Prabang, &c.) In cases of theft, double the value of the beast or thing stolen has to be paid to the late owner, as well as the fine to the court. If an elephant is stolen, a fine of 200 rupees has to be paid to the chief by the culprit. If a man cannot pay the fees, award, and fine, he is put into chains, and forced to saw wood, or do other work, receiving no pay or food from the officials whilst a prisoner. He has to beg in chains for his food, and prisoners in chains are frequently seen begging in the market-place, or from house to house. The prisoners are thus fed at the expense of their friends and relations, or, if they have none in the vicinity, by the charitably disposed. The imprisonment lasts until the man is released by the payment of the award and fees, whether by himself or by his friends, and seldom continues more than two or three years, for he is generally released, if impecunious, at the intercession of the lord whose serf he is.

In relation to the hills lying to the east of the city, which I sketched before leaving, the Chow Phya told me the following legend:—

In the time of Gaudama Buddh, Kom-ma Rattsee (the Siamese Komara-pat—the god Rudra, in the Rig Veda, who was worshipped by the ancient Aryans), a famous magician, demigod, and doctor, visited Lakon, and informed the princes and people that by his medicines and charms he could add beauty and restore youth and life to any one, however he might have been dismembered and mangled. A decrepit old prince, who was verging on dotage, and longed for a renewal of his youth, begged the magician to experiment upon him. The doctor, after mincing him up, prepared a magic broth, and, throwing the fragments into it, placed it over the fire. After performing the necessary incantations, the prince, rejuvenated and a perfect beau, was handed out of the pot. He was so pleased with his new appearance, and the new spirit of youth and joy pervading him, that he entreated the magician to reperform the operation, as he thought the first chopping up having been so successful, still greater benefits would accrue from its repetition. On the magician refusing, he clamorously persisted in his request. The demigod, annoyed at his persistence and his covetousness, accordingly minced him up and put him into the pot, where he remains to this day. The hill where the Phya, or prince, was dipped, is called Loi Phya Cheh (the hill of the dipped Phya); and a hill near it is known as Loi Rattsee (Russi), after the magician. Another of the hills is known as Loi Mon Kow Ngam (the hill of the horns of the beautiful wild

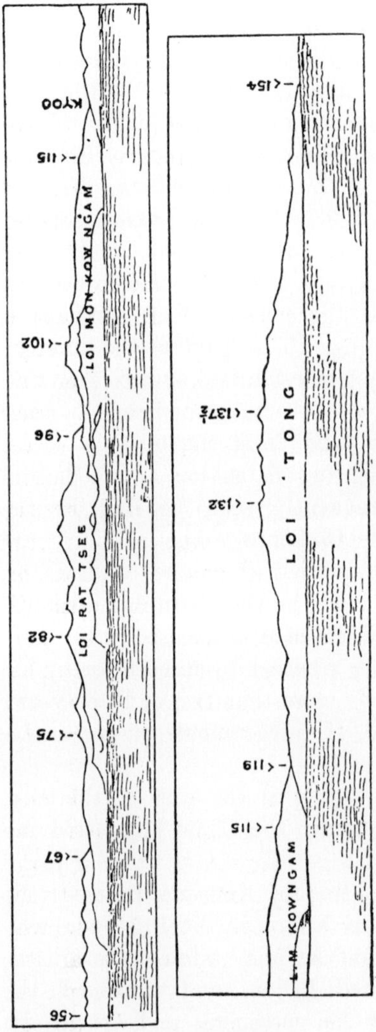

View of hills east of Lakon.

cow). Poo Chow, the celebrated Lawa monarch, is said to have been killed by the cow whilst pursuing it. He is the tutelary spirit of the district, and is worshipped by the people. The hill on which he was slain is known as Loi Kyoo Poo Chow (the hill of the pass of the revered Chow). *Poo,* or *pu,* is a term of high esteem, and means a paternal grandfather.

After relating the legend of Muang Ngow, which I have already referred to, he told us that of Lakon, which runs as follows: There was once a Lawa living on the verge of the Lakon State, when the whole of the country was covered by a dense forest. Hearing that Gaudama Buddh was visiting the site of Wat Lam Pang, the Lawa hastened to procure some wild honey, and placing it in the joint of a bamboo, slung it to the end of a shoulder-pole, formed from the branch of a Mai Ka Chow tree, and proceeded on his way to the Buddh. The country through which he passed is known as La-Kaun, the Lawa's walk (from *la* or *lawa,* and *kaun* or *kon,* walk). After eating the honey, the Buddh planted the bamboo joint in the ground, and from it sprang a great clump of yellow-stemmed bamboos, which still flourishes near the *Wat,* or temple. The branch of the tree being driven by the Buddh into the ground, with its thin end downwards, sprouted and became a tree, still thriving on the spot, bearing leaves reversed from their natural position. The tree, bamboo, and temple are objects of pilgrimage, and are worshipped twice a-year, in the second and sixth months.

He then related a modern joke about Phra Chedi Sow, the sacred twenty pagodas, situated five miles to the north-west of Lakon. These pagodas are likewise the site of pious picnics. An observant pilgrim happening to count them, could find but nineteen. Over and over again he counted, thinking that he must be mistaken, but his tally was always the same. At last he applied to the abbot for an explanation, and was assured that the twentieth pagoda was at Ban Wang Sow, the village of twenty pools, distant some miles to the south of Lakon, where there is a pagoda. This the old Chow Phya considered to be an immense joke.

After nearly splitting his sides with laughter over this humorous tale, he said that there was a legend about a small lake in the neighbourhood called Nong Wen (the lake of the ring), which we might perhaps like to hear. On our assenting, he said the name arose from the following circumstance: A youth wandering through the woods with his sweetheart became unseemly in his attentions, and thereby deeply offended the local spirit, who, to punish them, caused the ground to sink gradually under their feet. The couple fled in great fear. The young man in his terror grasped the girl's hand, and she, in her hurry to get away, wrenched it from him with such force that her ring fell off and came to the ground. The ring sinking, became a round pool—the Ring Lake.

Komara-pat, the god of medicine, mentioned in the first legend, is sacrificed to by all doctors in Siam at the expense of their patients, and in the stories told of him, seems to have many of the qualities of the Aswins, two grotesque personages in the Rig Veda, who were the general practitioners of medicine amongst the Aryans. In the Rig Veda they are described as brothers of the sun, and travel in three-cornered, three-wheeled cars drawn by asses. They are depicted as half-comic, half-serious personages, with very long arms, and are concerned in every odd legend in the Veda. To a holy man who was beheaded for revealing to them forbidden science, they presented a horse's head, and stuck it on his neck in place of his own head. They enabled the lame to walk and the blind to see, and restored an "aged man to youth, as a wheelwright repairs a worn-out car." These professors in healing seem to be the progenitors of the jugglers, magicians, and quacks found in all ages, not only in the East, but in Europe.

A Siamese doctor, according to an account given by a medical missionary, is distinguished from other folk by his medicine-box, wrapped up in a piece of figured muslin or some silken or woollen fabric, holding half a bushel, more or less, of pills and powders, carried under his arm or in his little skiff, or in the arms of a single servant. As the customs of the country require physicians to remain day and night with their patients while suffering under grave diseases, it is impossible for them to attend upon many persons at a time. Doctors are therefore far from being in the possession of a lucrative practice, and few are lucky enough to be able to save sufficient to enable them to acquire a teak-built house, surrounded by an orchard, and support two or three wives, together with a growing family.

Polygamy among them is accounted a mark of opulent distinction, and is looked upon as a favour which has descended to them by virtue of good deeds performed in previous states of existence.

The Siamese, according to the same authority, put diseases down to disturbances in the four elements, *ahpo* (water), *lom* (wind), *dacho* (fire), and the earth. Water produces dropsy; wind produces rheumatism, epilepsy, apoplexy, headache, flatulency, colic, inflammation, &c.; fire produces all kinds of fevers, measles, boils, smallpox, &c.; and the earth, by its invisible and impalpable mists and vapours, induces cholera and other terrible plagues. The spirits, both good and evil, have great power over these four elements internally and externally, and can produce a multitude of bodily ailments. The people, knowing that they have accumulated much demerit in their present state of existence as well as for their sins in their innumerable previous existences, feel themselves at the mercy of these spirits, and do all they possibly can to propitiate them.

The doctors use four general classes of medicines to combat the disturbances that are caused by the four elements. These are chiefly derived from the vegetable kingdom, and from such kinds as are indigenous to their country. A small proportion of their medicines are imported from China, and purchased from Chinese apothecaries. Barks, roots, leaves, chips, orchard-fruit, and herbs, constitute the great bulk of their *materia medica*. Next to these they employ articles of medicine belonging to the animal kingdom, such as bones, teeth, sea-shells, fish-skins, snake-skins, urine, eyes of birds, cattle, cats, and the bile of snakes and of numerous other animals. Lastly, but less frequently, they employ articles from the mineral kingdom, such as stones, saltpetre, borax, lead, antimony, sulphate of copper, table-salt, sulphate of magnesia, and, very rarely, mercury. Besides the above, aloes and gamboge, and a few other gums and resins, are occasionally used.

The dependence of Siamese physicians, in waging war with disease, is more upon a large combination of ingredients in a prescription than upon the power of any one or two of the same. Hence they often have scores of components in a single dose. One hundred and seventy-four ingredients were counted by a missionary in one prescription, which was ordered to be taken in three doses.

They employ their vegetable combinations chiefly in the state of decoction or infusion. A common way of speaking of the quantity of medicine which a person has taken is to say that he has swallowed three, five, or more pots of it—each pot containing from two to four quarts. And a common way of paying the doctor is by the potful, from 30 to 60 cents each. The form of pills is esteemed a more select mode of administering their vegetable medicines; but as these are more expensive and troublesome to prepare, patients are charged more highly for them.

Medical practitioners in Siam are all, with rare exceptions, self-taught, or mere empirics. If a man wishes to try his fortune as a doctor he reads a native medical manuscript or two upon some kind of disease, and quickly ventures to practise, following the directions of the book. If he happens to be successful in a case, or nature has cured the person in spite of his treatment, he trumpets his triumph abroad, and asserts that he has rescued his patient from death; and the Siamese, who, with all their native cunning, are easily gulled in medical matters, credit his reports, and his fame is assured. The ignorance of the physicians is safeguarded by the fact that all the cures that take place in connection with the use of their physic are attributed to it, and all failures to cure are supposed to result from the malicious interference of evil spirits, wizards, witches, or something else beyond the power of human skill to contend against.

Physicians are paid by results; and a bargain is struck to pay so much if the patient is cured, before the case is undertaken. If the doctor appears to have done his best, and has been very attentive, the people, even in case of the death of the patient, evince their gratitude by a valuable donation, as well as by small gifts whilst the patient is being treated. It is very seldom that "a job of healing" is undertaken for less than 8 ticals (a tical is worth two shillings), or for more than 20 ticals. The price may run up to ten or even twenty times the amount of these sums, in an inverse proportion to the reduction of the hope of effecting a cure, as the disease progresses. The pledges given are always verbal; but as there is never any want of living witnesses to attest them, the successful doctor can claim their payment by law, and in case of default of money, goods, or chattels, he may seize any of the family of the patient or relations dependent upon him or her under the age of twenty, and employ the youth or maiden as his bond-slave in lieu of interest of the debt until it is paid.

Over and above the amount of the pledge, the law allows the practitioner to demand in all cases of successful treatment the customary fee, which uniformly amounts to 3½ ticals, equivalent to seven shillings in English money. This fee is called *Kwan-Kow Kaya*, and is divided, like its name, into two parts. The *Kwan-Kow* consists of a proffer of 1½ tical (three shillings) in silver, made by the patient or his friends. This forms part of the offering for propitiating the primitive teacher of medicine, the demigod Komara-pat, who is believed to exert influence in the spirit-world over diseases. A wax candle is stuck upright in a brass basin or earthen bowl, and the money is planted in the candle. Then a small quantity of rice, salt, chillies, onions, plantains, &c., is placed in the same vessel, and an incantatory form is recited over it by the physician. No Siamese doctor will enter on the treatment of a patient, however trifling the disease, without paying his respects in this manner to the father of medicine.

The second part of the fee, termed *Kaya* (literally, the price of medicine), is 2 ticals, equivalent to four shillings, which is the supposed legal cost of the medicines that may be given in the treatment of the case, be it little or much.

The law having joined these two parts of the custom together, they must be exacted together. These two amounts remain in charge of the friends of the patient until the physician has worked the cure; and if he fails, he cannot claim the money.

Another legal method by which Siamese practitioners increase their incomes is by acting as priests to the demons who are supposed to cause disease. They take advantage of the universal superstition that the deceased spirits of mankind have power to cause, as well as cure, disease; and that they can be propitiated by offerings. The people credit the doctors with the power to tell whether these oblations are required or not; and for each time that he is at the trouble of making such offerings, he may legally claim, in case of cure, three shillings from his patient. This oblation is called *Kraban*, and is performed as follows: The doctor moulds little clay images, sometimes of men, women, or children; sometimes of elephants, horses, oxen, or swine; and sometimes of silver or gold coin; and places them on a little float, or stand made of plantain stalk, or leaf. Interspersed among them, he puts a little rice, salt, pepper, onion, plantain, chillies, seri-leaf, and betel-nut, and lights up the whole by placing a small candle on the stand. Thus arranged, he carries it into the street, and lays it down by the wayside; or, if the house faces the river or canal, he sets it afloat, and leaves it to take care of itself. The fee for making this sacrifice is called *Soo-a Kraban.*

The listlessness of the Siamese and other Shans with regard to contagious diseases is astonishing. They seldom take any care to avoid contact with leprous persons, who are quite common in their families; and until 1840, when vaccination was introduced by the American missionaries, they had no thought of shielding themselves or their children from their most terrible scourge, smallpox. Even now, when the utility of vaccination is explained to them, many shrug their shoulders and carelessly reply, "Tam boon tam kam,"—follow good, follow evil—which implies that they must submit to whatever happiness or sorrow their deserts bring them.

One of the great causes of disease amongst them is, doubtless, the uncleanliness of their dwellings and furniture. It might be inferred that a people so fond of bathing, and so particular in washing their persons and clothes, would be equally clean in their houses. But such is not the fact. They scarcely ever scrub the ceilings, walls, or floors of their dwellings. You may see dirt upon the walls and posts of their houses, layer upon layer, the accumulation of years. The floors, if made of plank, are always of a dingy dirty colour, yet polished with a varnish made by the dirt of their bare feet continually rubbed in with other filth. Here and there in the floor you will see holes conducting to the lower storey, which they use as spittoons, and for other purposes.

The houses of the nobles and wealthier classes have one room, or more, carpeted with grass matting, which hides the holes above mentioned, and such rooms are pretty well furnished with spittoons, generally dirty beyond description. When the floors are of split bamboo, the ordinary flooring of the poorer classes, one has a clear view of the filth beneath the floor, as the interstices between the slats are many and often large.

A peculiar concentration of filthiness is to be found in Siamese bedrooms, especially so if they are occupied by invalids. The sick have little strength or spirit to give attention to the cleanliness of their persons, much less to their bedding, and their relatives are little disposed to care for these things. It is fortunate that their rooms are well ventilated through chinks in the walls, floors, and roofs ; and that the continually accumulating filth is quickly dried, and is thus probably deprived of much of its inherent power to engender disease.

The missionary stated that, having visited the sick at their homes for twenty-nine years, he might truthfully say he had not seen a clean mattress, pillow, or mosquito-bar oftener than once in twenty visits, and then only among his Christian flock. The bedrooms amongst the masses of the people were generally horribly untidy. Their mattresses and pillows, having never had a sheet or pillow-case put over them, and having been used for months, and sometimes years, without any kind of washing, were generally brown and greasy as smoked bacon. Their mosquito-curtains, which when new were white, looked as if they had been long smoked in a chimney. The unmistakable marks of bed-bugs were thick and black enough to throw a European lady, or even gentleman, into hysterical fits at the sight. The Siamese think it wrong to kill their bugs, so merely take them up tenderly, and drop them into a little cocoa-nut oil, which soon gives them their quietus; or place the infested mats in the sun, so that the unacclimatised pests may die of sunstroke.

After such a description of the loathsome habits of the Siamese, it is refreshing to return to the Christian Chow Phya, whom we left squatting on the floor, telling us tales about the country. Before he left, I asked him to draw me a map showing the position of the different streams entering the Meh Wung, from the source of the river to its junction with the Meh Ping. On its completion, he gave me the names of 112 villages lying in the basin of the river, and said there were many more whose names he could not recollect. Fifty-four of these villages lay to the north of the city, and the remainder to the south in the portion of the valley that will be traversed by our proposed railway. Villages containing less than thirty houses were not included in his list.

Elephants, he said, took 13 days in travelling from Lakon to Raheng; 4 days to Muang Peh; and 5 days from Muang Peh to Muang Nan. In following the White Elephant route from Lakon to Raheng, the road is easy, and no hills are crossed between the two places. This portion of the country which will be traversed by the railway was surveyed by Dr Paul Neis in 1884, and a copy of his survey has been submitted to the Government and Chambers of Commerce with the other maps, included in our "Report on Railway connection of Burmah and China."

The Rev. David Webster, of the American Baptist Mission, whom I had met at the Siamese frontier-post on the Thoungyeen river, and subsequently shared quarters with at Zimmé, has been very successful amongst the Karens in the hills neighbouring Lakon. This field was only opened out in 1881; and in 1885 he had 161 Karen converts in these villages amongst his congregation. I have never met a missionary more in earnest than Mr Webster. He and his wife and their golden-haired little daughter seem utterly regardless of creature-comforts, and make long journeys among the hill-people, bearing all sorts of inconveniences in order to carry out their good work. I cannot speak too highly of all the American missionaries I had the pleasure to meet in the country. Although Dr Cushing was ailing with incipient smallpox, which had not yet declared itself, we could with difficulty persuade him to refrain from visiting the Karen villages occupied by the Christians, although they lay at a considerable distance from our route.

Mr Webster has frequently suffered from malarious fever, and in his report, dated Lakon, February 10, 1885, gives some interesting particulars as to his views on the subject. He says: "It is noticeable that different localities have each its own peculiar type of fever. This that I have just experienced is entirely new to me; yet it has not had a very bad effect, except that I am weak, and not as usual inclined to much exertion. As far as fever is concerned, I do not see that we have much to choose between places. In some places some men are healthy and others are sick. Much more depends on the person than on the place, I think; and, again, as much depends upon the exposure to heat, fatigue, cold or wet, and to the lack of really good food, as upon anything else in the locality." Although all my companions got fever at one time or another, I am thankful to say that I remained free from it; the only effect the malaria seemed to have upon me was to loosen for a time every tooth in my head, which is hard lines enough when one has to munch hard biscuits or even ginger-bread nuts.

Many of the tribes between Zimmé and the Chinese frontier are Karen, and in a pamphlet published in 1881 by by Dr Cushing, he states that "the Karens in this direction, towards Zimmé and beyond towards China, are very numerous, probably more numerous than all the Karens in British Burmah." It is therefore likely that a very large field for missionary work will be opened up by our assuming control of the Shan States lying between the Salween and Meh Kong rivers.

When saying good-bye to the Chow Phya, we asked him to send the Chinese monopolist to us, so that we might learn something of the taxation and trade of the State. On his arrival he told us that he paid the Government of Lakon 12,000 rupees for the right of levying taxes, amounting to 10 per cent of the value, upon all exports from the State, other than timber; and one of his employees informed us that the bargain left this monopolist a clear gain of 10,000 rupees. His district includes Muang Ngow, Muang Penyow, and the other provinces of Lakon. The value of the exports, outside teak and other timber, must be about 300,000 rupees.

The principal exports from Lakon to Bangkok consist of teak, sapan-wood, hides, horns, cutch, ivory, and stick-lac; to China, raw cotton, rhinoceros-horns, soft deer-horns, which are used for medicine, gold-leaf, saltpetre, ivory, and brass tinsel-plates. Lakon imports from Muang Nan rock-salt; from Kiang Tung, lead, steel swords, steel ingots, walnuts, lacquered utensils, and opium; from Zimmé, cloth, crockery, betel-nuts, and pickled tea; from Muang Peh, raw cotton, tobacco, cotton cloth, betel-nut, and cutch; from Luang Prabang, gum-benjamin, stick-lac, raw silk, and fish spawn; from the Chinese province of Yunnan, opium, bee's-wax, walnuts, brass pots, ox-bells, Chinese silk piece-goods, silk jackets and trousers, silk jackets lined with fur, figured cloth, straw hats with waterproof covers; and from Muang Penyow, paddy and rice. Nine or ten Chinese boats leave Bangkok for Lakon monthly, each bringing goods to the value of between 9000 and 10,000 rupees every trip. This implies an import trade from Bangkok, chiefly in English goods, of 90,000 rupees a-month. The monopolies for opium and gambling were farmed by another Chinaman, who pays the Government 3000 rupees, and is said to make a clear profit of 10,000 rupees. The only tax levied direct from the people is one basket of paddy for each basket that is sown.

Mr Carl Bock, who visited Lakon in 1881, states in his book that "the country about Lakon is apparently rich, not only in timber, but in minerals. Near the town are some very rich iron-mines; and I also saw a quantity of galena ore, of which I was assured the mountains in the neighbourhood were full. Copper is also found in the district. The natives are skilled metal-workers, and make their own guns."

In the evening we went to the palace to call upon the Chow Hluang. We found him seated on a raised dais, giving audience to several of the princes and head *phyas*. On our approach he got up and shook hands with us as we were introduced to him by Dr M'Gilvary. He appeared much interested in the subject of the railway, and after entering into particulars as to its construction, said that it would certainly do much to increase trade and enrich the people. Five or six thousand *Kamooks* could easily be hired for the earthwork, timber-cutting, and jungle-clearing. Those employed in the teak-forests were hired for 50 rupees a-year and their food, which cost about 3 rupees a-month. Lime was burned at Ban Kwang on the Meh Wang, and bricks cost only 30 rupees for 10,000. Carpenters received from 4 annas (fourpence) to 1 rupee a-day, and sawyers charged only 5½ rupees for every 169 feet sawn. From five to six Chinese caravans came yearly to Lakon from Yunnan, each accompanied by from 30 to 80 mules; and about 10,000 laden cattle and 20,000 porters frequented the city, coming from different directions, and passed through elsewhere. A large trade was done with the surrounding regions, and with Bangkok, Burmah, and China, but he was unable, or too indolent, to give me particulars of it.

Having got all we could out of the chief, we returned to Chow Don's house just in time to escape a tremendous thunderstorm, which soon cleared the air, and greatly reduced the temperature, which for some hours during the day had stood at 102° in the shade. Many elephants are bred in the Lakon State, and a great number are employed in the extensive teak-forests that are now being worked.

The next day the temperature was much lower, as the rain continued to fall until 9 A.M., and thoroughly wetted the ground. The greatest heat during the day was only 86°, or 16° less than on the previous day. Although in a hurry to get to Zimmé, I halted till the following morning, in the hope that Dr Cushing might be benefited by the rest, and spent the time in wandering about the place and collecting information.

CHAPTER XXIII.

PRINCE BIGIT'S EXPECTED VISIT—LEAVE LAKON—CICADAS AND THEIR MUSIC—A BATTLE-FIELD—DUPLICATE KINGS OF SIAM—TRUANT ELEPHANTS — DR CUSHING HAS SMALLPOX — A BEAUTIFUL DALE — A DANGEROUS PASS—WATER-PARTING BETWEEN THE MEH WUNG AND MEH PING—NUMBER OF VILLAGES IN THE ZIMMÉ PLAIN—THE MAI CHA-LAU TREE — PAGODA ON LOI TEE — A CART-ROAD — REACH LAPOON — THE GREAT TEMPLE AND CELEBRATED PAGODA — LAPOON BUILT LIKE ALADDIN'S PALACE—DESCRIPTION OF CITY — DESERTED FOR FORTY YEARS — VISIT THE CHIEF — LEAVE LAPOON — SCENE ON THE ROAD — REACH ZIMMÉ — REPORT OF THE R.G.S. ON MY SURVEY.

DURING our stay at Lakon, great preparations were being made for the reception and comfort of one of the King of Siam's brothers, Prince Bigit, who was on his way to Zimmé, *viâ* Lakon. The prince had been sent by the king to meet Mr Gould, who had been appointed British Vice-Consul to the Zimmé Shan (Ping) States, and to uphold the claim of Siam to some valuable teak-forests lying to the north-west of Raheng, in the valley of the Meh Tien, which were claimed by the chief of Zimmé as lying within his territories. Thousands of baskets of rice had been purchased by the officials in the neighbouring principalities, besides fowls, ducks, &c., from miles around, to feed the prince and his numerous retainers. Everything eatable was therefore very high-priced at Lakon, and it was nearly impossible to procure fowls, or even vegetables. One or two such visits would cause a famine in the land.

At daylight the next morning, April 16, we left the city, and after crossing the Meh Wung (350 feet wide, 10 feet deep, with $1\frac{1}{4}$ foot of water in the bed), continued for thirty minutes through the suburbs of the town, where several temporary buildings were being erected for the Siamese prince and his retinue. The suburbs, which line the river, and extend some distance inland, are extensive, and I think must contain fully double the population within the city walls. The river was alive with people—men, women, and children—fishing in lines with drop and fling nets.

We then proceeded in a direction a little to the north of east, and for five miles passed through, or near, extensive rice-plains, noticing many large villages fringing their borders. For the next three miles we marched through a plain in which many great *thyt-si* (black-varnish trees) were growing, all of which had great nicks cut out of their trunk, having their rounded bottoms charred for the sap-varnish to drip into. The loud rattle of the numerous cicadas in this part of the journey was nearly deafening.

These famous singers, celebrated by Homer and Virgil, are numerous in Burmah and the Shan States both in individuals and species, and are considered a delicacy by the Karens. Their notes are full, shrill, and continuous, swelling up like an Æolian harp so as to fill the air. According to Dr Mason, a celebrated missionary, botanist, and zoologist, who resided for the greater part of his life in Burmah, "The instrument on which this gay minstrel performs is a unique piece of mechanism—a perfect melodeon possessed only by the male, and which he carries about between his abdomen and hind legs. It consists of two pairs of plates comprising a shield for the box concealed beneath. Under these plates is a delicate iridescent covering, tensely stretched over the cavity, like the head of a drum; and attached to its inner surface are several musical strings, secured at their opposite extremities to another membrane at the posterior end of the box. The music is produced by the alternate contraction and expansion of these strings, which draw the tense concave covering downwards, with a rapid receding, the sounds issuing from two key-holes of the instrument, strikingly analogous to the action of the melodeon."

After leaving the varnish-trees, we crossed the Meh How near a village of the same name, and proceeded for a mile through a rice-plain, two miles in width, to the Hong Htan, the stream of the palm-trees (200 feet wide, 7 feet deep, with 9 inches of water in its bed), and halted for the night at a *sala*, or rest-house, in the village of Hang Sat, which is situated on the farther bank of the stream. Quartz gravel formed the bed of the stream, which rises in a great spur, some twenty miles to the north-west. Hang Sat lies forty-three miles from Zimmé, and 889 feet above the level of the sea.

Two great battles are said to have occurred in this neighbourhood in 1774, when the Zimmé Shans threw off the Burmese yoke. The first was between the Burmese and the Shans; the second between a Burmese army and a joint force of Shans and Siamese, who were led by two Siamese generals. These subsequently became first and second Kings of Siam.[1]

From the camp we had a splendid view of the main range of hills which divides the waters of the Meh Wung from those of the Meh Ping, its crest cutting the sky twelve miles distant to the west, and could see the entrance of the pass we were about to traverse lying nearly due west of us, and ten miles farther north the low dip in the hills forming its summit. To the north-west a great spur called Loi Koon Htan, that gives rise to the Hong Htan, ended about five miles off.

Our *sala* was only walled on three sides; and the rain falling heavily in the evening, and driving in upon us, nearly wetted us to the skin before we could rig up some plaids as a screen for our protection.

Next morning we were unable to start as early as we wished, because two of the elephants had broken their ankle-shackles in the night, and had strayed some distance before they were tracked and brought back. Rangoon creeper, the Chinese honeysuckle, abounded in the neighbourhood of the camp, and was in full flower. We continued for half a mile

[1] Up to August 1885, when George Washington, the second King of Siam, died, a duplicate king reigned in Siam in conjunction with the supreme monarch, and had much the same power as a Chow Hona has in the Shan States.

through the rice-plain, and then entered the forest. Two miles farther, after crossing the Meh Pan, we traversed some slightly rising ground, and descended to the Meh Sun close to its debouchment into the plain.

The Meh Sun, which we were about to follow for ten miles to its source, runs in a narrow valley bordered on either side by a teak-clad, table-topped mountain-spur trending in the direction of the stream, which runs from north-west to south-east.

Our first crossing of this mountain torrent was 38 miles from Zimmé, and 14 miles from Lakon, and lies at an elevation of 1049 feet above the sea.

After skirting the stream for some miles, we ascended to a *sala*, which had been erected for travellers on the crest of a small plateau-topped spur, and halted for breakfast. The rest-house was 34 miles from Zimmé.

Whilst we were breakfasting, Dr M'Gilvary noticed that small spots had broken out on Dr Cushing's hands. On his examining them, he said that there could be no doubt that they were smallpox. Dr Cushing said that they had been coming out for two days, and he was afraid that it might be the case. On calling the Shan interpreters, they at once agreed with Dr M'Gilvary, and we accordingly made arrangements as far as possible to cut off the chance of contagion from the remainder of the party. The two interpreters and Dr Cushing's servant, as well as the elephant-men, had suffered from the disease: we therefore put aside cutlery, crockery, cooking utensils, &c., for the invalid; arranged that the interpreters and his boy should wait solely upon him; gave up the rest-house to them; had a temporary shelter made for ourselves; and halted for the night, instead of making an afternoon journey.

The next morning we were off at daybreak, hurrying on towards Zimmé, where there was a doctor attached to the Presbyterian Mission. The beautiful dale which we were ascending reminded me of the lovely Derbyshire dells. The plateau-topped hills on either side were of no great height, and were wooded to their summit. The cool morning air bathed one's face, and everything around gave one a sense of exquisite pleasure. The fresh spring foliage spangled with dewdrops, partially hiding the silver-grey trunks of the trees; the dark-coloured water meandering over the white sand of the stream-bed, twisting and twirling round great granite boulders, and falling in little cascades; and the whole glistening in the early morning's sun, made a perfect picture. Even the leafless and ungainly teak-trees added beauty by contrast to the scene.

Leaving the stream where it forked near some *euphorbia* trees more than 40 feet high, which resembled gigantic cacti, we ascended the intermediate spur, and passed through a gap in the crest, 20 feet deep, which had been worn down by elephants and cattle in the course of centuries.

Our ascent along the spur was fraught with peril, as the hill was composed of friable earth, and great slips had occurred on either slope, frequently leaving a very narrow track, with precipices 80 and 100 feet deep close to its edge. Often there was only room for the elephants' feet placed one before the other, and deep holes had been worn by their following each other in the same foot-tracks for generations. Whilst on this narrow path we had to give way for cattle caravans to pass us, and at one time we were nearly precipitated down a great slip by a caravan of forty laden cattle meeting at a bend in the track. There was room for neither to turn back; but, fortunately, we were on a ledge in the slope of the hill, and our great beasts managed to scramble up the side, although it seemed nearly impossible for them to mount it.

On our way we met two Chinamen on ponies, accompanied by four porters; and shortly afterwards 151 laden cattle on their way to Lakon. The summit of the pass lies 28 miles from Zimmé, and 2136 feet above the level of the sea.

Our descent to the plain of the Meh Ta lay down the narrow valley of the Meh Sow, a stream that rises near the summit, and is bounded on either side by hill-spurs, having their crests about two miles apart, and sloping nearly to the stream-bed. For the first two miles the track led, for the sake of shortness, over several cross-spurs, and then descended to the Meh Sow, where the torrent was 40 feet wide and 2 feet deep, and flowing down its granite bed in a series of beautiful cascades.

The air was scented with the fragrant yellow blossoms of the padouk trees, and teak crested the spurs where the Meh Sow debouches on the plain. Leaving the stream near its exit from the hills, we continued through a forest of *eng* and *thyt-ya* (the Indian Sal tree), until we reached the Meh Ta. This river is 200 feet broad, 9 feet deep, with 6 inches of water, and enters the Meh Hkuang a few miles above its junction with the Meh Ping.

Having crossed the Meh Ta, we halted for the night at a couple of *salas* close to the bank, and to Ban Meh Ta.

Leaving the next day, we marched through a gap between the sandstone hillocks; near which the direct road to Zimmé leaves our route. Here we met twenty-four laden oxen. Two miles farther we commenced the ascent of the spur that divides the affluents of the Meh Ta from those of the Meh Hkuang. The ascent and descent were steep for some little distance from the crest. A tunnel through the spur would only need to be a few hundred yards long.

Two miles and a half from the crest rice-fields commenced, and from thence to 15 miles beyond Zimmé nearly the whole plain is under cultivation, and villages[1] are numerous. Continuing through the plain, I halted to ascend a knoll named Loi Tee, that juts up from the plain some distance beyond where a low spur from the hill we had last crossed ends. Loi Tee is about 100 feet high, and is crested by a celebrated pagoda and temple, from whose grounds a magnificent view is obtained of the country. Dr M'Gilvary and the remainder of the party, with the exception of Moung Loogalay and my guide, went on with Dr Cushing, whilst I got off my elephant to visit the shrine.

The broad brick staircase, 700 feet long, which led up to the platform of the pagoda, was roofed in a similar manner

[1] During my various journeys I passed through or near 222 villages in the portion of the Zimmé plain lying between the entrance of the Meh Teng, into the Meh Ping on the north and the junction of the Meh Hkuang with the Meh Ping on the south—including those on the various branches of the river.

to the one leading up to the Shway Dagon pagoda at Rangoon; and several men were employed repairing it in expectation of a visit from the Siamese prince. The temple was beautifully decorated with gold-leaf, tinsel, and glass of various colours. A wooden horse of full life-size was standing saddled on the platform near the pagoda, reminding one of the enchanted flying horse in the 'Arabian Nights.'

A raised cart-road 10 feet wide leading from Loi Tee to the ford over the Meh Hkuang, opposite the south entrance-gate of Lapoon, had recently been repaired, and, with its continuation towards Zimmé, was the only good made-road outside a town that I met during my journeys. After following this road for two and a half miles, we crossed the river (which is 250 feet broad, 10 feet deep, and had 9 inches of water in its bed), and entered the city. Five minutes later we halted at the house of Chow Don, the Siamese Assistant Judge, which is situated close to the Wat Hluang or Great Temple of Lapoon, where we put up for the night. The north gate of the city lies 12 miles from Zimmé, and the bank of the river is 1028 feet above the sea.

After breakfast, I wandered about the city visiting the pagodas and temples. The Great Temple, the finest seen by me in the Shan States, is 150 feet long and 65 feet broad. The posts of the centre aisle are $2\frac{1}{4}$ feet in diameter, and 60 feet high from the floor to the wall-plate. They are coloured with vermilion, and decorated with gold-leaf. The woodwork of the temple is beautifully carved and gilded, and richly inlaid with glass and tinsel of various colours; and the floor is flagged with rectangular slabs of marble. No expense seems to have been spared in building, adorning, and preserving the temples at this city. Many fine bronze images have been dedicated to the temples, besides the ordinary heavily gilded brick and plaster images: one of the latter, a reclining image of Gaudama, was 36 feet long.

At the entrance of the enclosure containing the Wat Hluang and the Pra Tat, or pagoda containing sacred relics, are two Rachasis, the fabulous king of beasts, one on either side, sheltered by ornamented roofs; and at each of the four corners of the pagoda are guardian spirits, sheltered in the same manner, and honoured by having an immense gilt umbrella erected in front of them. A large copper gong in the grounds measured 7½ feet in circumference, and had a magnificent tone.

The pagoda, which is said to be of stone and very ancient, is mentioned in one of the Buddhist books, and is held in great reverence by the people and by pilgrims from the neighbouring States. It rises in gradually diminishing rings to a height of 80 feet, and is covered by gilded copper plates, each 18 inches long and 12 inches wide. On the top of its spire is a handsome *htee,* or series of umbrellas which rise in a cone of five tiers. To each tier are suspended numerous small sweet-toned bells, whose clappers have large light tongues of thin metal attached to them, which are swayed by every motion in the air, the slightest breeze causing the bells to tinkle.

The pagoda is surrounded by a double paling formed of square copper rods, hollow inside; and at every 10 feet is a pillar of the same metal, surmounted at the top with a ball. Close to the railings are eight cast-iron lanterns intended to resemble temples, one of which is in the form of a junk; and cast-iron tables have likewise been erected near the base to receive the offerings of the devout. The pagoda is said to have been marked out by the two holy men, Wathoo-dewah and Tuka-danda, A.D. 574, at the time when, by their prayers and superabundant merit, they raised from out of the earth the walls, gates, and ramparts, and sunk the fosse of Lapoon. Two years later, having collected the people from the surrounding forests and hamlets, they raised Zammaday-we, daughter of the King of Vieng Chang, the capital of Soroaratatyne, and widow of a prince of Cambodia, to the throne.

It was about this time, according to the chronicle of Muang Mau, a Shan kingdom in the Upper Irrawaddi valley, that Kun Ngu, the third son of Kun Lung, the chief of Muang Mau, founded La-maing-tai, a city neighbouring Zimmé; and it may be that this prince married the queen, and gave rise to the first known Shan chieftainship of

Zimmé. After thirty-five kings of this line had reigned, the chief, perhaps of a new line, Adutza-woon-tha, built the pagoda only 7 cubits high; while each of his successors, during six reigns, added 7 cubits to its stature; and a princess completed the work by topping the pagoda with a gold cap and a handsome gold umbrella.

When visiting Lapoon in 1837, M'Leod heard that a copper-mine existed at Muang Kut, which had been filled up on the hill being struck by lightning.

Lapoon is of irregular shape, and between 2½ and 3 miles in circumference. It is surrounded on the three sides not facing the river by a wet ditch from 40 to 65 feet broad, and is enclosed by a brick wall, varying outside from 15 to 23 feet in height, and on the inside from 13 to 18 feet. The parapet of the surrounding wall is 4½ feet high and 2½ feet thick, and is loopholed for musketry. The city, which is neatly laid out and beautifully wooded, lies 3½ miles inland to the east of the Meh Ping. From A.D. 1558, when the Zimmé States became tributary to Burmah, till 1774, when they accepted the protection of Siam, Lapoon remained, except during short periods of rebellion, under the Burmese. From 1779 to 1820 the city was deserted, owing to frequent raids of the Burmese and Burmese Shans. It was re-established in the latter year by Chow Boon Neh, the youngest of the seven brothers who ruled in Zimmé, Lakon, and Lapoon, and whose descendants still govern these States.

A Shan queen.

In the evening I called on the chief, who holds the title of Chow Hluang. His palace consists of four buildings—one separate, and the others forming three sides of a hollow square. The buildings were of the ordinary type of the residences of the nobility, and had tiled roofs, and appeared to be substantial structures. On ascending to the verandah, I found the chief squatting on a carpet spread on a dais, or raised portion of the floor, giving audience to several of his chiefs and retainers, and surrounded by his wives. Around him were his emblems of rank, consisting of gold spittoons, betel utensils, trays, water-goblets, &c. He was lounging with his elbow on a three-cornered cushion, enjoying a large cigarette, and being cooled by two pretty women, who were seated 12 feet behind, wafting the air towards him with long-handled fans.

He was an elderly, iron-grey-haired man, courteous in his manner, and far more intelligent-looking than the supreme chief of Zimmé; but he had enjoyed a good dinner, and evidently did not desire to enter into a long discussion upon trade. After ordering mats and pillows to be brought for us, he said that doubtless the projected railway would be an excellent thing for the country, and would bring many pilgrims to the pagoda. He was a great advocate for improved communications, and asked me what I thought of the new bridged cart-road which I had followed from Loi Tee. Of course he would do what he could to help forward the railway, but he hoped that it would soon be commenced; for if not, he was so old that it would not enrich him. Seeing that it was hopeless to get information from him, as he was trying not to yawn between each sentence, we shook hands and returned home.

As soon as it was light on the morning of April 20th, I left Lapoon; Drs M'Gilvary and Cushing having started some time before, so as to reach Zimmé in the cool of the day. The road to Zimmé leads for the whole twelve miles through villages with barely a break in the houses between them; and the fine fruit-trees, and beautiful bamboo clumps in the gardens bordering the road, form a magnificent and shady avenue.

It is pleasant journeying amongst human beings and their habitations after a tour in the forest. Here a temple resplendent with gold like a herald's coat, shone out from the trees; and long, thin, red and white prayer-streamers, suspended from the tops of bamboo poles, waving in the air, called the attention of the passers-by to the place of prayer. There a gang of peasants were at work furbishing up the road, and making everything neat for the approaching visit of the prince. A little farther on, close to an ancient temple and pagoda, was a great avenue of *thyt-si* trees, with the lowest branches 50 feet from the ground, and great notches in their trunks for collecting the varnish. Even the bamboos were in fresh leaf. Parrots, doves, woodpeckers, black mocking-birds with their long tail-feathers, mynahs, and myriads of butterflies, as well as crows and sparrows, enlivened the scene and gave a zest to the journey. Here a light-coloured buffalo stretched out its neck, and sniffing the air, would approach and cast a surly glance at me, as much as to say, "You're an intruder, and have no business here." There a group of wayfarers had spread their morning's meal in the centre of the road, and had to be avoided, as they made no pretence of getting out of our way, but merely continued squatting and gazing at us. Just beyond, an offering to the spirits is spread on a small tray, consisting of a clay elephant, rice, and seri-leaves. The whole way was alive with objects of interest, and several fine monasteries and temples were noticed at some distance from the road.

It was nearly 4 P.M. when I reached Dr M'Gilvary's house, as I had halted for nearly three hours on the way for breakfast, and for the pleasure of watching village life, and enjoying myself under a beautiful grove of shady trees.

My circular journey to Kiang Hai and back, not counting the detour to Kiang Hsen, was 299½ miles in length. The cartographer of the Royal Geographical Society who plotted the survey found that its commencement and conclusion were only 1⅕ mile apart, and reported as follows: "I must confess that during my long experience I have never met with any survey executed with only a prismatic compass and watch which has given such highly satisfactory results."

CHAPTER XXIV.

HOUSE FOR DR CUSHING BUILT IN TWO DAYS—FUMIGATION AND DISINFECTION — BRIBERY AND EXTORTION AT FRONTIER GUARD-HOUSE — TRAVELLERS DELAYED—MR WEBSTER'S JOURNEY—TRADE BETWEEN ZIMMÉ, BANGKOK, AND MAULMAIN ; ENHANCEMENT OF PRICES—COMPARISON BETWEEN RUSSIA AND SIAM — OPPRESSION AND TYRANNY CAUSES CUNNING AND DECEIT—SIAMESE THE GREATEST LIARS IN THE EAST—AN AMUSING INTERVIEW WITH A PRINCE—RELIGIOUS BUILDINGS IN ZIMMÉ—DESCRIPTION OF MONASTERIES—BARGAINING WITH AN ABBOT—PALM-LEAF BOOKS—EVIL PRACTICES OF MONKS—SENTENCING THE DESCENDANTS OF CRIMINALS TO SLAVERY—BEGGING FOR MEALS—GIVING, A PRIVILEGE—RULES FOR THE ACOLYTES—SHAVING THE HEAD AND EYEBROWS—TEACHING IN A MONASTERY—LEARNING MANNERS.

A FEW days before my return to Zimmé the Rev. Mr Martin arrived with his wife from Bangkok, and occupied the half of Dr M'Gilvary's house which had formerly been placed at my disposal. It was therefore arranged that Dr Cushing should be placed in a house in Dr Peoples' grounds, where he could receive proper nursing and medical attendance. This building had been erected as soon as it was known that Dr Cushing was suffering from smallpox. With plenty of labour and materials at hand, such a house, built of bamboos, with mat walls and flooring and thatched roof, can be easily completed in two days.

A wealthy Chinaman who had for some years worked the Government spirit and opium farms, and owned a large vacant teak-built, shingle-roofed house near the Presbyterian Mission, had courteously placed it rent free at the disposal of Mr Webster on his reaching Zimmé with his wife and little girl from where we left them at the Shan frontier-post.

The house being very roomy, and the Websters without fear of contagion, half of this building was handed over for my use.

On seeing my elephant halt outside his garden, Dr M'Gilvary came out to bid me welcome and let me know what arrangements had been made. He advised me to have a grand fumigation of myself, servants, and things, and to be revaccinated as soon as possible. He had already been purified, and was going at once to Dr Peoples to be vaccinated.

On reaching the monopolist's house, I was welcomed by Mr and Mrs Webster, and by little Sunshine their daughter, but would not shake hands with them until I had been fumigated and freshly rigged out. I at once sent out for sulphur, and with my boys was soon in a closed room, surrounded with its fumes. All of our things were disinfected by being washed with a strong solution of carbolic acid. After my short quarantine I had tea and a long talk with the Websters, who had been detained for a week after we left the guard-house, owing to their conscientious objections to bribing the official in command of the guard.

This Jack-in-office, therefore, instead of aiding them as was his duty, had purposely prevented the neighbouring Karen elephant-owners from hiring their elephants to Mr Webster, all the time telling him that he could not force the men to let him have the animals. The Christian Karens accompanying Mr Webster warned him that he would have to get the elephants through the grasping official, as part of the hire was looked upon by him as his perquisite, and the Karens dare not hire them without his leave. Such behaviour on the part of the frontier officials is a serious hindrance to trade and communication, and should be strongly represented to the Siamese and Shan Governments. Even when tired out by Mr Webster's persistency, and threatened with being reported to the Zimmé chief and the King of Siam, the official only allowed the Karens to let him have elephants to carry his things for two short marches, at the end of which he had to halt for four days to procure a fresh relay. In the short journey from the guard-house to Muang Haut, he was thus obliged to change his elephants no less than five times. From a copy of Mr Webster's journal, I found this route struck eastwards from the guard-house, and was the same as that followed by M'Leod in December 1836.

After tea Mr Webster accompanied me to the Mission dispensary to call on Dr Peoples and be vaccinated. Although twice vaccinated during my stay at Zimmé, both operations proved ineffective. This could not have been due to the lymph, as it took well on Dr M'Gilvary, notwithstanding that he had been successfully vaccinated the previous year. I was glad to hear that Dr Cushing's attack was a slight one, and that the crisis was over. On visiting him, he seemed quite cheered up by being in cosy quarters and under medical supervision, and assured me everything had been done for his comfort, and that he hoped to be about in a few days, and able to leave for Bangkok.

Early the next morning I called on Mr Wilson, who had taken great trouble in finding out the prices of various articles at Maulmain, Bangkok, and Zimmé, and the cost of conveyance. From the written statement made by him it appeared, by the difference in prices, that articles sent from Zimmé to Maulmain were enhanced on arrival according to the following percentages: Elephants, 25 per cent; bullocks, 100 per cent; ponies, 70 per cent; embroidered silks (one grade), $122\frac{2}{3}$ per cent; embroidered silks (another grade), 100 per cent; embroidered cotton cloth, 150 per cent. Imports to Zimmé from Maulmain were enhanced on arrival as follows: Gold-leaf, 75 per cent; gold cloth, 15 per cent; broad cloth, 100 per cent; flannel, $32\frac{1}{2}$ to 50 per cent; copper *chatties* (or pots), 100 to $133\frac{1}{3}$ per cent. Exports from Zimmé to Bangkok were enhanced on arrival as follows: Ivory tusks, 30 to 45 per cent, according to size; stick-lac, $42\frac{7}{23}$ per cent; gum-benjamin, $13\frac{1}{3}$ per cent; opium, $41\frac{3}{17}$ per cent; cutch, $22\frac{2}{3}$ per cent; hides, $46\frac{2}{3}$ per cent; horns, $46\frac{2}{3}$ per cent; bee's-wax, $15\frac{1}{2}$ per cent; honey, 100 per cent; nitre, $33\frac{1}{3}$ per cent.

Imports from Bangkok to Zimmé include figured muslins, red muslins, bleached and unbleached muslins, guns, powder, shot, caps, lead, bar-iron, nails, sulphur, kerosene oil, candles,

Chinese crockery, matches, cotton yarn, green flannel, which were enhanced at Zimmé by between 12½ and 67 per cent above their price in Bangkok—the percentage varying according to their value, bulk, and weight. Salt, which is a bulky, small-priced article, is enhanced 510 per cent.

After thanking Mr Wilson, I called on the missionary ladies who shared the house with him, and exchanged my light literature for some of theirs that they had read. Amongst the books I thus acquired was 'Russia,' by Sir Mackenzie Wallace, which I had not had the pleasure of previously reading. I found it a most interesting work, and was much struck with the strong resemblance that the superstitions and customs of the Finnish tribes bear to those of the Shan and other people in Indo-China.

Take, for instance, Sir M. Wallace's description of the old religion of the Finnish tribes, and compare it with the superstitions still reigning in Eastern Asia—particularly in China and Indo-China. Then look at the similarity between the power possessed by the Khozain, or Head of the Household in Russia, and that of the Kumlung, or Head of the Household in the Shan States, as described in chapter xii. The laws of inheritance, the procedure for selecting a bride, and the peculiarities of serfdom and slavery, are likewise strikingly similar in the two regions.

Even the tyranny and oppression of the upper classes over the serfs in each country has been similar, and has had a like effect in fostering the habit of perjury and lying. In chapter xxi. Sir M. Wallace accounts for the proneness of the Russian peasant to lying and perjury by stating: "In the ordinary intercourse of peasants amongst themselves, or with people in whom they have confidence, I do not believe that the habit of lying is abnormally developed. It is only when the peasant comes in contact with authorities that he shows himself an expert fabricator of falsehoods. In this there is nothing that need surprise us. For ages the peasantry were exposed to the arbitrary power and ruthless exactions of those who were placed over them; and as the law gave them no means of legally protecting themselves, their only means of self-defence lay in cunning and deceit."

He goes on to say: "When legitimate interests cannot be protected by truthfulness and honesty, prudent people always learn to employ means which experience has proved to be more effectual. In a country where the law does not afford protection, the strong man defends himself by his strength, the weak by cunning and duplicity. This fully explains the fact—if fact it be—that in Turkey the Christians are less truthful than the Mahometans."

The Siamese, who for centuries have suffered from the *bad* old rule—

> "That they should take who have the power,
> And they should keep who can"—

are reputed to be the greatest liars in the East, and pride themselves above all things upon their cunning and duplicity.

After looking through the young ladies' albums and library, and talking over their recent journeys into the district, which were made without other protection than their own Shan servants, I said good-bye, and returned home just in time to receive Chow Hoo-a Muang Kyow[1] —the fourth in rank of the chiefs of Zimmé—the father of Chow Nan, who conducted us to Kiang Hai.

The Chow came in state, accompanied by fifteen attendants bearing his gold betel-boxes, water-goblets, and other paraphernalia of rank. On his ascending the stairs, I rose to meet him and exchange the usual greetings—"*Chow, sabira?*" ("Prince, are you well?") "*Sabi, sabi!*" ("Well, well!"). Having no interpreters—Mr and Mrs Webster being out, and my Shans in attendance upon Dr Cushing—the remainder of our conversation was chiefly in dumb show, owing to my knowing only a few sentences of Shan, and my visitor being acquainted with neither Burmese nor English. The interview was therefore more amusing and less instructive than it otherwise might have been.

We, however, got on very well together, sipped our tea,

[1] The prince at the head of the Gem City.

nibbled at biscuits, smoked cigars, drew the usual map with matches on the table, and haggled over the lie of the country. I thus managed to extend my knowledge of the geography of the State—the more so as he frequently explained himself in Shan, and I was beginning to understand much of the language used on such occasions, although still very weak in the power of expressing myself. Then I endeavoured to explain the use of my surveying instruments, and showed him the sketches I had made during the journey, and he seemed to be much interested. Whether interested or not, the visit under the circumstances was evidently rare fun to him; and he was pleased as a schoolboy would be when I presented him with a watch and a few other articles.

Zimmé may be said to be a city of temples and monasteries, and has no less than eighty temples within its walls and suburbs, which were mostly built during the Burmese *régime*. The monasteries are built in the Burmese style, and consist of a hall divided into two portions: one part level with the verandah, where the scholars are taught; and the other part, where the monks receive their visitors, two feet above the level of the rest of the building.

When the monastery is a large one, cloisters serving as dormitories, and separated by a central passage, surround two or three sides of the hall. In smaller buildings the monks sleep in the hall, and their beds may be seen rolled up, with those of the acolytes and schoolboys, round their pillows against the wall.

In the porch of one of the buildings, I noticed fresco-paintings illustrating the Jataka of Naymee picturing the punishments in the Buddhist hells for various sins. People were being thrown by black torturers into the fire, and thrust down with pitchforks; one man was being bled by a huge leech; another, fastened upright between two posts, was being sawn in two, whilst a dog was at the same time gnawing at him; three people, with their elbows fastened behind and their legs in chains, were being led by a black demon or jailer to punishment; and there were many other fearful sights.

When the monasteries are built of teak, the posts are sometimes of large girth, and the floor is raised 8 or 10 feet above the ground. If the staircase leading up to the broad verandah is of plastered brickwork, the parapets are sometimes coped with great *nagas* or dragons, or otherwise ornamented and finished off at the foot with images of ogres, *rachasis*, or other fabulous animals. If the staircase is of wood, the sides, like many other parts of the building, are generally beautifully and fantastically carved with mythological beings intertwined in the scroll-work.

On your entering a monastery the abbot does not rise, but, if accustomed to Europeans, he shakes hands, and calls for a mat for you to sit on, and three-cornered pillows to rest your back and elbows. After the usual compliments, and having partially satisfied his curiosity as to your purpose in visiting the country, where you have been, where you are going, and as to your age, he will very likely tell you his eyesight is much impaired, and more than hint that a present of a pair of spectacles would be acceptable.

If in search of curiosities, you may then express your admiration of the row of images of Buddha standing on a raised stand against the wall in the background, and ask permission to examine them. Before the images you will see offerings of taper-candles, flowers, and prayer-flags; and you will notice perhaps that the largest image is made of alabaster, in which case it has been carried all the way from the famous quarries at Moway, which are situated in the range of hills above Sagain in Upper Burmah. Standing about this image, or on a lower shelf, will be other images, some of wood or clay covered with gold-leaf, some of silver having a core of a hard resin, others of soapstone, and some of terra-cotta, the latter resembling Roman Catholic saints in their sculptured niches.

If you wish to bargain for any one of these, the abbot will express himself shocked, and will say that he cannot part with it, as it has been offered to by the people. If you pull out some silver coins, and say that you much wish to have the one you have chosen, he will most likely begin to boggle his eyes, and will perhaps send his scholars off to play, under the pretence that they are a nuisance to you, and, as soon as their backs are turned, commence to haggle over the price like an old Jew. Even when you have come to terms with him, he will, to salve his conscience, exact a promise from you to treat the image with respect, for, if not, ill will happen to you as well as to himself.

Then you may notice several bundles of palm-leaf manuscripts at his side, and two or three manuscript chests near at hand, and express your curiosity as to their contents, which are generally birth-stories of Gaudama, or sermons preached by him, both in Pali or else Shan translations, and explanations by various learned writers. The leaves of these manuscripts are formed of strips, 2 inches wide and 20 inches long, cut out of the leaves of the corypha, or book-palm, rendered smooth and pliable by water and friction. Each collection of leaves is enclosed between two boards, sometimes beautifully carved and gilded, with two wooden pegs, one near each end, to keep the leaves in correct sequence, and to allow them to be raised one after the other as required. When not in use they are either bound round with a crocheted ribbon about an inch and a half broad, with the name, titles, and distinctions of the owner worked on it—or enclosed in a square piece of silk, often with narrow slips of bamboo worked in to give it stiffness.

Some of the larger monasteries have a handsome building erected in their grounds, and set apart for a library, in which are to be found, besides religious books, medical treatises, astrological and cabalistic books, and some treating of alchemy. Such books are not allowed in the monasteries in Burmah. In Siam the study of alchemy has led some of the monks to coin false money. In the Shan States the monks are generally more lax in their observances and rules than in Burmah, and, if rumour is to be credited, are frequently more immoral than laymen; but violations of the laws of chastity are less frequent in Siam than in the Shan States, as the monks in Siam, on their sin being exposed, are severely punished.

In Bangkok, when adultery or fornication is proved

against a monk, the culprit is publicly caned, and then paraded round the city for three days, a crier going before him proclaiming his crime. He, and his posterity after him to the utmost remote generation, are then condemned to cut grass for the king's elephants for life. The woman is condemned to turn the king's rice-mill for life, and the same punishment is imposed upon her posterity from generation to generation for ever.

When a man becomes a monk he dissolves all secular relations, and cannot be called away to do *corvée* labour. A husband ceases to be the husband of his wives, and, by the act, his wives are absolved from all obligations towards their husband. Even a king on becoming a monk, if only for a few days, must abdicate the crown and throne during the time that he is in the monastery, and be recrowned and remarried on returning to secular life.

In Siam, the only way a *prai-luang* can escape the three months' *corvée* labour exacted from him by his Government master is by persuading that master to allow him to become a monk. When a monk, his life is one of ease and often of indolence. Early in the morning, about daybreak, he is aroused from slumber by the beating of the great gong, drum, or bell attached to the monastery, and, after washing his face, puts on his yellow robes, suspends his iron begging-bowl over his shoulders, hanging under his left arm, and his fruit-bag on his right elbow, and leaves the monastery, by boat or by land, a little before sunrise.

As he passes along the river or streets, the charitably disposed stand opposite their houses with a basin of smoking rice, curry, pork, venison, eggs, fish, fruit, betel-nuts, seri-leaves, tobacco, and cheroots. When the monks approach, sometimes as many as 10 or 15 in a line, the donors salute them reverently. As the first monk approaches, he removes his upper yellow robe from the hidden begging-bowl, and, still keeping his eyes on the ground, takes off its conical cover, and holds it out to receive one or two half cocoa-nut shells full of rice. Then, after closing his bowl and flinging his robe round it, he extends his fruit-bag for the remaining donations. The donor then murmurs an inaudible blessing, and the monk moves on, giving place to his successor. Thus they proceed from house to house, never making a request, or giving thanks, or even uttering a word. It is considered a favour by the people to be allowed to accumulate merit by making these offerings to the monks. When the monks have collected sufficient for their day's requirements, they return to the monastery, where they can regale themselves upon the food until noon, after which they must fast until sunrise the next morning. The abbot and other monks of more than ordinary rank do not beg, but have their daily wants supplied by the pious in their neighbourhood.

In case a monk requires anything else besides his daily food, he goes at a later period of the day, and silently stands for a few minutes near the house of the person he hopes to obtain it from. On seeing the monk, the person salutes him respectfully, and asks him what he needs. The monk replies, "My body has met with the necessity" of such a thing, which he names. If the person is unable or unwilling to present it to the monk, he bows low before him, at the same time clasping his hands in front of his face, and says, "Let it please thee, thou lord of favours, to proceed onward, and bestow thy compassion upon somebody else." The compassion, of course, is the privilege of supplying the particular want of the monk. No monk may, by the rules of his order, ask for anything until he has been requested to name his requirement.

The inmates of the monasteries are divided into three classes—the monks, the *nanes* (or acolytes), and the pupils. The rules or commandments designed for the monks are 227 in number, and are given by Colquhoun in his interesting work 'Amongst the Shans.'[1] The rules for the *nanes* are as follows: Take no animal life; do not steal; have no venereal intercourse; do not lie; drink no intoxicating liquor; eat no food after mid-day until daybreak the next morning; adorn not the body, even with flowers, nor make it pleasant by perfumery; be not a spectator at theatrical or musical performances; sleep not on a bed raised higher

[1] Page 219.

than one cubit (19½ inches); touch not silver or gold, or anything which passes for money.

Youths may be admitted as *nanes* at any time above seven years of age, but cannot become monks before being fully twenty years old. To become a monk a man must pass immediately from being a *nane*. If he has been a *nane* at some previous time, he must still become one again, and be reinstituted, before he can enter the ranks of the monks. Persons can be admitted as *nanes* or monks at any time in the year, except from the first evening of the eighth (Siamese) waning moon until the middle of the eleventh. The period which includes the rainy months of the year is termed Wasa, and is the great annual harvest-time for making merit. It is during this season that the monks may not absent themselves for a single night from their monastery. More people become monks in the first half of the eighth month than in any other month of the year.

Previous to being admitted as a monk, or even a *nane*, the candidate has the hair shaved from his head and eyebrows; and, if he has a beard, has it plucked out by the roots. This ceremony is repeated twice a-month by the monks and *nanes*, on the day preceding the full and new moon of every month. The shaving day is called "Wan Kone."

The pupils are taught by the monks either in the hall of the monastery, or in a building erected for the purpose in the temple grounds. The parents select the monk by whom they wish their son to be taught, and the monk takes his pupils under his special care; and they are fed and lodged in the monastery. When they have learned to read and write their native characters, they have to study the Cambodian character in Siam (the character in which the Siamese sacred books are written), and the Pali character in the Shan States.

Some of the lads, while in the monastery, learn the first rules of arithmetic, others medicine, some the sacred books, and all the rules of manners. In this latter respect our English board schools might well take a lesson from the rules of the Buddhist monasteries. The rules of etiquette are called Sekiya-wat, and include the adjustment of their robes; walking and sitting in a graceful and becoming manner; how to sit and rise up decently; the attitude of body and mind in which they are to partake their food; behaviour to their superiors and inferiors, and to the pagodas and images; how to behave themselves when begging, and when in the presence of the laity, especially in that of the fair sex.

CHAPTER XXV

LEAVE ZIMMÉ WITHOUT INTERPRETERS—BORROW A TENT—REACH BAN PANG KAI—THE CRY OF GIBBONS—LEGEND—A PRIMITIVE PAGODA—THREE KINDS OF PAGODAS—DESCRIPTION—LOW PLATEAU DIVIDING MEH LOW FROM MEH WUNG—BRANCH RAILWAY FROM LAKON—THE HEAD SOURCES OF MEH WUNG—A STORM—TEAK—REACH MUANG WUNG—COCKLE'S PILLS—A TEMPLE AT NIGHT—TOWER MUSKETS—A PLAGUE OF FLIES—MOOSURS—DR CUSHING LEAVES FOR BANGKOK—HIS EXCELLENT ARRANGEMENT—TRANSLATOR OF THE BIBLE INTO SHAN—LOSS OF SHAN INTERPRETERS—MR MARTIN JOINS PARTY—BAU LAWAS IN SOUTHERN SIAM—ARRIVAL OF MR GOULD—ELEPHANT TITLES—DINNER AT THE MARTINS'—A PRESENT OF CIGARS.

AFTER being detained five days at Zimmé in the hopes of one of the missionaries being able to accompany me to the sources of the Meh Wung, the Princess Çhow Oo Boon kindly hired me some of her elephants, and I started on the morning of April 26th, without interpreters, accompanied merely by the elephant-men and my own servants. Natives of India have an astonishing power of quickly learning sufficient words and sentences of a strange language to allow them to express themselves more or less fluently to the people of the country. As Jewan, Veyloo, and Loogalay were not exceptions to the rule, and I had acquired some little knowledge of the language, I thought we should be able to manage very well.

As the rains had set in, and we might expect showers every night, I borrowed a good-sized bell-tent from one of the missionaries, which, on a pinch, would contain myself and two of the servants; while the other one could curl himself up in an elephant-howdah, and shelter himself beneath its cover.

I followed the route which was taken by M'Leod in 1837, when on his way from Zimmé to Kiang Tung, as far as Ban Pang Kai, a village 9 miles to the south of Viang Pa Pow, which we had visited when proceeding to Kiang Hai. The height of the pass over the divide between the Meh Hkuang and the Meh Low crossed by the route is 3413 feet above the sea.

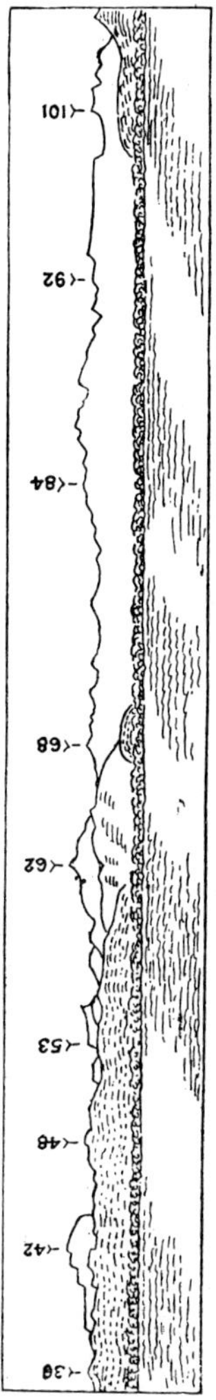

During the morning, before reaching Ban Pang Kai, we were accompanied by the howling of the gibbons which infested the evergreen forests; and I halted for a few minutes to take down their cry, which ran thus: Hoop-hoi, oop-oi, oo-ep, oo-ep; hoo-oo-oo, oi-e-e-e, hoi-e, oop-oop, oi-oi-oi-oi, oop-oi, oi-oi-oi-oo, oop-oi, hoi-hoi-hoi, hau-au-au. For miles on the journey these were the only sounds heard in the forest, and even the notes of some of the birds vociferated in the early morning seemed to be imitated from this cry. One calls koo-a-woo, at-a-woo; another, koo-a-koo, koo-a-hoo; another, koo-wa-ra, hoo-wa-ra; another, hoop-pa-pook; and another, hip-poo-hill, hip-poo-hill.

The Shans call the gibbon hpoo-ah (husband), from the similarity of its cry to that word, and account for its wailing as follows: In a former existence a woman, who afterwards was born as a gibbon, lost her husband, and becoming distracted, wandered through the forest rending the air with her cries—hpoo-ah! hpoo-ah! (husband! husband!). When she was born as a gibbon, she continued the cry, which has been kept up by her descendants ever since.

View of the hills to the north-east of Zimmé from Pen Yuk.

Ban Pang Kai lies 49 miles from Zimmé, and 2058 feet above the sea. Although only a small village, it possesses a temple, the roof of which was anything but water-tight, as the thatch required renewing. A large white ant-hill served as a pagoda, and had offerings of flowers placed before it. It was the most primitive, and most correct to the original design, that I had ever seen, as, according to the monks, Gaudama left no instructions with reference to pagodas, but merely said that a small mound should be raised over his bones in the form of a heap of rice.

The Siamese word "Chedi," for a pagoda, is derived from the Pali word "Chaitya," and means the offering-place, or place of prayer; and the Shan word "Htat," or "Tat," and the Siamese "Săt-oop," for a pagoda placed over portions of Gaudama's body, such as his flesh, teeth, and hair, is derived from the Sanscrit "Dhatu garba," a relic shrine. In Siam there are three classes of pagoda: the Pra Săt-oop, which is placed over remains of Gaudama; the Pra Prang, placed

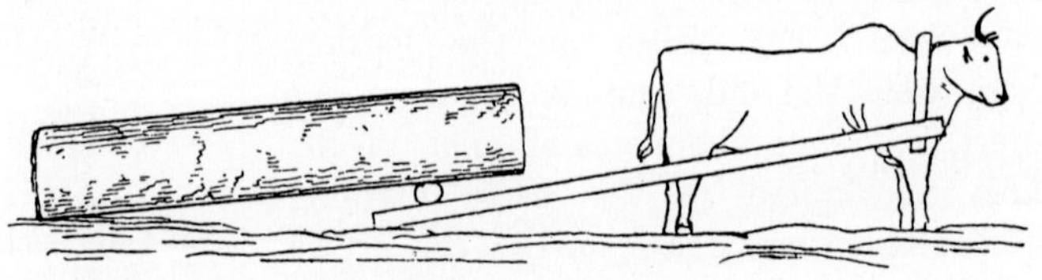

Ox drawing timber in forest.

over his utensils; and the Pra Chedi, placed over his personal apparel and that of his disciples. The pagodas are made of either brick or stone masonry, plastered over with a cement formed of lime, sand, and molasses, the latter rendering the plaster very hard and durable. Sometimes it is built over a core of earth, which is apt to cause the brickwork to crack as the earth settles. The bases of these pagodas are either square, circular, hexagonal, or octagonal. The structure rises in a taper form by regular square or rounded gradations to a small spire, from 20 feet in height to 150, and the apex is surmounted by a handsome *htee*, or gilded series of tapering umbrellas.

Leaving Ban Pang Kai, we struck eastwards, and after crossing the rice-fields of the village, ascended 90 feet to the crest of the plateau which divides the valley of the Meh Low from that of the Meh Wung. The crest lies only three-quarters of a mile from the village, and 2148 feet above the sea. A branch line could be run without difficulty from Lakon, up the valley of the Meh Wung, and over this plateau into the upper valley of the Meh Low, which will be able to support a large population when the fine plains and plateau are again brought under cultivation, and irrigated from the neighbouring streams.

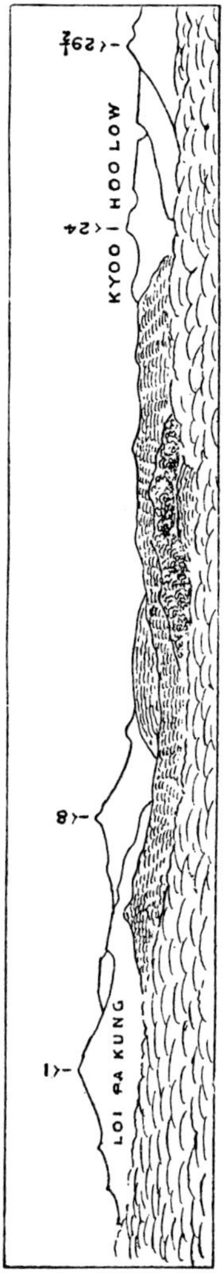

At 51 miles I sketched the head of the basin of the Meh Wung. Loi Mok, and its spur, Loi Pa Kung, lay about 15 miles due north, and the pass over the Kyoo Hoo Low, which leads into the valley of the Meh Ing, about the same distance to the north-east.

View of the head of the basin of the Meh Wung.

After crossing a valley in the plateau drained by the Meh Kee-ow,—a stream with slate and shale in its bed,—we passed some large blocks of limestone piled up like Druidical remains, close to the head of the valley. Here a thunderstorm commenced, and the rain began to pour down in torrents, soon making my followers look like drowned rats. From 53 miles the path passed for a mile amongst a series of limestone peaks, which stand up like skittles from the plateau, and are called Loi Pa Chau. These ended at the edge of the plateau, which was wooded chiefly by pine and teak trees, some of the latter being 16 feet in girth. The trees must be of great age, as a circumference of 6 feet denotes a life of one hundred years. At the point where the path commences to descend from the plateau, a road leading to Penyow, *viâ* Loi Mun Moo, leaves to the right. Descending the slope for a mile and a half through a forest of great teak-trees, many of which had been lately girdled, we reached the fields of Ban Huay Hee-o. A mile and a half farther across the

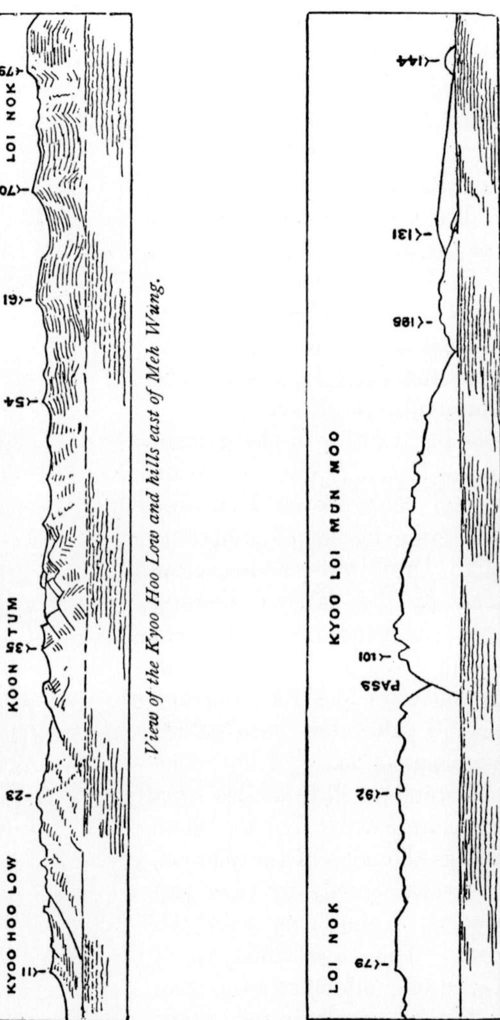

View of the Kyoo Hoo Low and hills east of Meh Wung.

View of Loi Mun Moo pass and hills east of Meh Wung.

plain brought us to Ban Mai, the headquarters of the governor of Muang Wung, which is a province of Lakon.

We put up for the night in a large and beautifully decorated temple, near the bank of the Meh Wung, which is here 80 feet broad and 9 feet deep, with 1 foot of water flowing in its bed. Ban Mai is 57 miles from Zimmé, and 1462 feet above the sea, or less than 700 feet lower than the water-parting separating it from the Meh Low. Just before reaching the village, I sketched the hills lying to the east of the Meh Wung, which divide it from the valley of the Meh Ing.

My head was aching with a bad bilious attack when I arrived, so I determined to go without dinner, and took a couple of Cockle's pills. These pills are simply invaluable in such cases, and I never travel without them. As soon as my things were unpacked, I sent for the governor, and procured the names of the villages in the Muang, and got him to make a map on the ground with matches to show me the position of the villages and streams.

The scene was one not easily to be forgotten. The magnificent posts covered with red lacquer and ornamented with gold, increasing in height with the tiers of the roof; the centre and side aisles lengthening out in the gloom; the chancel in the distance, with its great gilded image of Gaudama,—were shrouded in darkness, save for the dim religious light cast by my two wax candles.

Next morning the governor sent me a present of fowls and vegetables, accompanied by a guard of honour, armed with Tower muskets marked with G. R., a crown, and London, to attend me as far as Ban Pang Kai. Whilst sketching the hills at the head of the valley, my hands were absolutely gloved with flies, and you could hardly have put a pin between the flies on the backs of my attendants; but luckily they were innocuous, and did not lust after our blood. I halted for the night at the temple of Ban Pang Kai. Another heavy thunderstorm, accompanied by rain, happened in the evening. The roof of the temple was so leaky, that I had to protect my bed from the drippings with waterproof sheets.

Whilst halting for breakfast on the following day, near the hot springs on the Meh Low, I had my chair placed some distance from the camp under a great Mai Hai tree, which was dropping its damson-like fruit. A Moosur, with black turban, trousers, and jacket, passed by, and was shortly afterwards followed by another, who, startled at seeing me, looked about suspiciously, and clutching his gun, brought it to the front as he sidled past me. A little later, on returning to the camp, I found both of the men sitting round the fire, having an amicable smoke, and an attempt at a chat with my boys.

I was glad to hear on my return to Zimmé that Dr Cushing had so far recovered as to have been able to leave for Bangkok on April 30th. The thoughtful kindness of this missionary in taking over from me the management of the commissariat and camp arrangements during our journeys, together with his skill in keeping the loads of each elephant separate, and having only such things unpacked as were immediately required, enabled me to start by daybreak every morning (except when we were delayed by the carelessness of the elephant-drivers, who occasionally allowed their animals to stray), and I was thus able to make longer journeys and do more work than I could otherwise have done.

I trust that the knowledge he was able to collect of the various dialects of the Shan language, and the information he gained about the customs and habits of the Ping Shans, will be a full recompense to him for the constant and enthusiastic manner in which he took up those matters. It is only by acquiring a thorough knowledge of the languages, habits, customs, and superstitions of the people, that missionaries can hope to influence and convert them. The noble work that Dr Cushing has done in translating the Bible into Shan will greatly aid his fellow-missionaries in Christianising and civilising not only the Shans but the neighbouring tribes who understand their language. The greatest field for missionaries in Indo-China lies, undoubtedly, amongst the non-Buddhist hill-tribes, where so much good work has already been done by the American Baptist, the American Presbyterian, and China Inland Missions.

Dr M'Gilvary, and Dr and Mrs Peoples, were away in the district when I arrived, and Mr and Mrs Webster were out. Dr Cushing had taken the two Shan interpreters, one of whom was his writer, to Bangkok with him, and my servants soon went off to the bazaar, leaving me alone in the house. The third chief of Zimmé, hearing of my return, called to pay me a visit, which proved as amusing as my interview with the father of Chow Nan.

On calling on Mr and Mrs Martin, they invited me to dinner the next evening; and Mr Martin expressed himself willing to accompany me on my next journey, and believed that Dr M'Gilvary had made up his mind likewise to do so. This was indeed good tidings, and I at once accepted the proposal. I am indebted to this gentleman for a very interesting diary that he kept for me during the journey.

I then visited Mr Wilson, and in the course of conversation he told me that when journeying three days by boat above Kanburi, on a western branch of the Meh Klong, a river that empties into the east of the Gulf of Siam, he came across a Bau Lawa village containing thirty houses, and the people said there were three or four of their villages in the neighbourhood. The villages could be reached in one and a half day by elephant from Kanburi. This was interesting, as it shows how far south the villages of this tribe extend.

The next day Dr M'Gilvary returned, and Mr Gould, the British consul, arrived in the afternoon. I found that an order had been issued by the Chow Che Wit, the head chief, precluding elephants from leaving the district, so I went to the palace with Dr M'Gilvary to obtain permission to hire some for my intended journey to Moung Fang. The chief was out, but luckily we met him in the city, driving slowly in his carriage, and accompanied by many attendants. On his giving us the necessary permission, we called on the Princess Chow Oo Boon, who kindly consented to lend us six of her finest elephants. These were honoured with names: Poo Hot, Poo Kao, Poo Hao, Ma Ap, &c. The largest ones were over nine feet in height.

The dinner at the Martins' proved a great success: beautiful orchids and flowering creepers, daintily and tastefully arranged, ornamented the table, and the courses were so admirably designed and cooked, that one would have thought a *cordon bleu* had had control of the kitchen. There could be no doubt that the lady of the house was an excellent housewife, and on this occasion had not only superintended and assisted in the cooking, but had herself arranged the table. If I had been a believer in magic, I might have imagined that Mrs. Martin was the owner of Aladdin's ring, and had used it for our benefit.

Next day I called on Mr Gould, and had a long chat with him. Had I been possessed of the annals of my family, like the chief of Kiang Hai, I would have certainly called for them, and inscribed his name there in capital letters as a benefactor, as he gave me, joy of joys to a smoker, fifty excellent cigars, which were a great treat to me, for mine had been finished for some weeks, and I had been forced to regale myself with country-made cigars and cigarettes, which are certainly not remarkable for an enjoyable aroma or a pleasant flavour.

CHAPTER XXVI.

LEAVE FOR MUANG FANG—THE TEMPLE OF THE WHITE ELEPHANTS—TRAINING ELEPHANTS—EVENING SERVICE IN A TEMPLE—LEGEND OF WAT PRA NON—SNAKE AND SIVA-WORSHIP—CARAVANS—STICK-LAC TREES NOT CUT DOWN—THE 400 FOOTPRINTS OF BUDDHA—WILD TEA—VISIT TO SHAN LADIES—LOW DRESSES—RULES OF HOSPITALITY—WORSHIPPING THE MANES—A ZYLOPHONE—IMPLEMENTS OF EXPECTANT BUDDHA—STRAINING WATER—LEGENDS OF LOI CHAUM HAUT AND LOI KIANG DOW—THE PALACE OF THE ANGELS—DEMONS CANNOT HARM CHRISTIANS—CHRISTIANITY A GREAT BOON—ACCIDENT TO ANEROID—A VICIOUS ELEPHANT—FOOT-AND-MOUTH DISEASE—SNARES FOR DEMONS—A PANORAMA OF HILLS—SOURCES OF THE MEH PING AND MEH TENG—A RIVER PASSING UNDER A MOUNTAIN—MUAN HANG AN ANCIENT LAKE-BASIN—RIVAL CLAIMS OF PING SHANS AND BRITISH SHANS OR NGIO—THE UPPER DEFILE OF THE MEH PING—A MOONLIGHT SCENE—ENTANGLING DEMONS AT THE FRONTIER—A CHINESE FORT—LOI PA-YAT PA-YAI—MAPPING THE COUNTRY—DR M'GILVARY'S SERMON—REACH KIANG DOW—PETROLEUM AT KIANG DOW AND MUANG FANG.

On the afternoon of May 7th everything was packed, and after collecting together at Dr M'Gilvary's we started, crossed the river above the bridge, and halted for a few minutes at the dispensary to load a large tent that Dr Peoples had kindly placed at our disposal. We then proceeded along the broad road that skirts the city on the north as far as the White Elephant Gate, and then turned northwards along the White Elephant road, which is 35 feet wide, and kept in excellent order.

A quarter of a mile from the city we passed Wat Chang Peuk, the temple of the White Elephants, which contains two whitewashed life-sized images of the front, head, shoulders, and fore-legs of these animals. Each stands under a masonry arch closed up at the back; one faces the north, and the other the west. Fresh grass and flowers had been placed by devout passers-by in the curve of the elephant-trunks. These effigies, as well as those of two ogres, and a Russi in the grounds of the Wat Hluang at Zimmé, were erected as a protection to the city in 1799.

Half a mile farther we passed a beautiful temple decorated with red lacquer, and profusely gilded, which had been lately built by Princess Chow Oo Boon. The *mai chalau* trees, which are numerous, were in full blossom, and many beautiful orchids were suspended from the smaller trees. At 3½ miles from the bridge over the river, which I now mile from, we halted for the night at Wat Pra Non, the temple of the reclining Gaudama. Our march after leaving the city skirted the rice-fields of the Zimmé plain on the west.

As we passed the elephant stables of the Zimmé chief, I noticed the mode in which they train a refractory animal. He is confined in a pen barely large enough to admit his body, constructed of two strong post-and-rail fences, like the parallel vaulting-bars at a gymnasium. Between these, which are slightly inclined towards the front, the elephant is squeezed, and then enclosed and forced to be obedient.

The abbot of the monastery, who had held his post for thirty years, courteously allowed us to occupy an out-building of the temple. On going to the evening service we found the great, richly gilded image of Gaudama reclining on its right side, supporting its head with its hand, and covered by a star-spangled canopy. The image was forty-seven feet in length. The walls, ceilings, and pillars of the temple were tastefully decorated with gilt on a red lacquer ground, resembling the rich Japanese wall-papers now in vogue. The monotonous chant of the monks, and the great taper candles alight before the image, reminded me of a service in a Catholic cathedral.

After the service I asked the abbot whether there was any history attached to the monastery; and in reply, he related the following legend: "During the existence on earth of the third Buddh, he came and lodged under the great mango-tree, near whose former site this temple stands, when a Yak, with the usual ogre propensities, not knowing that he was a Buddh, came to attack and devour him. On learning his mistake, the Yak made obeisance, and the Buddh gave him his blessing. One of the Yak's teeth—Yak's teeth are as large as wild-boar tusks—fell out, and the Buddh presented him with a handful of his hair, and told him to place it in the hollow of the tooth, and bury it in the Hoo Nak, or dragon's hole.

The Yak then requested Buddh to preach a sermon for his benefit, but he refused, saying: "Another Buddh will come at some future time and do so." Having said this, he departed on his merciful mission to the universe.

When Gaudama the fourth Buddh came, he rested on the mango-tree, which had fallen down from age. On the Yak approaching to devour him, Gaudama remonstrated with him as the former Buddh had done, and told him that he was a Buddha. The Yak refusing to believe this, as the former Buddh was of enormous size, and Gaudama was small, Gaudama by his *aiswarya* (supernatural power derived from accumulated merit) expanded to the size of the former Buddh. After the Yak had worshipped, and received Gaudama's blessing, another of his tusks fell out, and after having some of the Buddh's hair placed in it, was buried, like the first one, in the dragon's hole. On the Yak asking Gaudama to preach him a sermon, he consented to do so if the Yak would build him a place of shelter, and fetch him some cool water. The Yak, calling two other friendly ogres to help him, at once made the sheltering-place; and proceeding a little distance to the south-east of the site of the monastery, dug the deep pool which is known as Nong Luang Kwang, and brought water for the Buddh to bathe and drink.

Gaudama then preached a sermon, and foretold that the Yak in a future existence should be born chief of Zimmé, and the two friendly Yaks should be born kings of Siam, and their descendants should reign for many generations. When the prophecy was fulfilled, the Yak, who became in his after-existence King of Zimmé, built the great reclining image in Wat Pra Non. After preaching and prophesying, Gaudama left, and proceeded to Ko-sin-na-li, where he entered Neiban.

Another peculiar belief of the people is in the power of snakes. *Naga*, or snake, worship, which was the State religion in Upper Burmah from A.D. 924 to A.D. 1010, still exists in the Shan States to the east of it, and even in Northern Siam. On one of his journeys in the Shan States, Dr Cushing found himself in an unpleasant predicament through killing a viper that he saw sunning itself on the bank of a lake. The Shans declared that it was the guardian spirit of the lake; it never bit any one, and had always been allowed to go and come when and where it liked.

Another case of snake-worship I heard of whilst staying in Bangkok. It appears that a certain temple in Kampheng Phet contained a large bronze image of Phya Nakh, the king of the Nagas, which was said to be very ancient, and was held in high veneration by people for miles round. A German merchant chancing to visit the temple, thought how extremely well the image would look in a German museum, and accordingly determined to annex it. Waiting till night had fallen, he proceeded quietly to the temple with his boatmen, and tried to carry it off. Finding that it was too heavy to remove entire, he broke off the head and the lower portions of the arms, together with the hands, the fingers of which were covered with rings, and carried them away. There was a great outcry the next morning, and the matter was reported to the King of Siam, who was highly indignant at the ruthless destruction of an object of veneration, and, after some correspondence, had the parts that had been carried away returned. From a photograph of the head and hands I thought that the image must be one of Siva, as it had the mark resembling the third eye on the forehead, and a serpent above the crown, which I fancied might be intended for a flame of fire; but I was assured by a gentleman who had seen the body and the pedestal, that the twining snakes about them left no doubt that the image was intended for the king of the Nagas. An entire image of such a Siva, or else snake-god, was seen by Mr Bourne near Ssumao. The horrid image was "seated on a white ox, with a sash composed of human heads round its breast, and armed with a trident and bell. It had six arms covered with snakes, and three faces, with the usual scar in the middle of the forehead replaced by an eye. An intelligent native told us it was the local god. And to the remark that he was of dreadful aspect, he replied 'Yes; he is just like that.'"

That Siva—whose text-books are "those singular compounds of cabalistic mystery, licentiousness, and blood, the Agamas or Tantras"—was worshipped in the Zimmé Shan kingdom as late as the middle of last century, is evidenced by the 'History of Lakon,' which states, that "at this time the chief priest of the temple, called Wat Na Yang, was a sorcerer, conjuring spirits by the means of the skulls of persons who had died a violent death. He came to be considered a man of extraordinary merit, and was consulted by every one." Comparing this statement with Dr W. H. Mills's translation of the Prabodha-chandra-udaya, Act 3, that appeared in J.R.A.S. No. 61 of 1837, I think there can be little doubt on the matter. The translation runs thus—

"With flesh of men, with brain and fat well smeared,
We make our grim burnt-offering,—break our fast
From cups of holy Brahman's skull,—and ever
With gurgling drops of blood that plenteous stream
From hard throats quickly cut by us is worshipped
With human offerings meet, our god, dread Bhairava [Siva]."

We were lulled to sleep by the chanting of the pupils in the monastery, and were awakened, soon after four o'clock the next morning, by the tolling of the temple bells, two in number, each of bronze, with inscriptions on them. One bell was three feet in diameter at the mouth, and the other two feet. As the sun rose, and our elephants were being loaded, a procession of men, women, and children was seen approaching across the plain, bringing the day's food for the monks and their pupils, and small bags of sand to trim up the paths in the temple grounds. A magnificent *padouk* tree was in full flower near the temple, round which clustered numerous bees, making the air musical with their humming.

Leaving the temple, we continued skirting the rice-fields

until we crossed the Meh Sa (60 feet broad and 9 feet deep, with 1 foot of water) close to its entrance into the Meh Ping, at 6½ miles. On the way we met ten loaded elephants accompanied by two of their big babies, and numerous caravans of laden cattle, some conveying tiles to Zimmé. Most of the cattle had bells of metal or bamboo hung round their necks to enable them to be easily traced when straying in the forest; and the leaders had a bow, or arch, of bent wood fastened above their shoulders, from which was suspended a metal bell 10 inches high and 4 inches long, and 2 inches broad at the mouth. The orange-shaped fruit on the *nux-vomica* trees had been largely consumed by hornbills.

For the next mile and a half, until we reached the Meh Lim, we skirted the river. The temples in the villages were beautifully ornamented with carvings, and decorated with red and gold; and the gardens were fragrant with the scent of pomelo and orange-trees, now in blossom. In the fields we noticed many *pouk* (stick-lac) trees,[1] and I was told by Dr M'Gilvary that, as there was a heavy penalty enacted for cutting these trees down, they are left standing wherever the jungle is cleared.

The Meh Lim, which enters the Meh Ping from the west, with its affluents the Meh Peum and Meh How, drains a great area of country, including some extensive plains. Two days' journey above its mouth this river passes through a gorge, which is celebrated for its 400 footprints of Gaudama, called *Pra Bat shee-roi* or *Prabat see-hoi*. M'Leod mentions these in his journal as *Pa-bat Sip hoi*, and accounts for the name by saying that "the four Buddhs have each trod on the identical stone, the prints of each succeeding one being smaller than the preceding one." I procured the names of nine villages and an ancient city called Muang Ka on the Meh Lim, and of seven villages on the Meh How and Meh Peun. Tea is said to grow wild on the hills neighbouring these rivers.

Leaving the Meh Ping, we journeyed nearly due north, thus avoiding a long bend of the river. A mile from our crossing of the Meh Lim, a low hill called Loi Chong Teng,

[1] *Butea frondosa.*

about two and a half miles long, and surmounted near its southern end by a pretty pagoda, cropped up from the plain a mile to the west. Here we caught a glimpse of the summer palace of the Zimmé chief, which lay about 3½ miles to the north-east, near the village of Wung Muang.

The foot of the hill was fringed by a line of villages embedded in beautiful groves of fruit-trees. After passing the north end of the hill, which drew in towards our path, we halted for breakfast at the village of Nam Lin, situated 11½ miles from Zimmé. The spurs from the main spur which separates the Meh Peun from the Meh Ping jutted into the plain four miles to the west of the village, and the plateau-topped low range to the east lay four miles distant, reducing the width of the Zimmé plain to about seven or eight miles at this spot, from whence it gradually decreases to the defile.

On our way to the village we halted for a few minutes to gain information about the valley of the Meh Lim, and, accompanied by Dr M'Gilvary, I ascended the steps of a substantial-looking house, and crossing the verandah, entered the reception-hall. Here we were welcomed by an old lady, her daughter, and four granddaughters, the last of various ages from fourteen to twenty-four. All were evidently in gala array, their hair neatly dressed and decked with flowers, jewels on their fingers and in the cylinders in the lobes of their ears, bracelets on their wrists, and handsome gold chains round some of their necks, but without jackets, or any other covering from the waist upwards, excepting a handkerchief round the old lady's top-knot.

In the Lao provinces of Siam, which lie in the basin of the Meh Kong to the south of Luang Prabang, it is the rule amongst the Shans that a woman whose husband is absent must not offer hospitality. In all cases before hospitality is offered, the master of the house must first worship the manes by lighting taper candles, and incense, and offering prayers, the stranger waiting until the ceremony is finished. The Ping Shans are not so strict, and no remonstrances were made at our unexpected entrance. The young ladies, at a hint from their grandmother, at once brought clean mats and three-cornered pillows to make us comfortable, and their mamma offered us her silver betel-box, which contained all the necessaries for a quid, which, I need not say, we thankfully declined.

All seemed anxious that we should have correct information, even the youngest daughter breaking in to mention the name of a village which the others had forgotten. There was no timidity, no shyness, no awkwardness, and apparently no self-consciousness, amongst the neat and comely little damsels. Their demeanour was courtesy itself, and their manners and deportment were as graceful and perfect as could be found in any drawing-room in Europe.

In the temple where our breakfast was spread I noticed a native zylophone, made of eighteen sonorous strips of hard wood fastened side by side by strings and suspended over a boat-shaped sounding-board, which had been hollowed out of a small log. There was a rough gradation in the tones of the successive pieces, but no adherence to our musical intervals.

When calling on the abbot, I asked him the uses of six wooden implements, painted red, standing about five feet high and placed in a rack. They were evidently part of his

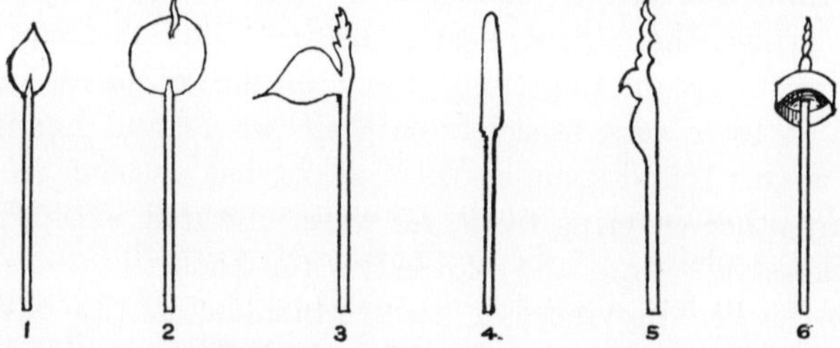

Implements for the use of expectant Buddhas.

paraphernalia, but not intended for use. The abbot replied that they were for the use of Buddhas or expectant Buddhas. Nos. 1, 2, and 3 were to shield his face when worshipping, No. 4 for washing his clothes, and No. 6 for his umbrella. The use of No. 5 has escaped me, but it somewhat resembles a bishop's crosier.

The abbot was a fat, sleepy-looking old gentleman, who considered it trouble enough to answer our questions without asking any in return. On noticing the sieve used by the monks to strain insects from their drinking-water, to save them from the sin of destroying animal life, Dr M'Gilvary told him that, notwithstanding the sieve, thousands of animalculæ remained in the water, and were thus consumed daily by him, and this was evident by looking at a drop of water through the microscope. The abbot merely shrugged his fat shoulders, and, with a glimmer in his eye, replied that as long as he could not see them it made no matter, so he need not grieve over it. The balustrades in the verandah of the monastery had evidently been turned with a lathe.

Half a mile beyond the village I caught sight of Loi Chaum Haut (the mountain with the top drawn in), an

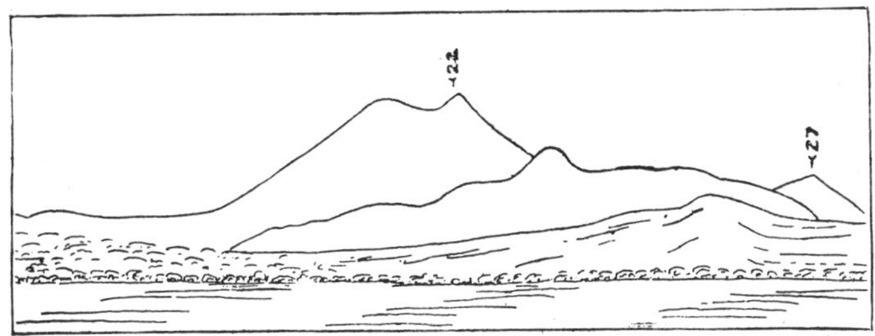

View of Loi Chaum Haut.

isolated mountain seemingly rising some 5000 or 6000 feet above the plain. It lies to the east of the Meh Ping, and is about 1000 feet lower than Loi Kiang Dow, the precipitous mountain that stands, a monarch amongst the hills, to the west of the river. A legend relates that formerly Loi Chaum Haut was higher than Loi Kiang Dow, and that this annoyed Phya In, who straightway pressed its head down until it was considerably lower than the more sacred Loi Kiang Dow, in which is the entrance to the Dewahs' country, where the great genius Chow Kam Doang resides, who is the guardian spirit of the Zimmé States. At the close of Gaudama's dispensation (a *tha-tha-nah* or 5000 years), Chow Kam Doang will be born as Phya Tam, and re-establish the Buddhist religion for the next *tha-tha-nah*.

According to another legend, Gaudama Buddha, in a former state of existence, was born on Loi Chaum Haut, and an aqueduct was constructed by the Yaks to bring water to him from Ang Sa Lome, a lake that is said to exist on the summit of Loi Kiang Dow. The aqueduct, unless it was a siphon, must have been 6000 or 7000 feet high, a creditable, but hardly credible, piece of engineering work.

The entrance to the Dewahs' country is said to be by a cave that has its exit in Loi Kat Pee, a spur of Loi Kiang Dow. Not far from the cave a stream, 13 feet wide and 2½ feet deep, issues from the foot of the hill, and is doubtless connected with the stream in the cave. According to the legend: "After entering the cave and proceeding several hundred yards, you come to a stream, about chest-deep, on the other side of which is an image of pure gold, as large as life. Unless a man has superabundant merit he will instantly expire if he attempts to pass the stream. A month's journey through the cave brings you to the Dewahs' country and the city of the Yaks, which is ruled over by Chow Kam Doang. There you have but to wish to obtain all you can desire."

This Vimana, or palace of the angels, is thus described in the 'Book of Indra,' one of the most ancient of the Siamese law books: "There is a celestial abode in the Dewah heavens, an aerial dwelling covered with gold and gems, with roofs resplendent with gold and jewellery and finials of crystal and pearl. The whole gleams with wrought and unwrought gold more brilliant than all the gems. Around its eaves plays the soft sound of tinkling golden bells. There dwelt a thousand lovely houris, virgins in gorgeous attire, decked with the richest ornaments, singing melodious songs in concert, whose resounding strains are ceaseless. This celestial abode is adorned with lotus lakes, and meandering rivers full of the five kinds of lotus, whose golden petals as they fade fill all the air with fragrant odours. Round the lakes are magnificent lofty trees growing in regular array, their leaves, their boughs, and their branches covered with sweet-scented blossoms, whose balmy fragrance fills the surrounding air with heart-delighting odours."

The people of this fair palace, according to my informant, feed on angel's food, which he materialised to a close resemblance of that described by Thomson in "The Castle of Indolence"—

> "Whatever sprightly juice or tasteful food
> On the green bosom of this earth are found,
> And all old Ocean genders in his round:
> Some hand unseen these silently displayed,
> E'en undemanded by a sign or sound;
> You need but wish; and instantly obeyed,
> Fair ranged the dishes rose, and thick the glasses played."

Dr M'Gilvary once entered the cave with Nan Inta, one of his converts, and the latter crossed the stream, but could not find the golden image. The atmosphere was very damp, and fetid with bat odour, and they were glad to get out of the cave without proceeding farther. The Shans say that Nan Inta was wanting in merit, and therefore could not see the image; and they account for his not dying instantly by the fact that he was a Christian, over whom the spirits of the country have no power. As the religion of the people is merely belief in the power of evil spirits to work them harm, the best thing, even for their worldly happiness, would be for them to become Christians, and thus free men—free from the worst tyranny that exists on this earth, the tyranny of superstition, which keeps its victims slaves, darkens their lives, and induces them to perpetrate all kinds of inhuman actions. I never understood what a great boon Christianity was to the world until I recognised what heathendom was, and how it acted on its victims in the interior of Indo-China.

Chow Kam Doang—or, to give him his full title, Chow Pee Luang Kam Doang—is the guardian spirit of the district: buffaloes and pigs are yearly sacrificed to him. It is strange to find these genii, who, like the Semitic gods, have wives and children, worshipped by the same people who sacrifice to the Turanian spirits, who have neither wives nor children, are neither male nor female, know not law and kindness, and attend not to prayer and supplication, but have to be humoured like fretful children to keep them in a good temper. Indo-China and China appear to have been the meeting-place of religions, and the people have shown not the slightest objection to try one after the other in case of ill health and distress. Nearly every superstition that has ever existed, and traces of nearly every religion, are to be found in the country.

We continued through the rice-plain to Wat Lum Peun at 16¼ miles, where we intended to halt for the night, but, finding it out of repair, we left the route, and turning eastward for a mile and a half, camped for the night, pitching our tent on the bank of the Meh Ping, in which we enjoyed a good bath.

In unloading my elephant, the driver carelessly threw my large aneroid barometer, with which I took intermediate heights betwixt my boiling-point stations, to Moung Loogalay, instead of carefully handing it down, as had always previously been done. Loogalay failed to catch it, and it came to grief, throwing me back upon a smaller aneroid which I had frequently tested and found less reliable, and making me doubtful of the succeeding aneroid observations.

Next morning Dr M'Gilvary's elephant showed temper when it was being mounted, starting off suddenly, and nearly throwing him when he was half-way up the rope-ladder. He therefore selected another animal. At the place where we subsequently halted for breakfast it again got in a passion whilst being bathed by the mahout, and, shrieking loudly, rushed, with him luckily still on its back, into the forest, and it was some time before it was brought under control. When at length we got off, I walked back to the Wat to recommence the survey, whilst my companions made a short cut, striking the route farther north. I left the rice-plain at the Wat, and entered the small-tree forest. This stunted forest was evidently the outcome of a few years, as the land bore signs of being formerly under rice, little ridges dividing it into fields, and small irrigating-canals intersected the path.

Near the village of Long Ka-mee-lek I noticed a *ta-lay-ow* fixed upon a tree, and under it a written order stating that as the elephants of the Zimmé chief were grazing in that direction, no other elephants or oxen were to pass that way. On asking the elephant-drivers the reason of the order, they said that foot-and-mouth disease was raging amongst the cattle in the country, and the order was to prevent the elephants of the chief from incurring infection.

Hills to the north of the Zimmé plain from the Meh Teng.

These *ta-lay-ows* are frequently placed, suspended from sticks, about the paths leading to a camp, house, or village, so as to entangle any evil spirit and prevent it from proceeding to perpetrate harm. They are generally made of slips of bamboo plaited into an open lattice-work; but where bamboos are not to be had, cane, or even twigs, take their place.

After passing two more villages, and a road leading westwards to Muang Keut, distant about a day's journey on the Meh Teng, I crossed that river near the village of the same name, and halted to sketch the hills and fix their position. The Meh Teng was 70 feet broad, 10 feet deep, and had $2\frac{1}{2}$ feet of water at our crossing, which was distant 21 miles from Zimmé.

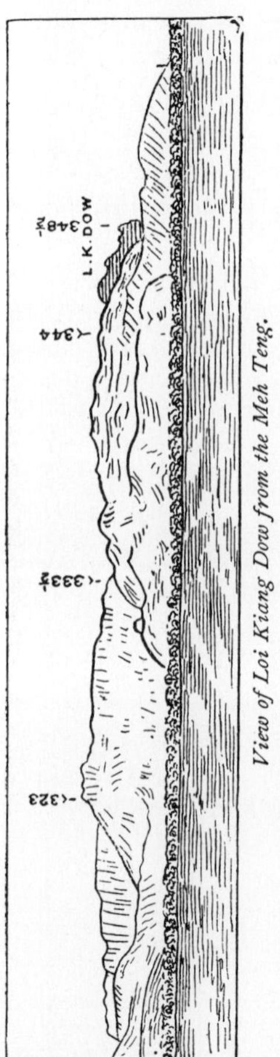

View of Loi Kiang Dow from the Meh Teng.

The panorama of hills stretching from north to west was magnificent. Towering thousands of feet above the plain, they seemed to be the remains of the great arm of a plateau separating the sources of the Meh Teng from the upper waters of the Meh Ping. The plateau had been gashed across by the hand of time, and now formed an intricate maze of partially precipitous and apparently isolated hills. Six miles distant, due north, was the great spur which once connected the plateau with Loi Chaum Haut, and through which the Meh Ping has broken its way to the Zimmé plain. Over the head of the spur, near its junction with the body of the hill from whence it springs, appeared the precipitous head of Loi Kiang Dow, here 16 miles distant. A little to the south of west a great valley extended as far as the eye could reach, in which lie many ruined cities, Ken Noi, Muang Hâng, Muang Kong, Muang Keut, and others whose names are now forgotten.

The Meh Teng rises in Loi Ken Noi, a range of hills that, springing from Loi Too-ey, stretches southwards, separating the affluents of the Salween from those of the Meh Ping. The Meh Ping rises in the armpit formed by the junction of these two hills, and its head is separated from that of the Meh Teng by the broken chain of hills called *Loi Lin Koo,* of which Loi Kiang Dow is the monarch, rising head and shoulders above the rest.

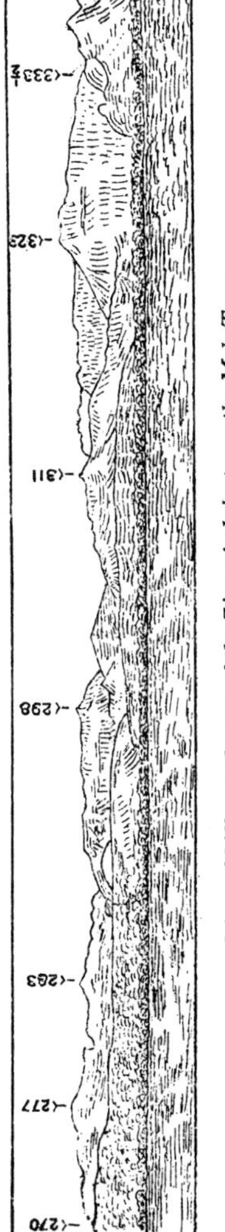

View of hills north-west of the Zimmé plain from the Meh Teng.

Loi Too-ey is said to be the highest mountain in the country, and forms part of the spinal range which divides the waters of the Meh Kong, or Cambodia river, from those of the Salween. Just to the north of this mountain a freak of nature has occurred, such as is frequent in Western China and Indo-China,—the upper sources of the Meh Hang, which naturally belong to the drainage of the Meh Ping, have percolated through a fault in the great range of hills, and now find their way by an underground passage into the Salween. Before this passage was made, the head-plains of the Meh Hang formed the bottom of a great lake which was, and is still partially, drained by the Hua Sai, a branch of the Meh Soom into the Meh Ping.

Two ancient cities, Muang Hâng and Muang Teung, and several villages, are situated in the old lake-basin which forms part of the British Shan States; it is solely occupied by Burmese Shans, and was included in the Burmese Shan States under the name of Muang Hâng. The upper parts of the Meh Ping and Meh Teng valleys are likewise occupied and owned by Burmese Shans, although claimed by the Zimmé Shans as part of their

State; and I was told that the possession of the basins of the Meh Pai and Meh Fang is also a moot question and a subject of quarrel between our subjects and those of the Siamese. These questions will have to be fixed by the Boundary Commission appointed for demarcating our frontier with Siam.

Leaving the Meh Teng, we crossed a low plateau partially crowned with teak-trees to the Meh Ping at a point where the river is contracted to 70 feet in breadth. Continuing through the teak-forest, we skirted the Meh Ping, the hills on either side gradually drawing in, until at 28½ miles the defile commenced, the slopes of the spurs fringing both sides of the river. Shortly afterwards we halted for the night, near a stream of petrifying water, which had turned the gravel in the river-bed opposite its mouth into a bank of conglomerate, and forced the river to take a rectangular bend, cutting into the hill on the opposite bank.

Our camp was situated in a wild spot which appeared to be closed in by hills on all sides. Many of the trees were giants of the forests, with great buttresses springing out from the trunk several feet from the ground; others were being slowly strangled by creepers of large girth, which, twining round their trunks and branches like gigantic snakes, sprang in great festoons and wreaths from tree to tree, making the forest in places appear one vast tangle. The Rangoon creeper crested some of the trees with its pretty flowers; and beautiful flowering shrubs, creepers, and trees were in full blossom. From beneath the branches of a great tree called *mai ngoon*, great semicircular beehives were suspended, and the pegs that had been driven into its trunk to serve as a ladder for the honey and wax collectors, looked like knots on the tree, being overgrown and hidden by the sap. As the moon rose over the hills, and shed its delusive beams amongst the trees and on the water, the beauty of the scene raised one's poetic fancies, and made one nearly believe it the effect of enchantment.

The next morning we continued up the gorge, at times crossing and recrossing the river. On passing the boundary between the provinces of Kiang Dow and Muang Ken, which crossed the path at 32 miles, I noticed a small wooden altar on which had been placed offerings of grass and flowers. The boundary was marked by a rude gateway made of two posts connected at the top by a narrow network of strings, under which the elephants passed. On inquiry I learned that the network was intended to entangle evil spirits proceeding along the path, and thus protect the territory from demons coming to work harm from the neighbouring province.

Loi Chaum Haut from Ban Meh Meh.

Just beyond 33 miles the hills retire, and the gorge ends near the village of Ban Meh Kap. A mile farther we crossed an ancient Chinese fortification called Viang Hau, consisting of two ditches one encircling the other—about 40 feet broad, and from 10 to 15 feet deep —and an intermediate rampart. A suburb of Ban Meh Meh is situated within the enclosure. Shortly after passing through the fort we halted at the temple of the main village for breakfast. Here I had a capital view of the hills to the east which divide this portion of the Meh Ping from its eastern branch, the Meh Ngat.

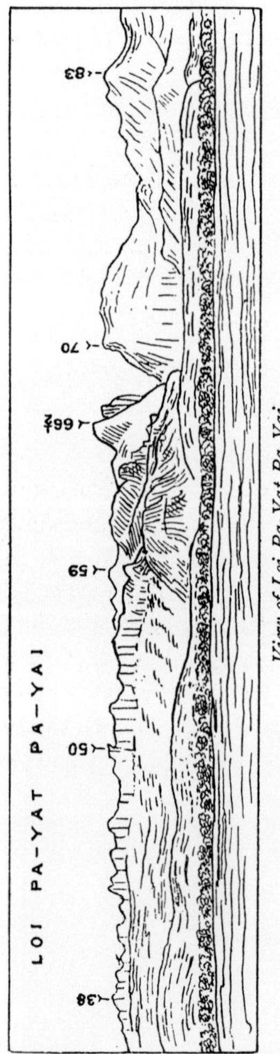

View of Loi Pa-Yat Pa-Yai.

To the north of the gap through which the road leads to Viang Pow (Pau) is a great plateau, the crest of which is edged by a narrow range of mural limestone cliffs called Loi Pa-Yat Pa-Yai, through which the Meh Pam passes in a gap after draining the plateau lying between the Meh Fang and the Meh Ping. To the south lies Loi Chaum Haut and its spurs, and to the east of them the beautiful province of Viang Pow, which I passed through on my return journey.

Whilst I was sketching the hills and fixing their positions, the villagers came crowding round me, and peeped from all directions at the picture I was making. When I had finished, I made the most of the opportunity by getting the head-men into the temple to make a map of the country with matches and bamboo strips on the floor. All were very good-natured, and I learned from them the position of the sources of the Meh Ping, Meh Teng, Meh Hang, Meh Pai, Meh Nium, Meh Pam, and other streams. All were intent upon my having correct information, and various villagers were sent for who had travelled in different parts of the country. After I had finished the map, Dr M'Gilvary asked the people to listen quietly to him, and preached to them the glad tidings that the world was ruled by a God of love, and that belief in Him would relieve them from their gross fears and senseless superstitions.

In the afternoon we continued through the rice-plain for a couple of miles, and then passing through the southern gate of the palisaded city of Kiang Dow, entered the city, and shortly afterwards, turning to the right, left the enclosure by the east gate, and camped for the night on the bank of the Meh Ping.

A short distance before reaching the city, Dr M'Gilvary noticed traces of what he believed to be petroleum on the bank of a small stream. In connection with this I may mention that Chow Rat, a first cousin of the Queen of Zimmé, who was intrusted with the settlement of Muang Fang, brought specimens of a black encrustation found in the district of Muang Fang, which Dr M'Gilvary forwarded to a professor of Davidson College, North Carolina, who had it examined. It was pronounced to be indicative of rich petroleum wells. If petroleum exists at Kiang Dow as well as in Muang Fang, places 40 miles apart, the field is likely to be a large one; and other fields may be found to exist on the line of our proposed railway.

CHAPTER XXVII.

KIANG DOW—INVASIONS OF BURMESE SHANS—PRECIPITOUS HILLS—MUANG HANG UNDER THE BURMESE—VIANG CHAI—CATCH A KAMAIT—ENTERING MONASTIC LIFE—INQUISITIVE PEOPLE—REACH MUANG NGAI—VIEW UP THE RIVER—A SHAN PLAY—VISIT THE GOVERNOR—LEAVE MUANG NGAI—HOT SPRINGS—LOI PA-YAT PA-YAI—A STORM IN THE HILLS—DRAINAGE FLOWING IN THREE DIRECTIONS—UNDERGROUND STREAMS—DIFFICULT PASS—SINKAGE OF GROUND—A SACRED CAVE—LEGEND OF TUM TAP TOW—VISIT THE CAVE—AN UNPLEASANT NIGHT—LARGE GAME—THREATENED WITH BEHEADING—LEGEND OF THE HARE-LIP—BUILDING A HOUSE—CHINESE FORTS—TRICHINOSIS—REACH MUANG FANG.

THE city of Kiang Dow, which is barely a quarter of a mile square, is situated 37 miles from Zimmé, and is 1254 feet above the sea. The whole province contains only 250 houses, 75 of which are in the enclosure. The city is said to have been resettled in 1809 by seven householders from Ban Meh Lim, which we passed eight miles from Zimmé, and was destroyed by Chow Phya Kolon, a Burmese Shan chief, in 1869 or 1870. On his retiring, it is said to have been at once reoccupied. According to the governor of Viang Pow, whom I subsequently met at that place, two invasions of the country occurred in recent years: one in 1868-69, when Chow Phya Kolon, the chief of Mokmai, a Burmese Shan State to the west of the Salween, burned six villages in his State; and another in 1872, when the same chief again invaded the district, and burned two villages. Chow Phya Kolon was said to be living in 1884 as an acolyte in a monastery in Moné.

About this time, 1868-72, there appears to have been a general downward pressure of the Ngios (Burmese Shans), for, besides the above-mentioned movements, Chow Phya Roy Sam—whose brother A-Chai is at present the chief of Muang Hăng, a State in the upper valley of the Meh Teng —burned Muang Ngai, and drove the Zimmé Shans out of the province in 1869; and as I have previously stated, the upper valleys of the Meh Ping, Meh Teng, and Meh Pai, have been resettled by Burmese Shans, and are under the rule of their chiefs.

Whilst the elephants were being unloaded, I crossed the river so as to sketch Loi Kiang Dow, which lies nearly due east and west, and is seen on end from the city. It rises, like the rock of Gibraltar, straight up from the plain, to five times the height of that rock, and can be seen on a clear day from the neighbourhood of Zimmé, 36 miles distant, looming up over the hills, through which the river has cut its way. Its crest towered up apparently to more than a mile above the plain, and we guessed its altitude to be 8000 feet above the sea, or considerably higher than that of the great hill behind Zimmé.

The sun was setting over the great precipitous hill as I sketched it, and I had hardly completed its outline and that of Loi Nan (the Lady's Hill), which lies parallel to it, and due west of Ban Meh Kaun, before the sun went down, forcing me to take the angles the following morning. On the north side, as seen from beyond Muang Ngai, Loi Nan looks like a gigantic fortress frowning over the plain.

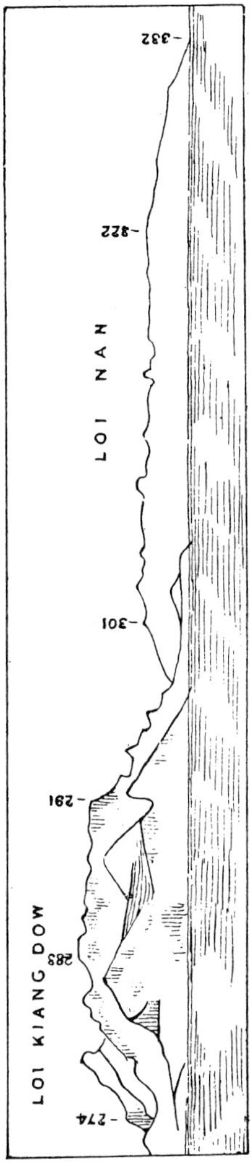

Sketch of Loi Kiang Dow and Loi Nan.

In the evening the governor of Kiang Dow, who has the title of Pau Muang (Father of the State), came with his brother to pay us a visit, and gave us some information about trade routes and the upper course of the river. He told us that the Burmese Shans held the upper valleys of the Meh Ping and Meh Teng, and that the villages in Muang Hăng belonged to them. The nearest Ngio villages on the Meh Ping were two days' journey up the valley, and were called Ban Sang, and Tone Pa Khom. The road to Muang Hăng, he said, passed in a defile through the hills, and crossed no range. Mr Gould, who subsequently visited this Muang, found this information was correct.

The next day being Sunday, I halted, according to agreement with my missionary companions, who made it a rule never to travel on Sunday, unless it was necessary to do so. Before breakfast we strolled to the ruins of a city called Viang Chai, some distance from Kiang Dow, where we found a pagoda 25 feet square, built of laterite that appeared to be of ancient date. This Viang was surrounded by a rampart and two ditches, one 40 feet wide and 15 feet deep, and the other 20 feet wide and 10 feet deep. There are said to be three Viang Hau (Chinese cities or forts) in the neighbourhood. When returning, I noticed a man resembling a Kamook, but with wavy hair, sitting with a group of people who were gazing at us; and on inquiry I was glad to learn that he was a Kamait, and seized the opportunity to arrange for taking his vocabulary early the next morning. In the afternoon Dr M'Gilvary and Mr Martin held a service, after which we wandered about and had a talk with the villagers.

The following morning the Kamait came accompanied by two companions. I was surprised to find that the Kamait language has a closer affinity to Bau Lawah than to Kamook, although the Kamooks and Kamaits have long been close neighbours. The three languages are evidently derived from a Mon stock. I was so taken up with the translation of the Kamait's vocabulary, that on its conclusion I gave orders for the loading of the elephants, altogether forgetting that we had not had our early morning's meal, and was humorously remonstrated with by my companions. This was soon served, and we left the city by the north gate.

After passing through some rice-fields and a teak-forest, we crossed a low flat-topped spur for about a mile, when we came to the Huay Sai, a small stream which forms the boundary between Kiang Dow and Muang Ngai. Fresh flowers had been placed on an altar erected on the stream-bank. Just before crossing the stream a road leaves the path for Muang Fang. The boundary cuts the path at 40 miles from Zimmé. A mile farther we came to Ban Meh Kaun, and breakfasted in its temple.

A play had been held the previous night at the village in honour of two young men who had become acolytes at the monastery. The temple grounds were crowded with visitors from the neighbouring villages, and a great many offerings had been made to the monks. These were heaped up in the temple, and consisted of new yellow garments, three-cornered and oblong pillows, mats, rugs, water-jars, and tastily arranged bouquets of flowers. Some of the nosegays were built up round the stem of the fruit of a plantain into the form of a large cone.

On visiting the temple to bargain with the abbot for two handsomely worked three-cornered pillows that my companions had set their hearts on, he told us that the receipts accruing to him from the play were over a hundred rupees. In conversation with the monks, Dr M'Gilvary was told that it would most likely be countless ages before they would attain the much-wished-for state of Nirvana, and that one transgression at any time might relegate them to the lowest hell to begin again their melancholy pilgrimage. After hearing this I could not help thinking of the young men newly entered into the monastic order—who were sitting devoutly on the raised dais, telling their beads and muttering religious formulæ,—how hopeless their task seemed to be! a very labour of Sisyphus. Yet there they were, attired in new yellow robes, with a scarf of new red print calico crossing their breast and left shoulder, sitting each on a new mat, with a new betel-box and water-jar before him, trying to look solemn whilst enjoying what must have been the sweetest moments of their life, surrounded by numerous admirers, who seemed to envy them their vocation.

Returning to breakfast at the temple, we were followed by an inquisitive but good-natured crowd of men, women, and children, who, after watching the boys dish up our meal, gazed at our mode of eating, and watched every morsel that we put into our mouths, wondering why we did not eat, like them, with our fingers, and had clean plates, and knives and forks, for every course.

After breakfast I gave the children a treat of biscuits and jam, and distributed a few hanks of beads amongst them, whilst Dr M'Gilvary preached to the people outside the temple. We then had the elephants loaded, and left for Muang Ngai, which was only a mile distant. Passing through the city, we camped for the night at two *salas* outside the north gate.

The city of Muang Ngai is surrounded, like Kiang Dow, with a strong stockade, and contains 100 houses. It is situated a mile to the west of the Meh Ping, near where the river alters its direction from south-east to due south. The view up the valley of the river is shut in by a low plateau covered with high-tree forest on the right; in front, as far as the eye can reach, three sharp peaks are seen on the horizon, in the direction of the source of the river, which is said to lie nearly due north-west, about 50 miles distant in an air-line; to the left, the country appeared a jumble of hills, all dwarfed by Loi Nan, which stood up thousands of feet above the plain, with its bold precipitous head facing the city at a distance of about six miles.

After sketching the hills, I visited the remains of the ancient city of Kiang Ngai, which lies three-quarters of a mile to the north-west, and is said to have been built by the Lawas, under a chief named A-Koop-Norp, who is still worshipped as the guardian spirit of the district, and has pigs sacrificed to him. On returning to Muang Ngai we had dinner, and were invited by a Shan gentleman to a play that he was giving that evening in the open air.

The play turned out to be far inferior to any that I had seen in Burmah. The only performers were three young men, dressed in their ordinary costume, who were squatted on a mat waving lighted tapers, whilst they chanted some legend or romance. The actors were accompanied by musicians playing on the Laos organ or pipes. When tired of the dreary performance, we accepted the invitation of one of the head-men, an old acquaintance of Dr M'Gilvary's, to visit his house, which overlooked the play, where we soon had a larger audience than was present at the performance, and were served with rice wafers and molasses cakes, handed to us on red lacquered wooden salvers.

View up the valley of the Meh Ping from Muang Ngai.

A great stack of pillows, mats, water-bottles, betel-boxes, fans, and other articles, lay in the corner of the verandah ready to be offered at the monastery the next day. Before we left, the son of the governor came to tell us that his father would be pleased if we paid him a visit that evening, as he had heard we were leaving early the next day.

We accompanied the young man, and were courteously received by the governor, Chow Phya Pet (*Pet* is Shan for a diamond), a fine-looking old gentleman, seventy-eight years of age, who said he had resided in the city ever since he was twenty-five years old, when there were only two houses in it. The city had been burnt by the Ngios (Burmese Shans) fifteen years before, in 1869. The Ngios were under the leadership of Roy Sam, the governor of Muang Hăng, the State in the upper valley of the Meh Teng. Muang Hăng was subsequently deserted, but had lately been resettled by A-Chai, a brother of Roy Sam, and now had twenty houses in it. Another play was being acted at the governor's, and we recognised one of our mahouts amongst the performers.

The governor told us that his *Muang* contained 2000 inhabitants, chiefly witches who had been turned out of Zimmé; other people were therefore reluctant to settle there. being afraid that the witches might work them harm, Amongst his people were 200 fighting (or full-grown free) men. Some of the teak-forests belonged to the Chow Che Wit, and one to Chow Ootarakan of Zimmé. The forests are worked by our Burmese subjects.

Leaving Muang Ngai the next day, we turned east, and crossed a low table-topped hill formed of soft sandstone, until we reached the Meh Ping. When crossing the river (which was 100 feet broad and 10 feet deep, with 1¾ foot depth of water, and a sandstone bed), I was amused by seeing the leading man on foot pull his foot quickly up as he stepped in a hot spring, but not saying a word for fear the others should miss doing likewise. The crossing lay 43½ miles from Zimmé, and 1444 feet above the sea. Small canoes can reach this place, but cannot proceed farther up the river.

From the river we crossed a low spur, and ascended through a teak-forest along the south bank of a stream called the Meh Na Oi, until we reached the crest of the plateau, and passed through a gap in Loi Pa-Yat Pa-Yai,—the limestone cliffs that fringe the edge of the plateau, which lies 300 feet above the bank of the Meh Ping. *Pa* means rocks; and *Yat* and *Yai*, in a straight line. The line of cliffs is precipitous on both sides, and lies nearly due north and south. Pine-trees were occasionally seen in the forest.

For the next six miles we skirted the eastern face of the cliffs, the streams on our right draining into the Meh Pam, which enters the Meh Ping a mile to the south of Muang Ngai. As we left the cliffs to descend to the Meh Poi, a heavy shower of rain came down on us like a deluge, from a low-lying cloud which capped some of the neighbouring peaks. The broken rainbows on the mist, and the battle between sunshine and cloud amongst the crags and peaks, made such a scene of beauty and grandeur that even the stolid elephant-drivers stopped their animals and shouted with delight.

We halted for the night at Pang Pau, on the banks of the Meh Poi, which lies 2357 feet above the sea. This stream rises a few miles off to the north-west, not far from the gap through which the Huay Sai passes from Muang Hang. The Huay Sai, flowing to the Meh Ping, which empties into the Gulf of Siam, and the Meh Hang, which enters the Salween, flowing into the Indian Ocean, both rise in the same plain, which is only separated from the Meh Fang, which drains into the Cambodia river, flowing into the China Siam by the range we were about to cross.

Next morning, after crossing the Meh Poi, we ascended a spur to the Pa Too Din (or Earthen Gate), the pass over Loi Kyoo Pa Săng. During the ascent it was raining heavily. The crest of the pass is 58¾ miles from Zimmé, and 2645 feet above the sea; and the hill is composed of a soft sandstone.

Descending the slope for a quarter of a mile, we reached the bottom of the valley, which is said to be merely a long pocket in the hills, its drainage passing in underground passages beneath them. From the bottom we immediately commenced to ascend to the Pa Too Pa (or Stone Gate), which we reached after a toilsome climb of just one hour, the horizontal distance being barely half a mile. The slope was formed of hard blocks of trap-rock, with an outcrop of non-crystalline metamorphic rock. The path up the ravine was so steep and slippery in places that it seemed impossible for any animal less agile than a man to ascend it. Our elephants proceeded slowly but surely, keeping, like links in a chain, so close together, that one felt if one should slip he would carry the others with him. The path is not more than 18 inches broad, and is strewn with great rocks. It is said to be the most difficult pass in the country. Its crest lies 59½ miles from Zimmé, and 2916 feet above the sea. Mr Archer gives the altitude as 2750 feet above the sea; and Mr Gould, as 1600 feet above Zimmé. There may be a slight error in my height on account of atmospheric disturbance and a dense mist.

Not far from the head of the pass, on the northern side, are two natural wells called Hoo Low, of great depth—one 6 feet and the other 10 feet in diameter. A pebble took four seconds in reaching the bottom. Two miles of easy descent among limestone hills brought us to the plain of Nong Vee-a, bounded on the north-west by a fine precipitous hill of mural limestone, called Loi Tum Tap Tow, rising about 1200 feet above the plain.

Four miles from the summit of the pass, two great depressions in the ground, called *Boo-arks*, occur,—one 250 feet in diameter and 25 feet deep; and the other, 300 feet long, 250 feet broad, and 8 feet deep. These have evidently been caused by the subsidence of the ground into underlying caverns in the limestone formation. Near these we left the path and crossed the plain for about half a mile to visit the sacred cave of Tum Tap Tow, which is situated not far from the north end of the hill. It was in this cave, according to M'Leod, "where the last Buddh (Gaudama) is said to have rested after a surfeit of pork which caused his death." Further particulars of this legend accounting for the name of the cave were related to us, whereby it appears that, on hearing of Gaudama's death, a number of his disciples shut themselves in this cave, and contemplated his perfections so intently as to become unconscious of the pangs and cravings of hunger, and thus also attained Neiban (Nirvana) —the state of forgetfulness and perfect rest.

On dismounting at the foot of the hill, we camped for breakfast, and then started on foot to the cave amidst a heavy shower of rain. Before we had proceeded 50 feet, we found that we should have to wade nearly up to our waists in the icy-cold water flowing out of the face of the hill, and therefore returned to rearrange our toilets. I put on a Burmese Shan costume, topped by a waterproof coat; Mr Martin wore a flannel shirt under a coat, and a Siamese *panoung* or petticoat; whilst Dr M'Gilvary draped himself in a gossamer waterproof, and carried a pair of sleeping-drawers to put on when he reached the cave. None of us wore shoes or stockings, and the sharp fragments of limestone in the path made us walk very gingerly.

After leaving the brook, we scrambled up a slope of shattered limestone and great blocks that had tumbled down from the cliff until the path lay up the face of the precipice, when it became so difficult as to make me rather dread the return journey. On reaching the entrance, we found it ornamented with stuccoed figures of spirits, having bird bodies, and elephant tusks and trunk in lieu of a beak.

Inside was a lofty cavern lighted by a natural skylight. On a raised platform in the cave was a great reclining image of Buddha, some 30 feet long, and around it a number of figures representing his disciples. Numerous small wooden and stone images of Buddha had been placed by pious pilgrims about the platform. Pillows, mattresses, robes, yellow drapery, flags, water-bottles, rice-bowls, fans, dolls, images of temples, dolls' houses for the spirits, and all sorts of trumpery, were lying together, with fresh and faded flowers that had been offered to the images, and were strewn in front of them. A steep ladder led up to niches near the roof of the cave, in which other images were enshrined.

My companions, who were full of ardour, determined to explore the inner recesses of the cave, and accordingly lighted their torches and proceeded farther into the bowels of the earth, whilst I enjoyed a quiet smoke amongst the gods. Down they went, creeping through narrow low passages, over rocks, and along ledges, with chasms and pits lining their path as the cave expanded, bottomless as far as they could judge by the faint light of their torches, but really not more than 20 or 30 feet deep, until they could get no farther, and had to return, having proceeded about an eighth of a mile.

Two deer sprang up from the long grass close to us when we were returning to the camp, where we were glad to change our clothing and have a good rub down after our wade through the icy water. Before we had finished, the rain again came down in torrents, and we had to climb into our howdahs to complete our toilets.

The *Boo-arks* mark the western edge of the great plain through which the Meh Fang runs on its way to join the Meh Khoke, which passes Kiang Hai, and enters the Meh Kong, or Cambodia river, below Kiang Hsen. Two miles to the north-east of the *Boo-arks* we reached the Meh Fang. and camped for the night. The river at our camp was 30 feet wide and 6 feet deep, with 1½ foot of water. Our crossing was 65½ miles from Zimmé, and 1747 feet above the sea. Much of the plain, as well as the low plateaux fringing it, are covered with teak-forest, and many of the trees are of great girth. A small deer sprang up from the long grass nearly at my elephant's feet as I approached the camp.

Here we passed the most unpleasant night we had yet spent, as we were troubled with rain, heat, and mosquitoes. The elephant-drivers, being piqued with my Madras boys ordering them about, chucked their clothes and bedding into a puddle. The boys dawdled as usual, instead of at once erecting their leafy shelter for the night, and they and their bedding got thoroughly drenched, and we had to make arrangements for their comfort in our tent. To increase our misfortunes, our Shan followers had appropriated our fowls on the sly, and we had to be satisfied with tinned soups and meats. The first leeches we had seen on the journey were found on our ankles when we took off our boots.

Next morning we continued our march down the plain,

passing some brick ruins and a *Viang Hau*, or Chinese fort. A mile beyond the fort we reached Ban Meh Kih, where the road to Zimmé *viâ* Viang Pow and Muang Ken joins the route. The village, the first that we had seen since leaving Muang Ngai, contained only sixteen houses. At another village we were told that game was very plentiful. Wild cattle, larger than buffaloes, come in droves from the hills to graze in the plain, and rhinoceros and elephant roam about the hills. Pigs were, however, the greatest pest of the country, as they rooted up the crops.

We halted for the night at Ban Meh Soon, a village situated near two *Viang Hau*, and in a good-sized rice-plain. The *Viang Hau* to the south of the village was the smallest that I had seen, being only 300 feet square. It is surrounded by a ditch 30 feet broad and 15 feet deep. A hundred cattle, laden with tobacco and pepper for Zimmé, were encamped near the house we put up in. We had been travelling all day through a fine plain many miles broad. Our camp was 76½ miles from Zimmé.

After we had settled ourselves in the empty house, a villager came to inform us that the house belonged to the chief of Muang Fang, and that anybody who slept in it would have his head cut off. As rain was threatening, we determined to risk the penalty; and we were soon glad we had done so, as the rain poured down in torrents.

On the head-man of the village coming to pay his respects, he told us that the Meh Fang flooded its banks on both sides between Ban Meh Soon and Ban Meh Mou, but that the inundation only lasts a day and a half. A similar flood happens between the city of Muang Fang and the Meh Khoke. Every basket of rice sown in his fields yielded at least a hundred-fold. He said the country was full of ancient cities whose names had been generally lost. Viang Ma-nee-ka was situated about 12 miles to the north-east of Muang Fang.

The legend attached to Viang Ma-nee-ka relates that a governor of Muang Fang had a daughter who would have been lovely if she had not been so unfortunate as to be born with a hare-lip. When she grew up, the thought of her deformity so preyed upon her mind that she left the city and made her home on the banks of the Meh Ai (the river of Shame), and founded the city of Ma-nee-ka (Hare-lip). There is a superstition that joints of bamboo cut for drinking the water of the Meh Ai should be cut straight across, if cut diagonally, the drinker will incur a hare-lip.

In connection with the new house we were in, I asked the head-man how long it would take in building. In answer, he said it took one man five days to make the thatch for a house 25 feet square; and three men five days to make the mat and bamboo floor and walling, cut the bamboos and posts, and build the house, including a verandah 10 feet square. More men could complete the house in less time. In walking about not far from the village, Mr Martin came across the lair of a tiger in the high grass, and Dr M'Gilvary found the tracks of wild hog.

We were awakened the next morning to the sound of gibbons wailing in the neighbouring forest, and were detained for about an hour and a half owing to one of our elephants having strayed in search of pastures new. Soon after starting we passed through a *Viang Hau*, where huge teak-trees were growing, and met a caravan of fifty oxen laden with tobacco for Zimmé, having brought rice thence for the new settlers in Muang Fang. One of the leading oxen wore a mask, formed like a cage, of thin strips of wood painted red, and surmounted by a bunch of pheasant-tail feathers; another had a mask made of tiger-skin, and surmounted by peacock's plumes.

We halted for a few minutes at the village of Ngio-Kow, containing ten houses, and found many of the people suffering from trichinosis, owing to their having feasted on a wild hog, which they had pickled and eaten raw. We subsequently learned that all the people of Viang Pow had suffered from the same cause two years before, and that it had caused the death of two of them.

Continuing through the forest and some large savannahs, we reached Muang Fang and passed through the fortified courtyard into the city, where we halted at a rest-house which was placed at our disposal.

CHAPTER XXVIII.

MUANG FANG—DESERTED FOR 200 YEARS—PROCLAMATION RESETTLING THE PROVINCE—POPULATION—SETTLEMENTS OF NGIO OUSTED BY SIAMESE—LAND YIELDING 250-FOLD—RUINED CITIES—320 RUINED TEMPLES—PURLOINING IMAGES—MR ARCHER'S REPORT—METHOD OF FORMING NEW SETTLEMENTS—SEPARATION OF RACES IN THE CITIES—COLONIES OF REFUGEES AND CAPTIVES—CHINESE SHANS AS LABOURERS—CITY SACKED BY THE BURMESE—GOVERNOR AND WIFE DROWN THEMSELVES—COST OF CARRIAGE—DR TIGER THE HUNTER—BARGAIN FOR A DAGGER—SWORN BROTHERS—CAMBODIAN AND KAREN CEREMONIES—THE AUGURY OF FOWL-BONES—PASSING MERIT BY COTTON-THREADS—FIRST HAIR-CUTTING IN SIAM—LAO MARRIAGE—VISIT THE RUINED CITIES—FALLEN IDOLS—PUTTING FUGITIVES IN CHAINS—A DEER-HUNT—SKETCHING THE HILLS—VISIT TO BAN MEH HANG—OUT OF PROVISIONS—FEVER AND DYSENTERY—MAHOUT ATTACKED BY VICIOUS ELEPHANT—SPREADING CATTLE-DISEASE.

THE city of Muang Fang, the capital of the province of the same name, forms part of the ancient city of Viang Fang, and measures 5950 feet from north to south, and 2700 feet from east to west. It lies 83 miles from Zimmé, and 1621 feet above the sea, and contained, at the time of my visit, 250 houses.

The roof of the *sala* where we put up being out of repair, we sent word to the governor asking him to have it put to rights, and learned that he was absent in the district, but that his brother would at once have the roof seen to. Shortly afterwards, the brother arrived and gave the necessary instructions. In the course of conversation, he told us that Muang Fang, after being deserted for over 200 years (according to Mr Archer's informant it was destroyed by the Burmese about 1717), was resettled in 1880 under Chow Rat Sam

Pan, a first cousin of the Queen of Zimmé, who was allowed by the Chow Che Wit to issue the following proclamation :—

"The Proclamation of Chow Rat Sam Pan Ta Wong, who has received authority from the Chow Luang (of Zimmé), Chow Oo-Pa Ra-Cha (second chief), and Wang Na (the whole body of the court or council of chiefs), proclaims to all people to inform them, that it may be known everywhere, that on Tuesday of the first month, the seventh of the waning moon of the civil era 1242, Pee-Ma-Kong, they have given orders that as Kiang Hsen [1] has already been established, while Muang Fang is still unpeopled, and the territory is vast for the people to seek a living, and if they were to think it advisable that the country should be settled in the same way as Kiang Hsen, it would not be fair, and because it is undoubtedly proper that it should be settled as our country; wherefore the Royal authority is granted to me to proclaim that whosoever wishes, or prefers, to go up and settle at Muang Fang, there shall be no obstacle thrown in his way. In the case of a serf of any prince or officer, they, their masters, shall not forbid this; their lords and officers shall give their consent. The serfs are not to be hindered from removing, as they will be still engaged in their country's service.

"This proclamation does not apply to slaves, temple serfs, the right and left body-guard of the king, nor to the city watchmen, jailers and jail-guard, nor to the Ngio-Kolon (the Ngio, or Burmese Shans who invaded the country with Chow Phya Kolon, and settled there after being taken prisoners); all which classes are forbidden to leave their present abodes. But the Ngio who came from Muang Peut, Muang Sat (Burmese Shan States on the Meh Khoke), in the reign of Chow Luang Poot-Ta Wong, are not forbidden. Again, when the country is established, there shall be no restriction thrown in the way of the people making a living, with the exception of the honey-trees and forest (teak, &c.), which are to be owned as heretofore. If, however, fresh honey-trees and forests are met with, they are to be divided among the rulers.

"If anybody wishes to settle in Muang Fang, let him be enrolled in my list of names; and let no one forbid them, until they number 1000 fighting men (free-men between twenty years and sixty years of age). If more than 1000 apply, the Government has power to restrain them. This proclamation is made on Sunday, the fifth day of the waning of the fourth moon in Pee-Ma-Kong 1242, and is submitted to Tow Tun Nun Chai to carry out."

---

[1] The province of Kiang Hsen, not the city; the latter was only reoccupied in 1881.

This Tow at the time of my visit had become Chow Phya Chai, the head judge and district officer of Muang Fang. On asking the Chow the population of the province, he said he could not tell exactly, because they did not count the women and children, but there were 630 fighting men upon the list. There were 250 houses in the city, and 411 in the Muang, and each house contained on an average from 7 to 8 people. This would give a gross population of over 3000 souls.

View looking south-west from Muang Fang.

He said that the Ngio (Burmese Shans) had held possession of, and settled in, the upper valley of the Meh Teng ever since 1870; and that up to the year before, there were some of their villages in the lower part of the valley of the Meh Fang, but the Zimmé Shans had forced them to retire from Muang Fang, and meant ultimately to drive them out of Muang Nyon and Muang Ngam. As these two provinces form part of the Burmese Shan State of Muang Sat, and have never been included in the Zimmé possessions, the talk of this Chow must have been either sheer brag, or the Zimmé Shans intended at that time to provoke and commence hostilities with their Burmese Shan neighbours.

The land in the province, according to our informant, was very fertile, yielding fully 250-fold what was sown. The inundation that occurs near the banks of the river will probably cease when the land nearer the hills is brought under cultivation, and the water is spread over the fields by means of irrigation - channels. When giving us the names of the three ancient cities, Viang Fang, Viang Soop Tho, and Viang Prah, built touching each other at Muang Fang, he said that the country contained many ruined cities, and at one time must have been very populous.

Mr Archer, who journeyed through the province in 1887 when on his way to Kiang Hsen, was of the same opinion as the Chow. In his report he states:—

" That the valley of the Meh Fang formerly contained a large population is proved by the most reliable evidence—the number of temples in ruins strewn close to both banks down to the junction of the Mé Khok (Meh Khoke); and that the country was well cultivated is shown by the present stunted vegetation. But the land close to the river is said to be at present so subject to high floods that no cultivation is possible: this curious fact may be due to some impediment of recent formation in the lower course of the river (perhaps fishing-dams). There is, however, still a large extent of country well suitable to cultivation, and labour alone is required to bring the province to its former state of prosperity. I was informed that 320 ruined temples have been counted within the province, and this number probably includes all; innumerable figures of Buddha strewn about these ruins are left undisturbed. I may, by the way, mention as an instance of the wrong impression made on an important people by unscrupulous travellers, that I was told by some of the earlier settlers and by officials of the province, that a 'former British consul' had purloined a number of Buddhas from the temples." This remark referred to a European traveller (Mr Carl Bock), who several years ago attempted to take away some of these images.

In reference to the reoccupation of States that have been deserted for a long period of years, Mr Archer makes some interesting remarks. In his report he says:—

"It is interesting to notice how these settlements are effected by the Laos (the Siamese call the Shans in their dominions outside Siam proper, Lao or Lau, which is given in the plural only by Europeans as Laos), as it may illustrate the manner in which the present capitals of these States were founded within recent times. The site generally chosen for the future capital is close to or on the banks of the principal river, and it is of primary importance that the surrounding country should be a fertile plain well suitable for rice cultivation. The capitals of these provinces are, therefore, almost always situated in the midst of a flat low country, but on ground sufficiently elevated to secure them from high floods. In the case of Muang Fang, however, the city lies at the foot of the hills on the Meh Chan, and at a little distance from the Meh Fang: this position was probably chosen in order to avoid the too heavy inundations of this river.

"Where the new settlement is on the site of a former city, the old embankment or wall, if any such remain, is kept as the boundary of the new town, and in time a wooden palisade, perhaps about 12 feet high, is put up; later, if the new city has greater pretensions, this is replaced by a high brick wall, either entirely, as in the case of Nan, or partly, as in Chiengmai (Zimmé) and Lakhon. The site having been fixed upon, the laborious task of clearing the jungle is begun; all, or nearly all, the trees are felled, the roads are marked out, and alongside the settlers are allowed to choose a piece of the ground. A rough shanty is generally put up at first, and round it are planted bananas and other quick-growing plants; the grounds of the old temples are not encroached upon, and the principal *wats* (monasteries) are often reoccupied by priests.

"Many of the new-comers first reside in the capital, but as by degrees they have opportunities of becoming better acquainted with the surrounding country, they begin by cultivating the most promising land in the neighbourhood; others join them, and thus villages are founded; and when a longer residence and increased population have given a feeling of greater confidence and security, settlements are gradually formed farther from the capital. A large body of immigrants, or a number of families from the same locality, generally form a separate settlement—especially if they are of different race from the original settlers; and if they settle in the capital, they usually have a separate quarter allotted to them.

"This is characteristic of all the settlements in Siam, both in the larger cities and in the provinces. In Bangkok the inhabitants of the different quarters have gradually become amalgamated; but not far from the capital the colonies of former captives of war still retain their language and customs, and keep up little intercourse with their conquerors. In the northern country the separation is as complete, and the town of Chiengmai (Zimmé), for instance, is divided into numerous quarters, inhabited almost exclusively by people of a different race; and many of the villages in the province are also colonies of refugees or captives.

"A settlement of this description entails considerable labour, and it is curious to note from what a distant source Muang Fang draws its labour-supply. At the time of my visit (early in 1887) to the province, most of the hard work of clearing the jungle was done by a band of several hundred hired labourers. These men belong to a people called by the Laos, Thai Yai, or Thai Lueng (Chinese Shans from the Chinese Shan States lying to the east of Bhamo), the inhabitants of the country tributary to China lying north of the (Burmese) Shan States, close to Yunnan and Burmah. They had followed the course of the Salween as far as

Mehongson (Muang Houngson on the Meh Pai), the western frontier province of Chiengmai, and thence had come across country to Muang Fang. Some of them return to their country with only a year's earnings, but they are soon replaced by fresh arrivals. They are said to be better and hardier labourers than either the Ngios or Laos, and they will probably be employed with advantage in the construction of public works in Burmah."

Returning to my conversation with the Chow, he said that the city was sacked by the Burmese general Soo Too after a siege of three years and three months—the people escaping to Zimmé. At that time Phya Pim-ma-san was the Chow Luang (governing chief), and his wife was named Nang Lo Cha. The night the city was taken, the governor climbed up a tree, hoping to escape detection; but being espied, was made prisoner, and fastened up with his wife and two favourite officers. When morning came they were all missing, and were found drowned in a well which is still pointed out. This seems to be an adaptation of the story of the Mongol Prince of Yunnan, who, when the army sent by Hungwu, the first Emperor of the Ming Dynasty, in A.D. 1381 captured Yunnan-Fu, with his family and minister drowned themselves in the neighbouring lake.

He told me, with reference to the cost of carriage, that the charge for bringing each bucket (25 lb.) of rice from Viang Pow to Muang Fang—a distance of 40 miles—varied between 8 annas in the dry season and 10 annas in the rainy season, which gives an average of 1¼ rupee a ton per mile, or forty times as much as is charged for conveyance by rail in Burmah.

As my companions wished to have a hunt after big game, the Chow sent for a celebrated hunter called Mau Sau, or Dr Tiger. Whilst awaiting his arrival, Mr Martin noticed that the man who had been sent as a guide with us from Bau Meh Soon, carried a knife with a handsomely carved ivory handle. On asking what he would sell it for, the man said that he had made it himself, and that Mr Martin might have it for 5 salungs (1 rupee and 12 annas). On Mr Martin drawing out several from his pocket, the man reflected for a while, and then remarked that the Nai was rich, and yet had only given him 5 salungs; but when Mr Martin remarked he had given him all he had bargained for, he had nothing to say, and took his departure.

The hunter gave me a good deal of information about the country, and indicated the position of the sources of the various rivers. He said he would gladly take my companions the following day to a place in the hills where game was plentiful, if Dr M'Gilvary would arrange with the governor—who would be back later in the afternoon—for beaters.

On my noticing that several of the men wore pieces of cotton thread tied round their wrists, Dr M'Gilvary told me that it was a bond of friendship showing that the wearer was a sworn companion to another man. It is the custom in many parts of Indo-China for men to enter into these solemn friendships. It exists in Cambodia, and likewise amongst the Karens and other people. Amongst the Koui, in Cambodia, the ceremony is performed before the village elders. Five taper candles and five sticks of incense are lighted to call the spirits to witness the act; cotton threads are wound about the wrists of the young men to produce a mystical tie between them. Holy water is then imbibed by each of the oath-takers, and the ceremony is concluded. In Forbes's 'British Burma' he gives an account of this ceremony amongst the Karens, which runs as follows: "There exists a singular institution of brotherhood among them, and to a certain extent among the Burmans, although I believe the latter have borrowed it from their wilder neighbours. When two Karens wish to become brothers, one kills a fowl, cutting off its beak, and rubs the blood on the front of the other's legs, sticking on them some of the feathers. The augury of the fowl's bones is then consulted, and, if favourable, the same ceremony is repeated by the other party; if the omens are still auspicious they say, 'We will be brothers—we will grow old together—we will visit each other.'"

The practice of passing merit and mystical influence by the means of thread from one person to another seems to be of Brahmin origin, and enters into many ceremonies in

Siam. In describing the ceremony of the first hair-cutting, Dr House says: "The ceremonies begin with the priests (monks) chanting in chorus their prayers, seated cross-legged on mats on an elevated platform, a thread of white cotton yarn passing from their hands around the clasped hands of the kneeling child and back to them again, serving as a sort of electric conductor to the child of the benefits their prayers evoke." Amongst the Lao branch of the Shans, the passing of cotton round the wrists forms the sole marriage ceremony.

In the afternoon we strolled about the old cities, which covered a great extent of ground. Numerous ruins of religious buildings testified to the wealth of the inhabitants in former days. Thousands of costly images, generally of bronze, representing Buddha sitting, standing, and recumbent, from life-size to a few inches in height, lay about in all directions. Some were minus their heads, some had fallen on their faces, some were half-buried in the debris, all were without worshippers and utterly neglected. The broken fragments showed that the bronze was a mere shell, for the images were filled with a core of black sand. The walls and gateways of the ancient cities are fast being destroyed by the ravages of the pipal tree, and large trees are now growing in the moats.

On returning from our ramble, we found Dr Tiger waiting to conduct my companions to the Chow Phya, who had now returned. On their return they said arrangements were being made for a great deer-drive the next day, when they hoped to get a big bag of game. The Chow Phya had told them that any settlers at Muang Fang who deserted the place and returned to their old quarters would certainly be put in chains, as they were now part and parcel of Muang Fang.

Next morning the beaters came, numbering twenty men, and carrying thirteen guns. My companions were eager for the sport, and became nearly tempestuous because they were detained for two or three hours after daybreak before the whole party was together. At last they were off; Dr M'Gilvary and Mr Martin on elephants, and the remainder on foot. For two hours they journeyed to the north-east,

Junction of the Meh Fang and Meh Khoke valleys.

and then left the path. A few minutes later they came upon an unsavoury odour, and Dr Tiger cocked his gun and looked sharply about; and then, rummaging in the grass, drew out the carcass of a deer on which a tiger had been breakfasting. This was encouraging. A few steps farther, one of the men spied a deer standing close by in the grass. He took careful aim, but his wretched flint-lock missed fire, and the deer was off. At the same moment another sprang from under the feet of Mr Martin's elephant, and got away unshot at.

The missionaries then dismounted, and sent the elephants a short distance away, and took up the stations assigned to them by the hunter. The drivers then approached in a big semicircle, but nothing appeared, and my friends again mounted their elephants, to cross some damp low ground to another part of the plain. Suddenly a deer sprang up close to Mr Martin, and he fired and missed. Meanwhile the men started another, which likewise escaped. The projecting hood of the howdah, together with the presence of the mahout on the elephant's head, doubtless helped to spoil the aim of the mounted sportsmen, particularly as the elephants got excited with the sport. In the next drive one of the men got a shot, but when he went to pick up his deer it started up and disappeared in the long grass. After lunch they made tracks homeward. On the way the hunter got one shot, Dr M'Gilvary four, and Mr Martin two more, and at least half-a-dozen deer got away without being fired at. They arrived tired and hungry, with a good many empty cartridges, but with no game.

In the meantime I had stayed behind to sketch the hills, fix their positions, and take the diurnal curve from the aneroid barometer and boiling-point thermometer, and had not the heart to chaff my companions when they returned with empty bags. The plain of Muang Fang averages 7 or 8 miles in width, and is over 30 miles long.

The next day being Sunday, Dr M'Gilvary and Mr Martin made it a day of rest, and stayed behind visiting and preaching to the people, whilst I journeyed five miles to the north-east to sketch the country from Ban Meh Hang, where I obtained capital views of the junction of the valleys of the Meh Khoke and the Meh Fang, the rivers meeting about 15 miles to the east-north-east. At the same time I got a view of the Loi Tum Tap Tow, now 22 miles distant, and two other limestone bluffs that jutted up in the plain.

On my return I proposed to my companions to visit Muang Hang, which was said to be about three days' journey due east from Muang Fang, and the sources of the Meh Ping and Meh Hang, and see where the latter passed under the hills; but circumstances were against us—our oatmeal, biscuits, sugar, tea, cocoa, chocolate, kitchen-salt, treacle, and milk, had all been consumed or appropriated by the nimble-

View up the Meh Fang valley from Ban Meh Hang.

fingered elephant-men, who seemed to consider that they had a right to feed themselves surreptitiously at our expense on the route. Vayloo and Jewan had fever, and Loogalay had dysentery. To put a finishing touch to our disasters, the driver of the vicious elephant had somehow provoked its anger, and the animal had knocked him down and tried to kill him with his tusks. Luckily he had escaped with a few bruises, a damaged hand, and a grazed side. So we had to give up the extra journey, and settled to return by Viang Pow and Muang Ken.

A large caravan of cattle was encamped close to us during our stay at Muang Fang, and had been spreading foot-and-mouth disease through the country by contaminating every camping-place it halted at. Several of the animals died of the disease during our stay at the city. There is no Contagious Diseases Act in force outside our possessions in the East, so the fell plague would be further spread as the caravan proceeded.

CHAPTER XXIX.

LEAVE MUANG FANG—MY COMRADES HUNTING—THOSE BOYS AGAIN: PANIC-STRICKEN FISHERWOMEN — WATER-PARTING BETWEEN THE MEH PING AND MEH KONG—RAILWAY FROM ZIMMÉ TO MUANG FANG AND KIANG HSEN—A FREAK OF NATURE—TREE EIGHT FEET BROAD —A DEER-LICK—BED WITHOUT DINNER—ILLNESS OF MISSIONARIES — SITTING ON A SNAKE — HEAD OR TAIL, QUERY — EMIGRANTS CARRYING SPINNING-WHEELS—CROSS THE MEH NGAT—A BEAUTIFUL PLAIN—VIANG POW—VISIT FROM THE GOVERNOR—NGIO RAIDS—LOLO AND KAREN VILLAGES — EFFECT OF MONOPOLIES — PEOPLE DESERTING MUANG FANG — OFFICIALS COLLECTING TAXES FOR MONOPOLISTS—NO GAMBLING AND OPIUM DENS—COST OF CARRIAGE — EXPORT OF RICE — ONE SON-IN-LAW IN ONE HOUSE — TRADE-ROUTES—LEAVE VIANG POW—THE DEFILE OF THE MEH NGAT—ACCIDENT TO ANEROID—A FINE VIEW—AN ARISTOCRATIC GOVERNOR —POPULATION—WILD TEA—LIGHT TAXATION—FREE FROM VICES—PUT UP WITH A SHAN CONVERT—WOMEN WELL TREATED AMONGST THE SHANS—CUTCH-TREES—REACH ZIMME.

We left Muang Fang on May 19, returning to Zimmé by a route five-eighths of a mile longer than that by which we had come. The first night we halted at Ban Meh Kih, where the two routes diverge. A mile beyond the village we commenced skirting the low plateau which intervenes between the Meh Fang and its eastern fork, the Meh Ta Loke. After crossing some low spurs of the plateau, which rises as it proceeds south, we again reached the Meh Fang, and halted on its bank in a valley about a quarter of a mile broad, and near a stream which bore traces of oil upon its waters. The hills about here are of sandstone.

During the morning's march we passed five laden elephants on their way to Zimmé, and met a caravan of fifty laden cattle. The forest on portions of the plateau was composed of pine-trees. My companions amused themselves on the way by making small detours through the long grass, and started many deer, which, however, they failed to bag. The forest along the route was generally so dense, and the path was so crooked, that angles had to be taken by me every two or three minutes, which is fatiguing work.

The Meh Fang, which we crossed after breakfast, was 60 feet wide and 6 feet deep, with 1 foot of water. Its bed is composed of pebbles coming from sandstone, slate, granite, and quartz formations. The crossing was 61½ miles from Zimmé, and 1954 feet above sea-level. A little farther on we crossed a bend in the river in which a number of men and women were fishing, who, scared at our appearance, scuttled away as fast as they could—the women screaming with terror at the sight of my Madras servants. These boys were always amused at the horror and panic their black faces inspired in the women.

After crossing the bend we left the river, and for the next mile gradually ascended to the summit of the water-parting that separates the affluents of the Meh Fang, which flows into the Meh Kong, from those of the Meh Pam, which joins the Meh Ping below Muang Ngai. The summit of this pass is 59¼ miles from Zimmé, and only 2158 feet above the sea. A railway from Zimmé to Muang Fang, and thence to Kiang Hsen, would certainly be aligned up the valley of the Meh Pam, and over this pass into the basin of the Meh Fang. The rise from the latter river to the crest of the pass is only 204 feet.

In ascending the pass I noticed many palms, resembling small cocoa-nut trees, and seeing that they were in blossom, asked a man to get me some of the flowers, when he refused flatly, saying, "Whoever touched them would certainly suffer from the itch." The wood of this palm is used in the construction of weaving-looms. The jungle was very dense, with aroids, ferns, and wild plantains scattered through the undergrowth. There are many plants in the jungle that one has to be chary in handling. Some blister the hand, while others are covered with prongs like fish-hooks. When riding, the eyes have to be kept constantly on the look-out, or your head-covering will be carried away and your coat torn into ribbons by these snares for the unwary.

The Shan States afford constant surprises, and one was before us as we looked to the west in descending the pass. Although we had crossed the water-parting, the high range of mountains which we had passed over on our former journey at the Pa Too Pa was still to our right, and we were now at the head of a valley worn out of the plateau formation at the foot of its slope. The range is here called Loi Pa Chan, and is limestone overlying sandstone, the latter rock appearing in the stream that drains the valley. The left side of the valley, from its easy slope, seemed especially made for railway purposes.

At 56 miles, Loi Pa Chan, which for the last 3¼ miles had been frowning down upon us, suddenly ended, and a mile farther we crossed the stream that drains the valley we had been traversing, having fallen only 288 feet in our easy descent from the crest of the pass. We shortly afterwards reached a low spur from the eastern hills, and crossed it to the Huay Pong Pow. We then followed that stream to Pang Pong Pow, and halted for the night. The trunk of a banian-tree not far from the camp was 8 feet in diameter, or more than 25 feet in girth.

The ground near the camp is boggy, with a strong smell of sulphur, the earth greasy and slimy, the strata a black shaly rock. The place is a deer-lick, and the caravans of cattle which passed through the camp early the next morning, taking rice to Muang Fang, so enjoyed licking the puddles that they could hardly be driven from the place. These pools are said formerly to have been a great rendezvous for wild cattle and other animals. Many trees in the neighbourhood of the camp were covered with the beautiful blossoms of the Rangoon creeper, and I noticed the single camellia of Burmah growing wild among the grass.

On halting for the night, we were so tired and weary that we at once fell upon sardines and cold rice, without waiting for dinner to be cooked, having had a very poor breakfast. When dinner was at length served, I was in bed, and my companions on their way there. The edge was off our appetites; sleep was dulling our senses,—so the boys enjoyed the dinner, while we enjoyed repose.

In the morning Mr Martin had a touch of the fever from which he had previously suffered. Dr M'Gilvary had long been endeavouring to ward off recurring visits of the same enemy by taking quinine in teaspoonfuls. The Shan servants accompanying the missionaries, as well as my men, likewise had it at times, and I alone remained impregnable. I was very thankful for my immunity from it, as otherwise I could not have stood the constant strain upon my attention.

Leaving the camp, we crossed a spur to the Huay Pun, and proceeded for a mile up its course, rising 339 feet, to the crest of the pass over the range which links on the Pa-Yat Pa-Yai plateau to the eastern hills. This range of hills separates the waters flowing into the Meh Pam from those flowing into the Meh Ngat. The crest of the pass lies 51 miles from Zimmé, and 2277 feet above the sea.

Whilst sitting on a stone taking the height with the boiling-point thermometer, a snake, called Shin Byee in Burmah, wriggled from under it. The men said the bite of the snake was deadly, and that it possessed two heads, one where its tail should be. On using my magnifying-glass I proved to them that this was a delusion, though the shape and marks on the flat end to the tail gave some reason for the general belief. A number of emigrants passed us here on their way to Muang Fang; the women, like good housewives, were carrying their spinning-wheels on their backs.

We descended the pass to the Meh Ngat, and after breakfast continued up the valley of that stream for a mile and a half, when we crossed it near where some men and half-a-dozen women were fishing in the stream. These hurried away as fast as they could put foot to ground, and hid themselves in the forest. Our crossing was 48 miles from Zimmé, and 1676 feet above sea-level; and the river 30 feet broad and 4 feet deep, with 6 inches of water in its bed.

Leaving the stream, we marched over the low plateau round which the stream turns to enter the great plain of Muang Pow (Pau). On reaching the plain we had a magnificent view of Loi Chaum Haut and its eastern spurs, and could see the head of Loi Kiang Dow peeping over the hills I had sketched at Ban Meh Meh. To the east of the plain, which averages 12 miles in length and 8 miles in width, spur after spur was seen stretching in a south-easterly direction to the range in the background that divides the waters of the Meh Ping from those of the Meh Low. To the south the Meh Ngat breaks through the hills in a long defile, and to the north appeared the hills we had passed on our journey. Nothing could be more peaceful than the aspect of this beautifully situated plain. It seemed to be cut off from the turmoil and din of the world by the surrounding mountains,—a place one might long to retire to—

> "Where rumour of oppression and deceit,
> Of unsuccessful or successful war,
> Might never reach me more."

But history tells a different tale: this pleasant little valley, encircled by beautiful parks of trees skirting the foot of the surrounding hills, has been the theatre of many a hostile raid, and its inhabitants are migrating from it, being discontented with the imposition of monopolies which they consider to be oppressive.

Owing to the sparseness of the present population, only a small portion of the rich plain was under cultivation; but it had evidently at one time been nearly entirely under rice, as only a few stunted trees, chiefly *pouk* (the stick-lac tree) and *mai cha-lau,* were scattered about it. After marching through the plain for 3 miles, we entered the north gate of Viang Pow, which is situated 44 miles from Zimmé, and 1426 feet above the sea. The city was surrounded by a newly constructed palisade raised above a low rampart, and by a ditch 10 feet broad and 1 foot deep.

Continuing along the main road of the city, we halted at a *sala*, nearly opposite the court-house. On hearing of our arrival, the brother of the governor, who was setting out the site of a new house, sent to borrow a compass so as to test whether he had guessed the true north and south. On proceeding to the spot, I found the posts had been placed only 5° out of the true magnetic meridian, giving the same error that appeared in the alignment of the main street. The city is well laid-out, the roads are broad, and the whole place has an aspect of neatness and order.

In the evening the governor paid us a visit, and told us that Viang Pow was established as a *Muang*, or separate governorship, by the chief of Zimmé, in 1870: previous to that time the villages had been under the direct control of Zimmé. In 1868-69, Phya Kolon, a chief of the Ngio (Burmese Shans), raided the district, and burned six villages; and again in 1872, when they burned two more villages.

The *Muang*, according to him, contained 900 houses occupied by Shans: 200 of the houses were within the palisades of the city. It likewise included two Kiang Tung Lawa (Lolo) villages, and three Karen villages. Although over a hundred householders had lately removed to Muang Fang, he had remaining under him over 1000 fighting-men. In the city and district there were four temples, containing in all eight monks. Asked why the householders had left his *Muang* for Muang Fang, he became quite excited, and said it was because of the monopolies lately granted by the chief of Zimmé on spirits, pork, and tobacco, and the imposition of a tax upon stick-lac. The people had given up collecting lac since the tax was imposed; and even cotton-planting was being neglected, as the people thought a tax would also be levied on it.

On my inquiring how the monopolists levied their taxes, he replied that the officials of the district agree to sell the spirit for the Zimmé monopolist, adding a thirtieth to the price for their trouble. The people are not allowed to distil liquor for sale, or even for private use. The monopoly on pigs brings into the monopolist one rupee for each pig killed for spirit-worship, and one and a half rupee when killed for ordinary consumption. One-tenth of this amount goes to the officials for collecting the tax. The tobacco monopolist mulcts the people to the extent of one-fourth of the amount that is sold. This last tax, if not an exaggeration, is certainly most oppressive; but, outside this, I do not see that the people have anything to growl about. The taxation in the Shan States is far lighter than in Siam, and the people are in every way much better off than there.

One thing the governor said he was very proud of, and that was, there was not a single gambling-hell or opium-den in the *Muang*. Monopolists had tried to establish these vices amongst the people, but by common consent they had all set their faces against them, so the disconcerted monopolists had to shut up shop and leave in disgust. As to trade, he said there was little doing except the export of rice to Muang Fang; the cost of carriage to that place was 8 annas a bucket in the dry season, and 10 annas in the rains. A bucket weighed 25 lb., and an ox carried exactly 3 buckets, or 75 lb.

Previous to the establishing of Muang Fang, purchasers from Zimmé bought the surplus rice at a rupee for 8½ buckets; but in times of scarcity, like 1884, the people received a rupee for 5 buckets. No import duties are levied in the district. When telling us of the average number of people in each house, which, according to him, was six, he said that amongst the Zimmé Shans only one son-in-law is allowed at the same time to live with the wife's parents. When the second daughter marries, the first removes to a house of her own.

The journey from Viang Pow to Kiang Dow takes only one day. To Ban Nong Kwang, on the Meh Low, the journey is done in three days. The range of hills crossed on the latter route, according to him, is as easy, and about the same height, as those crossed between Muang Fang and Viang Pow. An ancient city called Viang Wai (the city of rattan-canes) is situated 8 miles to the west of Viang Pow.

The next day we left Viang Pow, and continued through the plain some distance to the east of the Meh Ngat until the plateaux on either side commenced to draw in at 39 miles, when we crossed the river, which had enlarged to 55 feet in breadth and 8 feet in depth, with 1½ foot of water in the bed, and is 1300 feet above the sea. Up to this point the plain had continued from 9 to 7 miles broad. Several villages and large tracts of rice-fields were passed.

Near the hills the plain had the appearance of a beautifully timbered park.

On a low plateau that rises some twelve feet above the fields, *padouk* trees were in flower, and numerous cat-tail orchids adorned the branches of the smaller trees. The *Mai ma-kate*, a shrub bearing both white and yellow jessamine-shaped flowers, and the Rangoon creeper, were frequently seen, as well as the tree bearing the gooseberry fruit, and a small tree with fruit resembling lemons in scent, colour, and shape. This latter fruit is held in high esteem by the Shans for its

View across Muang Ken and the valley of the Meh Ping.

supposed healing qualities. I noticed the men plucking it as they went along, and scrubbing their skin with it. At one place, when passing some clumps of stunted trees, we came suddenly upon a group of Karen villagers, who, with their cloth blankets hooded over their heads and clutched round their bodies, reminded me strongly of pictures of gnomes in the Black Forest.

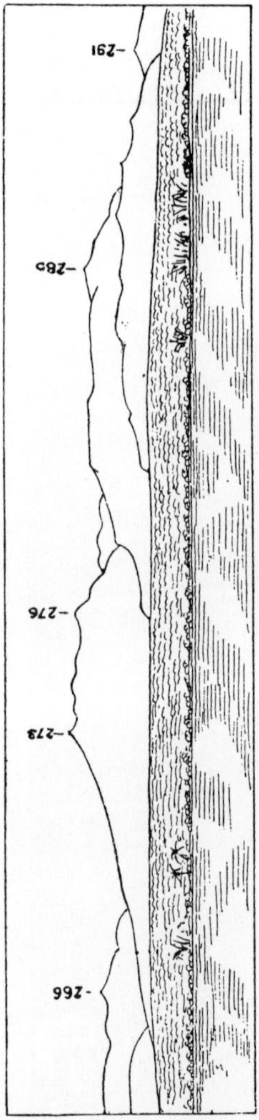

Hills west of the Meh Ping at 11.55 A.M. 23*d May.*

A little beyond Ban Huay Ngoo, we began to cross the plateau-topped spurs from Loi Chaum Haut, which, with the spurs from the eastern range, draw in and enclose the Meh Ngat in a defile. In crossing a stream near the village, my elephant gave a sudden plunge, and my last aneroid barometer came to grief, slipping off the mackintosh sheet upon which I was sitting, and tumbling to the ground; so I had to leave off taking intermediate heights between my boiling-point observations. This did not so much matter, as the Meh Ngat is an affluent of the Meh Ping, and I had no more water-partings to cross on the journey.

From the crest of the final spur, we had a magnificent view across the plain of Muang Ken to the plateau-topped hill, Loi Tat Muang Ken, which partly separates it from the Zimmé plain. Over the end of the hill and beyond it the splendid panorama extended along the broken hills lying to the west of the Meh Ping, and stretched as far as the eye could reach up the valley of the Meh Teng. Whilst I was sketching the view and taking angles to the hills, my companions were hurrying on to Ban Perng, so as to get breakfast ready by the time I reached that place. Ban Perng lies 21 miles from Zimmé, and is the principal village of Muang Ken, and the head-quarters of the governor. My companions, whilst breakfasting under some fruit-trees, had been discomforted by a storm of rain which came pelting down upon them before they could remove into a house. My sketches had delayed me till long past noon, so the boys had to dish up a fresh meal for me. Whilst I was eating it, Dr M'Gilvary and Mr Martin paid a visit to the governor, and brought him back with them for me to interrogate.

The governor was a distinguished-looking, white-haired old gentleman, very courteous in his manner, interested in his province, and perfectly willing to impart any information in his power. He said his *Muang* contained 400 houses, and over 400 fighting-men. The people gained their livelihood by cultivating rice, pepper, tobacco, and fruit-trees (chiefly oranges), and by fishing. Timber is only felled for local use, not for export.

On my asking if tea was cultivated in his district, he replied that it was not cultivated, but that it grew wild on some of the hills, notably on Loi Oo-um, one of the spurs of Loi Chaum Haut, and on the hills near Viang Dong, an ancient city on the Huay Chang Tai, situated six hours' journey to the west of the Meh Ping. A great deal of tea was cultivated, according to him, on the hills to the east and the west of the Meh Khoke above the entrance of the Meh Fang. A ruined city called Viang Koo-an lay between the Meh Ping and Viang Dong; he knew of no other ruined cities in his neighbourhood.

The taxes are very light in this *Muang*, consisting of a basket of paddy for each basket sown; and the monopolies consist of only pork and tobacco. The monopolist takes a rupee and a half on each pig slaughtered for ordinary use, and one rupee if it is killed for spirit-worship; on tobacco he takes a quarter of a rupee on each hundred tobacco-plants. There are no spirit, opium, or gambling farms in the district;

the people being addicted to none of these vices. A tax of ten rupees is levied on the sale of an elephant, half of which is paid by the seller and half by the purchaser.

Having thanked the governor for the information, we had the elephants loaded, and resumed our march. We shortly afterwards crossed the Meh Hau Prat (a stream 30 feet wide and 10 feet deep, with 1 foot of water), which drains the valley of Muang Ken. We then proceeded across several spurs from Loi Tat Muang Ken, and reached the Zimmé plain at 16 miles, near the village of Ban Hom Luang, in whose fields I halted to sketch the hills lying to the west of the Meh Ping, and to the south of the valley of the Meh Teng.

From the village to Zimmé is one great rice-plain, containing numerous villages, and beautified by orchards and by flowering shrubs, notably the *Mai cha-lau,* which in parts gave the fields the aspect of gardens of standard rhododendrons. It soon became so dark that I had to close the survey for the night, and hurry on to Ban Meh Set, where I found my companions accommodated in the house of Noy Sing Kat, one of Dr M'Gilvary's converts, and was hospitably entertained by Cheen Tah, his wife, he being absent from the village. The house was full of small red ants, which got through our mosquito-curtains and made us pass a miserably restless night, not improved by the sound of a ceaseless downpour of rain.

In conversation with Dr M'Gilvary after dinner, he told me that women were very well treated amongst the Shans, quite as well as amongst the Burmese, and this is particularly noticeable in cases preferred by women against men in the courts; the woman's word being taken as indisputable evidence. Child marriage is unknown in the country; divorces are very rare; marriage is a matter of choice, and not of trade; and the aged are respected by their relations and cared for.

On noticing a quantity of chips heaped up in the yard, I learnt that they were for boiling down to make cutch, and that a small thorny tree which I had frequently seen in the plains and forest, was the *sha* of Burmah, the tree from whence the cutch of commerce (the catechu of medicine) is extracted. The natives use this extract as an astringent to chew with their areca-nut and seri-leaf, which, with a little

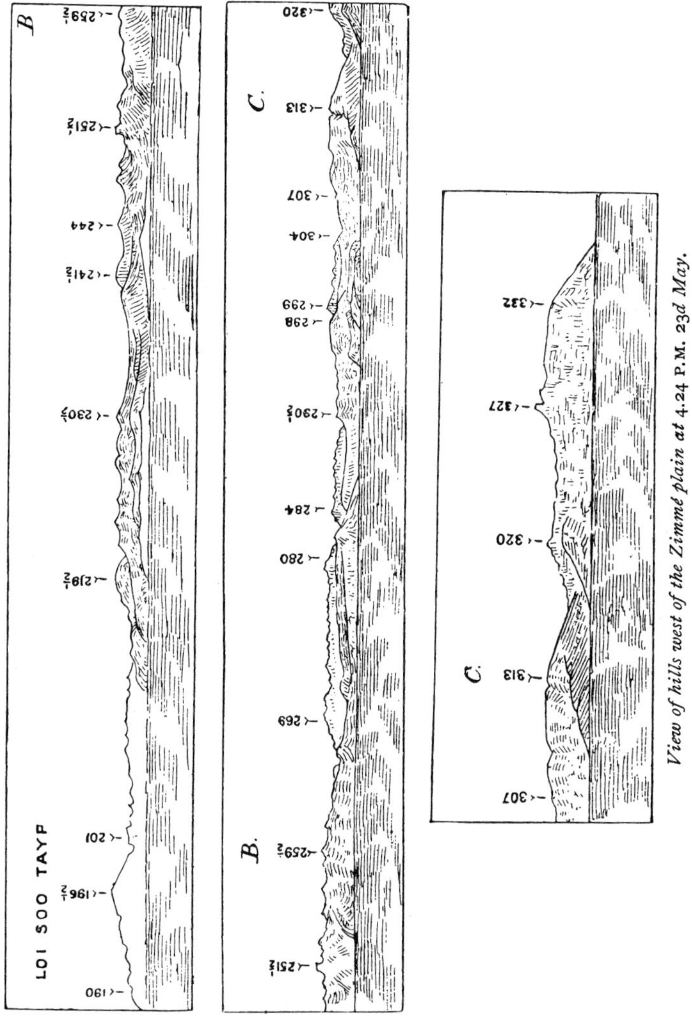

View of hills west of the Zimmé plain at 4.24 P.M. 23d May.

tobacco and slaked lime, form their betel-quid. Men, women, and children are addicted to betel-chewing, and where spittoons are not in use, expectorate about through chinks in the floor. This habit causes their gums to contract, loosens their teeth, gives their teeth and saliva a gory aspect, and renders even the fairest of the fair uncomely to European eyes.

Next morning I went back to the place where I had left off my survey, and continued it through the plain, passing several villages, until we reached the Meh Ping, and crossed it to Ban Meh Sa, which I had passed through on my way to Kiang Dow. Here I was only too glad to leave off work and enjoy myself during the remaining seven miles which separated us from Zimmé, by watching village life, and looking at the picturesque houses and temples framed in beautiful orchards, which formed an avenue to the bridge over the river.

On reaching Zimmé I put up in the Chinaman's house, which was still vacant.

CHAPTER XXX.

OFFERING TO THE GOOD INFLUENCES — THE SPIRIT IN SLEEP — THE CEREMONY OF TUM KWUN — SPIRIT - WORSHIP OF PING SHANS — ARRANGEMENTS FOR LEAVING—VISIT SIAMESE PRINCE—A GATLING GUN AS AN ORNAMENT—RAILWAY ROUTES—NUMBER OF FIGHTING-MEN—DISMISS LOOGALAY—PRETTY PAGODAS—BOXING AND WRESTLING —THE BRIDGE BREAKS—PRESENTS FROM CHOW OO-BOON—A LOVER'S LUTE—LACE PRIZED—DR CUSHING'S VIEWS ON THE PING SHANS— CONNECTION WITH SIAM — TAXATION — *CORVÉE* LABOUR — SERFS — SLAVES PURCHASED FROM RED KARENS—DEBT SLAVES IN CHAINS— RELIGION—FIELD FOR MISSIONARIES.

ON visiting Mr Wilson, he told me Prince Bigit, the half-brother of the King of Siam, had arrived, and that great preparations had been made for *Tumming* his *Kwun* or *Kwan*. On my inquiring what *Tum kwun* meant, he said *Tum* meant "the act of offering," and *kwun* the good influences which are supposed to pervade every part of the body, keeping them in good health. Any ailment in any part of the body is put down by the Shans to the departure of the *kwun*, or good influence, appertaining to that part.

If a person whilst on a journey, or in the fields, or elsewhere, becomes ill and has to return home, the spirit-doctor, when called in, immediately directs the person's relations or friends to carry offerings to the place where the *kwun* departed, and, after sacrificing to the *kwun*, beseech it to return to the sick man's body, and again perform its good offices.[1]

[1] The *kwun* among the Shans has a resemblance to the *ka-la* or guardian angel believed in by the Karens. The Karens believe that everything living, vegetable or animal, possesses a *ka-la*, which still remains with the soul of the plant or animal after its body is destroyed, and accompanies a man to his future abode of bliss or punishment. Its place is on the head or neck of every

The *Tum kwun* that had occurred was an offering to the *kwun* of the prince to induce them not to afflict him by taking their departure. At the same time, special offerings were made to the demons to keep them in a good temper, so that no harm might come to him.

A description of the ceremony of *Tum kwun* as performed on Siamese princes when visiting Zimmé in 1859, and seen by him, was given by Sir Robert Schomburgh, formerly her Majesty's consul at Bangkok, in the Siamese Repository of 1869, which runs as follows:[1]—

"Chao Operat (the second chief of Zimmé) had expressed a wish to present some gifts, according to Lao custom, to the young Princes Ong Teng and Ong Sawat who were with me. The ceremony took place in the large *sala* adjacent to our residence. The Deputy Viceroy (Chow Ooparat) did not come himself, but sent one of his high nobles accompanied by some other officers of rank.

"Two pyramids of flowers, consisting of three rows, one above the other, but each smaller than the preceding, and the whole about 5 feet high, were carried before the procession. Then came two smaller ones of more intrinsic value, each of the branchlets of the pyramids ending in a kind of network with a rupee in it. There were fifty of these on one tree, and forty-one on the other, the missing one having probably found its way to the fob of one of the attendants, or rather to the corner of his girdle.

"The pyramids having been placed in the middle of the *sala*, a number of dishes with legs of pork, fish, eggs, fruit, vegetables, &c., were placed around them. Ong Teng and Ong Sawat squatted on the ground near the pyramids. One of the noblemen then stepped forward, and having seated himself near the young princes, he made his salaam and took a book out of his girdle, and read a homily or prayer of ten tedious pages addressed to Buddha, invoking him to

human being. As long as it remains seated in its place the Karen is safe from all attacks of evil spirits; but if it is enticed away by others, or jumps down and wanders away during the body's sleep, then follow sickness and death. If a man is sick or pining away, his spirit is supposed to be wandering, and has to be enticed back with an offering of good.

[1] Siam Repository, 1869.

protect the young princes during their journey, and to vouchsafe their safe return to their parents and friends.

"The prayer finished, he tore down one of the long cotton threads which were hanging from the branches of the larger pyramids, and taking the end part, about four inches in length, in his hands, he passed the rest from the wrist of Ong Teng to the end of the boy's forefinger, murmuring all the time some sentence or incantation. He then tore off the short end which he had kept in his hand, and threw it away, for in it, according to their superstition, all the evil was embodied, winding, as already mentioned, the long part of the thread around the wrist as a talisman.

"The same operation was gone through with the left hand. Some of the noblemen who were present followed his example, and the second prince, Ong Sawat, having been performed upon in a similar manner, the ceremony was over. Not the slightest decorum was observed during it, the people present talking, smoking, and making jokes while the exhortation was being read."

From Mr Wilson I learnt that the Zimmé Shans believe that all evil and good spirits had their origin in human beings, and that the heavens, hells, and earth are peopled with spirits and ruled over by lords or kings. This belief is similar to that in ancient Chaldea, where, 2000 years before our era, Anu was worshipped as the lord of the heavens, Bel as the lord of the visible world, and Hea as the lord of the sea and the infernal regions.

The spirits in the heavens, or abodes of bliss, are governed by two kings, a court, and deputy-governors and officials, as in the Shan States at present. The kings are known as Phya In (in India called Indra, and in Burmah Thugra or Thagya) and Phya Prom (Brahma). The heavens are peopled by the Tay-wa-boot (male Dewahs), or male angels; the Tay-wa-da (female Dewahs), or female angels; and the departed spirits of all whose merit on earth gave them the right, so long as their stock of merit lasts, to enjoy the heavenly realms.

The good spirits, besides those who are in the heavens, include: Firstly, the Tor-ra-nee, or female angels of the earth, the ministering angels to all those whose object on earth is the acquisition of virtue and merit. When Phya Mahn (Dewadat), or the devil, with his evil spirits attacked Gaudama, the Tor-ra-nee came to his rescue, and wringing out their hair, caused such a flood as swept away the attacking force. Images of these angels wringing out their long hair are frequently seen in the temples, and their hair is supposed to receive all the scented water and frankincense that is offered to Buddha. It is to gain their assistance that a cup of water is always poured out whenever an offering is

Hanuman, king of monkeys. *Prom or Brahma.*

made. Secondly, the deceased spirits of meritorious kings and rulers down to the *Kenban,* or second officers of a district. Thirdly, the spirits of deceased Buddhist monks. Fourthly, the ancestors to the second generation, male and female, of monks. Fifthly, and lastly, the virtuous and meritorious departed spirits of the rest of society. The deceased rulers are called Pee Soo-a-ban, or guardians of the different districts and villages. The deceased monks are known as Pee Soo-a-wat, or spirits that protect the temples.

The King of the Earth, Phya Wet Sawan (Vishnu), who

lives in heaven, has control over the good and evil spirits that reside in the world and its atmosphere, and a system of government similar to that in the heavens. His four Tow Chet-to-loke, or ministers who record acts in his three courts and make reports to him, have under them, as agents of justice, the *Pee Hai,* the spirits of malaria and cholera; the *Pee Sook,* who are blind and are the spirits of small-pox; and the *Pee Pong,* who produce rheumatism.

The other evil spirits of the earth are: Firstly, the *Pee Mer Mor,* which possess sorcerers and soothsayers. These

Phya Lak. *Phya Wet Sawan (Vishnu).*

are the spirits of deceased physicians, and people possessed by them are called in in cases of theft or loss. Secondly, the *Pee Kah,* the wizard-spirits of horse form. Thirdly, the *Pee Hong,* who are in two classes: the headless, who are the ghosts of decapitated people; and the ones with heads, who are the spirits of those who have been killed by animals. Fourthly, the *Pee Pai,* who are the spirits of those who die from abortion, miscarriage, or childbirth. If the child dies with the mother, its spirit joins hers in its rambles, endeavouring to harm the living. The first objects of their search are their husband and father, whose death they do all they can to accomplish. Sometimes the man endeavours to escape by becoming a monk in a monastery away from his home. This belief, like most of the superstitions in Indo-China, is also current in China. Only last year I read of a case in Peking where the seven orifices in the head of a woman who had died in childbirth were burnt with a large stick of ignited incense to prevent her spirit from plaguing her husband.[1] Fifthly, the *Pee Koom ngeun*, the spirits who watch over hidden treasures. These are the spirits of misers who had during their life hid money and precious stones in the earth. On their death, their spirits are not allowed to join the ancestral clan, but have to haunt their buried treasure and watch over it.

Then there are the *Pee Pa*, or spirits of the jungle, who are the spirits of those who have died when absent from their home. Their numbers are recruited as follows: If a king, prince, or other ruler, dies whilst passing through the forest, his spirit must of necessity wander about the place where he died. No merit-making can accrue from any religious service over his corpse. The disembodied spirit, not allowed to join the ancestral spirits, wanders about in its desperation, and endeavours to cause the death of all who pass its way. If it succeeds, his victim's spirit has to become its companion and subject—thus a clan with its chief is formed; and passage through the jungle becomes more and more dangerous as time runs on. No one dying in the forest has the privilege of returning home and joining the ancestral spirits; he, or she, is for ever destined to be a *Pee Pa*, or evil spirit of the jungle.

The late King of Zimmé, the persecutor of the Christians, died on his way back from Bangkok; and therefore, according to the people, has become a *Pee Pa*. Mr Wilson gave me the following description of his funeral: The day after

[1] The Karens sometimes bury an infant alive with its mother; and amongst the Kakhyens, a wild tribe in the north of Burmah, if a woman dies within seven days of childbirth, the corpse, living child, house, and every article in the house, are burnt. The child may be adopted by a stranger, but it must not remain in the village, and no Kakhyen will have anything to do with it.

his death, the king's body was put in a coffin. The face and limbs were covered with gold-leaf,[1] which fitted so closely as to leave the features perfectly recognisable. The ordinary custom whereby the corpse should have been placed in a sitting posture was not adhered to in his case. Over the body was placed a loose robe of the purest and richest white damask. The inside of the coffin was lined with white, and the outside was covered with a gold cloth of the finest texture.

The corpse not being allowed to enter the city—no corpse is—was conveyed to the king's river palace by a large procession of soldiers, priests, and people on foot, and of princes on ponies and elephants. Near the front of the procession was an elephant of the second king, wearing its brightly polished silver trappings. Farther back came the coffin borne on a gilded bier, and surrounded by a large number of yellow-robed monks. Behind it was carried the vacant throne, bearing on its seat the royal crown. Next came a groom leading the pony the king used to ride, and after it, without a mahout, the favourite royal elephant—its huge body ornamented with rich trappings of gold. Following these were the members of the royal family and the near relatives. As the corpse came in sight, a number of princesses who were waiting in the public *sala* began in modulated tones the wailing for the dead. Every evening a company of priests assembled to chant the prayers for the dead, each receiving some gift at the close of the service.

The king of the infernal regions is known as Phya Yomerat, and his ministers, officers, and malefactors as Pee Narok. Pictures of the damned suffering in the Buddhist hells embellished the walls of many of the temples: the ideas are derived from one of the ten Great Zahts, or mystery-plays, in which a pious prince is shown the horrors of the various places of punishment.

Mr Scott (Shwé Yoe), in his book 'The Burman,' gives

[1] It is strange to find a custom in vogue many centuries ago in Egypt still practised amongst the Shans in Indo-China. In Egypt frequently the whole skin of the embalmed body was covered with gold-leaf; in other cases the face, the eyelids, and sometimes only the nails.

a description of some of the tortures, which he rightly says is sufficient to make one's flesh creep. Men devoured by five-headed dogs, by famished vultures, by loathsome crows, the flesh being renewed as fast as the foul creatures tore it away; others crushed beneath the weight of vast white-hot mountains; stretched on fiery bars, and cut up with burning knives and flaming saws, flame entering at the mouth and licking up the vitals; fiends all about, hacking, hewing, stabbing, lacerating the body; fiends with fiery hammers crushing the bones at every stroke: all are depicted in the temples—and much more.

The Buddhist hells and the Buddhist heavens have, however, little to do with the real religion of the people. Buddhism has next to no hold upon them; it is merely a veneer covering their old Dravidian and Turanian superstitions, which, as we have seen, are brought into play in their everyday life, and in the times of sickness and death. With the spirit-worshippers in China and Indo-China, as amongst the ancient Finnish (Turanian) tribes in Russia, described by Sir Mackenzie Wallace, the religious ceremonies have no hidden mystical signification, and are for the most part rather magical rites for averting the influence of malicious spirits, or freeing themselves from the unwelcome visits of their departed relatives. Amongst the Finns in Russia, many even of those who are officially Christians proceed like the Shans at stated seasons to the graveyards, and place an abundant supply of cooked food on the graves of their relations who have recently died, requesting the departed to accept this meal, and not to return to their old homes, where their presence is no longer desired. Another strong resemblance between the practices of the Finns and the people of south-eastern Asia lies in the fact that "they do not distinguish religion from magic rites; and they have never been taught that other religions are less true than their own. For them the best religion is the one which contains the most potent spells, but they see no reason why less powerful religions should not be blended therewith." Thus the Chinese and Indo-Chinese have acquired a thorough olio of religions and religious superstitions.

Phya Mahn, in the Shan pantheon, is very much altered from the Mahn Min of the Burmese, and the Dewadat of the Pali scriptures; he still can roam about in heaven, and earth, and hell. Formerly, before his attack upon Gaudama, he had power over the spirits of all these regions, but could not bring his heavenly attendants with him to earth, nor take his earthly attendants with him to heaven. Since his ill behaviour he has no attendants in heaven, and must gain the consent of Phya Wet Sawan before any of the latter's evil spirits can join him in his progress upon the earth.

On my telling Mr Wilson that I wished to leave for Bangkok as soon as possible, as I had agreed to meet Mr Colquhoun there at the beginning of June, and that he might already be there, or on his way up the river to meet me, he said that he thought the best plan would be for him to make arrangements for the crews, and to charge me a lump sum for them and for the use of the comfortable house-boats belonging to his Mission. He considered that 500 rupees was a fair bargain, as it would include the return journey and the food of the men. To this I gladly assented, on the understanding that 200 rupees were to be paid down, and the remainder on my reaching Bangkok. He promised to have the boats ready for me to start on May 31st.

Next day I paid visits to the missionaries, and called on Mr Gould to ask him to accompany me to Prince Bigit's on the following day, and to arrange for the interview, which he promised to do. On reaching the house occupied by the prince, I found the drawing-room furnished with tables and chairs, and ornamented by a Gatling gun that he had brought with him either for defence or to astonish the natives.

After being introduced, and shaking hands with him, and asking him about his journey, and the direction he had taken, he said he was much interested in the subject of railways, and that he intended to visit Burmah at the end of that year or the beginning of the next, to see how they acted in that country. The telegraph was to be carried to Zimmé during the next dry season, and he hoped that would be the forerunner of railways.

He asked me what direction I thought a railway should take through the Shan States into Siam. I told him I had not seen the lower defile of the Meh Ping, but, from what I had heard, I was led to believe that it would be very expensive to carry a line through it to Zimmé, but that one could be carried from Raheng up the Meh Phit and through the defile crossed in 1837 by General M'Leod, to Muang Li, and thence to Zimmé. From Zimmé a line could easily be constructed *viâ* the Meh Pam across the low pass into Muang Fang, and perhaps from thence to Kiang Hsen.

A far easier line, and one that would be more convenient for tapping the trade of all the States, could be made from Raheng up the valley of the Meh Wung to Lakon, and thence *viâ* Muang Ngow, Penyow, Hpan, and Kiang Hai to Kiang Hsen. A branch line could be made from this line, either from Lakon or from near the mouth of the Meh Wung, to connect Zimmé with this main line. From Raheng the main line would proceed down the valley of the Meh Nam to Bangkok; and a branch line could be carried westwards from Raheng to the frontier to meet a British railway proceeding from Maulmain.

He then asked whether it would not be very difficult and expensive to construct a railway across the hills from Maulmain. I said of course it would be more difficult and expensive than the portion through the plains, but from the character of the country I had traversed when coming from Maulmain, I considered the difficulties could be overcome without great expense, and that the traffic which would pass over the line would certainly more than justify a very much heavier outlay than would be required. The traffic that might be expected to pass between Siam and Burmah would be so considerable as of itself to make the construction of the railway highly remunerative, besides being a great boon to both countries.

I then asked the prince whether he could give me an idea of the population of Siam and its Shan States. In reply he said he doubted whether I could even get the population of Siam from the Government in Bangkok, for nothing was accurately known about it. The estimate made by Sir John Bowring was very much too low. As to the population of the Shan States, all he knew was that Zimmé returned 80,000 fighting-men on the list forwarded to Bangkok; Lakon, 80,000; and Nan, 100,000. The Siamese Government doubles these figures, as the Shan chiefs return far too few on their lists, so as to have to provide fewer men in the case of war. I may here mention that the number given by Prince Bigit for Zimmé was 50,000 higher than the number given me previously by Princess Chow Oo-Boon. Slaves are not included amongst the fighting-men.

Whilst we were talking, tea and cigars were handed round. The Siamese commissioner said that he had received instructions from Bangkok a day or two after I left Zimmé for Muang Fang, to do all in his power to help me; that he had made inquiries about the trade and population of the Shan States according to his promise, but could get no reliable information. He was very sorry to disappoint me in the matter, but he had really done his best. I wonder if he thought I believed him—probably not!

After quitting the prince's abode I returned home, and found my Madras boys in a great state of excitement. They said Loogalay was a thief; that he was stealing my things, and selling them in the bazaar. They had watched him appropriating bottles of medicine from the stock which had been placed in his charge. As the boys had never liked Loogalay from the first, as he constantly tried to ride the high horse over them, I naturally doubted the truth of the accusation, and asked for full particulars.

Jewan said that Loogalay had put the bottles in his private *pah* (basket), and intended to sell them, as he had already sold others. I told them to fetch the *pah*, and had it uncorded before me, when I found several unopened ounce-bottles of quinine, bottles of chlorodyne, and pain-killer, and even boxes of Cockle's pills, besides the medicines which were in use by our party. I then said, "Very well; cord the *pah* up again, and put it in its place, and keep quite quiet about the matter."

Fowls, ducks, and other articles of food had been constantly stolen during our journeys by the elephant-men and porters, who glided about at night as noiselessly and cunningly as snakes, and were as expert and as little troubled by conscience as clowns in a pantomime. The boys, under whose charge the culinary live-stock and other provisions lay, were much nettled at finding their vigilance not only evaded but laughed at, and the game made more pleasantly exciting to the light-fingered Shans. They had therefore been brooding over this last iniquity, particularly as it had been perpetrated by Moung Loogalay, one of their fellow-servants, and half sullenly told me that, if the case was proved against him, either he or they would have to leave the party, because it would injure their characters if it were known that they kept company with a thief.

Loogalay was away all that day, and did not return till I had gone to bed. In the morning I called him, and asked where the quinine was. He said in his *pah*. I told him to bring it, and see what other medicines he had out of stock, as I wished to take count. He then brought me the opened bottles and boxes; and on my asking whether he had any more in his *pah*, he answered no!

I then told him to bring it. He saw his game was up, and became dumfoundered for a time, and even when he found his voice, could not find excuses. I told him I was very sorry to find him dishonest, particularly as I had expected better things from him; that of course I could hand him over to Mr Gould for trial, but that I would not do so, as I trusted his present uncomfortable plight would be such a warning to him as to ensure his honesty for the future; that of course I could not expect Veyloo and Jewan to consort with a thief; and that he must therefore make arrangements for returning to Maulmain with one of the caravans, and the sooner the better, and should at once see some of the Burmese foresters residing in Zimmé, and settle the matter with them.

Quinine was fetching about 10 rupees an ounce in the bazaar. Loogalay had seen me making presents of it to the chiefs, and parcelling it out amongst fever-stricken villagers.

He therefore may have looked upon his misdeed rather in the light of "picking" than of "stealing," and as appropriating what would have gone to others less deserving, in his own opinion, than himself.

Two days later he returned, saying that he had made the arrangements, and asking for the pay that was owing him for four and a half months' service. Having previously advanced him 85 rupees, I handed him the 50 rupees then owing, and wished him a safe journey and an honest career for the future.

A little beyond the bridge which crosses the river, a large pagoda near the eastern bank had recently been repaired, and was far more graceful in shape, and more exquisitely finished, than any other in the State. On each corner of its square basement was erected a smaller pagoda, covered with a handsome tartan of yellow-and-green-looking glass tinsel, which glittered in the sunlight; and in each corner, close to the smaller pagodas, was an image of the guardian spirit.

In the grounds I noticed a large stone slab with an inscription on it which might be worth while translating. Many such slabs, giving the date of the foundation of religious buildings, are scattered through the country, and contain the only reliable evidence about events that have happened in the country, recording not only the date, but generally the name and race of the ruler of the State. Some of these inscriptions are said to be inscribed in a writing now obsolete, which cannot be deciphered by the most learned living monk. If rubbings were taken of them, they could be compared with ancient Cambodian and other characters, and the clue found for reading their contents.

Whilst sketching the pagoda, a couple of Shans who had been watching me began sparring with boxing-gloves, joining tripping and wrestling in the sport. A crowd soon gathered round, and I became judge of the contest, tipping the winner of each round. Instead of hitting from the shoulder as English boys do, the blows were more roundabout, and oftener with the open hand than with the closed fist; both the knee and the foot were occasionally used. The wrestling, however, was very fair, and more in the Devonshire than in the Cornish and Cumberland styles.

The bridge over the river was in rather a shaky condition, the planks being loose, and only held in position by a wheel-guard on either side. One day during my former stay at the city, some laden cattle being driven across the bridge crowded together in the centre, and a girder and several of the rotten planks above it broke, and eight or ten of the bullocks were precipitated into the river 30 feet below, and some of them were seriously injured, as the river was shallow, being barely 3 feet deep at the spot.

Siamese wrestlers.

The centre span of the bridge was raised a step higher than the rest to allow the great boats belonging to the chief to pass under, and every time we drove over the bridge our pony-carriage had to be lifted on and off this step; and carts were prevented from crossing. A small expenditure in strengthening and slightly arching the bridge would make it fit for cart traffic, and thus enable carts to cross the river throughout the year.

A day or two before I left Zimmé, Dr and Mrs M'Gilvary asked me to dinner, together with Princess Chow Oo-Boon and her well-behaved children. The princess brought with her some beautifully embroidered Shan dresses as a present for my youngest sister; and her son presented me with his own lover's lute. This musical instrument is peculiar. It is formed of a black ebony-like stick resting on a bowl made of half a well-polished cocoa-nut shell. Near each end of the stick is a metal rest for the two brass strings of the lute. The top of the bowl is pressed against the chest, and serves as a sounding-board when the instrument is played. After admiring the presents and expressing my delight, I told the princess that it would give me much pleasure if she would allow me to send some little remembrance from England, and would let me know what she would like. In answer she said that if I could match some lace which she had got from Maulmain, or get some of the same quality, she would be very pleased, and that she would send me the patterns next day.

On showing the patterns to my sister in England, she said they were cheap rubbish, costing a penny for two or three yards; and she therefore purchased a quantity of far better quality, which I forwarded to Bangkok for it to be sent to Zimmé. By the next post I heard that the princess was dead; and a few months later she was joined by the Queen of Zimmé.

Before leaving Zimmé for Bangkok, it will be well to give Dr Cushing's views concerning the present state of the people. In his account of the journeys made with me, he says that "the Laos principalities are tributary to Siam; but all internal affairs are managed, for the most part, by the native princes. At first their connection with Bangkok was such that the native princes were absolute in everything that pertained to home affairs. Only in matters involving the relation of Siam to foreign powers, the triennial tribute, and the confirmation of princes in their rank and power, was the authority of Siam dominant.

"Of late years the power of Siam has increased gradually, so that now the Siamese commissioners residing at Zimmé exercise a great deal of influence and quiet authority in local matters throughout the principalities. Siam, however, does not treat these tributary States in the way that the Court of Ava treated its dependent Shan States, where extortion, oppression, and the fomenting of intestine feuds have been the policy of the occupants of the Burman throne. Hence the people lead a quieter and more peaceful life.

"The taxation is not heavy. One basket of rice for every fifty or hundred, as the custom of the principality may be, with a small assessment on each house for the tribute paid to the King of Siam, are the principal demands of the Government in the way of taxation, although a small sum may be levied for a special subject on some rare occasion.

"The most oppressive right of the Government grows out of the relation of the people to their rulers, by which they must perform Government work whenever called to do so. The whole of the people are in a condition of serfdom. They are apportioned among the princes and rulers in such a way that each one has his lord, to whom he must render a certain amount of service every year if called upon to do so. Although there are rules determining the frequency of call to service, these rules are easily overridden.

"No person can change his residence permanently, much less go out of the country, without the permission of his feudal lord. While, therefore, the people are a nation of serfs, there are many who are in the worse condition of abject slaves. These persons are the personal property of their master, to whom belongs the full result of their labour. Some of these are captives taken in war, or kidnapped by the Red Karens and sold to the Laos (Zimmé Shans).

"Others are slaves on account of debt. A man borrows twenty or fifty rupees, expecting to repay it. If he cannot do so when the money is demanded, he is summoned to court, where he is adjudged the property of the person who lent him the money. He is then loaded with chains about the neck and ankles, which he must wear in company with the worst fellows. His only alleviation is the privilege of choosing his master, in so far that he may persuade another man to buy him by paying the sum of his debt to his owner. The missionaries have liberated many from time to time by paying their debts, and allowing them to render an equivalent by work at fixed wages for a certain time.

"In religion the Laos are nominally Buddhist, but it is a question whether Buddhism has as much hold on their practical life as *nat*-worship.[1] They build fine temples, and the youth enter the priesthood; but they have none of the pronounced religious feelings and immovable bigotry of the Shans west of the Salween. They say that the precepts of Gaudama are the right thing to accept, but who can observe them?

"While in the priesthood there is none of that strictness which exists in the more northern Shans. The priests visit the houses of their friends, often remaining over-night at them. They work for wages even, and in each monastery there is a money-box belonging to the priest and one to the monastery.

"In the Kengtung (Kiang Tung) principality, where the people call themselves Kheun, and are the link between the Shans and the Laos, the priests go so far as to ride ponies. As the handling of money and the touching of a pony are two of the seven great sins forbidden to priests by Gaudama, it is needless to say that the Shans (to the west of the Salween) look upon the Laos as very heterodox.

"All this looseness in religious practice makes the Laos more open to missionary work than are the Shans. They do not have that strong belief, that in listening to the tenets of another religion they may bring about a schism in the body of Buddha, and thereby commit a deadly sin. Certainly the outlook of the Laos Mission is very hopeful, not only in the number of converts gained, but in the readiness with which the people listen to the preaching of the truth.

"Missions to the Karens and Moohseus (La-hu or Mu Hseu) in Laos territory, and to the Kamooks in the region east of the Cambodia, would be remunerative, as these people are quiet, docile, and not bound by any strong ancestral religion like Buddhism."

[1] Spirit-worship.

CHAPTER XXXI.

APATHY OF SIAMESE OFFICIALS — PROPOSAL TO SURVEY PASSES BETWEEN SIAM AND BURMAH—MR WEBSTER'S OFFER—PREPARATIONS FOR BOAT-JOURNEY TO BANGKOK—BOATS AND CREW—KINDNESS OF MISSIONARIES — LEAVE ZIMMÉ — NUMBER OF VILLAGES—SHAN EMBROIDERIES—BUYING PETTICOATS—AN EVENING BATH—SHAMELESS WOMEN — PREPARING FOR THE RAPIDS — MORE BARGAINS — SCRAMBLING FOR BEADS—ENTER THE DEFILE—MAGNIFICENT SCENERY—GEOLOGICAL CHANGES — UNDERGROUND RIVERS — SUBSIDENCE AND PERIODS OF UNREST—AN EARTHQUAKE-BELT—LIMESTONE CLIFFS—A CHINESE SMUGGLER—ROPED DOWN THE RAPIDS—PICTURESQUE CLIFFS—PRECIPICES A MILE HIGH—A WATERFALL—THREE PAGODAS —OFFERINGS TO DEMONS — SPIRITS OF THE JUNGLE — FORMING SPIRIT-CLANS — ALLURING TRAVELLERS TO DEATH — LASCIVIOUS SPIRITS—M'LEOD'S ROUTE—SHOOTING DANGEROUS RAPIDS—KAMOOK LUMBER-MEN—THE PILLAR-ROCK—PASS TO BAN MEH PIK—SKETCHING THE GOVERNOR—PATH TO MAULMAIN—SEARCHING FOR RUBIES—A SAMBHUR DEER — LEAVE THE DEFILES — ENTRANCE OF THE MEH WUNG—PATHS FOR THE RAILWAY—SILVER-MINES—REACH RAHENG.

BEFORE leaving Zimmé I made a round of calls to thank the Shan princes and the missionaries for rendering my visit so pleasant, and for their kindness in collecting and giving me information about the trade and the country. Every one, with the exception of the Siamese authorities, had shown themselves eager in making my explorations a success; and even the Siamese commissioner, although apparently too indolent to interest himself in my doings, had certainly thrown no hindrance in my path, and was as communicative and truthful as I had been led to expect before leaving Burmah.

By noon on May 31st everything was in the boats, and the missionaries came to see me off and hand me their mail for Bangkok. Mr Webster assured me that if I determined to zigzag across the various passes over the hills which divide Raheng and Zimmé from the British frontier, during the next dry season, he would gladly be of the party, and would be useful in communicating with the Karen villagers who inhabited that region. To this I gladly consented, on the understanding that the exploration would not be carried out unless I could collect sufficient funds for the purpose—which I am sorry to say I was unable to do.

The boats were mat-roofed and flat-bottomed, and about 40 feet long by 6 feet broad. The one occupied by me had a good-sized room at the stern, in which I could stand up and look over the lower roof which sheltered the rowers. Under the floor, which was constructed of movable planks, was placed part of the baggage and some cargo that the boatmen were carrying down as a private speculation. In the other boat were the boys and the remainder of the baggage. Part of the stern of this boat was used as a kitchen; I was therefore not afflicted with the smell of the cooking, and my boat was not inconveniently crowded.

Each crew consisted of a steersman and four rowers, and a Chinaman accompanied us in a similar-sized boat: the three crews were thus able to help in dragging each boat in sequence over the rocks, and in slackening its progress by hauling on to ropes when passing down the worst of the rapids. Before leaving, I procured a list of sentences in Shan and English that would be useful to me on the journey, and Dr M'Gilvary and Mr Martin secured for me a most intelligent *paynim* or steersman, who had frequently made the journeys with missionaries, and was therefore well aware of the ways and requirements of Europeans.

Mrs M'Gilvary, Mrs Martin, and Mrs Peoples vied with each other as to who should provide me with the choicest delicacies for consumption on the journey, and the young ladies supplied me with light literature for my idle moments. It is not surprising that, after experiencing such constant kindness from the Americans in Zimmé, I determined, if I could get Mr Colquhoun to accompany me, to return home through America, and spend three or four months in travelling about in that country.

In the afternoon of June 3d we reached Muang Haut, which lies 82 miles from Zimmé, and is the village where I exchanged elephants for boats on my journey to Zimmé. On the way between Zimmé and Muang Haut, I passed and took the names of fifty-nine villages. Twenty-five of these lie between Zimmé and the mouth of the Meh Hkuang, the villages bordering that part of the river being nearly conterminous; other villages were hidden from view by the long, low-lying, orchard-clad islands, which are numerous for some miles below the city.

We passed Muang Haut, and halted for the night at Ban Nyang, a Karen village situated on the west bank, 84½ miles from Zimmé. For 24 miles below Ban Nyang the river continues very tortuous in its course—cliffs of sand and rounded gravel, remains of the old lake-bottom, occasionally skirting the river on either hand. Leaving early the next morning, we continued down the river, which is beautifully wooded on either bank with great clumps of plumed bamboos, which seem to grow to perfection in the neighbourhood, owing perhaps to the heavy mists which rise from the river, and passing Nong Poom, a suburb of Ban Nang En, we stopped for breakfast at the main village.

Ban Nang En, the village where the body of the levanting princess was washed ashore after her bold leap with her lover from the cliff at Pa-kin-soo, with its suburbs contained seventy-four houses. In wandering through the village, noticing the beautifully embroidered skirts worn by the women, I told my steersman to call the women together and let them know that I wished to purchase some of their handiwork. Soon the shore was thronged by people, some with new garments, and others carrying one just stripped from their person and replaced by one of a plainer nature. The designs would have done credit to the best of our art schools at home, and the colours were blended and chosen with exquisite taste. On showing specimens of the skirts to Mr Helm of Manchester, he was much struck with their beauty, and after looking at the texture of the skirts, which were made in three pieces, through a magnifying-glass, said that the top piece was of English manufacture and the two lower portions by native looms. The prices asked were so low, and the embroidery so extensive and so carefully done, that the women could have earned barely a shilling for a fortnight's work. I therefore presume that the embroidery is carried on in spare moments as a labour of love, like the fancy-work that employs the fingers of our young ladies at home, and is not expected in any other way to repay the labour expended upon it. Some were worked with silk, some with cotton, some with wools, and others with gold and silver threads, the latter being naturally the most expensive.

After passing four more villages, two of which were suburbs of Ban Nang En, we came to Ban Ta Doo-er, a village on the east bank, 100 miles from Zimmé, where the road from Muang Li crosses the river at a ford. Here two streams, the Meh Tan and the Meh Yee-ep, enter the river from the east, near a great cliff of sand and sandstone which skirts the river on the same bank for about a mile downstream. After passing three more villages, a great tree-clad spur from the Bau plateau, called Loi Kern, was seen extending close to the west bank near Ban Chang, a village built on both sides of the river, where we camped for the night.

Whilst sitting in my arm-chair enjoying a smoke after my bath, and waiting for dinner to be served, the young women of the village came trooping down to the river to fetch water for household purposes; and afterwards returned chattering and laughing, and, to my consternation, in a twinkling disrobed themselves within a few yards of my chair, and skurried into the water like so many young ducks. I thus gained absolute proof that some at least of the Zimmé Shans wear clothing solely for the sake of warmth, and are as devoid of shame as Adam and Eve were in Paradise.

Beyond the village the Meh Hat enters from the east, and $2\frac{1}{2}$ miles below the village the Meh Lai joins the river from the west. The latter stream has its source close to that of the Meh Teun, and drains the great bay of country lying between Loi Kern and Loi Hin Poon, the latter hill forming part of the great broken limestone plateau through which the river passes, tumbling down numerous rapids in a deep cliff-bound gorge to the great plain of Siam.

Ban Meut Kha, the frontier village of Zimmé on the west bank of the river, which lies immediately to the south of the Meh Lai and 109 miles from Zimmé, contained fifty houses. Whilst I was at this village sketching the north entrance of the gorge, and waiting for the pilots who were to steer our boats through the gorge, and to fix great bamboo fenders on either side of the boats, in order to increase their buoyancy and save them from injury during the passage, my steersman, thinking I might require some more embroideries, and perhaps with the hope of taking toll from the women, wandered through the village advising the people to hurry to me with any garments that they had for sale. In a few minutes my boat was stormed by the female population, and even when starting, fresh relays were so anxious to secure a purchaser that my men had actually to hustle them out of the boat. I, however, partly compensated those who were disappointed by distributing the remainder of my beads and bead-necklaces amongst them. It was as good as a play to see the scramble as I threw them on the bank.

A mile down-stream on the east bank of the river is the village of New Htow, below which the Huay Kay-Yow enters from the east, after draining the north-eastern portion of the great plateau through which we were about to thread our way. As we proceeded, spurs from the hills on either side began to approach, occasionally ending with bluffs at the edge of the stream, the rock exposed in some of their faces appearing more like trap than limestone, the strata being much contorted and veined with quartz.

Just before the first rapid, which occurs at 113½ miles, a great rock pierced by two flat-arched caverns juts up from the bed of the stream; and a little farther a spur, Loi Hin Poon, ends in a bluff 60 feet high, which has its face riddled with caves and adorned with stalactites.

After passing the second rapid the scenery becomes bold, and great precipices of mural limestone, with their red and black mottled faces beautified by lichens, mosses, and stalactites, occasionally are seen on either side. A mile farther the defile may be said to commence, the hills coming to the bank on either side, and on the west rising sheer from the river's edge in precipices 1000 feet high; similar cliffs soon afterwards skirt the river on the east.

Beyond Loi Panya Lawa, the hill of the Lawa chief, is a bold bluff with a face strongly resembling a gigantic sphinx. This cliff lies on the west of the river, and its face for some distance has been scooped out at the foot for 15 and 20 feet in width by the action of the strong current. The precipice on the opposite bank resembles a gigantic Norman castle with rounded towers jutting out from its face. The strata in these cliffs are pitched up vertically, as though they had been bodily turned over on their side.

Beyond the castle-cliff the precipice on the west bank changes its aspect, and looks as though it had been punched up or telescoped from below, one precipice rising above another, and another above it, with a slope at the foot of each, appearing as if before the subsidence of the tiers the slopes had been continuous.

There can be no doubt that the great ravine has been caused by sinkage into caverns and underground passages worn out by water, the hills subsiding into them during a period of violent earth-action. An earthquake-belt extends right up the Malay Peninsula through Burmah and Siam into Yunnan and Szechuen. The whole region is still in a period of unrest, as is evidenced by the numerous hot springs passed by travellers, and the earthquakes which frequently occur in this region.

We halted for the night at the hamlet of Ban Kau, which is situated 123 miles from Zimmé, in a small valley which is drained by the Huay Kau. The precipice facing the village was grotto-worked by the action of the lime-water, the grottoes overhanging in great masses giving the cliffs a honeycombed appearance.

At Ban Kau the river makes a westerly bend for 4 miles, and then continues nearly due south for 19 miles, until it is joined by the Meh Teun.

The next morning we passed six rapids before we reached Ban Sa-lee-am, the last Ping Shan village on the river.

Below it the river-banks are under the direct control of Siam.

Soon after leaving the village we halted for breakfast at a barrier of rocks 6 feet high, through which a passage had been made for boat traffic. Here I noticed slate and shale outcropping from the bank and forming the base of the mural limestone, which was much veined with quartz. The cliff on the east of the river below the barrier rises about 600 feet, and is known as Loi Pa May-yow, the Cliff of the Cat. Its name is derived from the great mottled patches of lichen on its face representing figures of cats, tigers, and other animals to people with a fertile imagination.

Between the barrier and Loi Chang Hong, three rapids are passed. Down the last, boat after boat was let down by a rope, the crews of my boats and of that belonging to the enterprising Chinese smuggler who had attached himself to our party in the hope of escaping the custom-houses on the river, tugging at the rope to check the speed of the boat.

Loi Chang Hong is remarkable for its castellated appearance, three grand semicircular buttresses and one of smaller diameter rising 1200 to 1500 feet from the edge of the river. Near the top of the precipice is a great cave about 100 feet high, and on the opposite bank the cliff protrudes for some distance over the stream.

The scenery in the neighbourhood is the boldest and most beautiful in its grandeur that I have ever seen. The cliffs are tinted with red, orange, and dark-grey. Great stalactites stand out and droop in clusters from their face, whilst their summit is crowned by large trees, which, dwarfed by the distance, appear smaller and smaller as the depth of the defile increases. Pale puffball-shaped yellow blossoms of a stunted tree like a willow, shed their fragrance from the banks, where small bays are formed by streams conveying the drainage of the country. Beautiful grottoes have been fretted out by the current near the foot of the cliffs, and are covered with moss and ferns which drip drops of the clearest water from every spray.

The cliffs on the west bank are here 3000 feet high, and rise in great telescoped precipices. At 141 miles the hill on the west retires, leaving a narrow plain for about a mile. On the opposite side of the river, the cliff towers up seemingly to more than a mile in height, the trees on its summit looking like small bushes from the boat. This great precipice is named Loi Keng Soi, and from a chink in its face a waterfall comes leaping and dashing down. Its last great leap is a sheer descent of 500 feet. A short distance beyond the waterfall, far up the cliff, the figure of a gigantic horse is seen standing in a natural niche. When it was sculptured and by whom, tradition fails to tell.

On the west bank of the river, near the end of the cliff where the hill retires and forms a small valley, is a pagoda, and two others are seen cresting the low part of the next hill, which gradually rises into a great cliff near the thirteenth and fourteenth rapids, down which we had to be roped. This cliff is surmounted by three ear-like pinnacles: 2000 feet of rock had lately fallen into the river from the face of the precipice on the opposite bank.

Before leaving the pagodas the boatmen went off in a body to make their offerings and worship. The demons in the defile are evidently much dreaded by the Shans, for at our various halting-places offerings, accompanied by lighted tapers and libations, were habitually made to the local demons before the men ate their meals.

It is no wonder that the deep ravines of this great defile are full of terrifying potentialities to people ridden by such nightmare superstitions as are believed in by the Shans. Such places, according to them, are infested by *Pee Pa* or jungle demons, the spirits of human beings who have died when absent from their homes. These endeavour to cause the death of others by the same means as caused their own. Their victims have to join the company or clan of demons to which the successful demon belongs. Thus the clan increases in numbers, and is ever becoming more potent for mischief.

The way in which the *Pee Pa* allure travellers to their death varies according to their tribe. The *Pee Pok-ka-long* cause deep sleep to fall upon weary travellers, and then lead tigers to kill them. At other times they allure them to a tiger's den by imitating a human voice. Or they enter the body of a wild pig, stag, or even a reptile, and entice the traveller to follow them to meet his death. The *Pee Ta-Moi* have power over the atmosphere, and cause sudden darkness in order to force a traveller to camp in a dangerous locality infested by wild beasts. The *Pee Ee-Koi* produce fever with their breath.

Pee Pok-ka-long (*jungle demons*).

The *Pee Song Nang*,[1] who are more feared than the other *Pee Pa*, are the spirits of two dissolute princesses, who, after leaving their father's palace on the sly, were lost in the forest, and perished. These spirits, like those in the spell-bound forest in Milton's "Comus," have

> "Many baits and guileful spells
> T' inveigle and invite the unwary sense
> Of them that pass unweeting by the way."

Should travellers succumb to their wiles, they die on the instant, and become for ever their companions. These spirits assume such beautiful faces and figures, such winning ways, and such melodious voices, that it is said no man within their influence can withstand them. Great precautions are therefore taken to keep them at a distance. In every path leading to our camping-places, figures made of twisted twigs or bamboos were set up so as to delude these lascivious spirits and keep them at a distance. Other offerings are made to the rest of the jungle demons, varying according to the supposed inclinations of the spirits.

[1] The Pee Song Nang, if belonging to the primitive Turanian spirits, so generally believed in by the Shans, are neither male nor female spirits. All such spirits, unlike the ancient Chaldean deities, have neither husbands, wives, nor children, and are utterly devoid of any of the good points appertaining to human beings. They know neither law nor kindness, do not listen to prayer and supplication, and are merely objects of dread to the people. They are sacrificed to only to keep them in a good humour, and to prevent them wreaking their vengeance and spite upon the people.

The next morning we reached the mouth of the Meh Teun, which drains an area of country 55 miles long and 15 miles broad, lying between the Meh Ping and the crest of the range which separates the affluents of the Salween from those of the Meh Nam, and forms the spinal range of the Malay Peninsula. This stream was followed by M'Leod for some distance when on his return from Zimmé to Maulmain in 1837. From the junction of the Meh Teun the Meh Ping trends in a north-easterly direction for 5 miles, and then runs nearly due east to 159½ miles, when it again turns to the south.

Close to the mouth of the stream is the fifteenth rapid. Some distance beyond it the river is contracted by two great rocks protruding from the west bank, and another from the east bank, which must at one time have extended across the stream, and formed a formidable barrier to boat traffic. This barrier is known as Vin-a-tum.

A short distance farther another rapid occurs at the entrance of the most dangerous part of the defile, which is here formed by Loi Teun on the south and Loi Ap Nang on the north. The bold red-coloured precipitous face of the latter hill has been cut into for a depth of about 30 feet by the fierce current of the next rapid.

The boatmen were here seen at their best. The pilot and the steersman both laid hold of the long broad oar that formed the rudder, and the other men held long bamboos to prevent the boat from dashing against the side as we rushed under and alongside the overhanging cliff. The seven minutes taken in descending this rapid must have carried us more than a mile, and the sensation was exhilarating and delightful. The slightest mistake on the part of the steersmen would have brought us to grief.

At the next rapid the cliffs on either side rose 3000 feet above the river, and the section of their summits so perfectly resembled each other that they looked as if they had only lately been rent apart.

After dashing down four more rapids, and being roped down the next one, we halted for breakfast where the river widens, near an island, to 1000 feet. Here the hills on both sides retreat for a time, and I noticed granite outcropping in the stream-bed, and forming the base of the limestone. Just below the island, which is called Song Kweh, is a very long rapid, down which we were roped; a passage had been made by heaping the boulders on the sides.

The next rapid lies a short distance above Ban Soop Tau, a long house inhabited by some Kamook foresters. Trusting solely to the current and our steersmen and the men with bamboos, we rushed along at railroad speed for three-quarters of a mile, doing the distance in four minutes. After passing

Loi Pa Khun Bait.

the house, which is situated 154 miles from Zimmé, we saw many teak-logs floating down the stream, and some Kamooks on elephants who were engaged in keeping the logs from stranding on the boulders, and edging them off when they did so.

A little farther we came to another rapid below which the hills again closed in—the one on the left afterwards retiring at a hamlet near the twenty-seventh rapid, the last that needed the use of the rope. The boat was allowed to rush along the edge of the cliff at the next one, at such a pace as to make me clench my teeth and bite through the cigar I was smoking.

Three miles farther the hill on the left again closed in, and we entered a defile and descended through rough water over a rapid that looked like a chopping sea. A mile farther we halted for the night in a bay of the hills close to the foot of Loi Pa Khun Bait—a pillar-rock about 250 feet high that rises from the foot of a hill near the east bank of the river. The hills had latterly become less precipitous, and the defile ended near the traveller's rest-house called Sala Bau Lome. The river had latterly varied from 300 feet to 120 feet in breadth.

A mile from the gorge some palmyra-trees on the west

Extremity of spur from the west range.

bank mark the site of a former village, and soon afterwards the pilots left us to conduct some boats up-stream. The valley between the last gorge and the next one is about 13 miles long and of considerable breadth. It is bounded on the east by the Loi Pa Kha range, and on the west by a bold plateau-topped range of hills known as Loi Luong, which separates the southern branch of the Meh Tuen from the Meh Ping.

After shooting two small rapids, and passing a couple of small villages situated on the west bank, we halted for breakfast near a great spur from the western range. This spur appears to be more than half a mile high, and precipitous near the end, where a great cave is seen high up in the cliff. I sketched the end of the spur from the foot of the eastern hills, which had now come to the river.

Two miles beyond the spur we reached the village of Soom Cha, whence there is a pass across the eastern hills to Ban Meh Pik, a village near the Meh Wung, through which roads lead to Zimmé and Lakon. Soom Cha is situated on the east bank of the river, and contained fifteen houses, besides a temple and pagoda, of the ordinary Shan type. Three miles farther we halted for a couple of hours at Ban Nah, which, with its suburb Ban Ta Doo-a, contained 135 houses.

On calling at the house of the Keh Ban, or head-man of the village, to get information, I was told that he had gone to the temple to worship. Following him there, I found him squatting on his heels before a wretched collection of images, holding up with both hands a brass tray with lighted tapers round its rim containing his offering. There he sat, without looking round or even moving, and had most likely hurried to the temple and turned himself into a worshipper on seeing my boats approach the landing, so as to avoid giving me any information. Suspecting this, I waited until I was tired of waiting, and then, seeing him still rooted to the spot, took out my pencil and made a sketch of him and the images; after doing which, I returned to the boat.

Ban Nah is situated on both sides of the river, the main body of the village and its suburb being on the west bank. From the village the path leaves for Maulmain, which was traversed by M'Leod on his return journey in 1837.

Two miles below Ban Nah we entered the last defile which severs the Loi Pa Kha range from Loi Wung Ka Chow, and is 4 miles long, ending at a ford called Ta Pwee, where there is a pagoda near the exit of the gorge on the western hill. Half-way through the defile the boatmen asked for leave to land, as they wished to search for rubies in a hill called Kow Sau Kyow on the west bank of the river, where, they told me, valuable gems were sometimes found. After scraping at the gritty ground for half an hour, they brought me a few small—very small—pebbles to look at, which looked more like garnets than rubies. Soon afterwards we camped for the night. Whilst I was enjoying my bath, a large sambhur deer swam leisurely across the river about 1000 feet from the boat, whilst my boys and the Chinaman were taking long and fruitless shots at it.

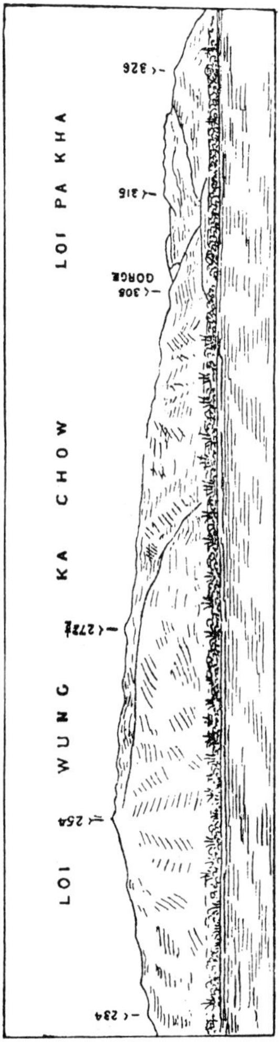

The next morning, 2 miles beyond the mouth of the gorge, I noticed a low plateau-topped, red-coloured bluff near the west bank, with three niches or caverns in its face, with a scaffolding along the entrances, and a ladder leading up to it. These caves formed the temples of a village of twelve houses which was situated to the south of the hill. After passing three more hamlets containing together between thirty and forty houses, from one of which—Ban Pah Yang Neur—I sketched the exit of the gorge, we reached the mouth of the Meh Wung, which is situated about 193½ miles from Zimmé.

Sketch at 188½ miles from Ban Pah Yang Neur.

This is the river along which the railway would proceed to Lakon. Another line could be made from near its mouth, proceeding through a short gorge near the source of the Meh Phit and the silver-mines to Muang Li, and thence to Zimmé, and from thence through Muang Ngai and Muang Fang, to join the main line at Ban Meh Chun in the Kiang Hsen plain.

Three miles beyond the village, at the mouth of the Mhe

Wung, I halted at Ban Meh Nyah on the western bank to sketch the hills lying to the east of the Meh Wung. From Ban Meh Nyah onwards, the villages are continuous on the west bank as far as a small hillock called Loi Dee-at Ha, which juts up from the plain at 206 miles, and is faced on the east bank by Loi Meh Pah Neh — a hillock shaped like a great letter L, one limb of which skirts the river for a mile and a half.

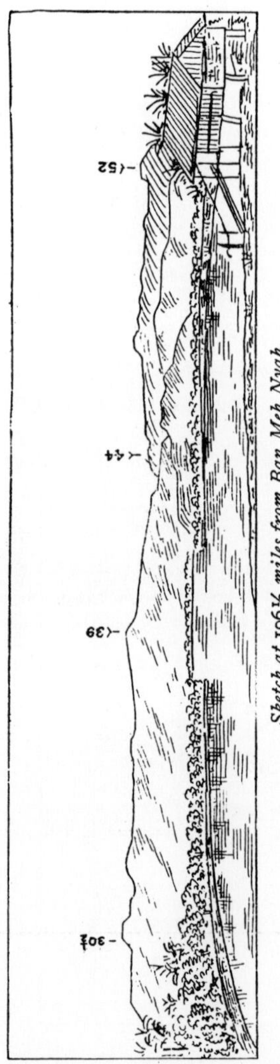

Sketch at 196½ miles from Ban Meh Nyah.

For six miles above Loi Meh Pa Neh the east bank is likewise lined with houses, imbedded, as is usual in Siam and its Shan States, in beautiful gardens containing palms, mangoes, tamarinds, and other trees. We halted for the night near a building erected on piles over the water at Ban Tat, for the monks of the neighbouring temple to repeat, at the time of the full and new moons, the ritual appointed to cleanse them from their sins, which, if report is to be believed, are by no means few.

From Ban Tat I sketched Loi Luong Sam Huay—the great hill-spur which juts out from the western hills, ending nearly due west of Raheng, and separates the Meh Tak from the Meh Tau. It is by this spur that the railway from Maulmain to Raheng would gradually descend from the crest of the pass over the spinal range which separates the drainage of the Salween river from that of the Meh Ping. The direction of the spur for some miles is due east and west, and it seems—particularly on its southern side—eminently fitted for the easy development of a railway to the pass. The pass is only 2400 feet above the level of the sea, or about 2000 feet above Raheng, and only 1770 feet above the bank of the Thoungyeen river at our frontier, which lies only 37 miles to the west of Raheng.

When the country through which this portion of the line will run is fully explored and accurately surveyed and levelled, it will probably be found that both the distance and estimated cost given by Mr Colquhoun and myself in our Report to the Government and the Chambers of Commerce, is considerably in excess of what will actually be required; because, in estimating this portion of the railway, we have assumed a length of 80 miles, or more than double the direct distance, and for 53 miles of the length have allowed about double the amount per mile that railways have cost in Burmah.

From Ban Tat we proceeded leisurely, stopping at several of the villages, to Raheng. The city and its straggling suburbs—some 10 miles in length—are beautifully wooded, lining the banks from 212 to 222 miles. The villages on the west bank are smaller and farther apart than those on the east bank, on which the city is built.

We halted at 215 miles, about half a mile above the house of the governor, opposite the house of Mr Stevens—an English pleader who had been for some years in the country, and is concerned in the timber trade.

CHAPTER XXXII.

THE FORMER GOVERNOR IN LEAGUE WITH DACOITS—TROUBLE ON THE FRONTIER — DACOITING BOATS — ADVICE TO A MISSIONARY — THE GOVERNOR OF PETCHABURI—A PETITION TO THE KING—ROBBING THE PEOPLE—MISGOVERNMENT OF A SIAMESE PROVINCE—MISSIONARY'S OPINION OF THE KING — EXTRAORDINARY FLOODS IN SIAM — THE SEASONS—FLOOD OF 1878 : VILLAGES WASHED AWAY—FLOOD OF 1831—ENTERING THE PALACE IN BOATS—BOAT-JOURNEYS FROM AND TO BANGKOK.

As soon as the boats were made fast to the bank, I called on Mr Stevens, and fortunately found him at home. He proved a highly intelligent man, well acquainted with the people and their manners and customs. He said the governor of Raheng was the pick of the flock of Siamese officials, and one of the few that was allowed an adequate salary, which had been granted him by the king so that he might not be induced to take to the evil practices of his predecessor, which had given rise to frequent complaints on the part of the British Government.

The late governor was a bandit in disguise. He was notoriously in league with the dacoits who infested his province, which neighbours our frontier, and his proceedings had been laid bare in a police case which was reported in the English newspaper at Bangkok. In the issue for March 1873 it was related that two men, Tah and Nai Ruan, whilst at a theatre near the governor of Raheng's residence, seeing the servants of one of the new governor's deputies loading a boat with goods, learned that the deputy was going to Bangkok. They then proceeded to a rest-house in a neighbouring village, and informed five others of their crew, one of whom was named Chi. Whilst conversing on the matter, Chi remarked to Tah: "When Pra Intakeeree [the former governor] was still in Taht [Raheng] we were in the habit of committing robberies, selling the plunder, and dividing the money thus acquired with Pra Intakeeree. If at any time complaints were made against us, Pra Intakeeree assisted us, and exonerated us from criminality. This ally of ours is now under accusation at Bangkok; we have no protector; we cannot enter the town, and must wander hither and thither in concealment: we must commit and multiply daring robberies, and thus make it manifestly true that Pra Intakeeree was not the patron of thieves. This will be the cause of his return to Taht, to be again our patron and protector." They accordingly waylaid the boat, fired into it, wounded the deputy and one of his children and killed a slave, and afterwards plundered the boat.

I heard many similar stories of the governors of the Siamese provinces. For instance, one of the missionaries whom I met in Bangkok was loud in his complaints about the evil doings of the governor of Petchaburi, a missionary station to the west of the Gulf of Siam, who was a brother of the Foreign Minister. He told me that when talking with the abbot of the monastery at that place about the power of Christianity in inducing men to lead virtuous lives, the abbot turned smilingly to him and begged him to concentrate all his labours upon the governor, because that personage was the perpetrator, by himself or by his crew, of most of the ill deeds in the province.

Four petitions had been thrown into the Mission-house by the people, one of which had been forwarded by my friend to the king, who despatched three commissioners to inquire into the case, the head one being reputed to be the honestest and most fearless man in Siam.

The commissioners stayed about six months, investigating various charges, and convicted 70 criminals, 27 of whom were the jailers, constables, and slaves of the governor. One of the men, named "Chat," had been convicted of murder by the governor, and should have been sent to Bangkok for execution, but having bribed the governor with seven catties (£56 sterling), he was allowed to roam about in chains, the anklets of which he could remove at will, as they were made of lead instead of iron. The complaints against the governor and Chat are summed up in the following petition, which was translated for me by the missionary :—

"*April* 6, 1883.

"We, Siamese, Laos, and Peguans, have consulted together as to our troubles. We believe the missionaries are wise, and are able to bring happiness to us. The Chinese tax-collectors receive but small salaries, therefore squeeze sums from the poor people. We complained to the governor of this province, but the tax-collectors had already bribed his Excellency, who therefore replied to his subjects: 'You must pay according to the demands of the tax-collectors [monopolists].' Thus they have great gain to send to China, and no benefit occurs to our country. The missionaries have never been known to impose upon any one, but desire all may be happy; teaching all to be wise, and freely caring for the sick and needy. Because of this we have had some happiness. We therefore beg you to help us now.

"At this time there is great trouble among the citizens of Petchaburi. Thieves and robbers are shooting many men and women. Liberated prisoners in chains, and some whose chains have been loosed, are plundering houses. Some of them are slaves of the governor. One named Chat, a notorious robber, freed from prison and now a slave of the governor, is prowling about, daily committing highway robberies all the way from the large bridge to Ta Ching, both from boats and on shore, never ceasing.

"Morning and evening the slaves of the governor, having been liberated, go to the temple Bandi It, the temple Chap Prie, the temple Poue, the temple Chan, and the temple Yai, and plunder various things, gold and jewels from the women, and as the women are bringing their sugar to market they seize it. The owners of the sugar recognise the thieves as slaves of the governor, and complained to the governor's head-wife, who brought out the parties not concerned. The sugar-women said these are not the parties. Then the governor's mother charged the sugar-women with making false accusations, and threw them into prison, compelling them to pay seven and a half dollars before liberating them.

"Thieves have stolen our cattle. The governor's mother received the said cattle. They were found in her possession, and proved to be ours. Notwithstanding this, we had to pay large sums to secure them. She is also accustomed to take bribes from litigants. The case then enters the court, and if not decided according to the bribe, she exercises her authority and sees that it is so decided.

"Litigants in his Excellency's courts, where cases are as yet pending, are required to render his Excellency service; if they refuse, wages equal to the service are exacted from them. His Excellency sends prisoners to cut bamboos belonging to citizens in the province, and sells or uses the same. They also go to bridges, halls, and temples to steal boards and timber to be used as fuel at his Excellency's place. If you doubt this, we beg you to go and inquire at Temple Chang. The slaves of the governor's head-wife have stolen from this temple, and even defiantly cursed the monks, and thrown stones against the monasteries. Her slaves have also stolen cattle, and placed them at her fields, Na Kok Sanook. The owners have traced their cattle to the said fields, but dare not take them, and sought to redeem them and failed. At these fields cattle are constantly butchered.

"Again, when the season arrives for flooding the rice-fields, the head-wife shuts off the canals so as to secure the water to her fields. Thus the farmers cannot secure water for their fields until hers are all worked. She is also accustomed to send out officers and draft farmers to till and harvest her fields. She has no mercy on the farmers. Her cattle are permitted to go over the rice-fields adjoining hers and graze upon the growing rice. On the owners complaining, she told them to drive the cattle away, and on their doing so, had them thrown into prison until they paid money to gain their liberty. Many persons have been thus arrested, oppressed, and hindered from work.

"We can no longer send our children to herd our cattle. Cattle have been forced from our children in as many as three or four different places in a day. They even come and steal our cattle from under our houses at night. These cattle-thieves are the governor's slaves and prisoners. Even a prisoner guilty of murder, plunder, and highway robbery has, for a consideration, been released by the governor, and is now plundering boats and houses along the markets. His name is Chat; he is now a slave of the head-wife.

"The cattle-thieves have been caught by the owners and handed over to the governor, their only punishment being four or five days' imprisonment. The chains were then taken off, the thieves were posted to deny the theft to the last, and the suit was decided according to his Excellency's interest. The informers have at such times been held at the governor's place, and been compelled to work night and day as though they were prisoners.

"At times we have been compelled to watch the prisoners, the prisoners having been previously advised to flee; this being done, the complainants have been thrown into prison instead of the prisoners. This being the case, who can dare to seize the governor's slaves on charge of theft? Whilst the owners were thus wrongfully in prison, the stolen cattle were sold. The owners have then gone to the buyers and proved their cattle, and begged to be allowed to redeem them, but the buyers refused. The owners have wept over their loss, not knowing what to do. Cattle-boats have taken away our cattle, one and two boat-loads a-day. How can we be happy? We beg to take you as our refuge. Give us peace, we pray; our hearts are filled with sorrow. It is of no use to cry to his Excellency!

"There is no one to catch the robbers and bring them to justice. Tow Poo Chow (the governor's son) sends out police at night. But these police are simply litigants, who work all day for his Excellency. The litigants bring the cases before Tow Poo Chow, but he is indifferent, and uses the litigants for his own purposes. The day police are instructed to arrest all persons carrying knives, and fine each offender two and a half dollars. If we carry our tool knives (for cutting bamboos, &c.) we are arrested. But the governor's people are allowed to carry knives, swords, and guns, and none dare arrest them.

"They go about oppressing the people. If we have meetings for merit-making, weddings, and hair-cuttings, they attend to curse us, and act like rowdies. These days are not like those of his Excellency the Kromatah [the Minister of Foreign Affairs, the former governor of the province]. It is beyond all endurance. We are but common people; we cannot write well, and beg you to put this in good form. We of the three languages [Siamese, Laos, and Peguans] have been greatly oppressed. We beg to take you as our refuge. We beg you to hear our words that we may have peace."

In sending me the translation of the petition, the missionary stated that "the petition was much longer than this, but with similar charges. It contains the request that it may be placed before his Majesty." And he says: "I sent the enclosed document to his Majesty. The king replied through his private secretary, expressing approval of my action, and determination to send a commission to root out the matter. The commissioners came, and were successful, finding things worse even than the petition stated. They also captured about seventy of the most notorious murderers and robbers. These are at present enjoying prison fare in Bangkok; but, strange to say, the governor is free, or at least virtually free. He is on trial, but at the same time in his place as governor. I fully believe his Majesty desires the peace and prosperity of his subjects; but much is concealed from H.M.'s eyes, and underlings are greedy for filthy lucre, and at the same time inefficient."

While conversing about the country, Mr Stevens told me that in making railways in the plains of Siam, the occasional extraordinary rise of the rivers, and the consequent inundation of the country, would necessitate high embankments. At Raheng, in November 1878, he had the opportunity of observing the highest flood that had happened during the lifetime of the inhabitants. In the plains of Siam, from November to May, scarcely a cloud obscures the sky, and no rain falls except in January, when the Siamese look for a shower, which is necessary for certain kinds of fruit which are then forming. From November to February the weather is delightful, being the cool season; but the thermometer is seldom lower than 64°. Even in March and April, the hottest months, the thermometer in Bangkok seldom rises above 98°. From November to May the north-east monsoon blows constantly; and from May to November is the wet season, when the south-west monsoon occurs, and showers fall almost every day. The rainfall in Bangkok during ten years' observations was found to vary between 39 and 73¼ inches, giving an average of less than 56 inches against 182 inches on the parallel coast of Burmah.

Rain being an unusual occurrence in Siam in November, Mr Stevens noted in his diary that on the 6th inst. it rained heavily throughout the day, many logs of timber were drifting down the river, and that the water, topping the banks, inundated the city. During the night the river rose three feet, and rain continuing throughout the next day, the inundation increased, and the elephants were removed to the high ground. On Friday the 7th, the heavy rain continued, and there was a great rush of water from the hills at the back of his house, carrying everything before it; fruit-trees and the slab palisade, besides 40 of his teak-logs, being washed away, and the floating grass drifted off the lake at the back of his house; and the house, although built on posts well rooted in the ground, was in great danger. In the evening he removed what he could into boats, and left for the night. Several of the villages in the neighbourhood were swept away, the houses floating down the river with the people in them. There had never been such a rise since Raheng was founded.

Some of the governor's buildings were destroyed; rafts of timber were drifting past from Lakon; and the inhabitants of Raheng and the neighbouring villages all took refuge in their boats. The river rose two feet above the floor of his house, or 8½ feet above the river-bank. Several rafts broke up below the city, and 140 houses were washed away.

The next morning was fine, and the people returned to their houses, as the water was falling rapidly. The flood rose seven feet in twenty hours, and on its fall left a creek three feet deep on each side of his house. There was a great loss of property. Rice was not to be had, and many of the people found themselves starving on the Monday. The flood continued right down to Bangkok, and rose 10½ feet on the fields a gunshot distance to the west of the river at Kamphang Pet, 4½ feet on the fields to the east, and the same height under the governor's house at that place.

In the 'Siam Repository' for July 1873, there is a description of the great inundation which occurred in 1831, which, like the flood described by Mr Stevens, was due to heavy rainfall in the north. The flood lay from three-quarters of a fathom to one and a half fathom on the rice-fields of the northern provinces, varying with the height of the land. Flowing southwards, it swamped the low lands in the neighbourhood of Ayuthia, the former capital of Siam, to the varying depths of one and three fathoms, and the rice-fields and orchards of Bangkok to from three-quarters to one and a quarter fathom.

Within Bangkok the surface of the ground was covered to the depths of half and three-quarters of a fathom; and noblemen, great and small, whose duties required them to visit the king, paddled their boats to the doors of the inner palace buildings. Between Bangkok and Ayuthia, as the flood rose above the floors, which are raised several feet from the ground, the people elevated a temporary floor, and made egress and ingress through the windows. Some were obliged to erect the floor upon the roof-beams of their houses, and to enter and leave by the gable-ends. The great plains looked like a sea; and one night during a storm the drifting masses of floating plants, gathering against some houses, swept them away, many of the sleeping occupants perishing.

Boats from Raheng to Bangkok take from 6 to 8 days in the rains, and from 12 to 15 days in the dry season. Returning from Bangkok, boats take 20 days in the rains, and from 30 to 35 days in the dry season. They are longer proceeding up-stream in the dry season than in the rains, owing to the shallowness of the stream, and the numerous sandbanks in its bed.

CHAPTER XXXIII.

GROWTH OF FOREIGN COMPETITION FOR TRADE—NEED FOR NEW MARKETS—INDIA AND CHINA AS MARKETS—NECESSITY FOR CHEAP COMMUNICATIONS—ACTION TAKEN BY MR COLQUHOUN AND MYSELF—PROBABLE EFFECTS OF THE INDO-SIAM-CHINA RAILWAY—INDO-BURMESE CONNECTION IN COURSE OF CONSTRUCTION—REASONS FOR CHOOSING MAULMAIN AS TERMINUS FOR CONNECTION WITH CHINA—SIAMESE SECTION NOW UNDER SURVEY—EFFECTS OF CONNECTING MAULMAIN WITH SIAMESE RAILWAY—COST OF CONNECTION—PROSPECTIVE ADVANTAGES—CARAVAN-ROUTES FROM MAULMAIN TO RAHENG—ESTIMATE FOR BRANCH TO OUR FRONTIER—APPROXIMATE ESTIMATE FOR CONTINUING THE BRANCH TO RAHENG—COMPARISON BETWEEN PROPOSED BRITISH AND RUSSIAN RAILWAYS—BRITISH INTERESTS IN SIAM—MR SATOW'S LETTER—SIR ARTHUR PHAYRE'S OPINION ON OUR DUTY TO PROTECT SIAM—CONNECTION OF BURMAH AND SIAM BY RAILWAY THE BEST FORM OF SUPPORT—CANNOT ALLOW SIAM TO BE ABSORBED BY FRANCE—EFFECT OF SUCH ABSORPTION UPON BURMAH—OPINIONS OF SIR CHARLES BERNARD—CANNOT AFFORD TO HAND OVER OUR MARKETS TO FRANCE—OPINION OF SIR HENRY YULE—PAYING PROSPECTS OF THE BRANCH TO THE FRONTIER—SIR RICHARD TEMPLE'S OPINION—THE MOST PROMISING OF ALL FUTURE RAILWAY LINES—EFFECT OF PROPOSED LINES—SIR CHARLES BERNARD'S PROJECT—COMPARISON BETWEEN MAULMAIN AND BHAMO ROUTES—TAKAW ROUTE—KUN LÔN FERRY ROUTES—THE MAULMAIN ROUTE OR NOTHING—IMPORTANCE OF THE QUESTION.

In these days of commercial rivalry, when foreign nations are competing with us in every neutral market in the world, when Europe and North America are being closed against our goods by prohibitive tariffs, and the Royal Commission appointed on the late depression of trade has placed on record its opinion that over-production has been one of the prominent features in the course of trade of recent years, and has urged us to display greater activity in searching for and developing new markets, we cannot afford to neglect any advantage we possess for the extension of our trade.

The seaboard and navigable rivers of the world give access to only limited areas for commerce. To open up new markets, we must penetrate the great and populous but landlocked interiors of the unopened continents of Asia and Africa, and our vast colonial possessions, with railways thus providing cheap means of communication in the extensive areas that are now shut off from our commerce by the prohibitive cost of carriage.

India and China, the largest and most densely populated markets yet undeveloped, contain together 700,000,000 inhabitants—one-half the population of the earth. These consist of civilised people, with their commerce uncramped at their ports by prohibitive tariffs, who would gladly become our customers if by cheapening the cost of carriage we could place our machine-made goods at their doors at a less price than they can acquire local hand-made manufactures.

Since 1881 my friend Mr Colquhoun and I have been striving our utmost to interest the public in the great and yet undeveloped markets of the East. We have tried to impress upon Government and the mercantile and manufacturing community, that Great Britain is in possession of certain advantages which render her the envy of competing nations. She is in possession of India and Burmah, and is thus the next-door neighbour to the landlocked half of the great and populous empire of China.

We have endeavoured to awaken, and have awakened, an intelligent interest in the subject of the importance of connecting India with China by a railway; and by exploration have proved to the satisfaction of every one who has studied the question, that a practical route between these two great empires exists, and that along that route a railway can be constructed at a reasonable cost, which would tend greatly to enhance the commerce of Great Britain and India with its Eastern neighbours—Siam and its Shan States, and the western half of China.

When this railway is constructed, its inland terminus at Ssumao will assuredly form the nucleus of a system of Chinese railways which will spread through the western, central, and southern provinces of China. One of these lines would be made to join our terminus at Ssumao with Pakhoi, the southern treaty-port in the China Sea, and thus complete a through line from the Persian Gulf to the China Sea by a railway extending solely through British, Siamese, and Chinese territories. This line would pass through and develop the richest part of Asia, foil the designs of the French, who are hoping and endeavouring to oust our trade from Southern China and Central Indo-China, and give us vast markets for the future expansion of British and British-Indian commerce.

Our project divides itself into two portions—the Indo-Burmese and Burmo-Chinese railways. The first involves the connection of the Indian and Burmese systems of railways by a line joining the railways in Northern Assam, *viâ* Mogoung, with the Rangoon and Mandalay line, together with an extension of that railway from Rangoon to Maulmain. The connection of Rangoon with Maulmain by railway has since been advocated by Sir Charles Crosthwaite, the present chief commissioner of Burmah, so far as proposing that its first section should be surveyed and put in hand by the Government of India.

The connection of the Indian and Burmese railways *viâ* the Patkoi pass met with unreasonable opposition; but actual exploration, carried out by the Government, has lately proved that, as we have averred all along, the route is the easiest, cheapest, and most feasible that exists for the connection of these two systems of railways. The section of the line from Sagain—a town opposite Mandalay—to Mogoung, is already sanctioned, and about to be commenced; and the other portion of the railway will doubtless be taken in hand as soon as the first section is completed.

The second portion of our project is the connection of Burmah with Siam and China by railway. Our study of previous explorations, followed by exploration-surveys conducted by myself in Siam and its Shan States, and by my colleague Mr Colquhoun through Southern China and by the Bhamo route into Northern Burmah, afforded positive proof that the path for a railway from Burmah to China should have its western terminus at Maulmain. By starting from that seaport, the following advantages would be gained:—

1. The difficult country lying between the Irawadi and Salween rivers in Upper Burmah would be entirely avoided, because Maulmain is situated near the mouth of the Salween, and on its eastern bank.

2. By proceeding eastwards from Maulmain, you cross the hill-ranges by the best route, as can be seen by comparing the Bhamo route, which trends eastwards over an alpine country from Bhamo at the navigation head of the Irawadi river, with the Takaw route, lying 230 miles to the south of the Bhamo route, and with the Maulmain route, which lies 350 miles farther to the south. It is evident that the farther you go to the north, the more difficult do the routes leading from Burmah to China become.

3. The line from Maulmain, owing to the easy country through which it passes, could be constructed at a fraction of the cost of any line projected from Upper Burmah, and would have the advantage of easier gradients throughout, and would be the shortest possible route for connecting Burmah with the capital of the Chinese province of Yunnan.

4. The line from Maulmain, from its shortness, would possess great advantages in competing with the lines projected by the French from their Tonquin seaboard, and would thus enable us to carry our goods from Maulmain to Ssumao, the frontier-post of South-western China, for £3 a ton, or about one-twentieth of the average tariff now charged upon our goods by the French customs in Tonquin.

5. The line from Maulmain would likewise connect with the projected system of Siamese railways, and thus tend greatly to the advantage of Burmah, and to the development of British trade throughout Central Indo-China.

6. The Siamese system of railways projected by us, and now being surveyed and estimated for the King of Siam by English engineers, if joined on with Maulmain by our projected branch to the frontier, would connect our seaport of

Maulmain with Bangkok, the capital and chief seaport of Siam, thus affording us more rapid mail communication with China and Australasia, and would complete more than two-thirds of our projected railway to China. The remaining 230 miles could be cheaply constructed, and would open up the British States lying to the east of the Salween throughout their length, and thus give us an easy control of the country.

The branch line which we propose for the connection of our seaport of Maulmain with the Siamese system of railways at Raheng, as I shall proceed to explain, would probably cost less than one and a half million sterling,[1] the cost of fifteen average miles of English railway. Half of this line lies in Siamese territory, and the other half in the Indian province of Burmah; and approximately half of the cost would have to be defrayed by the King of Siam, leaving only three-quarters of a million sterling as the charge to the Indian Government.

This branch alone would open out to our seaport of Maulmain the nine million inhabitants of Siam and its Shan States, and would, together with the Siamese line to Kiang Hsen, greatly decrease the cost of carriage to our British Shan States lying to the east of the Salween, which are believed to contain about one and a half million inhabitants. It would likewise greatly decrease the cost of carriage to the Chinese province of Yunnan, and thus, by lowering the prices, tend greatly to increase the number of our customers. The journey from Maulmain to our frontier at Myawadi, on the Thoungyeen river, is performed by porters in four days, and by cattle caravans in about eight days.

In referring to the route from Myawadi to Raheng, the 'British Burmah Gazetteer' states that "the route between them, being much frequented, is clear and open, and the journey can thus be performed in two days."

The hills between the Thoungyeen and Raheng were sur-

[1] The length of the branch line is estimated at 160 miles, the cost at one and a half million sterling, which is equivalent to Rs. 136,363 a mile, taking exchange at 1s. 4½d. The 108 miles opened in Upper Burmah up to December 31, 1888, cost, according to the last "Administration Report on the Railways in India," only Rs. 50,349 per mile.

veyed for the King of Siam some years before my visit; and the copy of the survey, which was lent me by the governor of Raheng, showed no less than eleven distinct caravan-routes crossing the hills: the passes crossed are said to be low, the greatest height attained by Mr Ross on his journey from Maulmain *viâ* Myawadi to Raheng did not exceed 2400 feet above sea-level; and I was informed by some of our leading foresters who worked the forests in these hills, that the routes traversing them were quite as easy as those crossing the range which separates Maulmain from our frontier at Myawadi.

Myawadi lies 60 miles east of Maulmain, 40 miles west of Raheng, and 630 feet above the level of the sea. It is separated from Maulmain by a range of hills over which the caravans clamber by a pass having its summit 1600 feet above sea-level, or 800 feet lower than the pass between Myawadi and Raheng. The ascent, however, from Myawadi to the crest of the Raheng pass is reduced by 630 feet—the height that Myawadi lies above the sea; and the descent to Raheng by 400 feet—its height above the sea-level.

Sir Charles Bernard, when chief commissioner of Burmah, estimated the cost of connecting Maulmain with our frontier station of Myawadi by railway at 105 lakhs of rupees, which, at the present rate of exchange, 1s. 4¼d., is equivalent to £710,938, or less than three-quarters of a million sterling; and he informed me that he had received a letter from Mr Satow, our consul-general in Siam, giving his opinion that "Siam would be ready to carry out its part of the Burmah-Siam railway if the Government of India expressed its willingness to connect the two countries by railway at the frontier."

As Myawadi is one-third less distant from Raheng than from Maulmain, and the country to be crossed is barely more difficult than to Maulmain, it is not likely that the cost of the section from Myawadi to Raheng would exceed that of the portion from Maulmain to Myawadi: therefore the expense of joining the terminus of our section at Myawadi with the Siamese main line at Raheng would not exceed three-quarters of a million sterling; and the whole of the branch, from the main line to Maulmain, would not cost more than one and a half million sterling.

Unlike the projected and partially completed Russian line across Asia, which passes through the great deserts and wastes neighbouring the north of the Chinese dominions, our line would traverse the richest part of Asia. It would, as already stated, foil the designs of the French, who are striving to oust our trade from Southern China and Central Indo-China, and would give us vast markets for the future expansion of British and British-Indian commerce.[1]

The British stake in Siam already exceeds that of any other nation. According to Mr Satow, our fellow-subjects trading and working in that country comprise about ten thousand souls; and in his letter to Earl Granville, dated Bangkok, May 7, 1885, he stated that "nine-elevenths of the total export trade [of Siam], valued at nearly £1,650,000, is with Hong Kong and Singapore, and must contribute greatly to the prosperity of those two colonies. Of the imports, about £340,000 represents English manufactures; £200,000 products of British India; while Hong Kong sends goods, partly of British, partly of Chinese origin, to about the same value. From the Straits Settlements produce is imported to the value of £22,000, making in all £762,000, or over three-quarters of a million sterling.

"The imports from the continent of Europe are valued at £164,000, and from the United States £50,000. If we suppose the imports from Hong Kong to be equally divided between goods of British and Chinese origin, the result will be, articles produced in Great Britain and British possessions to the value of £640,000, against £314,000 from the continent of Europe, the United States, and China combined.

"The commercial interests of Great Britain in Siam, as compared with the rest of the world, are consequently—In

[1] Two hundred and seventy-five British steamers and 16 British sailing-vessels visited Bangkok in 1888, and only 17 French steamers and no French sailing-vessels. The gross sea-borne trade of Bangkok in the same year was valued at over four millions sterling, the imports at £1,657,708, and the exports at £2,598,901. The import of cotton manufactures was valued at £302,746, and cotton yarns at £40,936.

fixed capital, as 2 to 1; in steamers, as 8 to 1; in exports, as 9 to 2; in imports, as 2 to 1.

"It is further to be noted that the import duties are only 3 per cent *ad valorem*. If Siam proper were to pass into the hands of any European Power with protectionist tendencies, it cannot be doubted that the tariff would be greatly increased; and it is by no means improbable, if we are to judge by what has been proposed with regard to the trade of Tonquin, that differential duties would be imposed to the disadvantage of British trade."

After reading this report, it is not surprising to find the late Sir Arthur Phayre, who had been for many years chief commissioner of Burmah, writing to the 'Times,' in his letter dated October 12, 1885, that "I beg to add that British interests appear also to require that the King of Siam, so long the friend and ally of the United Kingdom, should be assured of support in the conservation of his independence and of the integrity of his dominions." No better assurance of support could have been given by us to the King of Siam than the promise of co-operation in the junction of the two countries, Burmah and Siam, by railway. Our trade with Siam would in that case vastly and rapidly expand, our fixed capital in the country would increase, and our railway route to China, which would pass through Northern Siam and its Shan States, would never be allowed to pass into French hands, and the French, knowing this, would cease all thought of further encroaching on the king's territories.

The strengthening of the French hands in Indo-China by the absorption of Siam would render France a more formidable antagonist, for it would keep a larger army in Indo-China and have a larger recruiting-field for its native auxiliaries. The absorption of Siam by France would place the French frontier within sixty miles of Maulmain; would render the country to the south of Burmah, between it and our Straits Settlements, French territory; would destroy our trade in Siam and its Shan States; stop the recruitment of cattle[1] and elephants from those countries, which are the

[1] In 1888, 27,118 bullocks were exported from Bangkok, and according to the last Consular Report, "the export of cattle overland to Burmah is said to

breeding-grounds for Burmah; would ruin our pedlars, foresters, timber-traders, and other fellow-subjects in Siam; and would block for ever our connection with China by railway.

There seemed to be every reason for making arrangements with Siam for connecting it with Burmah, and continuing the proposed railway to China; and if Sir Arthur Phayre had been still chief commissioner of Burmah, doubtless the advisability of pushing on the railway would have been strongly urged upon the Government. Unfortunately for the extension of our trade in the East, the reins of the province were in the grasp of an official of a different school. In a letter which I have leave to quote, Sir Charles Bernard gave me his reasons, in a very straightforward manner, for opposing the connection of Burmah with Siam by railway. He said: "I demur to the correctness of any statement that I 'had set my face against our being linked on to Siam.' I have distinctly and repeatedly said that I would gladly see a railway from Maulmain *viâ* Raheng to Bangkok and the Yunnan border. And I have repeatedly said that such a railway would do great good to that part of British Burmah, and especially to the port of Maulmain. But I have at the same time said that in my judgment that railway would be too dearly purchased if it involved a guarantee from India to Siam against French aggression. And I have also said that in my belief the railway from Maulmain to Raheng would not pay for many years; also, that there are other railways in Burmah and in India on which money from the Indian Treasury would be more usefully spent than on the Maulmain-Raheng line. If you or any one else can get British Burmah linked by railway to Siam, I shall regard you as benefactors to British Burmah. But, as you are aware, benefits can be bought at too high a price."

We have seen in Mr Satow's letter to Earl Granville that

be about double that from Bangkok." One hundred thousand head of cattle—buffaloes and bullocks—have died in a single year of cattle-disease in Burmah, and a large portion of the area of our province would have been thrown out of cultivation if it had not been for the supplies we were able to draw from Siam.

the interests of Great Britain in Siam are greater than those of any other nation—and, indeed, than those of the rest of the world combined. We have been warned by him that if Siam is allowed to pass into the hands of any European Power with protectionist tendencies, it would be the death-blow to our commerce in the country. We have seen that the late Sir Arthur Phayre considered British interests in Siam already sufficient to require us to assure the King of Siam of support in his independence, and of the integrity of his dominions.

The connection of Siam with Burmah by railway would certainly increase our stake in Siam by developing British and Indo-Siamese trade; but I fail to see how it would increase the responsibilities of the Government of India. Our trade is not in such a position as to allow us to hand over markets to the French. The Siamese dominions are at present nearly exclusively British markets, and it cannot be expected that the British nation will calmly stand by and see its goods turned out of those markets by our French rivals.

I was glad to find during the discussion of the paper in which I gave an account of my explorations before the Royal Geographical Society, that the India Council, as represented by Colonel (now Sir Henry) Yule, the most eminent authority on Indo-China, did not consider the French bugbear a sufficient reason for blocking the Burmah-Siam-China Railway, and with it, the extension of our commerce in South-eastern Asia. He said: "As to the projects themselves, described in the paper, I cannot now say much, for what I have to say will probably have to be said elsewhere [in the India Council]. I feel the difficulties that beset them—not engineering difficulties, but of quite another kind. Still, I cannot but hope that events which are even now [November 1885] upon the wing [the annexation of Upper Burmah and its Shan States] may help to clear the way for the execution of the projects which Mr Colquhoun had at heart, and on which he and Mr Hallett have expended an amount of thought and energy which I cannot believe will be in vain."

As to the statement by Sir Charles Bernard, that in his

"belief the railway from Maulmain to Raheng would not pay for many years," that is merely a matter of opinion, and estimates based upon opinions as to the prospective trade that would accrue to projected railways in Burmah have always proved below the mark. The paying prospect of railways in Burmah was officially allowed by the Government of India, in its despatch to the Secretary of State in January 1881, where it stated that—"The great financial success of the Rangoon-Prome Railway (a success almost unprecedented in railway construction in India) has demonstrated that railways in Burmah will, on account of the enterprising character of the people, and the great undeveloped wealth of the country, not only give large indirect returns in land, customs, and forest revenue, but will pay, within a very short period after being opened to traffic, a fair percentage of net income on their capital cost."

The line to our frontier, besides opening out and developing the country through which it passed, would have the advantage of conveying the traffic to and from the Siamese lines with which it would be connected; and when the line is extended to China, a vast increase of traffic would be ensured. There is not the slightest reason to doubt that when the Siamese railways are constructed, this branch line to our seaport would be the most profitable line in our Indian dominions. It would not be undertaken until the connection between Raheng and Bangkok is completed; and if opened up at the same time as the Siamese section of the branch, it is certain that it would in the first year far more than recoup the Government for the interest upon the outlay for its construction.

Sir Richard Temple, who has administered some of the largest provinces in India, in writing of our proposed line to China, gave his opinion that—"By all the accounts of exploration, also on a consideration of the commercial and political geography, this is *the most promising of all the future railway lines that can be devised.*" And in comparing our north-western frontier of India with our north-eastern or Burmese frontier, Sir Richard says: "The ways across the north-western frontier, from the British side, lead to nothing profitable for British interests. On the other hand, the ways across the north-eastern frontier lead to regions full of prospective advantage for British commerce and for British expansion in every way. . . . On our north-western frontier the railways are mainly for strategic or political objects, and only in part for commercial objects. But on this our north-eastern or Indo-Chinese frontier, the railways will be mainly for commerce, for the opening of new markets, for the spread of cultivation and habitation, for material development in every way." Our system of railways would act like arteries, developing the resources, mineral and agricultural, of all the regions they traversed, and would enable us to throw British goods right into the interior, and bring back in return the produce of Siam and China for shipment at Maulmain.

Let us compare this project with that which is favoured by Sir Charles Bernard. In his address to the Scottish Geographical Society in November 1887, some months before Sir Andrew Clarke had arranged with the King of Siam for the surveying of the Siamese system of railways, he said: "A railway is now being made, and will be open within eighteen months, to Mandalay. That line will doubtless be continued to Bhamo, 700 miles from the sea, and 35 miles from the border of China. The ancient route of traffic between Burmah and China was by Bhamo and the Irawadi valley. We ought to make the most of that route, and exhaust its possibilities, before we committed ourselves to creating another and a wholly new route. No doubt the lofty passes on the old path between Bhamo and Yunnan-fu are most serious obstacles to a railway on that route. But it might be possible to find much easier gradients if the Shweli valley and other valleys leading towards Sunning-fu, instead of to Tali-fu, were examined. A thorough examination of the country would take one or two seasons."

We have seen that the branch line for connecting Maulmain and Raheng will probably cost about 1½ million sterling. Mr Archer, our vice-consul at Zimmé, reported in 1887 upon the portion of our proposed railway from Raheng to China that lies in Siam and its Shan States, as follows :—

"*Best Route for Railway through Northern Siam.*—If the railroad were made to pass through Zimmé, the great mass of mountains between the city and Kiang Hai would probably prove a serious difficulty. But if it were to follow the valleys of the Meh Nam and Meh Wang as far as Lakon (our route), there would appear to be no great natural difficulties to overcome, and thence north-eastward to Muang Ngow the road would lie over easy undulating country. From Muang Ngow to Penyow the watershed of the Meh Nam and Meh Kong must be crossed; but it is of no great elevation (merely undulating ground), and I believe would not present any serious difficulties. Once this range is passed, the whole way to Kiang Hsen, and some distance farther northward, is on almost quite level ground, apparently highly suitable for a railway. This route I think preferable, not only because it offers greater natural facilities, but because a large portion of the country traversed is capable of great development, and it is evident that the advantages of a railway to these States are based, not on the actual wealth, but on the consequent development, of the country."

To learn the character of the country along our route between Kiang Hsen and Kiang Hung, we can turn to Garnier's account of the part of his journey skirting the river from Kiang Hsen to Sop Yong, a place half-way between Kiang Hsen and Kiang Hung. There were no serious physical difficulties noted by him on this part of his journey, and his party turned inland at Sop Yong simply because it was the rainy season, and the plains neighbouring the river were swampy. The only other European observer who has traversed any portion of our route between Kiang Hsen and Kiang Hung is Mr Archer, who, in his journey back from Kiang Tung in 1887, struck it at Muang Len (Lim, a place 35 miles to the north of Kiang Hsen). In the account of his journey he reports that "Muang Len has a more prosperous appearance than any Chiengtung (Kiang Tung) district I had yet seen. The valley is broad, and there are numerous villages with extensive rice-fields. These settlements are comparatively new, for, after the destruction of Chiengsen (Kiang Hsen) in 1803, Chiengmai (Zimmé) advanced up the valley of the Meh Kong and took off captives all the inhabitants they could find. The junction of the Meh Len with the Meh Kong is about a day's journey from the village where we encamped. From Muang Len to Huapong, also a prosperous-looking district, is a day's journey on a good road, mostly through bamboo forest; and the next day, May 31st, we passed through Hong Luk, crossed the Meh Sai, and reached Ban Tham in Chiengsen, about 10 miles below the Siamese fort. Hong Luk is a populous and well-cultivated district. In passing through Wieng Phan, just south of the Meh Sai, and close to the Siamese fort, I saw a settlement just being made in the jungle by Chiengtung people, who were busy putting up their houses."

From all information gained by explorers, it is evident that from Raheng northwards to Kiang Hung, a distance of 470 miles, the line for our proposed railway is exceptionally free from physical difficulties. Kiang Hung lies 2000 feet above sea-level. Near this important town the Meh Kong or Cambodia river will have to be crossed; and after crossing the river, an ascent of 2520 feet will have to be made by the railway along the slope of the Yunnan plateau to Ssumao, the frontier-post of China. The total length of this line from Maulmain to Ssumao is estimated at 700 miles.

Mr Colborne Baber's survey and levels along the Bhamo route, which proceeds from Bhamo—a town 700 miles from a seaport, situated at the head of the steamer navigation on the Irawadi—through Tali-fu to Yunnan-fu, the capital of the Chinese province of Yunnan, showed that the country traversed by the route was of an alpine character, and exceedingly difficult. The passes over the series of mountains between Bhamo and Tali-fu have their summit at a greater altitude than that of any of the passes over the Alps, with the exception of the Stelvio, which lies 800 feet above the level of perpetual snow. The Bernina, the next highest to the Stelvio, only rises 7658 feet above sea-level, whereas the pass between Bhamo and the Salween river lies at an altitude of 8730 feet; that between the Salween and the Meh Kong at 8166 feet; that between the Meh Kong and Chutung at 8510 feet; that between Chutung and the Shan-Pi river at 8410 feet; and that between the Shan-Pi and Tali-fu at 8090 feet.

To connect Bhamo with Yunnan-fu, the chief town of the Chinese province of Yunnan, would require a railway at least 967 miles in length. The stupendous cost of such a line can be judged from the report of Mr Colborne Baber, who surveyed and levelled the portion of the route lying between Momein and Yunnan-fu. He says—"The trade-route from Yunnan-fu to Teng-yuch (or Momein, the frontier-post of China with the Chinese Shan States) is the worst possible route with the least conceivable trade." Again he says—"I do not mean that it is absolutely impossible to construct a railway. By piercing half-a-dozen Mont Cenis tunnels and erecting a few Menai bridges, the road from Burmah to Yunnan-fu could doubtless be much improved."

The advocates of the Bhamo route assume that because the crow-line distance from Bhamo to Yunnan-fu is only 375 miles in length, these two places can be easily and cheaply connected by railway.[1] They seem not to have studied, or if they have studied, are unable to comprehend Mr Baber's report, maps, and sections, which were made by him when accompanying the Grosvenor Mission from Yunnan. These have been issued both by the Royal Geographical Society and as a Parliamentary Blue-book (China, No. 3, 1878), and are therefore easily accessible.

In the Blue-book the maps are drawn to a large scale, 3 miles to the inch, and the levels of the route above sea-level are written upon it, and given separately in a table on pp. 30 and 31 of the report. The country passed over by the caravan-route is clearly delineated on these maps. The track is seen traversing high passes, between great hills, towering up thousands of feet above the crest of the passes,

[1] A superstitious belief that the ancient trade-routes must necessarily be the best has always influenced Indian officialism. It overlooks the important fact that routes which were well adapted for caravan traffic may be quite unsuitable for railway communication; and also that the character and localities of commerce have changed since the ancient routes were opened up.

and crossing deep ravines and steep valleys, not in a level crow-line (that would necessitate viaducts many thousand feet high, at an expense in comparison with which the cost of the Panama Canal would be as nothing), but zigzagging up and down the valleys and ravines, and following the general contortions of the passes. Thus the crow-line of 375 miles is developed into 489½ miles for caravan traffic, so as to enable mules and human beings to clamber over the mountain-passes between the two places. To any competent engineer who studied the maps, it would be evident that the length of a railway with a ruling gradient of 100 feet to a mile, carried from Bhamo to Yunnan-fu, would be at least 967 miles.

Some of the ravines are so steep, that if the crow-line were adhered to, mules, or even goats, could not crawl up them. Let us take, for instance, the descent from the crest of the pass lying to the west of the Salween to the bridge over that river. The dead drop in a crow-line of one mile is 6300 feet, and a zigzag seven miles in length has had to be made up the face of the ravine to enable mules to ascend and descend it. Railway trains are neither flies, nor crows, nor mules, and therefore can neither crawl up precipices, follow a crow-line through the air, nor proceed up a mule-track. To ascend this ravine, this crow-line distance of one mile, the railway track, if straight, would have to be at least 63 miles long, in order to allow a locomotive to haul up a load equal to six times its own weight in addition to itself. The 100-feet-to-the-mile gradient up on the straight portions would have to be flattened at every curve of the zigzags: this means additional length, which, together with the necessary level-lengths which are required to give runaway trains a chance of being again brought under control, would add three or four miles on to the 63 miles mentioned above. It will be rather within than without the mark to allow 66 miles for the alignement of a railway over this single crow-mile of country.

The difficulties, so well described by Mr Baber, lie in Chinese territory, and it is not reasonable to expect that the Chinese would ever consent to undertake such a costly railway through such a poor and sparsely populated hilly region as is traversed by the Bhamo route.

The only other route from Upper Burmah to Yunnan that has been followed by Europeans is that from Hlinedet (Hlaingdet), a station about 80 miles to the south of Mandalay, *viâ* Kiang Tung and Kiang Hung, to Ssumao. In 1872 Dr Cushing ascended the Hlinedet pass to Poayhla, 4160 feet above the sea, and proceeded to Moné or Mong Nai, crossing four hill-ranges. From Moné he passed over three ranges of hills, and descended to the Takaw ferry, where he crossed the Salween. Between the Salween and Kiang Tung three or four ranges of hills, as well as four or five spurs, making eight ascents and descents, occur on the route, one of the passes rising to 6400 feet above the level of the sea, and another to 5500 feet. The country between Kiang Tung and Kiang Hung is equally difficult, the route crossing five mountains before reaching the Meh Kong river at Kiang Hung.

The Salween river might be reached from Poayhla by another route, swaying slightly to the north, if it is found possible to carry a railway across the Nattit pass, 4800 feet above sea-level. This pass, however, is so difficult, that it is feared it will prove an insurmountable obstacle. Anyhow, a railway from Hlinedet to the Salween will prove a most expensive undertaking; and the country to the east of the ferry, between it and the Meh Kong, although much easier than on the Bhamo route, is so difficult that it is in the uttermost degree unlikely that it will ever be traversed from west to east by a railway.

Two other routes—the ones that are at present apparently favoured by the Government for the connection of Burmah and China—converge on the Salween at the Kun Lôn ferry. One starts from Mandalay and proceeds eastward through Theebaw and Thoungze to the ferry; and the other, after ascending the Shan plateau by the pass leading from Hlinedet to Poayhla, takes a north-easterly direction to the ferry. Some of the difficulties on the first route are evidenced by the report of the Government surveyors on the portion of the route lying between Mandalay and Thoungze. From this it appears that the cart-road to Maymyo (Pyinulwin), a place 24 miles to the east of Mandalay, has had to be contoured to 44 miles, and ascends in this distance 3300 feet. The descent to Thoungze from Maymyo is given by our surveyors at 1600 feet, and the greater part of the ascent from the plain of the Irawadi is said to be very steep. Thoungze lies on the route to Theinni, and is only 40 miles in an air-line from Mandalay, or about one-fourth of the air-line distance from Mandalay to the Kun Lôn ferry, where the route would cross the Salween. The difficulties of the route, according to people who have traversed it, are said to be still greater beyond Thoungze. The great gash in the country, between 1100 and 1200 feet deep, called the Goteik defile, has to be descended by steps cut in the face of the rock for 800 feet to a natural bridge across the ravine, and, having crossed it, the precipice on the other bank has to be ascended in the same manner. The banks of the ravine are 3600 feet above the level of the sea. Between Thoungze and Theebaw, besides this ravine one descent of 800 feet and another of 1600 feet have to be made, as well as ascents of 1500 feet, 800 feet, and 900 feet. Even on reaching Theebaw you are only half-way to the Salween, and have not crossed the high range which divides the drainage of the Irawadi from that of the Salween.

I have no information as to the level of the country beyond Theebaw, but I find in the accounts of a journey from Theinni to the Kun Lôn ferry, that 20 miles out of the 52 miles is very difficult. Looking at these particulars, it will be seen that the ascent from Mandalay to the summit of the plateau at Maymyo is nearly double as great as the ascent from our frontier to the crest of the pass on the Maulmain-Raheng route, and the descent to Thoungze is nearly equal to that to Raheng. It is therefore evident that the difficulties to be encountered within 40 miles of Mandalay by a railway from Mandalay to the Salween must be considerably greater than those which would be met by the Burmah-Siam-

China Railway between our frontier and Raheng, and probably greater than those on the whole of the line from our frontier to Kiang Hung.

The second route starts from Hlinedet, and clambers the steep western flank of the Shan plateau to Poayhla, from which place the Kun Lôn ferry across the Salween can be reached by caravans by various routes, all of which are difficult. The northerly route over the Nattit hill is believed to be impracticable for a railway. Another, proceeding eastwards, crosses four ranges of hills before it reaches Mong Nai. It thence proceeds northwards to the ferry, crossing a very difficult range of hills before reaching the Salween. The portion of this route between Hlinedet and Poayhla, and between Poayhla and Mong Nai, presents serious obstructions to the construction of a railway. To avoid one of the hills between Poayhla and Mong Nai, and to cross the others by easier passes, Mr Scott, the assistant superintendent of the Shan States, proposes that the railway, after leaving Poayhla, shall take a great sweep southwards to Mong Hpai, and from Mong Hpai proceed in a north-easterly direction to Mong Nai. This will involve a railway distance between Rangoon and Mong Nai of about 525 miles, and, according to him, Mong Nai is distant 200 miles from the Kun Lôn ferry across the Salween. The distance from Rangoon to the Kun Lôn ferry would therefore be at least 725 miles, or a greater distance than Maulmain is from the Chinese frontier at Ssumao. The most serious obstacle between Mong Hpai and Mong Nai, according to Mr Scott, is "the deep gash in the hills made by the rapid waters of the Nam Pwon," and it is not yet known whether that "deep gash" can be avoided. Anyhow, the avoidance of the gash might add considerably to the length of the railway.

I have previously shown how difficult the country east of the Salween, along the Bhamo and Takaw routes, is—one line lying to the north of the Kun Lôn ferry route, and the other south. There is every reason to believe that the difficulties to be encountered on the Kun Lôn ferry route, although perhaps less than on the Bhamo route, will be greater than on the Takaw route.

The Bhamo and Kun Lôn ferry routes, which seemingly are the only ones finding any favour with Government, deal only with the country west of the Salween, are purely local routes, and can never be anything else, as their termini would still be on the western or Burmah side of the enormous physical barriers crossed by the caravan-routes from Upper Burmah to Yunnan. To talk of either Bhamo or the Kun Lôn ferry as on the Chinese frontier for the purposes of trade, is altogether misleading, as both these places are separated from the fertile and populous regions of Southern China by alpine country, over which the Chinese would never consent to carry a railway.

The more the subject is examined, the more evident does it become that the only possible railway connection between Burmah and China must be by the Maulmain route projected by us. It is a case of that or nothing.

The enterprise which we propose is big with promise, not only for the present but for future generations. Our policy, political as well as commercial, should be to develop by every means in our power our intercourse and intercommunication between India and China—between British manufacturers and millions of Chinese, Siamese, and Shan customers. A prudent and yet resolute readiness to undertake reasonable responsibilities, inseparable from the duties of a great commercial nation, should be the key-note of our national policy, and should be the badge of no particular party. It is for the commercial community and working classes to see that such a policy is undertaken and adhered to.

We are a nation of shopkeepers, and it is by trade that we live. Every nerve should be strained by the manufacturer and working man to gain for British commerce the great market existing in Western China. The French are already in the field to snatch it from us; surveyors and engineers are at work surveying and estimating for the railways from the Tonquin seaboard. The race in this case is to the swift, and it still remains to be seen whether

French or British enterprise will win the much-coveted prize.

It will be strange indeed if, with the advantage we now possess by the annexation of Upper Burmah and its Shan States, the press, the mercantile community, the manufacturers, and working classes of this kingdom, cannot induce the Government to make or guarantee the sections of our railway to China which lie in British territory, and thus throw open for British commerce the most magnificent, unopened, and available market in the world.

CHAPTER XXXIV.

LEAVE RAHENG—ISLANDS—ZIMMÉ SHANS IN RAHENG—SIAMESE WOMEN —MISLEADING STRANGERS—"SOW" AND "RAT" POLITE TERMS—REACH KAMPHANG PET—SALUTED WITH STONES—FOUND DEAD—BURMESE—VISIT THE GOVERNOR—THE FLOOD—POPULATION—A FEMALE INTERPRETER—LEAVE KAMPHANG PET—CULTIVATION—REACH PAK NAM PO—TOUNGTHOO PEDLARS—NAVIGATION ON THE MEH NAM—LOOP-LINE TO OOTARADIT—GAMBLING-HOUSE—A FRENCHIFIED MONK—SKETCHING A BEARDED SIAMESE—SIZE OF THE DELTA—JOURNEY TO BANGKOK—A LONG STREET OF VILLAGES—REACH BANGKOK.

WE left Raheng early in the morning of June 13th, and after forcing our way through the double file of boats which lined the banks, passed the fine plastered brick building, somewhat resembling Salween House at Maulmain, where the governor resides, and halted to sketch the south-eastern hills near Ban Ta Kare. A mile and a half farther I got a capital view of the hillocks lying to the east of the city. Seven miles from Raheng the villages forming its suburbs came to an end, and in the next sixteen miles we saw only two small villages or hamlets.

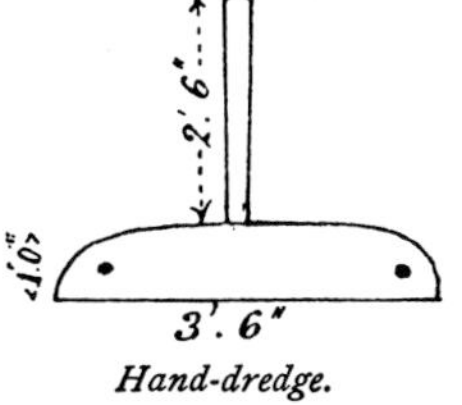

Hand-dredge.

The quicksand in the bed of the river during this stage of the journey, and as far south as the junction of the Meh Ping with the Meh Nam, was a constant cause of delay, as boat after boat had to dredge its way across drifting sand-banks, which closed up as they passed. The hand-dredge used consisted of a blade formed of a teak plank three and a half feet long and one foot deep, with a handle rising two and a half feet above it. One man pressed down the handle, and three or four others drew the blade along by two pieces of cord fastened through holes near its end. The remainder

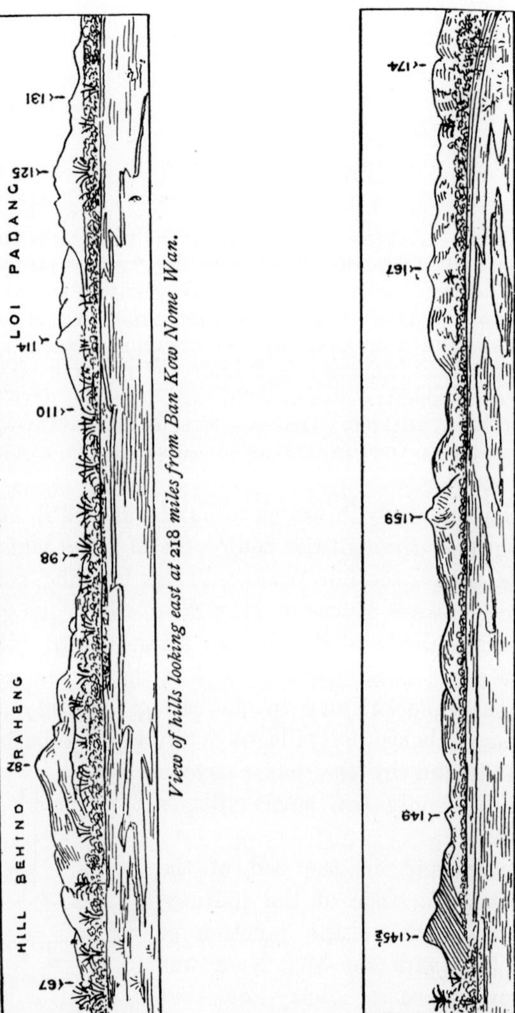

View of hills looking east at 218 miles from Ban Kow Nome Wan.

Sketch at 216½ miles from Ban Ta Kare.

of the men of the three boats aided the action of the dredge by loosening the sand with large teak-wood roofing shingles.

Owing to the swift current and drifting sandbanks, the

passage up-stream is very tedious, and boats from Bangkok to Raheng take between thirty and thirty-five days in the dry season. The river varies between 700 and 1000 feet in breadth; but at one place opposite a small hillock below the revenue station of Dan Wung Chow, which is situated at the border of Raheng with Kamphang, it is contracted for some distance to 400 feet. Near here we halted for the night, having made 17 miles in the day.

The province of Raheng is mainly occupied by descendants of Zimmé Shans, owing to its having formerly been part of the kingdom of Zimmé. Even in the city, more than half the people are Zimmé Shans and Peguans. As we proceeded southwards from Raheng, the daintily dressed Zimmé women, with their neat coiffure and pleasant faces, rapidly gave place to slovenly brazen-faced Siamese females, often made more repulsive by their recently shaven heads being covered with short bristles. All of these women whom we addressed on our way to Bangkok, asking the names of villages or for other information, answered us cheekily, and never by any chance digressed into the paths of truth. The men were but little better; and we had frequently to inquire the name of a village from half-a-dozen separate people before I considered it safe to enter it in my field-book. My steersman seemed to enjoy the game, and constantly hailed the women and small girls passing by in their little dug-out canoes, the women as *sow-ey* and the girls as *rat-ey*—*sow* being the polite Siamese term for a woman, and *rat* for a girl.

The following morning we continued for five miles through islands. Below the last island the villages became more numerous, fringing both banks for three miles out of the six to Kamphang Pet. Carts were seen in these villages, the first we had encountered since we left Burmah: they were remarkable for the size of their spoked wheels, which were fully six feet in diameter. Just before reaching Kamphang Pet we halted for a few minutes at Muang Ko, an extensive village on the opposite bank of the river, built on the site of an ancient city. The village possesses a fine temple and large pagoda. To the north of the village a stream called Krong Suen Ma enters the river, down which much teak is floated from the western hills.

Shortly after anchoring for the night at Kamphang Pet, whilst the boys were preparing dinner in the gloaming, a shower of stones was flung at the boat by some lads from the bank. All my men were quickly after them, but failed to catch the urchins, who retreated but to return and salute the boat in the same manner several times during the evening. As Veyloo happened to be hurt by one of the missiles, and a fresh supply of ducks and fowls was required, I determined to look up the governor before starting the next morning. Ten of my fowls had died since we left Zimmé, being found by the boys dead in the morning, and being considered unfit for my consumption, had been eaten by the boatmen. Fowls are apt to die a natural death, but rarely in such swift succession. I had been rendered suspicious by seeing the eagerness with which the boatmen besought Veyloo to give them a duck which had been found dead that morning, instead of chucking it overboard, as he threatened to do. I therefore told him to carefully skin it and see whether its neck had been dislocated, and this was found to be the case. I had that duck for breakfast, and need scarcely say no more fowls and ducks were *found* dead during the journey.

Near the governor's house I met Moung Byay, one of our Burmese subjects, and his wife, and had a chat with them. After some talk, he said he would be glad if I would come and put up with him for a day or two at his house at Wung Pa Tat, when he could give me a good deal of information about the country. I thanked him, and replied that I was sorry I could not afford the time, and said I would be much obliged if he would come and interpret for me at the governor's. He told me that the great flood of 1878 had risen ten and a half feet on his fields, which lay about a gunshot to the west of the river. The country to the east was higher, and the flood there was less than five feet in depth.

On reaching the governor's, I found him in the company of half-a-dozen of his head-men. He received me courteously, and appeared anxious to do what he could for me.

I told him of the reception my servants had met with, and made Veyloo show him the scar on his shoulder. I said it was the first incivility I had met in the country, and that such rowdyism did not speak well for the government of his province. He was evidently annoyed at the incident, and at once sent two of his officers to inquire into the circumstances, and see whether the lads could be traced. I then asked him about the flood, and he showed me the mark he had made on his own house in order to register the height. It was four and a half feet above the ground, and eighteen and a half feet above the water in the river, which was at the time of my visit fourteen feet below the bank.

I said I should be much obliged if he would order some fowls and ducks to be supplied to me at the market rate, as my supply was running short, and I wished to continue my journey in the afternoon. He at once put down four rupees on the mat before him, and each of the head-men put down one, and a couple of officers were despatched to purchase the birds and carry them to my boats. He assured me there were at least 3000 houses in the city—including the neighbouring suburbs Noung Palin, Muang Kow, and Nong Ping—and fully 30,000 in his province. Elephants take three days proceeding to Sukkhothai, and five days to Sawankalok on the Meh Yom: there are no mountains on the way, and carts can be taken to either place. During the conversation the wife of Moung Byay interpreted for me, and did so in a most intelligent manner.

After thanking the governor and his officials, and refunding the money they had given, I returned to the boats accompanied by the Burmese, who said they would be glad to receive me as their guest if I happened to be in the neighbourhood again. Having thanked them for their kindness, I sketched the hills; and the men having brought the fowls and ducks, I continued my journey, and halted for the night at Ban Wung Pone, close to a house that had been erected for the local demons, and had four yellow flags planted before it. The village lies 5 miles from the city and 261 miles from Zimmé.

The next two days, proceeding leisurely, I halted at several temples, at one of which I was presented with a stone head worthy of Grecian art; and at another I saw many fine bronze images of Buddha, which had been maliciously broken—perhaps when the Burmese invaded the country. Some of the abbots I subsequently met gladly sold me several small images of Buddha for a few two-anna and four-

View looking west from Kamphang Pet.

anna bits—equivalent to 2d. and 4d. One of the pagodas—that at Ban Wung Ken—was remarkable on account of its being ornamented with crockery plates four inches in diameter. This mode of decoration must be Chinese in origin. One of the large pagodas in Bangkok is similarly adorned. On the branches of a Mai Ma-kok tree near the crockery pagoda, some enormous beehives were suspended about 70 feet from the ground.

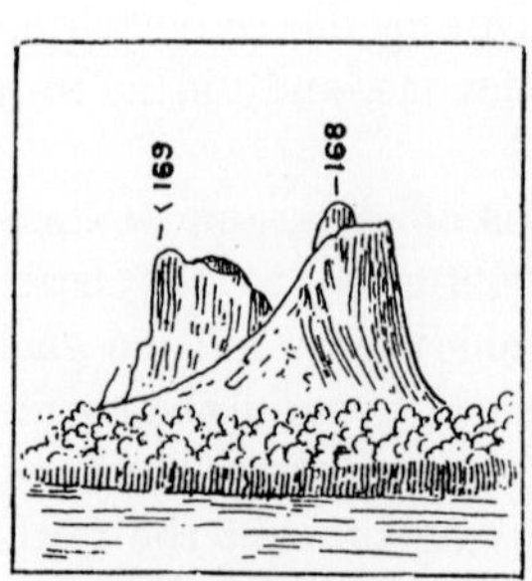

Loi Kow Chung.

On the morning of the 18th I halted at Ban Bung Kay-ow to sketch a hill of mural limestone about 2000 feet high, called Loi Kow Chung, which was seen on end three miles to the south-east of the village; and shortly afterwards passed some floating houses, resting upon rafts of bamboos, and occupied by a band of strolling players. The women had their faces daubed over with a ghastly white paste; and their fingers, as is the habit with well-to-do Siamese females, covered with rings; and gold, or most likely pinchbeck, chains thrown over their neck and shoulders.

The amount of jewellery and gold and silver ornaments worn by wealthy people in Siam—especially by women and children—is surprising. Children of the rich wear heavy anklets and bracelets of gold, those of poorer people of silver, and those of the poorest classes of brass. More often than not, lads and lassies so bedecked have not a rag of clothing on them. Clothes are not thought necessary for children in Siam until they reach seven or eight years of age.

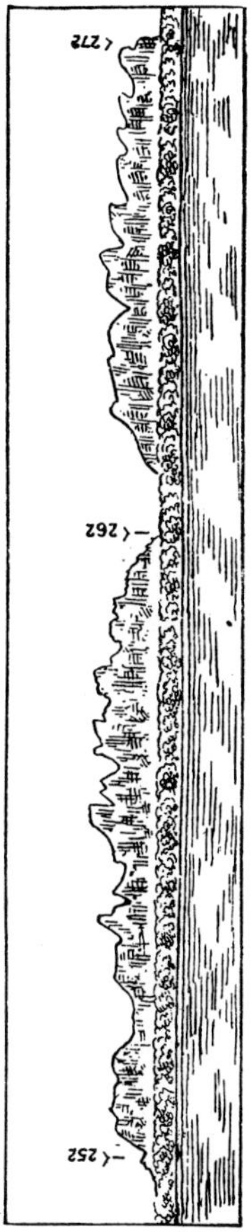

At Ban Ta Nyoo I sketched the front face of the limestone hill, and, 10 miles farther down-stream, Loi Kow Luong—the last great spur that approaches the river from the western hills. Sugar-cane, rice, cotton, and tobacco seemed to be the chief crops grown. The slopes of the river-banks, where flat, were planted with tobacco, pumpkins, and melons.

At Pak Nam Po, the town at the junction of the Meh Ping with the Meh Nam, I met some Toungthoo pedlars from Thatone in Burmah, and halted for an hour to enable the boys to replenish their larder. The water in the Meh Ping, from Zimmé downwards, had seldom exceeded 2 feet in depth.

Loi Kow Chung.

The Meh Nam below the junction has much more water in it, and large boats are able to sail up the stream nearly to Phichai (Peechai), and poling-boats can reach Ootaradit from Bangkok in twenty days. A steamer drawing 4 or 5 feet, according to Mr Satow, might do the same journey in four or five days. Above Ootaradit, owing to rapids in the bed, the Meh Nam is only navigable for dug-out canoes. Ootaradit is one of the termini for the Chinese caravans from Yunnan, and might be connected with the Siamese main line of railway by a loop-line from near Pak Nam Po, rejoining the main line near Muang Ngow. It could likewise be connected with a branch from Raheng, which would pass through Sawankalok and Sukkhothai—the ancient capitals of Northern Siam.

In the 84 miles between Kamphang Pet and Pak Nam

Loi Kow Luong.

Po, we passed fifty-four villages—many of them of considerable size; and during the whole of the journey from Kamphang Pet to Bangkok, we frequently heard at night reports of firearms from boats anchored near us, and on inquiry I learnt they were fired off to scare the pirates—bands of whom are said to infest the river. There are no river-police above Bangkok; the boatmen, therefore, have to carry arms to defend their cargoes. The policy of the Government seems to be to squeeze as much as they can out of the people, and to leave them a prey to the officials and to pirates; the officials, indeed, are said generally to be in league with the pirates, and to share the plunder with them.

When walking through Pak Nam Po, I had my attention drawn to the gambling-house by the band playing within its precincts and by the crowd in its neighbourhood. Whilst watching the gamblers, in order to comprehend the method of the game, a man at my side addressed me in Siamese. On turning, I found he was a young man dressed in the yellow robe of the monks, but wearing an imperial beard and small twisted-up moustaches after the French fashion. I addressed him in French, thinking he was a French half-breed from Cochin-China spying out the land in disguise, who had not had the heart to sacrifice his personal appearance beyond shaving his crown, but merely got a blank expression and some more words of Siamese. Not even a tell-tale shrug could I get out of him. If he was a Siamese monk, he was the only one that I ever saw so adorned.

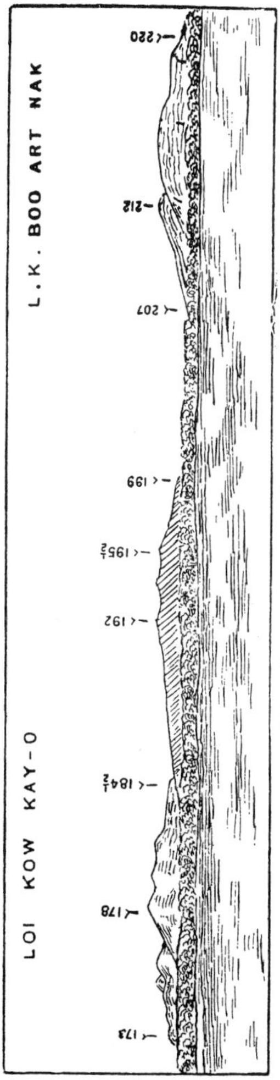

View from the junction of the Meh Nam.

Some of the Shan and Siamese laity neglect to pluck out their beards and moustaches; and I had an amusing interview with one of these hairy-faced men at Nakhon Sawan—a city about two miles below the junction of the Meh Nam. Whilst rambling about the place, I noticed a man with his hair parted in the middle, and with well-grown whiskers, beard, and moustaches, amongst the crowd of gazers who were accompanying me. I at once stopped to take his likeness, and, for fear he should bolt, kept him within 18 inches of me whilst I completed the sketch. The crowd formed a ring round us, nearly splitting their sides with laughter at one bearded man staring intently at and sketching another, and incessantly chaffing my victim.

Below Pak Nam Po the villages become more numerous, frequently lining one or the other or both sides of the river. For 55 miles below Muang In, and for 25 miles above Bangkok, the string of towns and villages on each side of the river may be said to be conterminous—one long street of houses. Nearly the whole population of the delta, which is about 130 miles long by an average of 50 miles broad, reside on the banks of the main river and its affluents.

Pak Nam Po is 338½ miles from Zimmé, and 204½ miles from the king's palace in Bangkok—the distance between Zimmé and the palace being 543 miles. The river for 173 miles from Pak Nam Po varied in width from 600 feet to 900 feet, and from thence to Bangkok was seldom more than 1000 feet in breadth. I reached Bangkok on June 28th, and put up in the hotel, where the manager did the utmost for my comfort and that of my servants. In fact, Veyloo was so pleased with hotel life that he subsequently took service with the manager.

CHAPTER XXXV.

MR SCOTT—VISIT TO THE LEGATION—ADEPTS AT INTRIGUE—MR ALABASTER ON SIAM—EVERYTHING TAXED—THE REVENUE—*CORVÉE* LABOUR—IMPOVERISHING THE PEOPLE—THE OLD SCHOOL DYING OUT—THE IRON-ROAD A MAGICIAN'S WAND—KING STORK—PUTTING A STOP TO CATTLE-THEFT—A PIQUANT STORY—CATTLE-LIFTING BY OFFICIALS—A LINGERING LAWSUIT—EXTORTING CONFESSIONS—TORTURE AT THE POLICE COURTS—THE LAST DAY'S AGONY—UNLAWFUL IMPRISONMENT—INSIDE A PRISON—IMMORALITY OF PRINCES—FIT COMPANIONS—BROTHELS IN BANGKOK—SELLING RELATIONS—CHANTING PRAYERS—FLOGGING WOMEN—THE BIGGEST LIARS AND THIEVES—SLAVERY IN BANGKOK

ON reaching the hotel I was glad to learn Mr Scott had arrived the previous day, and Mr Colquhoun was expected in about a week. During part of the Franco-Chinese war the former gentleman acted as Mr Colquhoun's secretary, and afterwards as correspondent for some of the home papers. For many years he had been in Burmah, and had earned a high reputation as a writer under the *nom de plume* of Shwé Yoe. His charming work 'The Burman' is elegantly written, and gives the best extant description of the habits, manners, and customs of the Burmese. I was pleased to find him willing to be my companion on future journeys of exploration, in case Mr Colquhoun and I could arrange for the necessary funds for carrying them out.

As soon as the boats were unloaded, I hired a house-boat from the hotel and proceeded up the river to call upon Mr Satow, our consul-general, and to receive the letters awaiting me. Mr Satow, previous to his appointment at Bangkok, had for many years been attached to our ministry in Japan, and is considered the best European authority upon that country. His library of Japanese works—comprising books from the earliest times to recent date, many of them beautifully illustrated — filled several large rooms, and necessitated his employing a Japanese librarian to attend to them. He gave me a hearty welcome, and subsequently, on Mr Colquhoun's departure for China, became my host for some weeks during my stay in Bangkok, and did all he could to make my visit pleasant. He proved to be a most agreeable acquaintance, a student both of books and men, and an admirable musician. He possessed great tact, and the rare capacity of rapid insight into the characters, mode of thought, and action of people with whom he came in contact. Without the latter faculty, our minister in Siam would be worse than useless, because the Siamese are adepts at intrigue, besides being malicious, cunning, treacherous, tricky, and untruthful beyond conception. I was informed by some of their European underlings that Siamese strategy had caused the removal of former British consul-generals, and that a similar victory could easily be attained again if the whim moved them. Unless backed up by our Foreign Office, our minister in Siam would be in a very unpleasant position.

Before returning to the hotel I visited the other members of our legation, Mr French, Mr Cording, and Mr Archer, and had a long and pleasant conversation with them. They gave me a good idea of the place and the people, and showed me many interesting articles of *virtu* which they had collected. I am especially indebted to Mr French for a beautiful collection of Siamese china which he enabled me to purchase, and to Mr Cording and Mr Archer for much of the pleasantness of my visit to Bangkok.

During the next few days I made a series of visits to various foreign consuls, missionaries, merchants, and gentlemen in Siamese employment, and gained much information upon the hindrances and prospects of trade, and the condition of the people of the country. Every one was of opinion that the state of the people could not be much worse than it is, and that it would be difficult to imagine any further hindrances to inland trade than already existed. Mr Alabaster, the confidential adviser of the king, who has since died, told me that nine-tenths of the non-Chinese inhabitants of Bangkok were slaves; that squeezing was so universal amongst the nobility, officials, and monopolists, that no man could become rich in the country unless he purchased an appointment, and thus became one of the rulers; and that justice in the courts was a farce—the heaviest purse, or the most powerful person, invariably winning the case: besides which, if a man was believed to be in possession of money, false charges were brought against him, directly or indirectly, by the officials, in order to wring the money out of him. The taxes of the country were farmed to Chinese monopolists, who, being in league with the officials, collected far more than their dues. Everything in the country was taxed—even bamboos, mats for thatching, and firewood. An old woman could not collect a few sticks into bundles for sale without giving up one-fifth of the bundles to the creatures of the monopolists. A man could not fish even in the sea without paying taxes on his boat, stakes, nets, lines, and hooks. The mesh of the Government net was so fine that it missed nothing; everything that was marketable was taxed in Siam. The revenue coming into official hands was known to exceed three millions sterling a-year, but only twelve hundred thousand of that ever found its way into the Treasury; and he believed that he was within bounds when he stated that between five and six millions were collected lawfully and unlawfully, by tax-gatherers and monopolists, from the people.

Outside foreigners and Chinese, all the people resident in the country who were not slaves were serfs, and unable to leave their districts without the permission of their Government masters. The majority of them were forced to work thrice a-year for a month at a time without recompense by their Government masters, or pay heavily for a substitute to be procured. This simply impoverished the people, not only from loss of time, but by preventing them from entering into trade and interfering with their agricultural pursuits. It was true that the king and Prince Devawongse—his most trustworthy and trusted minister—really desired the welfare of the country, and that their power was gradually increasing; but the vested interests of the deceased regent's family[1] were so great, and the nobility and officials were so generally vicious and corrupt, that considerable time and tact would be required to clean out the Augean stables of Siam. A railway might be the best way of strengthening the king's hands—it would certainly mean the death of serfdom and slavery, and act like a magician's wand in improving the position of the people; but it could never be made to pay if the present evil condition of the country continued.

The latest scandal that had occurred at the date of my visit was caused by the Lord Mayor of Bangkok, one of the half-brothers of the king, who governed the city as King Stork governed the frogs, by gobbling up all within reach of his beak. He was described to me as selfish, sensual, and depraved; a cold-hearted libertine, without the poor gloss and with none of the social attractions of a Lovelace, who gave way unrestrainedly to the indulgence of his appetites, and had as cruel inclinations as any devil yet depicted by monkish mind. On the plea of putting a stop to cattle-theft, he had issued an order that every owner of cattle must be able to show a written receipt indicating from whom they were purchased. He then, according to my informants, sent his satellites round to lift and convey to his own pastures the confiscated cattle, which of course included those bred by the peasantry on their own lands. Many of the cultivators had been thus, in one fell swoop, deprived of their only means of tilling their fields. To get rid of such a tyrant and his myrmidons would be like getting rid of the devil and all his angels. It was quite refreshing to me to hear some months ago that this scoundrel had been removed from

[1] The son of the late regent was then Kalahom, or Prime Minister of Siam, and the Kalahom's daughter is the king's first wedded wife, but without the rank of queen. The present queens, right and left, are half-sisters of the king, and full sisters of Prince Devawongse. The Kalahom, the Kromatah or Foreign Minister—who was a half-brother of the ex-regent—and the uncle of the king, who were the heads of the nobles that opposed progress, have been removed by death or resigned since my visit, and the king has no longer a pretence for delaying to propagate measures for the improvement of his administration and the welfare of his people.

his office, and that there was some talk of making Prince Devawongse Minister of Justice.

A story, worthy of enshrinement for its humour, was related to me by Mr Van Dyke, one of the missionaries at Petchaburi. According to him, the governor of that province having procured a prize bull, invited the people of his neighbourhood to bring their cows to be served by his noble animal; and after the cows had dropped, claimed the calves as his property, on the ground that his bull was their father. Another anecdote was told me by the same missionary: A man came from Ratburri to Petchaburi in search of four cattle that had been stolen. Mr Van Dyke advised him to look for them in the governor's fields. He did so, and found them grazing there, and returned and told the missionary it was no use taking any action for their recovery, as the thief was too powerful and would judge the case. He then set his face homewards. I could fill a good-sized book with similar stories of various governors and other officials which were related to me whilst in Bangkok.

The Rev. S. J. Smith, who edited a newspaper in Bangkok, gave me an instance of the extortion practised in the courts in the case of Sang, his head-printer. Six years before, Sang quarrelled and came to blows with a man, and each laid a complaint against the other in the court. Since then the two men had been called up periodically, forced to pay court-fees, and then sent back without their case being heard. It was likely to remain on the lists as long as money could be squeezed out of the men. The law as administered in Siam, evidently plays with its victims as a cat does with a mouse. Other missionaries gave me similar instances which had come under their notice.

From a European inspector of police in Siamese service, I learnt the method by which confessions were extorted in the police courts. If a man is arrested on suspicion of theft or other crimes, he is at once put in irons, and when brought before the magistrate, is questioned very roughly by the magistrate and his understrappers, and often asked most insolent questions having nothing to do with the case. If the truth of his answers is doubted, his face is slapped with the sole of a shoe until sometimes the blood flows from his mouth. If he does not then allow that he is guilty, his head is fastened in the centre of a bamboo yoke formed like a short ladder, his hands are tied in front of him to the yoke, one end of which rests on the ground, and he is made to sit down with his body inclined forwards and his legs outstretched. A rope is then fastened to his ankles and to a peg in front, so as to prevent him from bending his knees. Another rope is tied round his waist and to a peg some distance to the rear, and tightened so as to stretch the skin of his back as tight as a drum-head. He is then thrashed above the waist with a long cane, getting fifteen or twenty strokes. If he still avers that he is innocent, the strokes are increased to thirty: this is considered to be sufficient torture for the first day. The cane is drawn along the back like a whip, blood is drawn with the first stroke, and his or her back is completely lacerated at the end of the punishment. All the while the thrashing is going on, the magistrate, jailers, clerks, and other officials sit round about jeering at the man, and telling him he had better confess. The performance is varied by striking the presumed criminal on the tender parts of the hips and arms with a piece of raw hide the thickness of an inch, twisted like a rope, which, though as hard as iron, is slightly pliable. This often occurs between the lashes—ten lashes, then a hammering.

After his first dose he is left to cogitate for a whole day whether he will allow himself guilty or not. Then he is had up again into the yard of the court where the case is being tried, and trussed up as formerly and again flogged, getting ten or fifteen lashes. Should he still say that he is innocent, the number of blows is completed to thirty altogether, and he receives the usual intermittent hammerings. His fingers are clasped and beaten to a jelly with the hide, and if he does not then confess himself guilty, he is allowed another day's rest, after which he receives another ten strokes, and is again interrogated. If he is still obstinate, the tally of thirty strokes is completed, he being interrogated and hammered between each five stripes. This makes ninety stripes, the full number that a magistrate is allowed to give.

The above punishment happens when a man or woman is had up on suspicion. If the tortured person does not confess before the close of ninety strokes, he or she is considered to be innocent. According to my informant, such a case seldom happens, for nearly invariably innocent folk confess to having committed the crime merely to save themselves from the balance of the punishment. If on the third day the number of the strokes is verging on the ninety, and the victim is still obdurate, a piece of flat wood, one and a half inch broad, and a quarter of an inch thick, is placed on each side of the head above the ear across the temples, and the two ends of each are brought together and fastened like a loop-spring. The top of the bow is then struck. The vibration is nearly equal to striking the temple, and then passes through the whole system, causing great agony. This form of torture is said to occur at least once a-week in Bangkok.

After each day's punishment, the bamboo yoke is taken off, and the victim lies face downwards, whilst a friend or another prisoner tramples on the wounds to keep the swellings down: a wet cloth or wet rag, if handy, is then thrown over his back. If the ninety strokes are received by a prisoner without his confessing, he is still, though against law, kept in jail on suspicion to the day of his death, which, as the jails are the foulest holes that can be imagined, generally occurs within a few months. This unlawful imprisonment happens because the authorities do not wish it to be known that they have tortured an innocent person.

The best-kept and most commodious prison in Bangkok is said to be that of the Mixed Court, which I visited in the company of a member of one of the consulates. On our entry we found amongst the manacled and chained inhabitants—men and women sleep in the same den with a chain run through their leg-irons at night—a little girl, nine years of age, who had been in prison more than a year for losing a small boat she had been left in charge of,—a boat that had been swept away by the swift current of the river whilst the child had been thoughtlessly playing in the neighbourhood. On inquiry I learnt that the child would not be released until the boat was paid for, or until the hard-hearted prosecutor, who had perhaps forgotten her existence, chose to forgive the debt. If we had not visited the prison, in which the stench was so bad that we had frequently to go outside to get a breath of fresh air, the child would have rotted in that deadly atmosphere, amongst her perhaps equally innocent companions, until kindly released by death.

The state of morality amongst the officials in Bangkok may be judged from the fact that many of the princes and nobles treat the brothel-keepers, some of whom wear his Majesty's uniform, as bosom friends, and are seen riding in the same carriage with them. The description of the brothels in Bangkok, as given to me by one of the police inspectors, was most revolting. The prostitutes are all slaves, having been sold by their nearest relations in order to pay their gambling debts, or to aid their parents who are in the clutches of the law, the parents promising to buy them back as soon as they can. As a rule, they are said to be far more modest and particular than the same class of women in Europe.

Previous to being sold into a brothel, the girl has to be taken to the Lord Mayor's office, where she is asked if she consents to become a prostitute. Often, although hardly able to speak for tears, they dare not refuse, and a mere gesture is taken for consent. Their relations are allowed to flog them within an inch of their life, and if they do not die within fifteen days of their flogging, their death is not considered to have been caused by it. There is therefore no chance for a girl to escape her doom in the brothel. On being sold she has to declare that she was born before 1868 (the year when the king came to the throne), for otherwise she could not be sold for more than two guineas (22 ticals). The law is easily evaded, like every other law in Siam. If a girl says she is thirty-three or thirty-four when she is only fifteen, the officials would not take the trouble to question her assertion, and if they did, their conscience would soon be satisfied with a small bribe.

Every night when the house is closed, the inmates sit in a circle on the floor and sing or chant a prayer for their health and prosperity and for that of their owner. This in most houses is compulsory, but it becomes habitual to the girls. Each night one or two of the girls must, turn and turn about, provide oil for the lamps, and flowers for decorating the rooms, out of any presents they have received. If one of them has received no presents, she is considered by her owner to have been lax in her blandishments, and receives a good flogging. The howls of these poor creatures, together with the whish of the cane, is heard through the city in the early hours of the morning.

The magistrates in Bangkok have the reputation of being the biggest liars in the country, and the police are said to be the greatest thieves. So unsafe are the people from false charges and lawsuits, that they willingly become the slaves of the powerful in order to gain their protection. Thus, according to the inspector, not five per cent of the Siamese in Bangkok are in possession of their freedom.

CHAPTER XXXVI.

MR COLQUHOUN'S ARRIVAL—PRINCE DEVAN—CHARACTER OF THE KING—VISIT TO PRINCE DEVAN—MEMORANDUM ON THE RAILWAYS—GRANT REQUIRED FOR FURTHER EXPLORATION—INTERVIEW WITH THE KING—TERMS REQUIRED BY SYNDICATES—SIAM'S CREDIT—THE CONNECTION WITH BURMAH—EXCURSION INTO EASTERN SIAM—NAI SIN—AN OFFICIAL OF 2500 MARKS—POO BAH—GOLDEN OPPORTUNITIES—TRUMPERY FORTIFICATIONS—AFTER THE STORM—THE BANG PA KONG RIVER—LEGEND OF THE KOW DIN—AN INFATUATED MONK—CHINESE IN SIAM—ESTIMATE OF POPULATION—CHINESE IMMIGRANTS AND THEIR DESCENDANTS—MARKING THE PEOPLE—UNSCRUPULOUS GOVERNMENT-MASTERS—THEIR LITTLE GAMES—A VAST PLAIN—LITTLE CULTIVATION—LOVELY SCENERY—TRAMWAY TO THE GOLD-MINES—RETURN TO BANGKOK—DR M'GILVARY'S OPINION UPON THE PROJECTED RAILWAYS—ONE OF THE GRAND WORKS OF THE CENTURY.

WHEN Mr Colquhoun arrived, Mr Satow arranged an interview for us with Prince Devawongse. This prince, who is colloquially termed Prince Devan, like most Siamese is small in stature. His appearance was boyish, and although perhaps thirty years of age, he did not look more than twenty. He was then acting as private secretary to the king, filled the post of Chancellor of the Exchequer, and had the character of being a person of great tact, discretion, and ability. His post as confidential adviser to the king must have been a difficult one, because his Majesty, although well-meaning and even well-doing by spurts, is said to be infirm of purpose and irresolute, indulging in half-measures, and becoming wearied and languid before he has fully carried out a reform. There is therefore no continuity in his actions, and he becomes exasperated at constantly recurring abuses being thrust upon his attention. One cannot expect much continuous energy or backbone in a potentate who is credited with a harem containing about eight hundred wives and concubines.

Prince Devan, who is believed to be in earnest in wishing to reform the administration of the country and to ameliorate the condition of the people, received us courteously, and after shaking hands, offered us cigars and ordered tea to be served. We entered into the purpose of our visit, explained the advisability of opening up Siam by railways, and of connecting it with our seaport of Maulmain, and pointed out on a map the direction of the projected lines. He listened with great attention, discussed the matter intelligently, and remarked that his Majesty the king was fully awake to the importance of developing the resources of the country by means of railways. The king, he said, had always been well-disposed towards England, and would look favourably upon the project for connecting his dominions with Burmah. He would arrange an interview for us with the king, and would be obliged if we would send him a memorandum on the subject of the projected railways to lay before his Majesty before we were presented.

In the memorandum drawn out by us and forwarded to the prince we proposed[1]—

(1) A main line from Bangkok to Kiang Hsen.

(2) A branch line to Luang Prabang.

(3) A branch line to Korat.

(4) A branch line to connect the main line with Maulmain.

We pointed out the commercial, strategic, and administrative advantages of our projected system, and entered into the methods of construction, explaining that the railways might be executed by one of the following three methods:—

(*a*) By the State out of Government funds.

(*b*) By granting concessions (land, &c.) and a small guarantee.

(*c*) By granting a considerable guarantee, pure and simple.

[1] These railways, with the exception of the branch from Maulmain, are now being surveyed by English engineers, under Sir Andrew Clarke's syndicate, for the King of Siam.

We stated that should the king sanction the introduction of railways, it would be for his Majesty to decide on which system they should be constructed. If by either the second or third, we believed a private company could be formed in London to undertake the enterprise on moderate terms.

We then entered into the advisability of further explorations and surveys being carried out, and said if his Majesty thought fit to grant £3500 towards the Exploration Fund for their execution, Mr Colquhoun or I would be willing to carry them out without drawing pay from the fund, as our services had been volunteered and given gratuitously to the work. Copies of this memorandum were submitted through Mr Satow to the Foreign Office and the Government of India.

We found the king an intelligent-looking young man, about thirty years of age, erect and well built, with a handsome face for a Siamese, a slight moustache, and his hair cut and arranged, with its parting in the middle, in European fashion. Although understanding English, the king spoke in Siamese, Prince Devan acting as interpreter. Annoyed, perhaps, at Mr Colquhoun's plain-speaking letters to the 'Times,' his Majesty addressed his remarks chiefly to me. After entering very fully into our projects, and following the lines pointed out on the map, he said that the matter required careful consideration, and he must consult with his Ministers before determining upon his action.

Shortly after the interview Prince Devan assured us that the king had expressed himself strongly in favour of the railways, and would probably give his decision in a few days, on his return from his country residence, which he was about to visit. He likewise said his Majesty wished us to inquire in London and Calcutta what terms would be likely to be required by English syndicates who might be willing to undertake the projected railways, so as to enable him to judge whether or not it would be expedient to grant the required concessions. Mr Colquhoun replied that he was obliged to return at once to China, but I would remain in Bangkok to await the decision, and if his Majesty desired it, would be willing to negotiate the matter with secrecy and without delay.

Next day Mr Colquhoun left with Mr Scott, after giving me the names of people from whom I might gain the required information, and I removed from the hotel to Mr Satow's house. Having procured the intelligence by wire, I had another interview with the prince, and told him that the lowest terms mentioned had been a seven per cent guarantee, with free land for construction purposes, but that perhaps a smaller guarantee would be required if the king granted leave for the timber necessary for the undertaking to be extracted free of duty from the forests. He considered, or pretended to consider, the terms very high, and said that the Siamese Government could borrow money at an interest considerably less than the guarantee, and construct the railway itself, which he considered would be preferable, as the railways would then be theirs. I said I was not aware that Siamese credit stood higher than that of China, and that China had to pay about seven per cent for her recent loans.[1] He could, however, easily settle the question by telegraphing to their consul-general in London.

He then asked me whether I knew for certain that the Indian Government would be willing to carry out its part of the Burmo-Siamese connection, as it would be useless for the Siamese to construct their branch to the frontier if the Indian Government did not intend to meet and join the Siamese line. I replied that there could be no reasonable doubt on the subject. The Chambers of Commerce, who represent our manufacturing and mercantile communities, had for the last quarter of a century been constantly urging our Government to connect Burmah with China, and our projected connection *viâ* Northern Siam was the only feasible one that could be made. The cost of the branch to the Indian Government would be but small, the benefits to be derived from it would be immense; it was therefore most improbable that a great commercial nation like England would let slip such an opportunity for

[1] China has since been able to borrow at five per cent.

increasing its trade. He might entirely remove that doubt from his mind; for if the Indian Government were to hesitate in the matter, our commercial classes, who formed the voting power of our nation, would insist upon its being carried out.

After remaining for some time in Bangkok visiting the sights of the place, which have been fully described by Carl Bock in his 'Temples and Elephants,' and by other travellers, I made an excursion with Mr Satow into Eastern Siam in a steamer belonging to Nai Sin. Nai Sin, in his stockings—all Siamese nobles wear stockings, and are as proud of them and as fastidious in their choice as our fashionable ladies are of their bonnets — stood a miniature swarthy Bacchus, some 5 feet 3 inches in height, and considerably more in circumference. Like Poo Bah in the "Mikado," he held many dignified posts, was Deputy Lord Mayor, Town Magistrate, Commissioner of Rice Exports, and general go-between to the palace and to all distinguished foreigners visiting the capital. He bore the official title of Phya Thep Phaloo. His rank was denoted by 2500 marks, and he was proud of being a Siamo-Chinese and a near relation of George Washington, the late Chow Hona, or second King of Siam. When granted an audience with the king or with Prince Devan, Phya Thep Phaloo fetched you in his carriage, ushered you through the burlesquely clad guards, and acted as master of the ceremonies as far as the steps of the presence-chamber, and conducted you safely home again.

Surely one would imagine, until acquainted with the manners and customs of the place, that such a distinguished, trusted, and useful factotum would receive a salary for such multifarious duties a little above that of his theatrical representative, or at the very least above that of a parish beadle at home; but such was not the case. The Deputy Lord Mayor, Magistrate of the capital of Siam, High Chamberlain, Gold-Stick-in-Waiting, rejoiced in a pittance of 200 Siamese ticals a-year, the equivalent of £20 in English money. Such pay for such appointments, of course, implied nearly unlimited patronage, pickings, and such "insults" as Poo Bah and Siamese officials cheerily pocket. I do not assert that

Nai Sin profited by his many golden opportunities, but if he did not, and general rumour is to be believed, he forms nearly the single official exception in the realm of Siam.

Anyhow, Nai Sin looked the picture of a thriving and prosperous man, owned rice-mills and fields, houses and a steamer, wives, concubines, cattle and slaves, beamed with good-nature—or a very good semblance to it—was a capital companion, and gave me one of the pleasantest holidays I ever enjoyed in my life. By 5 A.M. we were on board the steamer, with our bedding, servants, and baggage, and in a few minutes were steaming slowly down the river in a thick mist which hid the beautiful orchards that skirt the river and delude the stranger as to the real size of the suburbs.

Two hours later we were passing Paknam and the pretty pagoda-decked islands in the river, and smiling at the trumpery fortifications that had been erected, under the supposition that they would tend to frighten a hostile fleet from endeavouring to enter the river. It is needless to say that one or two of our modern gunboats could not only silence these batteries in a few moments, but demolish the ludicrously armed and manned tin-pot vessels that his Majesty pleases to term his fleet.

Leaving the river, we quickly crossed the bar, and soon felt the unpleasant effects of a heavy swell, arising from a strong gale that had been blowing a few hours before. Passing junks partially dismasted, endeavouring to make headway with the remnant of their mat-sails which had been blown to tatters, and winding through fishing and mussel stakes driven into the bed of the sea, we were glad to enter the mouth of the Bang Pa Kong river and steam once more in quiet waters.

Journeying up the river, we passed several small villages, in which the space between the ground and the floor of the houses, some six or eight feet, was nearly filled with the shells of mussels, in which small pearls are frequently found, and reached the Kow Din, or "cut off" of the river, formed by a wood-cutter making a ditch for drawing his boat over the neck of a bend. The ditch rapidly widened, thus shortening the course of the river by several miles.

Nai Sin told me a story concerning this Kow Din. It appears that a few years ago, when the cut-off was yet only 70 feet in breadth, a famous Buddhist monk arrived at the place. Finding his progress stopped by the ditch being too deep to wade across, and believing in the power of his merit, he faced his disconcerted disciples and addressed them thus: "Stay where you are, and I, by the power of my merit, will become a bridge for you to pass over. After crossing this stream, you can restore me to my natural shape by pouring consecrated water upon my head." He then plunged into the river, and taking the form of a monstrous crocodile, stretched across from bank to bank. A mouse was never yet found to bell the cat. How could the infatuated monk expect such perfect faith in his disciples as to make them tread across such a horribly hideous bridge? Human nature had its way: no sooner was the miracle performed than the disciples, glancing at the huge reptile, as if by general consent fled homewards.

The Bang Pa Kong river is very serpentine in its course; so we did not reach Toon Chang, the village where Nai Sin had his mill, until three o'clock in the afternoon. The village was occupied by Chinese from Swatow—married to Siamese and Lao wives—and by pigs. The population of the various villages we passed on the river consisted chiefly of Cambodians, Cochin-Chinese, Lao, a few Siamese, and Chinamen. Chinamen in Siam seem to be ubiquitous. Half the population of the Meh Nam delta is Chinese, and very few of the people are without some trace of Chinese blood in them. The Chinese are neither serfs nor slaves, and can go as they will throughout the country. Mr Eaton, the able and painstaking American Baptist missionary in Bangkok, who attends to the Chinese section of the Mission, terms them the Americans of the East. They are the tax-gatherers, and, jointly with the king's favourites, the monopolists of the taxes of the country. Nearly all the trade is in their hands. They are the shopkeepers, shoemakers, bricklayers, carpenters, tailors, gardeners, and fishermen of Siam; the owners and agents of some of the steamers; the coolies employed in the mills; they man the cargo-boats and unload the ships; and are considered by Europeans the best servants in the country. They are frugal in their habits, quick to learn, and utilise everything. According to M. Gaston Rautier, in an article in a recent number of the 'Revue Française,' the most recent estimate of the population of Siam puts it down at about 10,000,000, roughly composed of over 3,000,000 Siamese, 3,000,000 Chinese, 1,000,000 Malays, 1,000,000 Cambodians, 1,300,000 Lao, and about 400,000 Peguans, Karens, and other tribes. The Chinese, therefore, form about a third of the population of Siam, and are nearly as numerous as the Siamese.

Chinese immigrants not European subjects are considered by the Siamese to be under their jurisdiction, and are subjected to the laws of the realm. After three years' residence, and at the close of every three years from that date, they have to pay a tax of 4¼ ticals, equivalent to 8s. 6d. They are exempted from *corvée* labour, and all other Government requisitions, except the ordinary taxes. Their children have the option of submitting to the triennial tax, or of selecting a Government master and becoming Siamese. The grandchildren of Chinese immigrants are classed and registered as Siamese, and are liable to *corvée* labour as soon as they measure 2½ sok, or 50 inches, to the shoulder, and are marked to one or other Government master. The mark is tattooed on the back of the right or left wrist, and all persons thus marked are liable to be called out in their master's department.

The people and the Government are both imposed upon by the unscrupulous officials. Marked men die. The master avers that the man had not served for a number of years, and claims arrears of money, equivalent to the value of the labour he has omitted to do, from his wife and family. As certificates for times served are not given, no available proof can be brought to show the dishonesty of the master's claim. Either the sum must be paid or a paper of indebtedness must be made out giving the master the power of selling the family, or as many of them as will cover the amount of the declared deficit.

Another mode of making money out of the people is as

follows: On receiving an order for the services of a certain number of men, the master calls many more than are required, and says he has to choose so many from them. They all naturally want to beg off: those who offer the smallest bribe have to serve. If instead of men being requisitioned, the order is for posts, or other materials, oppression comes similarly into play. Some years ago the king requisitioned ten posts from the minister of certain provinces, the minister ordered twenty from the governor, who ordered forty from the Samien, who ordered eighty from the masters of the *prai-luangs*, who made the *prai-luangs* cut a hundred and sixty, on the plea that some of them would be hollow or otherwise imperfect.

Nai Sin's mill is marked on the charts as the English mill, having been built and owned for many years by an English firm who employed him as their manager, until in time he became a partner, and ultimately owner of the mill. The Blue Mountains, to the south of the entrance of the river, had now faded into space, and the country had the appearance of a dead level. To the west the plain extends for more than 100 miles to the foot of the spurs of the Tenasserim range. To the east it reaches some 250 miles, with hardly a perceptible water-parting, then turning to the south-east embraces the Tali Sap, or great Lake of Cambodia. To the north and north-east it stretches 50 miles or more to the foot of the Dong Phya Phai, or forest of the Fire King, the fever-infested hills to the south of the Korat plateau. On the south it is bounded by the sea and by the Blue Mountains, which contain the celebrated sapphire-mines.

As we passed up the river we found the land on both banks cultivated as gardens, sugar-cane plantations, and rice-fields; and from the many straggling villages along the course of the rivers and canals, one would conclude that the country was thickly populated—but this is not the case. Agriculture ceases a short distance from the banks, and not more than one-twentieth of this vast and rich plain is under cultivation.

The scenery in Indo-China is indeed exquisitely beautiful: the streams wind continuously through ever-changing foliage; with here and there a house, pagoda, or temple peeping out from the trees; children playing on the banks; people going to and coming from market in their little dug-outs, the boats of the poor. Here and there a yellow-robed monk, paddled along by the pupils of his school, on his morning mission to collect from the religiously disposed the daily food for his monastery. Men, women, and children, seemingly fearless of the numerous crocodiles which infest the river, swimming about, laughing, screaming, joking, and splashing each other. A hop-o'-my-thumb astride of a huge buffalo, until the brute gets rid of him by rolling in the water. Here a gang of men and women fishing with baskets or with fling-nets. The whole scene teems with life, and the people seem gay notwithstanding the life they are born to. We continued up the river as far as the tramway leading to the deserted gold-mines, near where the telegraph line crosses the stream, and then returned to Bangkok.

On our arrival I found Dr M'Gilvary had written to the local newspaper strongly advocating the construction of the Siamese main line and its connection with Burmah. He gave his opinion in these words: "Considering its prospective influence on the civilisation and development of the whole of South-eastern Asia, and its probable, if not certain, extension to China, I verily believe it may be classed with the Suez Canal and the great American Pacific Railway as one of the grand works of the century."

I trust that the Governments concerned in the construction of the Burmah-Siam-China Railway may come to the same conclusion, and that this great work, so important for the extension of British trade and for the civilisation of South-eastern Asia, may soon be carried into execution.

APPENDIX.

BURMAH-SIAM-CHINA RAILWAY.

RESOLUTIONS OF CHAMBERS OF COMMERCE.

London.—On November 29, 1885, the following resolution was carried with acclamation : "That this meeting of the members of the London Chamber of Commerce and others interested in British trade with the East, having heard Mr Archibald R. Colquhoun's address, hereby accords its thanks to Mr Colquhoun and to Mr Holt S. Hallett for the valuable services rendered to commerce by them, with exceptional zeal and ability, in studying and reporting upon the new markets of Indo-China and China, and the best means of opening them ; and further, that the attention of her Majesty's Government be directed to the great importance of these Eastern markets, and of the services of Mr Colquhoun and Mr Hallett."

Manchester.—At the quarterly meeting of the Chamber, the President stated that the question of the projected railway from Burmah to Western China was one of the most important that had come before the Chamber for some years past. He thought that it might very well come before the Royal Commission on Trade Depression, who should insist, as far as they could, that our trade with Burmah and Western China should receive at all events the attention of the Indian Government. Before leaving this subject he thought he might make allusion to the services rendered gratuitously to British commerce by Mr Colquhoun and Mr Holt Hallett, and to the fact that no recognition of their work had been made by the Government. It seemed to him that it would not be improper for the Chamber to call the attention of the Government to the services which both gentlemen had rendered in the direction of promoting the interests of English commerce.

Leith.—On the 9th of December 1885, after careful consideration of the whole of the published facts about the Burmah-Siam-China Railway, the following resolution was passed: "The Leith Chamber of Commerce, after carefully considering the communications received from Mr A. R. Colquhoun, desires to record its sense of the value of the services rendered by him and by Mr Holt S. Hallett to commerce in the far East, and resolves to press upon the attention of the Government the importance of opening railway communication between Burmah, Siam, and Southern China in the interests of British commerce."

Tynemouth.—On the 11th of December 1885, the following resolution was unanimously adopted: "That this Chamber accord their thanks to Mr A. R. Colquhoun and Mr Holt Hallett for their valuable services rendered to British commerce by their zeal and ability in studying and reporting on the new markets of Indo-China and China, and the best means of opening them by railway communication; and that her Majesty's Government be requested to give substantial recognition for their services."

South of Scotland.—On the 5th January 1886, the Chamber wrote to the Secretary of State for India representing that, "Having had under their consideration certain communications relative to the establishment of railway communication between Burmah and Siam and in Western China, they are of opinion that such undertakings are of vast importance to the development of British commerce in those countries, and deserve the careful attention of her Majesty's Government. They trust that the numerous communications made to your lordship upon this subject will receive early and due consideration, and in this connection I am also desired to express the sense the Chamber entertain of the value of the gratuitous services rendered in the cause of British commerce by Mr Colquhoun and Mr Holt Hallett, and their hope that such services will not fail to be recognised by her Majesty's Government."

London.—At a meeting of the London Chamber of Commerce, held on the 14th January 1886, a resolution was passed requesting the Government to recognise the services to the trade of the kingdom by the explorations of Mr A. R. Colquhoun and Mr Holt S. Hallett in connection with the railway from Burmah to the south-west frontier of China.

Oldham.—At the annual meeting held on the 25th January 1886, it was resolved: "That in the opinion of this Chamber the opening out of new markets for British manufactures is of pressing importance at the present time, and that her Majesty's Government, in view of recent events in Upper Burmah, be memorialised in favour of the construction of a Burmah-Siam-China Railway as proposed by Messrs A. R. Colquhoun and Holt S. Hallett, or by any route which may be deemed more eligible." . . . "That this Chamber calls the attention of the Government to the services which Messrs Colquhoun and Hallett have rendered in the direction of promoting the interests of English commerce."

MANCHESTER.—At the annual meeting, held on the 1st February 1886, Mr J. L. Hutton, M.P., the chairman, called attention to the development of new markets with Western China through Burmah, and asked the Chamber to support the action of the Board in urging the Government to recognise officially the services which had been rendered in this respect by Mr Hallett and Mr Colquhoun.

MANCHESTER.—Extract from Annual Report for 1885: "If ever railway enterprise in those regions be developed—as suggested by Mr Colquhoun and Mr Hallett, and as this Chamber earnestly hopes—the traders of Lancashire at least will owe a deep debt of gratitude to those pioneers of commerce who have devoted their services voluntarily for the benefit of the country, for which, however, they have not yet received any official or honorary recognition."

LONDON.—Extract from Annual Report for 1885: "Both the commercial community and British reputation for progress are indebted to Messrs Colquhoun and Hallett for their unremunerated services to their country in pursuing these investigations. It is to be hoped that her Majesty's Government will duly recognise and reward their services, as an encouragement to both present and future commercial pioneers."

ASSOCIATION OF CHAMBERS OF COMMERCE.—At the annual meeting, held on the 23d and 25th February 1886, it was resolved: "That this Association strongly emphasises the importance of opening railway communication from the ports of British Burmah, *viâ* the Shan States and Siam, to the south-western frontier of China, and requests the Executive Council to urge, by deputation or otherwise, her Majesty's Government and the Government of India to give every possible facility and assistance in promoting such communication."

CARDIFF.—On the 18th November 1885, the following resolution was unanimously passed: "That this Chamber desires to support any well-considered scheme for the promotion of railways for the connection of Burmah with Siam and China, and that the secretary is hereby instructed to place this resolution before the Council of the Association of Chambers of Commerce."

HONG KONG, 1886.—To the Secretary of State for the Colonies. Resolved: "That this Chamber bring to the notice of the Secretary of State for the Colonies, the importance attaching to the explorations of Messieurs Holt S. Hallett and A. R. Colquhoun, in Burmah and the Indo-China States, and express a hope that the Government will support the construction of a railway as recommended by these gentlemen, with a view to opening up communication with Western China, which would prove of great commercial value to both countries."

MANCHESTER.—The following resolution was unanimously passed on September 30, 1885: "That, in thanking Mr Colquhoun for the important communications addressed by him to this Chamber, the president be authorised to express the regret of the directors that Mr Colquhoun was prevented fulfilling his engagement to address the Chamber on September 16. The directors also desire to express their recognition of the valuable services rendered to British commerce by the earnest zeal with which the importance of opening up communication with Western China and Eastern markets has been advocated by Mr Colquhoun and Mr Holt Hallett."

GLASGOW.—The president, at the request of the directors, informed her Majesty's Secretary of State for India that—"After careful consideration of a project submitted to the Chamber by Messrs A. R. Colquhoun and Holt Hallett, after explorations personally conducted by them in Burmah, Siam, and the Shan States, and for which thanks are eminently due, the directors of the Chamber have unanimously resolved to represent to her Majesty's Government the Chamber's sense of the general importance of establishing railway communications in British Burmah and Siam, as a means of opening up new markets for British commerce in those countries, and by probable ultimate extension in China likewise; and consequently also respectfully to urge on her Majesty's Government to encourage and assist the promotion of such a system of railways in British Burmah as may be best fitted to tend to the development of British commerce in the countries above referred to."

WORCESTER.—The Worcester Chamber of Commerce has written to the Secretary of State for India urging upon her Majesty's Government the importance of considering the present opportunity for opening up to our commerce the markets of China and Indo-China, and the construction, either by guarantee or directly, of a branch line of railway to the Siamese frontier.

LIVERPOOL.—In reply to the questions put by the Royal Commission on the Depression of Trade, the East India and China Trade Committee of the Liverpool Chamber of Commerce has recommended "that the surplus revenue of British Burmah should be employed in public works and for the benefit of the country, and not be remitted, as at present, to Calcutta."

Leeds.—The following resolution has been unanimously passed and been forwarded to the Secretary of State for India: "That in the opinion of this Chamber it is highly desirable that a system of railways should be carried out as soon as possible connecting India and China, as indicated by Mr Colquhoun."

The Bleachers' Association.—The following was amongst the recommendations to the Royal Commission on Depression of Trade: "We can only suggest that your Chamber calls the attention of the Commission to the opening out of new markets, particularly that of Southern China, as advocated by Mr Archibald Colquhoun, where we have every reason to think that a large market exists for piece-goods of all descriptions."

North Staffordshire.—Among the answers compiled by the North Staffordshire Chamber of Commerce to the questions issued by the Royal Commission on Depression of Trade is the following: Asked their opinion as to what measures could be adapted to improve the existing condition of trade, the committee reply: "By freeing the canals from the control and from the monopoly of railway companies; by developing the resources of India; by a close commercial alliance with our colonies; by opening out new markets, particularly that of South-western China, as advocated by Mr Archibald Colquhoun in his paper lately read before the London Chamber of Commerce; and by a check, if possible, to the further depreciation of silver."

Huddersfield.—In December 1885, the Huddersfield Chamber of Commerce had framed a series of answers to the questions sent out by the Depression of Trade Commission, and in reply to the question as to the remedy for the depression, the Chamber says it seems most desirable to encourage the opening of new markets and to afford every legitimate facility for trade in the markets already opened, and adds that the report recently made by Mr Archibald Colquhoun in reference to the possibilities of China and similar nations, deserves most careful attention.

Calcutta.—Bengal Chamber of Commerce, on 24th January 1886, again had under consideration the subject of the trade with Western China. The Chamber, while not pledging itself to Mr Colquhoun's or any other particular route, has urged that something should be done immediately to open up that trade, and has also expressed its sense of the great services rendered by Mr Colquhoun and Mr Hallett.

Bristol.—January 1886: "That this Chamber is of opinion, and considers it important, that a system of railway should as soon as possible be carried out connecting India and China, as advocated by Mr A. R. Colquhoun."

Hull.—On 24th February 1886, resolution introduced at the

Associated Chambers' Annual Meeting: "That, having regard to the great importance to British commerce of establishing communication with China through Burmese territory, this Association urge by memorial or deputation to her Majesty's Government the necessity of doing all in their power to secure this advantage."

Dundee.—Abstract of Report by Directors of Dundee Chamber, 31st March 1886. Resolved: "The directors, considering the importance of connecting Burmah with India and China by means of railways, and seeing that Upper Burmah has now been annexed, are of opinion that her Majesty's Government should encourage the construction of such a system of railways as may best develop the resources of those countries, and thus give additional outlets and new markets to British commerce."

Rangoon.—On 11th June 1886, at a general meeting of the Rangoon Chamber, attention was drawn to the valuable services rendered by Messrs Colquhoun and Hallett in directing public attention in Europe to the capabilities of Burmah and the adjacent countries as markets for English goods, and in pointing out the best means for extending British trade in Indo-China.

"The Rangoon Chamber has not as yet sent any formal acknowledgment of its sense of the importance of the services thus rendered, but now conveys the thanks of the Chamber for the work done, and expresses the hope that the Indian Government will see its way to granting to Messrs Colquhoun and Hallett some fitting recompense for an important public service thus voluntarily rendered."

Ipswich.—In February 1887, resolved: "That the suggestions for the extension of railway communication in India, and especially Burmah, are worthy of the strongest support from Chambers of Commerce, as offering a probability of an extension of trade from and to this country."

Liverpool.—East India and China trade section. On 23d March 1887, resolved: "That this committee is of opinion that the extension of railways in India and Burmah is very desirable in the interests of commerce, and the committee hopes that the Government of India will continue to give its best attention to the subject." Adopted by the Chamber.

Birmingham.—On the 26th May 1887, resolved: "That this meeting of the Birmingham Chamber and the mercantile community of the town considers that the connection by railway of India and China is of the greatest possible importance to the extension of British trade, and that Upper Burmah and the Burmese Shan States having been acquired by England, as the railway proposed by Messrs Colquhoun and Hallett would run entirely through British and Siamese territory, the Government should take the matter into their serious consideration with a view to the construction of the same without further delay. That this Chamber tenders its best thanks to Messrs Colquhoun and Hallett for the services they have rendered to this country in bringing this matter so forcibly before the attention of the commercial community, and urges the Government to adopt their suggestions and to make suitable recognition of their services."

LONDON.—On the 7th of November 1887, it was resolved that: "This meeting of members of the London Chamber of Commerce and others specially interested in Eastern trade, having heard Mr Colquhoun's final report on the prospects of railway communication between Burmah and South-west China, and considering that the economic value of Burmah would be greatly enhanced if approved lines of railway could be established, resolves, that her Majesty's Government be approached with a view to their urging upon the Government of India the great desirability of conceding a guarantee to any responsible private enterprise which may be prepared to undertake the construction of the approved lines; and further, that this meeting desires to express its sense of the high value of the reports of Mr A. R. Colquhoun and Mr Holt Hallett, which have placed the project in such a practical shape before the commercial community."

MANCHESTER.—The Manchester Geographical Society, on November 8, 1887, adopted the following resolution: "That the members of the Manchester Geographical Society tender their best thanks to Mr Colquhoun for his able address, and for the services rendered by him, and by his friend and colleague Mr Holt Hallett, in so constantly and forcibly attracting the attention of the mercantile community to the great importance of connecting British Burmah with Western China by railway. In the interests of British commerce this Society would urge her Majesty's Government to take this matter into serious consideration, with a view to the construction, without further delay, of the best and shortest route of railway."

LEEDS.—On November 9, 1887, the Leeds Incorporated Chamber of Commerce passed the following resolution: "That this meeting of the members of the Leeds Incorporated Chamber of Commerce, and others interested in the Eastern trade, having heard Mr Colquhoun's report on the projected railway connection between Burmah and South-western China, is of opinion that it is highly desirable, in the interests both of the Burmese and of British commerce, that the connection should be made, and would respectfully urge upon her Majesty's Government the advisability of conceding a guarantee to responsible private enterprises for securing a railway connection between those countries."

Glasgow.—On November 11, 1887, the Glasgow Chamber of Commerce passed the following resolution: "That the cordial thanks of the meeting be given to Mr Colquhoun for the important and instructive address he has just delivered, accompanied with an expression of the hope that a direct railway route may soon be opened up from Burmah to the frontiers of South-western China, and of the opinion that her Majesty's Government should be approached with a view to urging upon the Government of India the great desirability of conceding a guarantee to any responsible private enterprise which may be prepared to undertake the construction of approved lines."

Oldham.—On the 14th November 1887, the Oldham Incorporated Chamber of Commerce passed the following resolution: "That this Chamber again expresses its belief in the urgent necessity for opening up railway communication between British Burmah and South-west China."

Dewsbury.—On the 20th December 1887, it was resolved, that "The members of the Dewsbury Chamber of Commerce tender their best thanks to Mr Holt Hallett for his able address, and for the services rendered by him and by Mr Colquhoun in so constantly and forcibly attracting the attention of the mercantile community to the vast importance of connecting the British Burmese port of Moulmein with Siam, the Shan States, and China by railway; and that in the interests of British commerce this Chamber urges her Majesty's Government to take this matter into serious consideration, with a view to their carrying out this railway without further delay."

Halifax.—At the annual meeting of the Halifax Chamber of Commerce, held on January 18, 1888, the following resolution was passed: "That this meeting desires to place on record the appreciation of the members of the Chamber at the zeal and energy displayed by Mr A. R. Colquhoun and Mr Holt Hallett in not only considering but in reporting upon and surveying trade-routes between Burmah, Siam, and Western China. It would further urge upon Government the necessity of taking steps to bring into direct railway communication the vast and important interests existing in the South-western provinces of China and our Burmah possessions; and would further draw the attention of the Government to the services which Messrs Colquhoun and Hallett have rendered to the interests of British commerce in the East."

Newcastle and Gateshead.—The annual meeting of the Newcastle and Gateshead Chamber of Commerce was held yesterday, 27th January 1888, in the Guildhall, Sir C. M. Palmer, Bart., M.P., President, in the chair. There was a large attendance. Mr W. S. Daglish moved the following resolution: "That the best thanks of the members of this Chamber are due, and are hereby given, to Mr A. R. Colquhoun and Mr Holt S. Hallett for their able and exhaustive efforts to bring before the commercial community of this country the value of Burmah, Siam, and South-west India as new markets, and the best means of opening out the same; and this Chamber of Commerce would urge on the Government the advisability of making every effort to promote railway communications with and through these countries." Mr T. Omerod seconded the resolution, which was carried unanimously.

Blackburn and District.—At a meeting of the Blackburn and District Chamber of Commerce on February 8, 1888, the following resolution was unanimously passed: "That this meeting of the Blackburn and District Chamber of Commerce begs to express its high appreciation of the pioneer work of Mr Holt Hallett and Mr Colquhoun with regard to the railway communication between British Burmah and South-western China, and takes this opportunity to impress upon her Majesty's Government the importance of at once taking measures for the construction of a good practicable railway to connect those important markets with our Indian possessions."

Association of Chambers of Commerce.—Resolution passed at annual meeting, 21st February 1888: "That this Association requests the executive council to communicate with the Prime Minister and the Secretary of State for India, urging upon them—Firstly, To advise the Government of India to order an immediate survey of the railway routes to South-west China from Burmah, in order that railway communication may be opened without unnecessary delay.

Manchester.—At the ordinary monthly meeting of the Manchester Chamber of Commerce on April 24, 1889: "With reference to the address recently delivered by Mr Holt Hallett to a joint meeting of this Chamber, the United Cotton Spinners' Association, and the Manchester Geographical Society, it was arranged that a resolution in favour of more vigorous prosecution of railway enterprise in India should be submitted to the quarterly meeting of the Chamber to be held on Monday next."

Lord Salisbury on the Connection of Burmah with China by Railway.—The following letter from Lord Salisbury has been received by the secretaries of the Lancashire and Cheshire Conservative Working Men's Federation (Mr S. C. Nicholson and Mr F. W. Deacon), in reply to a resolution passed by the Executive Committee of the Federation after hearing Mr Holt S. Hallett's recent address, which resolution supported Mr Hallett's views, and urged the Government to encourage by every means in their power the extension of the railway system in India and Burmah with a view to opening out South-western China to British trade:—

"HATFIELD HOUSE, HATFIELD, *April* 20, 1889.

"SIRS,—I am desired by the Marquis of Salisbury to acknowledge your letter of the 13th instant. I am to say in reply that the Government would be very glad to see Burmah and South-western China united by railway, and fully believe that if such a measure could be carried into effect it would have the beneficial consequences which you indicate, especially to the industries of Lancashire and Cheshire. It is probable that when the existing Burmese railway is taken up to Bhamo it will receive a further extension up to the frontier, but no decision to this effect has yet been taken, as the possibility of such an undertaking must depend upon the conditions of the regions through which such a railway would pass. They have in past times been very disturbed, and the efforts to obtain a partial survey of the country, which have been made more than once by the Indian Government, have been frustrated by the uncivilised and turbulent character of the people. —I am, your obedient servant, R. T. GUNTON."

INDEX.

PRINTED BY WILLIAM BLACKWOOD AND SONS.